Social Media Law and Ethics

In this new textbook, social media professor Jeremy Lipschultz introduces students to the study of social media law and ethics, integrating legal concepts and ethical theories.

The book explores free expression, as it applies to students, media industry professionals, content creators, and audience members. Key issues and practices covered include copyright law, data privacy, revenge porn, defamation, government censorship, social media platform rules, and employer policies. Research techniques are also used to suggest future trends in social media law and ethics. Touching on themes and topics of significant contemporary relevance, this accessible textbook can be used in standalone law and ethics courses, as well as emerging social media courses that are disrupting traditional public relations, advertising, and journalism curricula.

Case studies, discussion questions, and online resources help students engage with the complexities and ambiguities of this future-oriented area of media law, making it an ideal textbook for students of media law, policy and ethics, mass media, and communication studies.

Jeremy Harris Lipschultz is a Peter Kiewit Distinguished Professor in the UNO Social Media Lab, School of Communication, University of Nebraska at Omaha. He is the author of *Social Media Communication*, 3rd edition; *Social Media Measurement and Management*; and dozens of other books and articles. He teaches communication law and policy, social media measurement and management, computer-mediated communication, and media entrepreneurship. Connect with @JeremyHL #smle2022 or #smc2021 on Twitter, and follow Social Media Communication on Facebook and Jeremy Harris Lipschultz on LinkedIn. Send questions to: Jeremy.Lipschultz@gmail.com.

Social Media Law and Ethics

Jeremy Harris Lipschultz

Routledge
Taylor & Francis Group
NEW YORK AND LONDON

First published 2022
by Routledge
605 Third Avenue, New York, NY 10158

and by Routledge
2 Park Square, Milton Park, Abingdon, Oxon OX14 4RN

Routledge is an imprint of the Taylor & Francis Group, an informa business

Library of Congress Cataloging-in-Publication Data
A catalog record for this title has been requested

ISBN: 978-0-367-89769-7 (hbk)
ISBN: 978-0-367-43781-7 (pbk)
ISBN: 978-1-003-02101-8 (ebk)

Typeset in Warnock Pro
by KnowledgeWorks Global Ltd.

Access the Support Material: www.routledge.com/9780367437817

Congress shall make no law respecting an establishment of religion, or prohibiting the free exercise thereof; or abridging the freedom of speech, or of the press; or the right of the people peaceably to assemble, and to petition the Government for a redress of grievances.
(First Amendment, 1789)

Contents

List of Boxes xi
Preface xiii

1 Social Media Freedom of Expression 1

Social Media Company Site Management of Users 4
Social Media Business Law and Ethics 6
Why Study Social Media Law and Ethics? 8
Essential Elements of Law 10
Essential Elements of Ethics 16
Law and Ethics in a Free Society 19
U.S. Legal Approaches 20
Comparative and International Law 21
Law Review Analyses 23
Ethical Frameworks and Issues 27
Online Resources 33
Discussion Questions 35
References 36

2 Student Free Speech Issues 41

Public High Schools 43
Colleges and Universities 44
Key Case Law 45

Current Student Political and Other Speech 47
Law Review Analyses 50
Ethical Frameworks and Issues 53
Online Resources 61
Discussion Questions 61
References 61

3 Influencers and the Federal Trade Commission 65

Principles of Commercial Speech Law 68
Transparency of Interests 72
Deception and FTC Guidelines 73
Key Case: *Lord & Taylor* (2016) 76
Ethical Frameworks and Issues 81
Online Resources 88
Discussion Questions 88
References 88

4 Advertising, PR, and Social Marketing 91

Social Media Commercial Speech in Advertising and PR Promotion 102
Corporations and Contracts 106
Ethical Frameworks and Issues 107
Public Relations Ethics 110
Ethics Across the Silos 111
Online Resources 118
Discussion Questions 118
References 119

5 Intellectual Property Rights 123

Copyright Infringement, File Sharing, and Fair Use 126
UK and Australia Copyright Law 127
Trademarks 128
Content Ownership 130
Copyright Scope, Fair Use, and Transformative Use 136
Law Review Analyses 139
Online Resources 146

Discussion Questions 146
References 146

6 Privacy, Data, and International Law 149

History of U.S. Privacy Law 153
National and International Politics 155
Understanding Privacy Law and Ethics 163
Other Personal Data 164
Illinois Biometrics Data Protection 167
Ethical Frameworks and Issues 169
Online Resources 175
Discussion Questions 175
References 175

7 Hate Speech, Revenge Porn, and Obscenity 181

Revenge Porn, Cyberbullying, and Obscenity 189
Key Cases 193
Ethical Frameworks and Issues 202
Online Resources 212
Discussion Questions 212
References 212

8 Defamation 215

False Statements 222
Global Approaches 222
Ethical Frameworks and Issues 224
Online Resources 226
Discussion Questions 226
References 226

9 Government Censorship 229

Prior Restraints 233
Law Review Analyses 235
International Consideration of Law and Ethics 239

Online Resources 246
Discussion Questions 246
References 246

10 Theories and Practices 249

Speech and Press First Amendment Law 250
Time, Place, and Manner Restrictions 256
Ethical Frameworks and Issues 262
Online Resources 263
Discussion Questions 264
References 264

11 Researching Law and Ethics 267

Legal Theories and Ethical Frameworks 269
Lingering Constitutional and Statute Law Issues 271
Research Law and Ethics Issues 273
Social Legal Research 274
Legal Structures and Other Factors 278
Online Resources 287
Discussion Questions 287
References 287

12 Future Issues 289

Growing Global Market Conflict 313
U.S. Constitution Passages 317
Online Resources 318
Discussion Questions 318
References 319

Glossary 323
Index 345

Boxes

1.1	California Prop 24 (2020)	12
1.2	Legal Process Overview	13
1.3	Challenging Facebook Monopoly Power	24
1.4	Thought Leader Stephen J.A. Ward	27
1.5	The Santa Clara Principles on Transparency and Accountability in Content Moderation	33
2.1	Case Study: Drafting a Student Conduct Code	54
2.2	Thought Leader Maurika Smutherman	56
3.1	The *Central Hudson* (1980) Test	69
3.2	Federal Trade Commission Social Media Scam Data	71
3.3	Federal Trade Commission Social Media Endorsement Guidelines	74
3.4	Thought Leader Tasha M. Davis	82
4.1	California Consumer Privacy Act of 2018 (CCPA)	96
4.2	How to Spot Misinformation or Disinformation Online: Ten Tips from the UNO Social Media Lab (@unosmlre)	100
4.3	The New Consumer Agenda: Strengthening consumer resilience for sustainable recovery	102
4.4	Thought Leader Emily Kinsky	112
5.1	The Case of Naruto and His Monkey Selfie	130
5.2	Case Study: Online Photos in the EU	137
5.3	Your Professor's Social Media, Course, and Research Content	140
6.1	Trump Executive Order and Legal Fallout	156
6.2	U.S. Magistrate WeChat Ruling	158
6.3	California Privacy Statute	165

6.4	Illinois Biometrics Law	167
6.5	Thought Leader Holly Kathleen Hall	170
7.1	Illinois Chapter 720. Criminal Offenses §-23.5	182
7.2	Updated Instagram Terms of Service	188
7.3	Cyberbullies and #MoreThanMean	190
7.4	U.S. Supreme Court Denied Certiorari in *Illinois v. Austin* (2019)	194
7.5	Case Study: Social Media Moderators	202
7.6	Facebook Mental Health Resources	206
7.7	Thought Leader William R. Davie	207
8.1	Sanford's "Red Flag" Words	218
8.2	Case Study: *Kogan v. Facebook, Inc.* (2020)	225
9.1	Thought Leaders Donnalyn Pompper and Molly Schwartz	239
10.1	Thought Leaders Timothy Barouch and Greg Lisby	257
11.1	The *Bobal* Ruling	272
11.2	#StopTheSteal Case Study	275
11.3	U.S. Supreme Court Justices	279
11.4	Thought Leader Ming Xie	281
12.1	*MalwareBytes, Inc. v. Enigma Software Group* (2020)	296
12.2	U.S. Senate Questioning of Twitter CEO	298
12.3	Case Study: Florida Target Anti-Mask Parade	305
12.4	Thought Leader Jasmine McNealy	308

Preface

Students may find communication law and policy to be a complex and difficult subject to master. At the same time, there also is a need to explore ethical dimensions within a social media communication (SMC) context. The malleable nature of regulation may challenge us to provide definite answers to many questions. In late 2020, for example, Facebook faced a Federal Trade Commission (FTC) and a 46-state lawsuit for using "illegal monopoly power and an 'unlawful scheme' to stifle competition, degrade personal privacy, and crush rivals" (Silverman & Mac, 2020, para. 2). It was unclear at the time of writing this whether the antitrust claims would survive in court and force the sale of Instagram and WhatsApp.

In 2020, and ahead of the election, the Federal Communications Commission (FCC) considered the Department of Commerce's Section 230 "petition for rule-making." Section 230 of the Communications Decency Act of 1996 was signed into law during dramatic Internet dot.com growth. The law provided immunity from lawsuit liability and helped social media companies launch their revolutionary communication platforms. The Save Journalism Project commented about Section 230 that the law gave social media companies a clear advantage over traditional journalism websites:

> Companies like Facebook use the shield of Section 230 against **liability** to actively push the most sensational and often deliberately false material and posts to optimize engagement among its users, while exploiting the content produced by news outlets. With the "liability shield" and "algorithmic sword"—neither of which news outlets can use—the journalism industry doesn't stand a chance. The pen is said to be mightier than the sword, but whoever said that didn't take into account the shield of Section 230. As big tech companies like Facebook have grown stronger and mightier, the pen has been sapped of its strength … The FCC has

> the power to enforce the requirements of Section 230 in a manner that levels the playing field and helps preserve The Fourth Estate. If Facebook wants to act like a publisher, it should be treated as such.
>
> (Save Journalism Project, 2020, para. 3)

The heart of this argument is that the Facebook computer algorithm that promotes some newsfeed content also silences voices, amounts to editorial decision-making, and is driven by advertising revenue. As a business, Facebook seeks to attract and maintain time on site by determining user interest and continuously gratifying them.

U.S. Supreme Court Justice Clarence Thomas has challenged the broad interpretation of 27 U.S.C §230 over more than two decades of Internet development: "[M]any courts have construed the law broadly to confer sweeping immunity on some of the largest companies in the world" (*Malwarebytes, Inc. v. Enigma Software Group*, 2020, p. 1). Commentators, however, were quick to rebuke his statement as not consistent with legislative history or U.S. Supreme Court case law (Masnick, 2020). Privately held social media companies exercise free expression limits of content bans through contract law with their users, and the First Amendment treats this differently from limited state action on protected speech by the government (Terry, Anderson, Wiley, & Memmel, 2020).

Facebook's billions of users may be exposed to misinformation, at the same time as audiences have lost an appetite for traditional local news. Around the world, online hate speech is a growing problem. India held a "closed-door hearing" with Facebook executives after reports that it "was allowing anti-Muslim hate speech" and "favoritism" among political parties (Saaliq, 2020). Cyberbullying also has sparked innovative attempts to fight back. One example is "the Polite Type," an international system that recognizes and rewrites hate, blurs text and seeks to promote equality in online spaces (Polite Type, 2021).

Existing law promoted entrepreneurial growth of social media platforms, and did not protect traditional news media from competition. Democracy, however, depends on informed voting. Social media posts have been free under the law to deceive and manipulate at the same time that ethics failed to create a sense of social responsibility for accuracy, truth, and transparency. When Donald Trump was banned for life from Twitter, many asked if a social media company should have the power to remove a sitting president from its site. There is a need to understand how the First Amendment has been interpreted by the U.S. Supreme Court and lower courts. Global development also depends on application of international law and norms.

The study of social media law and ethics expands on *Social Media Communication* (2021) and *Social Media Measurement and Management* (2020)). The rapidly growing and maturing academic field is strengthened by the Social Media Professors Facebook group with more than 1,900 members in two years. Additionally, Daxton "Chip" Stewart's excellent edited volume, *Social Media and the Law, A Guidebook for Communication Students and Professions,* 2nd edition (2017) encouraged an interest in social legal issues.

As author for more than two decades of a new communication technologies law chapter in the annual updates of W. Wat Hopkins' *Communication and the Law* (2021), I have seen how media law and ethics evolved because of Internet and social media communication uses.

Social Media Law and Ethics is organized slightly differently from traditional media law or ethics books, based on student interest in law and ethics research. This structure stems from my more than 30 years of teaching undergraduate and graduate students to research and write papers based on their interests and passion. Virtually every new social media legal issue – from data privacy to online hate speech – remains unresolved by U.S. and international courts, so it makes sense to discuss law within each chapter and then follow this with an examination of ethical boundaries beyond legal precedent. Law and ethics remain fundamental areas of importance that are required to fully understand media and information literacy in the 21st century.

Most students have a deep interest in their use of social media. This curiosity can be leveraged to learn from a practical approach about law and ethics. For example, the *Elonis v. United States* (2015) Facebook threats case engages students in criminal law issues evolving around state of mind of a person posting on social media sites. Similarly, the *Packingham v. North Carolina* (2017) case approaches the issue of registered sex offenders' use of social media, and the U.S. Supreme Court's First Amendment free expression democratic values.

The study of expressive conduct it involves the need to consider how governments increasingly attempt to place restriction on social media use. At the same time, individuals are publishers facing potential civil lawsuits or criminal charges. High school and college students face unique concerns about potential disruption of a classroom. Social media influencers must avoid deceptive advertising that does not have First Amendment or other commercial speech protection for legal products and services. Content creators, such as photographers, may need to fight for their property rights. Further, privacy rights are growing at the same time that news sites face new legal threats. Each chapter of this book reviews the law, and this is then followed by ethical analyses of key topics, such as cyberbullying and revenge porn. At the same time, the textbook considers how artificial intelligence (AI), natural language chatbots, **augmented reality** (AR), "deepfakes" video, and other new technologies will challenge traditional law and ethics. For example, crypto art NFT's worth millions of dollars are likely to spawn copyright claims. At the same time, sneaky "dark patterns" that make it difficult to unsubscribe have been banned in California. Students will be guided to deeply dig into a specific research topic, such as social media **memes** and the law, by learning how to read case law and law reviews.

As with the previous two social media communication textbooks in my series, this book was enriched by a collaboration with Sandy Shepherd Lipschultz. For nearly four decades we have been soulmates in search of understanding media communication, politics and civic life. I also dedicate this book to my grandfather, attorney Charles T. Kramer, and my grandmother, Tillie. They dutifully and ethically served clients in Chicago for more than 50 years. My longtime friend, Gerald A. Role, principal at Role Law Firm in Washington, DC, made an important contribution by graciously editing the glossary. Professor Greg Lisby at Georgia State, in addition to the "thought leader" section, contributed intellectual property insights. Decades ago, Professor Robert Spellman taught me much about law and journalism. At Routledge, Emma Sherriff patiently and professionally helped to edit and format the book. Helen Baxter, HJB Editorial, skillfully found important edits.

College of Communication, Fine Arts and Media (CFAM) Dean Michael Hilt supported a Faculty Development Fellowship (FDF) for me to write this book. My colleagues at the University of Nebraska at Omaha, Association for Education in Journalism and Mass Communication (AEJMC), and RFI Rural Prosperity Nebraska (RPN) have sparked new interest in the evolving social media legal and ethical issues.

Jeremy Harris Lipschultz
January 2021

REFERENCES

Malwarebytes, Inc. v. Enigma Software Group, 592 U.S. ____ (2020), at p. 1.

Masnick, M. (2020, October 13). Clarence Thomas Doesn't Like Section 230, Adding To His Anti-Free Speech Legacy. *TechDirt*. https://www.techdirt.com/articles/20201013/11283545491/clarence-thomas-doesnt-like-section-230-adding-to-his-anti-free-speech-legacy.shtml.

Polite Type. https://www.thepolitetype.com/.

Saaliq, Sheikh (2020, September 3). Facebook India Grilled Over Hate Speech, Allegations of Bias. *Associated Press*. https://apnews.com/d39c2b46ce80211bfd6431c3c13f51a5.

Save Journalism Project (2020, September 2, para. 3). Comment of the Department of Commerce's Section 230 Petition for Rulemaking. https://savejournalism.org/ 2020/09/02/ comment-on-the-department-of-commerces-section-230-petition-for-rulemaking/.

Silverman, C. and Mac, R. (2020, December 9). The US Government Says Facebook Needs to Sell Instagram and WhatsAapp. *BuzzFeed News*. https://www.buzzfeednews.com/ article/craigsilverman/us-government-facebook-monopoly-sell-instagram-whatsapp.

Terry, C., Anderson, J., Wiley, S.K., and Memmel, S. (2020, Fall/Winter). Free Expression or Protected Speech? Looking for the Concept of State Action in News, *UB Journal of Media Law & Ethics*, 8(2), 102–116.

Social Media Freedom of Expression

> *In sum, to foreclose access to social media altogether is to prevent the user from engaging in the legitimate exercise of First Amendment rights.*

—U.S. Supreme Court Justice Anthony Kennedy,
Packingham v. North Carolina (2017: 1737)

The state of North Carolina prosecuted more than 1,000 registered sex offenders under a law that made it illegal to use online sites that also had child users on them. Lester Gerard Packingham was a 21-year-old college student who had sex with a 13-year-old girl in 2002. He was indicted, pleaded guilty and was required to register as a sex offender. Under a state law passed in 2008, Packingham was banned from using commercial **social network sites** (SNS), including Facebook, that allowed anyone 13 or older to join. After receiving a traffic ticket that was later dismissed in 2010, Packingham went on his "J.R. Gerard" Facebook account wall and posted:

> Man God is Good! How about I got so much favor they dismissed the ticket before court even started? No fine, no court cost, no nothing spent.... Praise be to GOD, WOW! Thanks JESUS!
>
> (p. 1734)

A Durham Police Department officer connected the post to the traffic ticket. Packingham was indicted and convicted, but he did not serve time. Packingham later won his appeal to the U.S. Supreme Court based on the First Amendment value of the Internet and social **media communication**. While Packingham apparently never used Facebook to contact a minor, others have used powerful digital tools in harmful messages.

Anthony Elonis' wife of seven years took the couple's two young sons and left him in May 2010. He responded in the months that followed her filing for divorce by listening to violent music, changing his Facebook name to "Tone Dougie," and **posting** graphic, violent words and images that targeted him in a criminal probe by the Federal Bureau of Investigation (FBI). He would later claim that his social media posts were rap music lyrics protected under free speech law:

> "Little Agent lady stood so close
> Took all the strength I had not to turn the b**** ghost
> Pull my knife, flick my wrist, and slit her throat
> Leave her bleedin' from her jugular in the arms of her partner
> [laughter] ...
> And if y'all didn't hear, I'm gonna be famous
> Cause I'm just an aspiring rapper who likes the attention
> who happens to be under investigation for terrorism."
>
> (pp. 2006–2007)

Elonis' former employer, a Pennsylvania amusement park, had tipped the FBI to monitor his Facebook account. Elonis was indicted by a **grand jury** for threats, including those against his estranged wife, a kindergarten class, park employees, police officers and an FBI agent. Elonis was arrested and charged under 18 U.S.C. §875(c) – a federal statute that makes communicating "any threat" with the intent to "injure" another considered a crime. Under criminal law, his trial jury was instructed to determine whether prosecutors had proven that "a reasonable person" would interpret the words as threats. Elonis was convicted on four of five counts and served more than three years' prison time. He lost his Third Circuit appeal that claimed in a **pleading** that the jury should have been instructed to apply a "true threat" standard.

U.S. Supreme Court Chief Justice John Roberts in 2015 wrote the opinion: "The question is whether the statute also requires that the defendant be aware of the threatening nature of the communication, and—if not—whether the First Amendment requires such a showing" (p. 2004). Prosecutors had evidence that Elonis' ex-wife and former coworkers were afraid of what they considered "serious threats"

(p. 2007). The Court used **precedent** of previous case law to find that a criminal conviction requires evidence about the speaker's state of mind. Beyond online threats law, it is clear that online harassment of individuals is not ethical behavior.

Five years after *Elonis* was decided, social media legal and ethical issues had become much more complex. For example, ahead of the U.S. presidential election in 2020, Facebook banned some right-wing conspiracy QAnon accounts, "militia and anarchist groups that support violence" and other "hate speech" and "abuse" (Ortutay, 2020, para. 2). Twitter had previously acted to limit QAnon, and TikTok banned it from searches: "Google said it has removed tens of thousands of QAnon-related videos from its YouTube service and banned hundreds of channels for violating its policies" (para. 4). Hate speech, while difficult to define under the law, would frequently be judged by most as unethical and outside the norms of civil society. The First Amendment limits government state action **censorship**, but social media **platforms** are managed based on evolving rules that are contract law agreements between the sites and users. These are applied to practices and responses to user behavior. When it comes to the banning of hate speech or offensive content, Facebook, YouTube and other social media sites have a legal right to define community standards:

> [T]he difference between speech that is protected versus speech that is free is a core issue not only of the First Amendment, but of American government, society, and freedom as a whole. It is also, therefore, the starting block for understanding a second key lesson of free speech, namely that even protected speech is not without consequences. Although the government's ability to punish a person for speech after the fact is limited by the protections of the First Amendment, the same cannot be said about non-government entities, such as one's employer. This is also the case for online platforms and social media sites like Facebook, Twitter, Instagram, … they have every right to include or exclude content from their platforms.
>
> (Terry, Anderson, Wiley, & Memmel, 2020, p. 115)

These social media sites also have been protected by **statute law**, commonly known as Section 230, that limits their liability for content published. Increasingly, however, arguments have been made that Facebook and its billions of global users constitutes a public forum that should not be restricted by government or corporations. Donald Trump even threatened to veto defense spending unless Congress repealed Section 230, but the U.S. House later voted 335-78 in support (Romm, 2020). Nevertheless, Facebook is a somewhat closed and "gated" **community** from the more open Internet in which it resides. Even Twitter, that more resembles a public thoroughfare, increasingly exercised editorial control over content by flagging blatant misinformation.

SOCIAL MEDIA COMPANY SITE MANAGEMENT OF USERS

Twitter, a more open site than Facebook, allows users to block other accounts. President Donald Trump's lawyers were forced to ask the U.S. Supreme Court to reverse earlier decisions that he could not block @realDonaldTrump critics (Sherman, 2020). An acting solicitor general wrote: "President Trump's ability to use the features of his personal Twitter account, including the blocking function, are independent of his presidential office" (para. 3). However, Trump had been forced to unblock Twitter accounts after the Second Circuit found a public forum First Amendment violation (*Knight First Amendment Inst. at Columbia Univ. v. Trump*, 2018). After the president refused to unblock all accounts, a second lawsuit claiming viewpoint discrimination was filed (*Knight Institute, II*, 2020): "Defendants' blocking of the Individual **plaintiffs** from the @realDonaldTrump account violates the First Amendment because it imposes a viewpoint-based restriction on the Individual Plaintiffs' right to petition the government for redress of grievances" (p. 12). At times, the former president made official announcements on the account that grew to over 82 million followers during his presidency. Journalists and those writers with a **blog** or **vlog** are among those accounts that have been previously blocked while he was the president. Meanwhile, Twitter added new tools to allow users to limit who can reply to a tweet, and the issue was moot after Trump lost.

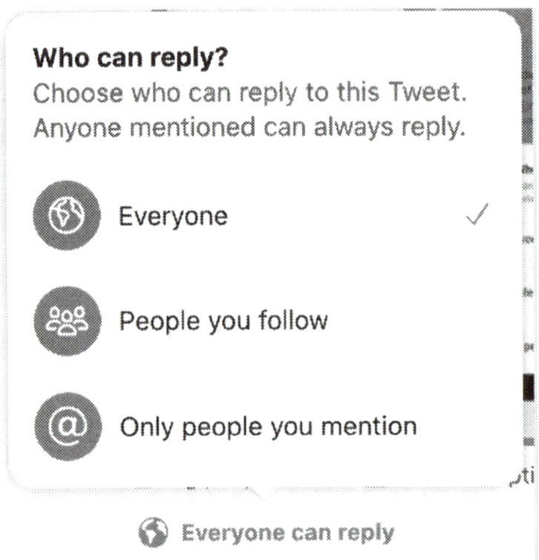

Twitter in 2020 allowed users to limit who could reply.

Photo courtesy @Twitter. https://help.twitter.com/en/managing-your-account/notifications-on-mobile-devices.

Twitter was among the most important social media sites to ban Donald Trump following his tweets amid deadly U.S. Capitol violence.

During and, indeed, after the 2020 election, Twitter used a variety of content flags on Trump's **tweets** that questioned the legitimacy of the election outcome – even after Joe Biden had clearly won more popular votes and enough electoral votes to claim the presidency (Brigham, 2020).

Trump was later required to remove three tweets that were "repeated and severe violations" of Twitter's Civic Integrity Policy. @TwitterSafety posted that an "unprecedented and violent situation in Washington, D.C." before lawmakers certified election results led to pausing the @realDonaldTrump account. Twitter also followed through with "permanent suspension," and most other major social media sites also halted access to the outgoing U.S. president.

In response to the Twitter lifetime ban on Trump, Poland threatened to fine social media companies censoring free speech, and German Chancellor, Angela Merkel, called presidential suspensions "problematic."

Twitter earlier announced that the official @POTUS account was to be given to President Biden moments after the inauguration (Scola, 2020). However, Twitter changed policies from four years earlier and decided that followers would not automatically go to the new president, vice president (@VP) and other official accounts (Fischer, 2020). The Trump @POTUS account was renamed @POTUS45 (para. 5). Twitter also notified @ POTUS followers "about the archival process," and offered "users the choice to follow the Biden administration's new accounts" (para. 6). Twitter also planned to reopen user account **verification** after a pause since 2017 of non-celebrities (Hutchinson, 2020a).

Journalism and media communication (JMC) students are trained to create and distribute content across a variety of channels and platforms. Between 2004 and 2018, about half of all traditional newsroom jobs disappeared, as hedge funds about into major newspapers (Arbel, 2021). Journalists were trained in law and **ethics**, but bloggers, citizen journalists and social media enthusiasts frequently lack formal media education and training. In some cases, so-called ghost blogging and commenting that lack **transparency** raise serious legal and ethical issues (Gallicano, Bivens, & Cho, 2014).

They need to understand legal and ethical risks in sharing news and information as a journalist, broadcaster, **public relations** practitioner, advertiser or social media manager. Even if you never work in media, it is likely that you already create and share personal social media and these posts open account users to legal liability and potential ethical lapses. The study of social media law and ethics includes understanding free expression history, student First Amendment rights, regulation of influencers, **commercial speech** and intellectual property rights, invasion of **privacy**, **obscenity**, **defamation** and censorship, and other issues. For each area of law, there are legal boundaries and consideration of ethical behavior. As Stewart (2017) observed, live streaming of rapes, murders, suicides and other crimes have presented new legal challenges. He identified a 2004 Classmates.com case in which an Oregon lawyer posed as a teacher and posted: "I get to hang out with high school chicks all day … I have even been lucky with a few" (pp. x–xi). The state's Supreme Court "publicly reprimanded him" in one of the earliest social media cases (p. xi).

SOCIAL MEDIA BUSINESS LAW AND ETHICS

For business people in the "gig economy," the power to share content to large audiences is both an opportunity and a challenge. There are issues when it comes to signing contracts, owning photographs and video through intellectual property law, and facing the possibility of violating privacy laws. Explicit consent under the law should be given in writing because **implied consent** is weaker evidence in a court case. In St. Louis, for example, Uber and Lyft passenger conversations in 2018 were surreptitiously live streamed on Twitch, and the driver, aged 32, claimed to earn $3,500 from monthly subscribers and donation. The driver said he stopped disclosing to passengers that they were being broadcast live because it did not feel authentic. The *St. Louis Post-Dispatch* called this "creepy" video (Lipschultz, 2020, pp. 175–176). Missouri law did not require consent to record someone, but passengers could file invasion of privacy lawsuits against the driver. Beyond legal liability, he failed ethical responsibility to be transparent and disclose financial interest in his **entrepreneurial** media.

Entrepreneurs may use **crowdfunding** to raise money for their social media project ideas. These appeals to followers, readers, listeners, viewers, and subscribers may leverage social network authority. When social media influence leads to a lawsuit, audiences may be asked to pay legal bills. Social media campaigns also may use **crowdsourcing** to leverage a social network for information to strengthen a story or position. There also were ethical concerns about the potential harm from publicly sharing home addresses and other private locations. The absence of clear federal social media law and regulation means that each of us must know state law that governs legal and illegal behavior within a jurisdiction.

During the Covid-19 pandemic, law enforcement used social media posts as evidence that business and personal travelers were properly following quarantine afterwards. Failure to do so led to some fines and confusion. In Australia, nonessential travel was banned, and police fined a husband and wife for violating stay-at-home rules after they posted photographs on Facebook during the strict lockdown. The photos, however, were from a trip the previous year. In infringement notices seen by *The Independent*, the couple was handed fines of AU $1,652 (£840.70) each for "failure to comply with a direction given to a person in the exercise of a power under an authorisation given under section 199" (Xie, 2020, para. 7). The fines were later revoked, but the couple was warned against further posting of old travel photos during the pandemic. The case goes to another important reality. Our social media posts can be viewed by police investigating crimes.

Just as people in some cities were required to wear a mask, the ubiquity of social media content means that sharing may sometimes intersect with the law or public shaming. For example, an Omaha, Nebraska bakery posted a photo in 2019 of a 14-year-old who allegedly took $15 from a tip jar. He was tackled by one of the owners, held for arrest, and the shop posted two photos on Instagram (Conley, 2019). The teen's mother filed a misdemeanor assault charge, and complained to the local newspaper. Nebraska law allows use of reasonable force to protect property, yet it did not explicitly address social media posting. Online comments can potentially be the basis for a **libel** lawsuit. For example, an online reaction to the story read: "Mom – get over yourself – your kid is a thief and it has nothing to do with color. Teach him the appropriate lessons at home and you won't have to worry about what behavior he exhibits while not at home. Shame on him." While U.S. citizens enjoy broad First Amendment rights for their opinions, online comments frequently cross normative ethical lines.

Before Covid-19 and social media, the world experienced severe acute respiratory syndrome (SARS). Text messages and email filled an early "media blackout" that "served to **fan** rumors" (Lee, 2005, p. 54): "Doctors and nurses, angry at government-orchestrated cover-ups, turned whistle-blowers and supplied more accurate figures of SARS casualties to the foreign media" (p. 56). Also similar to Covid-19, SARS triggered "alarming cases of prejudice against Chinese-Americans, as well as other Asians in different parts of the world" (pp. 56–57). In this sense, social media served to amplify what was already happening with online media and communication. The cases serve as studies in journalism, media, politician and public ethics.

WHY STUDY SOCIAL MEDIA LAW AND ETHICS?

Around the world, national leaders have restricted social media communication because it threatens their power. In Turkey, for example, strict social media rules were forced through the political process and into law (AFP, 2020). The regulation of social media followed laws to restrict broadcast and newspaper freedom: "If not, they face advertising bans, fines of up to 40 million Turkish liras (US$5.1 million), and – crucially – bandwidth reductions of up to 90 percent, making the platforms effectively unusable" (para. 7). The president had 16.7 million @RTErdogan Twitter followers, but he dislikes social media: "Twitter schmitter! he declared in 2014, vowing to "wipe all of these" platforms out (para. 8): "Twitter last year listed Turkey – along with Russia and Japan – among the top three countries responsible for 86 percent of all requests to take down posts" (para. 12). Turkey has blocked an estimated 408,000 sites, 40,000 tweets, 10,000 YouTube videos, and 6,200 Facebook posts (para. 13). At the same time, corporate and third-party social media **apps**, such as those created by defunct Cambridge Analytica and its collection of 87 million Facebook profiles, generated more than 100,000 documents in 68 countries, "that will lay bare the global infrastructure of an operation used to manipulate voters on 'an industrial scale'" (Cadwalladr, 2020, para. 2). There was evidence that social media continued to be used to target vulnerable voters in the 2020 U.S. presidential election. The power of social media to help or harm people should not be lightly taken.

College and university journalism and media communication (JMC) students may be required to study law and ethics within their academic programs. This may obscure the value of learning this highly relevant content. Social media law and ethics are basic to understanding advanced media and information literacy skills, critical thinking and **skepticism**, as well as useful knowledge to be an informed **citizen**:

> The more you are aware of how media operate and how they affect you, the more you gain control over those effects, and the more you will separate yourself from typical media users who have turned over a great deal of their lives to the media without realizing it.
>
> (Potter, 2008, p. xvi)

Potter was speaking about the social science of media effects research, but a similar argument can be made about social media law and ethics. Users of social media sites, such as Instagram and TikTok, are governed by contractual agreements with corporate owners. **Terms of service** (ToS) end-user agreement language may be legal under U.S. or other law, but applied practices by individuals, organizations, and companies may not be governed by reasoned ethical decision-making.

Hayes (2013) suggested that media and communication students should learn legal terms and key ideas: "Landmark rulings, precedent, and **strict scrutiny** are concepts essential to understanding how our American common law system of judicial review operates, how judges reason in general, and how they analyze First Amendment free speech and press cases in particular" (p. 2). Stewart (2017) noted that the courts have not fully addressed social media sharing and "voluntariness of social networks" because law "often seeks more rigid definitions and boundaries to regulate human affairs" (p. ix). Myers (2019) agreed with Judge Learned Hand that democratic citizenship depends on people knowing and obeying the law. However, laws – city ordinances, state and federal statutes or regulation and court opinions – are designed for *lawyers*. In an age of social media communication, lawmakers and the courts find it difficult to keep up with rapid technological change. The social media era has led to numerous lower court and higher cases being brought during the past decade, such as:

- In *Perkins v. LinkedIn* (2014), a Class Action settlement was reviewed over LinkedIn's use of users' personal contacts. Judge Lucy Koh reviewed whether a proposed settlement was fair, adequate, and reasonable. She noted the strength of the plaintiffs' case against LinkedIn and the cost of ongoing litigation. Later, in *Perkins v. LinkedIn* (2016), Judge Koh granted a motion for final approval of the settlement terms. She noted that: "LinkedIn has revised the disclosures relating to the Add Connections" that "now clarify that up to two Reminder Emails will be sent for each … invitation" (p. 6).

- In *Minnesota v. Tatro*, a state supreme court upheld the discipline against a mortuary science student for Facebook wall posts that she claimed were "satire," about a body in a lab in which she was studying. Amanda Tatro, who died in 2012, had violated student conduct code and program rules that were designed to professionally respect privileged access to human cadavers. The University of Minnesota focused on two social media posts:

  Amanda Beth Tatro: Gets to play, I mean dissect, Bernie today. Let's see if I can have a lab void of reprimanding and having my scalpel taken away. Perhaps if I just hide it in my sleeve … (November 12, 2009)

  Amanda Beth Tatro: Who knew embalming lab was so cathartic! I still want to stab a certain someone in the throat with a trocar though. Hmm … perhaps I will spend the evening updating my "Death List #5" and making friends with the crematory guy. I do know the code … (December 7, 2009)

While the postings broke no laws, Tatro was barred from the lab during an investigation, and two local television newsrooms interviewed her. Tatro was later allowed to return and take final examinations. Tatro testified that she did not understand that Facebook posts fell under a rule prohibiting blogging. Anatomy Laboratory Rule #7 specified that: "Blogging about the anatomy lab or the cadaver dissection is not allowable." Tatro's punishment included a grade of "F" in the course. Further, she was required to complete an ethics course, write a letter to faculty, and undergo a psychiatric evaluation. Tatro was placed on probation for the remainder of her undergraduate work. The Minnesota Supreme Court rejected Tatro's First Amendment argument, noting that she had signed a contract to follow lab rules:

> We acknowledge the concerns expressed by Tatro and supporting amici that adoption of a broad rule would allow a public university to regulate a student's personal expression at any time, at any place, for any claimed curriculum-based reason. Nonetheless, the parties agree that university may regulate student speech on Facebook that violates established professional conduct standards. This is the legal standard we adopt here, with the qualification that any restrictions on a student's Facebook posts must be *narrowly tailored* and directly related to established professional conduct standards … Accordingly, we hold that a university does not violate the free speech rights of a student enrolled in a professional program when the university imposes sanctions for Facebook posts that violate academic program rules that are narrowly tailored and directly related to established professional conduct standards.
>
> (p. 521, emphasis added)

The case was controversial because, similar to other recent decisions within the Eighth Circuit, high school First Amendment law was applied to public community colleges and universities within a professional training context. The alarming trend threatens to weaken established First Amendment protection for public school students, and an off-campus SnapChat profanity case is before the Court.

ESSENTIAL ELEMENTS OF LAW

If you have a driver's license, use a credit card, rent an apartment or sell on eBay, then laws impact actions. Of course, not everyone follows the law to the letter. For example, the Interstate highway near your home may limit speeds to 55 miles per hour. How many drivers have you seen go more quickly than posted speeds? Why is the law not always enforced? At what actual speed would you be likely pulled over and issued a warning or ticket?

One way to think about law is as a set of local, state, national and international rules and boundaries that govern human behavior through social control. When it comes to social networks that practice, **real-time social media engagement** through use of text, audio, **emoji**, photographs, lenses and filters, gifs, video and other tools, legal and ethical issues abound (Lipschultz, 2021). U.S. common or **constitutional law** is typically interpreted in the courts, whether it begins with a federal or state statute, regulation or dispute. We read cases to "find" the law. Law within a **case brief** is generally divided into four elements that law students learn to "brief" for the most important information (Makdisi & Makdisi, 2009, para. 4). For example, we can find the elements in an important U.S. Supreme Court precedent:

Facts. What happened between whom to elevate a dispute to the case? In the *Elonis* (2015) case, his threatening Facebook posts led to U.S. federal grand jury criminal charges. He was convicted on four of five counts, and lost at the Third Circuit Court of Appeals. The U.S. Supreme Court granted ***certiorari*** (cert.), which means they asked the lower court to send documents in order to hear the case.

Issues. What are the legal issues at stake in the ruling? The *Elonis* case turned on the proper evidence to determine a "true threat" under criminal law.

Holding/Decision. What was the vote of the court in applying rule of law? The Supreme Court voted 8 to 1 to reverse the Third Circuit and **remand** the case for further review. Justice Samuel Alito filed a separate opinion that partially concurred and dissented. Justice Clarence Thomas wrote the dissenting opinion.

Rationale/Reasoning. What was the reasoning by the court for the decision, and what language justified it? The Supreme Court found that:

> The fact that the statute does not specify any required mental state, however, does not mean that none exists. We have repeatedly held that "mere omission from a criminal enactment of any mention of criminal intent" should not be read "as dispensing with it." *Morissette* v. *United States*, 342 U.S. 246, 250 (1952). This rule of construction reflects the basic principle that "wrongdoing must be conscious to be criminal."
>
> (p. 2009)

Supreme Court decisions hold the highest precedent of stability over time in the law, but most disputes are not heard by the nation's highest legal authority. U.S. District and Appellate Court decisions, state courts, state and federal regulatory agencies, such as the Federal Trade Commission (FTC), presidential executive orders, and other national and international law may guide our understanding.

The government justifies regulation of business practices in an attempt to protect health and safety, as well as to guard against deception and fraud. Consider the car wrap scam that targeted college students. It lured them to "GET PAID TO DRIVE" with advertising on their vehicles, but it was an elaborate banking fraud (Lazarus, 2019, para. 2). Victims received fake checks to deposit and then told to wire money to a "specialist" (para. 3). The checks bounced, and the money wired from their bank account was gone.

Another area of concern is data protection. In California, for example, the state has been leaning toward the European Union (EU) data privacy protection framework. The Consumer Privacy Rights Act, Proposition 24, was passed by voters in 2020 to strengthen existing laws (Holmes, 2020). The amendments limit Facebook, Google and other companies from tracking by "allowing consumers to stop businesses from selling or sharing their personal information, including race, religion, genetic details, geographic location, and sexual orientation" (para. 3).

Box 1.1 California Prop 24 (2020)

California Proposition 24,
Consumer Personal Information Law and Agency Initiative (2020)

A **"yes"** vote supports this ballot initiative to expand the state's consumer privacy laws, including provisions to allow consumers to direct businesses to not share their personal information; remove the time period in which businesses can fix violations before being penalized; and create the Privacy Protection Agency to enforce the state's consumer data privacy laws.

A **"no"** note opposes this ballot initiative to expand the state's consumer data privacy laws or create the Privacy Protection Agency to enforce the state's consumer data privacy laws.

Source: Proposition 24 (2020, November). *Ballotpedia.* https://ballotpedia.org/California_Proposition_24,_Consumer_Personal_Information_Law_and_Agency_Initiative (2020).

State statutes, such as the law in California, may be challenged in state and federal courts, and there is little agreement among U.S. states about how to proceed with data privacy legislation. The federal government and its regulatory agencies have been slow and relatively weak in responding to the changing mobile and social context.

Box 1.2 Legal Process Overview

The U.S. has a "parallel" courts system that includes federal district trial courts, circuit courts of appeal, and the U.S. Supreme Court. Each state also has a court system that includes city courts, trial courts, intermediate state appellate courts and state supreme courts. Decisions may be appealed out of state courts to the U.S. Supreme Court when there are constitutional questions.

Within the parallel federal and state courts, there are civil and criminal cases. **Tort** actions by individuals can be brought as wrongs, such as a breach of contract. **Civil actions** may seek "at law" monetary **damages**, while "in **equity**" cases can force "remedies," such as requiring a specific behavior or stopping an action. Social media communication may harm someone, such as through defamation or invasion of privacy. Most "commentators had virtually ignored issues of *civil* liability, viewing threats to free expression as chiefly the product of *governmental* action, not implicated by private resort to the courts" (O'Neill, 2001, p. ix). That changed about two decades ago:

> The lateness of the emergence of free-speech litigation is a subject that invites much speculation, … the surprising recency of First Amendment case law makes more understandable the even later appearance in the courts of civil-liability claims involving free expression.
>
> (pp. 4–5)

Government officials may enjoy **absolute** or **qualified privilege**, which are forms of immunity from being named in defamation and other civil lawsuits for what they do while serving official duties. For example, presidential tweets and other social media posts may constitute protected speech while in office, but companies exercise editorial judgment.

Reputation has been increasingly valued in libel cases. At the dawn of Internet communication in the 1990s, Congress passed Section 230, and this insulated service providers from defamation civil liability, although plaintiffs may be able to seek the **identity** of defendant "anonymous posters" in cases claiming content "impaired the fortunes of business, or the value of its stock" (pp. 43–44). Defamation and invasion of privacy social media cases, in this sense, are similar to traditional legal issues faced by journalists. It is much more likely that social media posts could spawn a civil liability claim than the less common criminal law issues.

The state prosecutes criminal cases within **criminal courts**. Federal criminal cases are prosecuted by the U.S. Attorney's office; state prosecutors are known as district attorneys or state's attorneys. Most states have a unified court system, but some in the U.S.A. have a criminal court and separate civil court. In some criminal cases, a secret grand jury is called to consider evidence gathered by police to determine what criminal charges, if any, should be brought against a defendant. A county prosecutor, for example, could act as the plaintiff in a set of charges against a criminal defendant.

Four types of law must be considered: (1) **constitutional law** is fundamental, and the U.S. Supreme Court regularly considers First Amendment cases that raise constitutional issues; (2) **statute law** is passed by legislative bodies at all levels of government, and states increasingly enact laws that mention or impact social media use; (3) Congress has created **administrative law** agencies, such as the Federal Trade Commission (FTC), to regulate complicated areas; and (4) **common law** is "judge-made" through case decisions. The system began in England and spread through the colonies. In the U.S.A, common law can be found in state cases within areas not directly covered by the U.S. Constitution. Sometimes, federal courts are asked to decide "**diversity jurisdiction**" about where a case should be heard when parties to a lawsuit live in different states. Where common law is fairly rigid **positivism** and based on **precedent** or previous decisions, **equity law** seeks flexibility and fairness. The Latin phrase ***stare decisis*** uses precedent to seek consistency in the law.

At trial, juries or sometimes judges decide questions of fact. Cases may be filled with expensive and time-consuming pre-trail proceedings that can take years to resolve. First Amendment cases may be settled before trial, and it also is possible for a defendant to seek **"summary judgment"** to dismiss the plaintiff's allegations in a civil action where there essentially is no case. During a jury trial, a judge may apply law to reach a **directed verdict** that directs the jury to enter a verdict for one side in the case. A trial judge is expected to know the law, and the jury is instructed to apply it.

Sometimes a court decision declares rights in a **declaratory judgment** without financial "relief." During the "discovery" of evidence process, a judge may decide a point of law that could lead to a case being tossed out. Journalists or others having factual evidence can be held in **contempt of court** for failure to turn over confidential source information, and they may even be jailed for fulfilling their ethical responsibility of a promise to another.

A lower court ruling may be appealed by an "appellant" against the "appellee" opposing additional litigation, for example, because they won the original case. Following an appellate court ruling, the U.S. Supreme Court relatively rarely grants *certiorari*, which means that by granting "cert" the justices have agreed to hear the case. In a small percentage of federal cases, the Court orders that a lower court "send the papers" (files) to them. A U.S. Supreme Court decision has **controlling authority** in all federal courts. In cases not decided by the Supreme Court, each of the 13 courts of appeals establishes precedents for the courts within their respective circuits.

The First Amendment is a constitutional basis for freedom of expression. Federal courts also must consider the other nine amendments in the Bill of Rights. The Fifth Amendment due process clause requires compensation for private property taken for public use, and it values life, liberty and property rights. The Tenth Amendment reserves for states powers not taken by the federal government. In the area of biometric data privacy, for example, some states created law in the absence of federal action. Other constitutional amendments also may affect free expression. The Fourteenth Amendment applies to the states the First Amendment under what has been called "the **doctrine of incorporation**."

A U.S. Supreme Court decision has "controlling authority" over all federal circuits, as well as state courts facing federal issues. In some areas of law, such as on new technology questions, the Supreme Court has not issued a definitive ruling. Without clear court "**dicta**," the thirteen federal circuits may have conflicting law. A lawyer could cite law from another circuit, but it would be considered only "**persuasive authority**" and not controlling. The same is true for the use of common law decisions, law review articles or data.

The existence of conflicts is one reason that the Supreme Court may grant *certiorari* to clarify the law. The Supreme Court reads **briefs** arguing both sides in a case, hears brief oral arguments in an open court session, meets in a private conference to discuss and vote, and then issues an opinion. Rarely do all nine justices agree to an unsigned "***per curiam***" decision. A majority of justices may or may not agree on the ruling. In the case of a plurality opinion, there may be a number of concurring opinions. A justice voting against a ruling may write or sign onto a dissenting opinion. Cases are initially published in an unofficial reporter, such as *Supreme Court Reporter* (S. Ct.). Years later, the Supreme Court publishes its ruling the official *U.S. Reports* (U.S.). Important appellate decisions are published in the *Federal Reporter* (F.3d). Lower district court decisions may be found in the *Federal Supplement* (F.Supp.).

ESSENTIAL ELEMENTS OF ETHICS

It is possible that you will never be named in a lawsuit, but use of social media communication may present daily ethical issues. The University of Wisconsin-Madison Center for Journalism Ethics (2020) relates ethics to "correct conduct within society," "virtuous people, reliable character," "morality," and "the analysis, evaluation and promotion of correct conduct and/or good character, according to the best available standards" (para. 1). Because ethics also apply to corporations and other organizations: "Ethics is the difficult practical task of applying norms and standards to ever new and changing circumstances" (para. 3). Ethics may be personal, professional, or social, as we apply either a code of ethical rules or some other system to work through a problem in newer technologies, such as social media. Increasingly, global ethics of human rights may be applied to these issues: "Therefore, ethics is the dynamic, evolving activity of applying, balancing, and modifying principles in light of new facts, new technology, new social attitudes and changing economic and political conditions" (para. 9).

Ethicists have sometimes applied the Potter Box of: "(1) understanding the facts, (2) outlining the value inherent in the decision, (3) applying relevant philosophical principles and (4) articulating a loyalty" (Patterson & Wilkins, 2005, p. 90). This problematic framework, however, bogs down within a social media communication era of contested facts and truths. If social media ethics are "a communal thing, enacted individually within a shared morality," then it is possible to reduce rules or ethics codes to "a set of cultural ideologies rather than as philosophic immutabilities" (Koch, 2017, p.38). The lack of political consensus within maps of polarized social network clusters frequently is defined by disagreement on facts, values, decisions and loyalties – less grounded in coherent philosophies than **trending** topics of the moment. During the 2020 presidential election, Twitter flagged about 300,000 tweets for disinformation, including Donald Trump's frequent discredited claims about election fraud (Gordon, 2020). World leaders and candidates were allowed under Twitter to break its rules based on a "public interest" standard applied by the platform (Reuters, 2020, para. 2). Specifically, Twitter's Civic Integrity Policy (2020) was designed to prohibit users from "manipulating or interfering in elections or other civic processes" (para. 1). Twitter sought to "label and reduce the visibility" of posts "containing false or misleading information" (para. 1). The corporation claimed an ethical "responsibility" during national elections: "Any attempts to undermine the integrity of our service is antithetical to our fundamental rights and undermines the core tenets of freedom of expression, the value upon which our company is based" (paras. 2–3). Twitter essentially left false posts on the feed, but included disclaimers about content that "disputed claims that could undermine faith in the process itself," and other "misleading claims about the results or outcomes" – including "claiming victory before election results have been certified" (paras. 17–18). When Trump's tweets were later in the context of violence, the site escalated its response to required content removal, a timeout and then permanent suspension. The decision to label tweets impacted user behavior: "We saw an estimated 29% decrease in Quote Tweets of these labeled Tweets due in part to a prompt that warned people prior to sharing" (Gadde & Beykpour, 2020, para. 10). Twitter exercised corporate social responsibility (CSR) to provide context to what its users see on the site. Of course, social media use extends beyond campaigns and elections and to some of the most important social issues.

Frequently, we explore ethical judgment through case studies, such as those found within digital ethics. The University of Texas at Austin Center for Media Engagement (2020), for example, focused on public health doxing or flaming early in the Covid-19 outbreak. Students traveling for spring break led to trending hashtags, such as #Cabo44.

Posts via Twitter and Instagram, such as "Hi here is a thread of why you aren't pissed enough at Cabo44 using math and science," "2020 sucked A-S-S, then Texas Theta and their selfish members decided to exist," and "Endangering people's lives is not baddie behavior!!!," all of which aimed at shaming the travelling students, ran rampant throughout the blogosphere. This "flaming" (i.e., the online practice of posting insults, typically including profanity) quickly transformed into acts of "doxing" (also referred to as "doxxing") or publicly identifying the spring breakers involved so as to generate negative attention, as fellow Longhorns themselves demanded accountability (para. 2).

Identifying people in photographs and publishing this information may pose legal and ethical issues, such as economic inequality. *The Daily Texan*, a student newspaper, called labeled lack of social distancing as university misconduct. Some students, however, responded to the growing number of Instagram and Twitter doxing posts: "Perhaps the largest form of pushback against the doxing and public shaming was the response that some students were being falsely identified and accused" (para. 3). The debate also raised some invasion of privacy issues. Public shaming is a form of political activism, and social media shaming follows historic attempts to use media as a pillory on individuals by placing them in the public eye. An ethical examination might ask questions, such as: Does a pandemic justify any forms of doxing? Is doxing a form of cyberbullying? The redefinition of social media communication boundaries of privacy and human dignity go beyond individual cases: "To the extent that privacy as a moral good is known and appreciated in public life, the details of privacy protection in law, and in professional practice and user **interaction**, will be interpreted correctly" (Christians, 2019, p. 17). Social media present real-time problems, challenges, and opportunities for communication behavior.

Subramanian and Weare (2020) studied the digital health activism aspect of the #notokay Twitter **hashtag**. They noted that, "activist mobilization" requires development of "a common identity" (para. 5). The social media communication discourse challenged sexual violence and a culture of patriarchy. In a global human rights sense, such social movements exercise free expression to demand ethics and morality in society. Social media communication law and ethics is about how global interest in Facebook, Instagram, Twitter, LinkedIn, Snapchat, TikTok and other Internet sites frequently creates social conflict – some of which ends up in the courts. Laws are designed within nations to manage social behavior, limit chaos and create order, and articulate norms. The sites, such as Twitter, also have a responsibility to reduce chaos that might limit development of online communities. For example, it took Twitter more than a decade to add important details about direct messages (DMs) from accounts not followed by a user (Hutchinson, 2020b). The obvious change makes it easier to spot spam and online scammers. The data are found in a user's profile and include when they joined Twitter, number of following and followers, and any interests disclosed. Twitter told users: "[W]e're giving you more context upfront about who sent it, like how you're connected to the person on Twitter. And once you tap into the request, you'll see their profile info along with their message" (para. 2). Other sites, such as Facebook, also were testing context features within private messages (PMs).

LAW AND ETHICS IN A FREE SOCIETY

Internet digital law has begun to establish guiding precedent of rights and responsibilities. The law, regulation and policy landscape of voice commands, facial recognition, artificial intelligence (AI), natural language **chatbots** and robotics stand to redefine social media communication use. There are billions of webpages, social media users and posts. One estimate suggested that about 400 million people are active at any given moment and the monetization of communication behavior is valued in billions of dollars. From trillions of Google searches each year to the growing social media business spaces – Instagram and Facebook, TikTok, Snapchat, YouTube, LinkedIn and blogs – there is a growing understanding that legal and ethics issues surface every minute. Some will generate lawsuits. Other disputes will end with commentators debating ethics. Western ethics norms, however, do not fit with much of the global social media usage. About 80 percent of YouTube views, for example, are from outside the United States. Hundreds of languages fragment the Internet and social media communication with varying national law and cultural norms of freedom and responsibility.

The U.S. Federal Trade Commission (FCC) has warned bloggers to disclose financial interests when endorsing products or services, and it also reminded Instagram "celebrities" about disclosure rules. The FTC found that the hashtags #ad, #sp and #sponsored are not clear paid promotional disclosure of financial interests to followers and fans. In one letter, it wrote that if the marketer has a "material connection" affecting **credibility**, then clear and conspicuous disclosure is required. From an ethical standpoint, **customer relationship management (CRM)** based on loyalty and satisfaction should be open, honest and transparent when it comes to exchange of money or free branded goods and services.

The FTC may fine violators. While social media users have a lot of freedom, errors in judgment may spark litigation. At the same time, the U.S. Supreme Court has begun through recent cases to articulate how First Amendment rights are important because political speech happens online. The European common law tradition of judge-made law, one case at a time, has helped to establish an expectation of freedom of expression that had not existed under historic church and political rule.

U.S. LEGAL APPROACHES

One way to organize an introduction and study of U.S. communication law and policy is around key concepts and case law that are fundamental to First Amendment interpretation:

- Case law frequency balances an individual or group's rights of free expression and government regulation interests. The **balance of interest doctrine** has been refined over the years by legal scrutiny that emphasizes substantial or compelling interests required to outweigh First Amendment rights.
- The free trade or **marketplace of ideas** favors competition in search of truth (*Abrams v. United States*, 1919); however, the **clear and present danger test** addresses a threat of immediate harm as a justification for government restriction of free speech (Schenck v. United States, 1919). Prior to the 20th century, it was common for courts to apply a **bad tendency test** that restricted free expression based on any possibility that harm could be caused. The emphasis on harm was an application of normative ethics in the absence of First Amendment law.
- The **doctrine of preferred position** presumes state law constitutionality, except for the Bill of Rights and Fourteenth Amendment. States have a burden to prove that a law does not violate the First Amendment right of free expression. This is important because states moved to protect social media data privacy, and the U.S. federal government generally lags states in this and other areas that touch on free expression.
- Constitutional law generally prohibits government **prior restraint** that bans speech or publication before it happens (*Near v. Minnesota*, 1931).
- **Subsequent punishment** under libel law may address provably false defamation (*New York Times v. Sullivan*, 1964).
- A jury or judge at trial determines illegal **obscenity** under the *Miller* test. It applies an average person and contemporary community standards appeal to prurient interests; patently offensive sexual conduct under state law; and lack of serious literary, artistic, political or scientific value (*Miller v. California*, 1973). Historically,

so-called natural law may render **blasphemy** illegal, as disparaging words about churches, religion or gods.

- **Symbolic speech** and **expressive conduct** focus on constitutionally protected behavior, such as the burning of an American flag to represent political speech (*Texas v. Johnson*, 1989).
- Expressive conduct, such as burning a draft card, may be regulated, if there is a **compelling interest standard** other than stifling free speech (*United States v. O'Brien*, 1969).
- The *Brandenburg* test protects free speech advocacy for illegal behavior that does not rise to the level of immediate danger within a two-part context: the speaker history and the likelihood of illegal action (*Brandenburg v. Ohio*, 1969).
- The U.S. Supreme Court generally has found that a **gag order** attempting to halt the sharing of information about open court proceedings is unconstitutional because it freezes free speech (*Nebraska Press v. Stuart*, 1976). While this case applied to news reporting by journalist, it also controls First Amendment rights of social media users.
- Public high school and college students have strong First Amendment rights, as long as speech does not disrupt classrooms and the educational mission (*Tinker v. Des Moines*, 1969).
- **Commercial speech**, such as **advertising** for legal products and services, is protected under the First Amendment (*Central Hudson v. Public Service Commission*, 1980).
- The *Reno* court elevated Internet publisher First Amendment rights to as high as that of print newspapers (*Reno v. ACLU*, 1997).

There are a core group of First Amendment cases that dominate the U.S. legal framework, but it also is important to consider cross-national and comparative law within other countries, and emerging international law.

COMPARATIVE AND INTERNATIONAL LAW

The General Data Protection Regulation (GDPR), European data protection law, updated the European Union (EU) 1995 and 1998 directives, which left it to nation states to pass data privacy law. The EU regulatory approach, by way of contrast, sets binding EU legal standards. GDPR gave online users "more control over how their personal data is processed," and also created "new obligations" for an organization collected and using personal data (IT Governance, 2020, para. 5). GDPR, approved in 2016 and implemented in 2018, has six guiding principles of personal data. They must be:

1. Processed lawfully, fairly and transparently
2. Collected only for specific legitimate purposes
3. Adequate, relevant and limited to what is necessary
4. Accurate and, where necessary, kept up to date
5. Stored only as long as is necessary
6. Processed in a manner that ensures appropriate security (para. 16)

For most personal data, individuals must give consent for its collection. Organizations that collect data must follow contract language, protect vital and public interests and use data only for "legitimate interests" (para. 18). GDPR has driven compliance by U.S. social media companies, such as Facebook, as well as new U.S. state legislation. You have probably seen updated privacy notices posted by social media sites. These include company contact information, types of data processed, descriptions of company legitimate interests, any data transfer to third-party companies and how long data will be maintained. Under GDPR, user rights include rights to be informed about data collection, a right of data access, a right to correct errors, a "right to be forgotten" through data deletion, a right to move personal data and restrict its uses, a right to fight against direct **marketing** and a right to ask about data automation.

Facebook, Twitter and other social media sites, however, have increasingly used "dark patterns to nudge you toward giving away more of your data" (Pardes, 2020, para. 1). The use of popups that tells users they are in control of personal data sometimes end with a form of manipulation that leads them to consent to providing more information through "instant personalization" in the name of "a richer experience" (para. 4). For example, Facebook warned users against opting out of facial recognition:

> "If you keep face recognition turned off, we won't be able to use this technology if a stranger uses your photo to impersonate you." The button to turn the setting on is bright and blue; the button to keep it off is a less eye-catching grey.
>
> (Pardes, 2020, para. 4)

Examples of dark patterns include repeated site requests to turn on notifications, partial email messages with a link to return to the site, and difficult processes for deleting accounts (para. 5). Facebook, Instagram, Twitter, LinkedIn and other social media sites have all used these techniques. Increasingly, users seek to claim ownership of their data – a way to download, remove and store it. This is leading to emerging case law and law review analyses.

LAW REVIEW ANALYSES

Whitt (2020) noted that, since the 1990s early Internet, some analysts have been calling for "information fiduciaries" – independent agents who "would manage information deposited by end-users" (pp. 79–80). Whitt, a senior fellow at the Georgetown Tech Law and Policy Institute, noted that Facebook and other social media companies have been challenged on their claim of fiduciary responsibilities over data. In part, the legal and ethical issues relate to the fact that huge social media corporations, such as Google and Facebook, share none of the characteristics of a doctor–patient or other professional relationship: "The law of fiduciary relationships is a complex one, entwined with centuries of equity, torts, and other common law doctrine" (p. 86):

> The crucial linchpin of fiduciary obligation is what Frankel calls "entrusted power," affecting the existence, nature, and rules of such relationships… [A] fiduciary relationship is one in which one party exercises discretionary power over the significant practical interests of another. In fiduciary relationships, … "entrustors are always the vulnerable party."
>
> (p. 87)

It seems odd that Facebook would be open to taking on such an important professional obligation for its users, given that it requires loyalty and a **duty** confidentiality (pp. 97–98). Whitt (2020) noted that Facebook, in contrast, provides a lack of notice, legitimate consent, substance and accountability (p. 101). U.S. law has left questions about the relationship between social media users and platforms, and the sites have repeatedly not followed ethical principles grounded in **trust**, transparency and independence. A significant problem is the concentration of ownership by Facebook of Instagram and WhatsApp and the potential lack of competition within the social media marketplace. Still, recent continued growth of Reddit, Snapchat, TikTok and Pinterest offer a challenge to social media concentration. On a Pinterest board, for example, **pins** often reflect organic user interest in a variety of brands. Likewise, Reddit upvoting of a post seems more democratic than algorithm-based content that is pushed at users. However, any system can be subverted by **business-to-business (B2B)** agreements that may not be transparent. The U.S. federal and most state governments, meanwhile, have challenged Facebook in a claim that the company violated anti-trust laws.

Box 1.3 Challenging Facebook Monopoly Power

The United States government and 46 states took Facebook to court in an effort to force the sale of Instagram and WhatsApp. At the heart of the **complaints** were that Facebook "used illegal monopoly power and an 'unlawful scheme' to stifle competition, degrade personal privacy, and crush rivals" (Silverman & Mac, 2020, para. 1). New York Attorney General Letitia James claimed that Facebook "used its dominance and monopoly power to crush smaller rivals and snuff out competition, all at the expense of everyday users" (para. 2). During the decade that social media communication developed from a novelty into some of the largest global corporations, the regulatory system and courts were asked to decide if Facebook illegally eliminated competition. The Federal Trade Commission (FTC) added in a statement that: "Our aim is to roll back Facebook's anticompetitive conduct and restore competition so that **innovation** and free competition can thrive" (para. 6).

Earlier in the year, a U.S. House antitrust subcommittee revealed emails in 2012 sent between Facebook CEO Mark Zuckerberg and his chief financial officer (CFO) David Ebersman that showed concern about

- from: Mark Zuckerberg [redacted]
- to: David Ebersman[redacted], Mark Zuckerberg[redacted].
- time: Mon Feb 27 23:41:03 PST 2012 (1330414863647)
- subject: null
- body

One business questions I've been thinking about recently is how much we should be willing to pay to acquire mobile app companies like Instagram and Path that are building networks that are competitive with our own. These companies have the properties where they have millions of users (up to about 20m at the moment for Instagram), fast growth, a small team (10-25 employees) and no revenue. The businesses are nascent but the networks are established, the brands are already meaningful and if they grow to a large scale they could be very disruptive to us. These entrepreneurs don't want to sell (largely inspired our success), but at a high enough price -- like $500m or $1b -- they'd have to consider it. Given that we think our own valuation is fairly aggressive right now and that we're vulnerable in mobile, I'm curious if we should consider going after one or two of them. What do you think about this?

Damaging Facebook emails.

Courtesy UK Parliament, https://www.parliament.uk/documents/commons-committees/culture-media-and-sport/Note-by-Chair-and-selected-documents-ordered-from-Six4Three.pdf.

the potential threat from Instagram and other startups, as well as the need to buy them (Newton & Patel, 2020).

In another email Zuckerberg went further: "One reason people underestimate the importance of watching Google is that we can always just buy any competitive startups, but it'll be a while before we can buy Google" (para. 22).

In spite of the evidence, the Consumer Choice Center (2020) Deputy Director Yaël Ossowski responded that the FTC and states attorney general offices were "woefully misguided" (para. 3). Facebook "lawfully purchased Instagram for $1 billion" and "WhatsApp for $19 billion … Both services were acquired and already greenlit by the FTC, and have achieved inordinate amounts of success and user growth since" (paras. 4–5). However, a European Union investigation claimed that, far from being a consumers' organization, Consumer Choice Center was a covert lobbying group funded by big tobacco and business with a goal of promoting deregulation (Corporate Europe Observatory, 2017). In spite of this, it continued to receive media coverage in an effort to **influence** public opinion about social media companies.

In the case of WhatsApp, some competition exists from mobile SMS text messages, Facebook's Messenger, Snapchat, as well as Signal and other encrypted apps. The legal issue seems to be whether or not Facebook should be made to divest for its anticompetitive behavior in 2012 and 2014 – even if it failed to eliminate significant competition from Snapchat, Twitter, TikTok and other newer startups. Nevertheless, Facebook clearly had a strategy for market dominance that exploited user data privacy and unethically monetized it.

In *FTC v. Facebook* (2020), the FTC Act, 15 U.S.C. § 45(a) and 15 U.S.C. § 53(b) were **cited** to request "a permanent **injunction** and other equitable relief" (p. 1). Facebook reported annual revenues of $70 billion and profits of $18.5 billion (p. 2). As early as 2008, Zuckerberg emails expressed the view that "it is better to buy than compete" (p. 4). By 2011, the record showed that Zuckerberg concluded that Facebook had fallen behind Instagram – "a large and viable competitor to us on mobile photos, which will increasingly be the future of photos" (p. 4). The FTC complaint alleged that Facebook sought to "deter, suppress, and neutralize social networking competition" (p. 20). The FTC asked the court to order "divestiture" – sale of Instagram and WhatsApp to "one or more viable and independent business(es)" (p. 51).

In *State of New York v. Facebook* (2020) all but four U.S. states joined a lawsuit that claimed that under common law they had standing to use the Sherman Act, 15 U.S.C. § 2, the Clayton Act, 15 U.S.C. § 16, § 18, and § 26 to seek "injunctive and other equitable relief" (pp. 5–6). Their argument was that Facebook controls social media use of more than half of all U.S. people over the age of 13 (p. 6). The Google+ competitor, for example, ended because of "friend density on Facebook" (p. 15). The complaint alleged that Facebook exercised "monopoly" power in the social network marketplace (p. 71). Beyond the legal questions, the congressional disclosure of numerous Facebook executive emails over several years raises ethical concerns. Clearly, the competitive nature of Facebook led the company to cause harm to other startups that had innovated faster in the mobile app space, attracted younger users, and threatened Facebook's dominant market position. Rather than compete, Facebook appeared to conclude that their duty to stockholders would be to coerce buyouts rather than fairly compete in the marketplace. While Facebook has a fiduciary responsibility to shareholders to earn revenue and make profits, the scale of the business model may have squelched a lot of viable competitors.

Sources

Consumer Choice Center (2020, December 10). Yaël Ossowski email statement. https://consumerchoicecenter.org/.

Corporate Europe Observatory (2017, July 20). Big Tobacco and Right-Wing US Billionaires Funding Anti-Regulation Hardliners in the EU. https://corporateeurope.org/en/power-lobbies/2017/07/big-tobacco-and-right-wing-us-billionaires-funding-anti-regulation-hardliners.

FTC v. Facebook (2020, D.C. Cir., December 9). https://www.ftc.gov/system/files/ documents/cases/1910134fbcomplaint.pdf.

Newton, C. and Patel, N. (2020, July 29). "Instagram Can Hurt Us": Mark Zuckerberg Emails Outline Plan To Neutralize Competitors. *The Verge*.

https://www.theverge.com/2020/7/29/ 21345723/facebook-instagram-documents-emails-mark-zuckerberg-kevin-systrom-hearing.

Silverman, C. and Mac, R. (2020, December 9). The US Government Saysa Facebook Needs To Sell Instagram And WhatsApp. *Buzzfeed News.* https://www.buzzfeednews.com/ article/craigsilverman/us-government-facebook-monopoly-sell-instagram-whatsapp.

State of New York v. Facebook (2020, D.C. Cir.). https://ag.ny.gov/sites/default/files/ facebook_complaint_12.9.2020.pdf.

ETHICAL FRAMEWORKS AND ISSUES

Media ethicists offer models and concepts that may help extend our understanding of social media communication law and policy. The ambiguous nature of developing law, conflicting court decisions, proposed legislation and political context require that we identify social norms that begin with journalism and extend to social media communication.

Box 1.4 Thought Leader Stephen J.A. Ward

Stephen J.A. Ward.

Photograph courtesy Stephen Ward.

Digital technology, especially social media, has altered fundamentally how humans communicate. It also has altered fundamentally how we think about media ethics and law.

What *is* media ethics in a world transformed by individuals and groups employing digital media to promote their interests? What new notions and structures are needed for responsible publication in a digital universe?

These questions are urgent given that we live in a public sphere made increasingly toxic by government disinformation, extreme far-right groups, demagogic politicians, trolls, fixed ideologies, unswerving partisans and **fake news**. Yet, we also live in an era in which digital media can be used to inform humanity about its global problems and to empower the less powerful.

We can readily think about specific changes that would improve media, e.g., improving the fact-checking of claims. Such individual actions are laudable but, in my view, not sufficient. The resources of citizen, journalist, scholar, civic society and government need to be combined in a creative, collective manner.

But how? The first step is to rethink what media ethics is.

PUBLIC-DIRECTED ETHICS FOR A DIGITAL UNIVERSE

Since the origin of modern journalism ethics in the early 20th century, media ethics has been a "creature" of professional media workers. Ethics "belonged" to the professionals, who determined what norms to accept, and how they were updated and enforced. Media ethics was a professional-directed form of ethical self-regulation.

Today, this model cannot address many of the problems of our digital universe. Media content is produced outside profession newsrooms. Issues go beyond traditional concerns about the accuracy or bias of mainstream news media. We face society-wide, and globally, issues such as the interference of robotic disinformation programs in elections. Media ethics now includes questions about not only online behemoths, such as Google and Facebook, but also about the many smaller and experimental media "**startups**." Media ethics concerns how citizens are educated about media, and about how citizens use their media devices to inform or advocate. Moreover, media ethics needs to adopt an advocatory stance that promotes trustful channels of information and opposes those who make the public sphere a toxic domain. In sum, media ethics becomes a branch of communication ethics for digital, democratic society.

I propose we rethink media ethics as a *public-directed ethics system.* In this view, the public should play a central role in evaluating media content, helping to implement media education programs, and assisting in the formulation of new media guidelines. Public structures to carry out these functions should be created, e.g., media monitoring sites, and media councils. Initially, these structures could be anchored in agencies with knowledge of media, e.g., schools of journalism and communication, centers for ethics, and professional media societies.

The idea of a public-directed media ethics contains two basic notions:

Media ethics is a society-wide responsibility. The quality of a society's media system, defined by its reliability, inclusiveness, adherence to norms, and promotion of democracy, is a responsibility of all citizens, not just the mainstream media or government media regulators.

Media ethics is a collaborative system – a web of coalitions. At the center of a media system, there should be a web of coalitions, i.e., a network of individuals and groups that care about communication for democratic community. We need to *connect* across many boundaries. Media ethics becomes a responsibility not only of individual citizens but also of associations, such as academic institutions, schools of media, information professionals such as librarians, press councils, ombudsmen, media foundations and NGOs with an interest in good media, such as advocates for human rights and the protection of minorities. These structures could be organized around a central, administrative "hub."

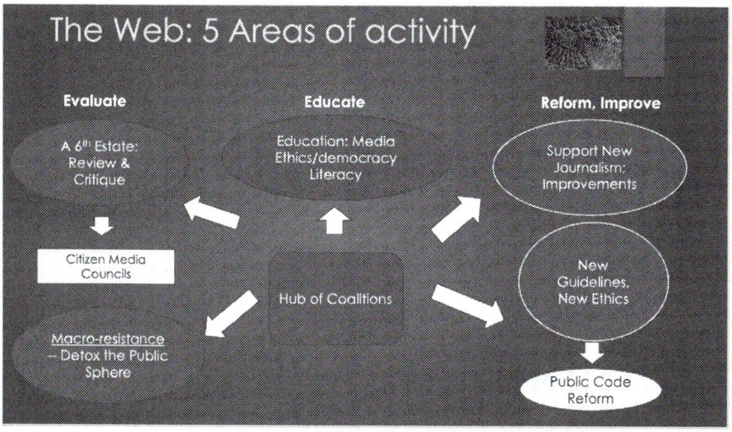

Five areas of activity.

Model by Stephen Ward.

The proposed model identifies five functions, or areas of activity, for this media ethics system. The functions fall under three categories: *Evaluate* media; *educate* about media; and *improve* (or *create*) guidelines for practice.

Evaluation includes the review and critique of public media and a "macro-resistance" to disinformation by exposing unreliable sources and fake news. I envisage a "sixth estate."* It would be a system of collaborating centers that contribute to a high-profile site or sites, well-known to the public as a trusted place in which to check media sources and debate media practice and policy. It would be a resource for media excellence and accountability. Among the coalition's functions would be not just fact-checking but "opinion-checking" – the evaluation of leading interpretations and perspectives in the news. It could maintain a "registry" of reliable and unreliable sources. This network could be anchored at a major school of journalism and/or a multidisciplinary center for democracy.

Evaluation includes the construction of what I call "citizen media councils" to stimulate public discussion about coverage of events and issues by media as a whole or by a media outlet. Unlike the older press councils, citizen councils would not be limited to the negative function of adjudicating individual complaints about individual stories by individual outlets. The councils would not be operated and financed mainly by the media industry and they would more effectively use social media to bring citizens together to openly debate the issue at hand.

The aim of education is to strengthen current efforts to create students and citizens who are informed, critical evaluators of media. Coalitions would lobby the education system and government to develop **media literacy** (and media ethics literacy) teaching in schools, starting at an early age. The coalitions could develop teaching modules to be

* *Note:* Originally, the fourth estate was the traditional mass media acting as a watchdog on government; the fifth estate is nonmainstream "'independent" media that, among other things, critique mass media. A "sixth estate" monitors and critiques all forms of media, including the fourth and fifth estates.

used not only in the classroom but also in media-awareness workshops organized by civic groups.

"Reform, improve" refers to a collaboration of professionals and citizens to create ethical guidelines for the use of new technology, such as virtual reality (VR), and guidelines for coverage of emerging or difficult social issues. It could be called "public code reform" since many of the guidelines would help to update codes of ethics. Democratic participatory processes, such as town hall meetings and citizen assemblies, gathered together in person or virtually, would allow citizens to engage the issues confronting their media system. Also, experts, NGOs, and government agencies can help these "reform sessions" develop guidelines on reporting such issues as mental illness, refugees, pandemics, and extreme groups.

Professional media would be an important part of the system, but media ethics would no longer be highly dependent on the always varying support of mainstream media for ethics. Media ethics would "belong" to citizens.

ACTIVE, DIGITAL CITIZENS

How this system should be realized and organized is open for experiment and discussion. For example, social media and digital communication can be used to create new mechanisms of public participation.

Practically, the construction of a public-directed system would encounter the same tough questions that confront any audacious project: How to persuade people to cooperate? What financial and administrative support would be needed? How to ensure that the intervention of public groups into media ethics is consistent with constitutional protections for freedom of expression and publication?

On the positive side, many elements of this system are already in place: codes of ethics, and guides on how to evaluate media systems. There are hundreds of media schools with teachers, scholars, and students; dozens of centers for media and democracy, fact-checking organizations, and NGOs already fighting online misinformation about immigrants and religion.

The object of this paper is not to settle these practical issues. My main aim is to plant the *idea* of a public-directed ethics system in the reader's mind. Another aim is to encourage citizens to adopt an active, empowering mindset. Democratic digital citizens are not powerless *if they act in a common cause*.

Stephen J.A. Ward is an internationally recognized author, media ethicist and historian of ideas whose research is on the ethics of global, digital media, the rise of extreme media, and its impact on democracy. He is Professor Emeritus and Distinguished Lecturer on Ethics at the University of British Columbia (UBC), Canada. He has written and edited ten books on media ethics, including the award-winning *Radical Media Ethics* and *The Invention of Journalism Ethics*. He is editor-in-chief of *The Handbook of Global Media Ethics* featuring chapters by 70 media scholars and journalists around the world. A former war reporter, he is founding director of the Center for Journalism Ethics at the University of Wisconsin, co-founder of the UBC School of Journalism in Vancouver, and former director of the Turnbull Media Center at the University of Oregon in Portland. He has won the President's Award for lifetime contribution to journalism from the Canadian Association of Journalists.

Professor Ward's emerging journalism ethics model could be *expanded* to better understand social media law and ethics. **Engaged journalism**, for example, emphasizes meaningful audience interaction. Starting with non-journalists also creating and distributing social media content to growing audiences, journalism ethics must be placed within a larger social, political and economic context. This appears to reject pure **objectivity** and the ethical theory of **determinism** that is a rejection of free will. The economic marketplace, in the longer term, seems to be based more on disruption of large corporate power than predetermined outcomes. In the shorter term, however, emerging powers – Google, Facebook, Apple and Amazon – do not always favor moral principles that would protect individual human rights. For example, a **Facebook Live** streaming video may quantify an audience on **Facebook Insights**, a **social media dashboard** similar to **Twitter Analytics**, but this lacks transparency with the research subjects' watching and engaging. Only Facebook may fully analyze a **user profile** or **social graph**, and we are not told all of the ways these data are maintained and used. Instead, the methods are treated as trade secrets. This turns people and their eyeballs into objects for profit within **social business**. While the industry-wide use of stories are promoted as disappearing after a certain amount of time, in truth, the data are maintained by Facebook and other corporations through cloud storage.

Students of social media law and ethics may apply theories, concepts, frameworks, and models through a variety of online resources and case studies. It is valuable to develop a mindset of constantly reading what is new. For example, The NATO Strategic Communications Centre of Excellence found it easy to pay Russian companies and buy thousands of likes, views, and shares for accounts, including those of two U.S. senators (Kinetz, 2020). Paid influence worked on all of the major social media platforms – Facebook, Instagram, TikTok, YouTube and Twitter. In an era of global health and environmental crises, misinformation and disinformation and political radicalization, we need international law to provide context and stability by establishing and practicing ethical values.

ONLINE RESOURCES

The Santa Clara Principles (2018). On Transparency and Accountability in Content Moderation. https://santaclaraprinciples.org/.

These were an attempt to outline "minimum levels of transparency and accountability" within online content moderation. In the absence of formal law and regulation, academics have called for self-regulation that applies ethical frameworks for communication.

Box 1.5 The Santa Clara Principles on Transparency and Accountability in Content Moderation

1. Numbers. Companies should publish the numbers of posts removed and accounts permanently or temporarily suspended due to violations of their content guidelines.
2. Notice. Companies should provide notice to each user whose content is taken down or account is suspended about the reason for the removal or suspension.
3. Appeal. Companies should provide a meaningful opportunity for timely appeal of any content removal or account suspension.

Source: The Santa Clara Principles (2018). On Transparency and Accountability in Content Moderation. https://santaclaraprinciples.org/.

Social media communication account users are governed by the terms of service (ToS) end-user contracts. These generally do not require sites to provide full justification and data transparency on the number of flagged posts, application of site rules and human review of decision-making and this can be very frustrating for users. Twitter, for example, made controversial decisions to flag content, delete accounts, and warn readers related to President Donald Trump's @realDonaldTrump false claims during the 2020 presidential election.

Pew Research (2020) found that most Americans (73 percent) think that social media sites censor political viewpoints, and the numbers are much higher for Republicans (90 percent). **Respondents** to a June, 2020 survey showed distrust for the executives running social media sites: "69% of Republicans and Republican leaners say major technology companies generally support the views of liberals over conservatives, compared with 25% of Democrats and Democratic leaners" (para. 4). Twitter's decision to label the president's tweets likely had some impact on the survey results. Respondents were split on the need to fact-check posts. In general, Republicans had less trust than Democrats in content review processes.

Hate speech on social media sites also is difficult to manage because of vague definition. Williams (2020) contended that lies, such as deep fakes' "doctored video," are allowed to remain on Facebook and other sites: "But when the leaders of social media companies are asked why they allow lies to spread, they hide behind claims of free speech for all" (para. 5). Corporate executives, too, also may be targeted in extremist conspiracy theories: "Today there is a far greater threat to honest debate – the flood of lies and distortion on social media" (para. 35).

Social media site activity also involves collection of massive amounts of user data. As there were attempts to monitor Covid-19 carrier patients, the problem of testing data breaches surfaced (Bonnet & Zionts, 2020). The inability to protect public health data from hackers suggests that every social media user also should be concerned. The frequent use of apps opens the possibility of continuous collection of location and other personal behavioral data. Too often, social media sites have not been transparent about the collection and use of user data. At the same time, public posts have a life of their own.

Robert O'Neill, for example, is the ex-Navy SEAL who may have killed Osama bin Laden. He tweeted a selfie photo not wearing a mask during a Delta Airlines flight while a marine behind him followed the rules (Langlois, 2020):

> Robert J. O'Neill @mkhooyah
> "I'm not a pussy." (August 19, 2020)
> "I am not the bad guy. I killed the bad guy." (August 19, 2020)
> "I just got banned from @Delta for posting a picture. Wow." (August 20, 2020)

O'Neill has been skeptical about the danger of Covid-19 and said the post was a bad joke. Even though he deleted the photo and apologized, Delta has banned more than 100 passengers from future flights for violating the Covid-19 rules. Yet Twitter took no action on O'Neill's account.

Beyond formal law and ethics, public opinion plays an important role in understanding social media communication. Australian musician, Nick Cave, for example, attacked the social promotion of "cancel culture" as having an "asphyxiating effect on the creative soul of a society" (Bakare, 2020, para. 1). His Red Hand Files newsletter took aim: "Political correctness has grown to become the unhappiest religion in the world" (para. 2). His concern was that cancel culture represented a lack of engagement with "uncomfortable ideas" (para. 3): "A force that finds its meaning in the cancellation of these difficult ideas hampers the creative spirit of a society." (para. 5). Cave (2020), in his open letter, values mercy in "any functioning and tolerant society" (para. 1), "free-ranging conversation" that expands "collective discovery toward a common good" (para. 2) and tolerance: "Without mercy society grows inflexible, fearful, vindictive and humorless" (para. 3). The #cancelculture hashtag on Twitter continued to be used over a long period of time and was connected to election differences between Donald Trump and Joe Biden's followers (Bond, 2020; NodeXL, 2020).

In the U.S.A., the First Amendment bolsters the common law concept that government shall not legally use prior restraint before publication of ideas, particularly most core political speech, yet subsequent punishment after publication is possible. From defamation lawsuits to others exercising free speech through boycott and cancellation, law supports the view that we generally favor more speech, not less. One defense in a libel lawsuit is that the content offered **fair comment** and public sphere criticism based on provably true facts. This common law defamation defense, and growing constitutional First Amendment protection for political speech, helps explain why social media channels are so robust. To the extent that cancel culture represents an attempt to stifle controversial speech, there may be ethical concerns.

DISCUSSION QUESTIONS

1. How should we determine state of mind during a federal online threat case? Should perceptions of fear by the victims of social media posts be considered?
2. Is a right to opt out of personal data collection enough to protect privacy, or should there always be opt-in provisions? Why or why not?
3. Do you favor the use of cancel culture to respond to the exercise of controversial views? Why or why not?

REFERENCES

Abrams v. United States, 250 U.S. 616 (1919).

AFP (2020, October 1). Turkey Applies Strict New Social Media Rules. *Bangkok Post*. https://www.bangkokpost.com/world/1994835/turkey-applies-strict-new-social-media-rules.

Arbel, T. (2021, January 1). Hedge Fund Alden Offers to Buy Tribune, Valuing It At $521 Million. *Associated Press*. https://apnews.com/article/business-new-york-media-newspapers-dcaafaefaf83b13b5f0b8b7aab11babc.

Bakare, L. (2020, August 12). Nick Cave: "Cancel Culture is Bad Religion Run Amok," Australian Musician Criticizes People's Refusal to Engage with "Difficult Ideas." *The Guardian*. https://www.theguardian.com/music/2020/aug/12/nick-cave-political-correctness-bad-religion-run-amuck-cancel-culture.

Bond, P. (2020, November 5). After the Election, Conservatives Brace for an Emboldened "Cancel Culture" Movement. *Newsweek*. https://www.newsweek.com/after-election-conservatives-brace-emboldened-cancel-culture-movement-1545212.

Bonnet, S. and Zionts, A. (2020, August 21). FBI Investigating South Dakota COVID-19 Patient Data Breach.*Rapid City Journal*. https://rapidcityjournal.com/news/fbi-investigating-south-dakota-covid-19-patient-data-breach/article_171b9b4c-e94d-555b-9d72-bb-4d40169ddb.html#tracking-source=home-top-story-1.

Brigham, B. (2020, November 14). Twitter Puts New Disclaimer on Trump's Tweets After He Lies About Winning Pennsylvania and Georgia. *Salon*. https://www.salon.com/2020/11/14/twitter-puts-new-disclaimer-on-trumps-tweets-after-he-lies-about-winning-pennsylvania-and-georgia_partner/.

Brandenburg v. Ohio, 395 U.S. 444 (1969).

Cadwalladr, C. (2020, January 4). Fresh Cambridge Analytica Leak "Shows Global Manipulation is Out of Control." *The Guardian*. https://www.theguardian.com/uk-news/2020/jan/04/cambridge-analytica-data-leak-global-election-manipulation.

Cave, N. (2020). What Do You Think of Cancel Culture? *The Red Hand Files 109*. https://www.theredhandfiles.com/what-is-mercy-for-you/.

Central Hudson Gas and Electric Company v. Public Service Commission of New York, 447 U.S. 557 (1980).

Christians, C.G. (2019). *Media Ethics and Global Justice in the Digital Age*. Cambridge: Cambridge University Press.

Civic Integrity Policy (2020, October). Twitter. https://help.twitter.com/en/rules-and-policies/election-integrity-policy.

Conley, A. (2019, November 25). Bakery Owner Holds Teen Down After Tip Jar is Stolen; Teen's Mom Wants Assault Charges Filed. *Omaha World-Herald*. https://omaha.com/news/crime/bakery-owner-holds-teen-down-after-tip-jar-is-stolen-teens-mom-wants-assault-charge/article_49ab36aa-b4f4-5275-967c-c4f22978e6be.html.

Consumer Choice Center (2020, December 10). Yaël Ossowski email statement. https://consumerchoicecenter.org/.

Corporate Europe Observatory (2017, July 20). Big Tobacco and Right-Wing US Billionaires Funding Anti-Regulation Hardliners in the EU. https://corporateeurope.org/en/power-lobbies/2017/07/big-tobacco-and-right-wing-us-billionaires-funding-anti-regulation-hardliners.

Elonis v. United States, 575 U.S. 723, 135 S. Ct 2001 (2015).

Fischer, S. (2020, December 22). Biden Won't Inherit Official White House Account Twitter Followers. *Axios.* https://www.axios.com/twitter-biden-wont-inherit-trump-potus-followers-007da822-c9bc-4c66-8f08-1a945aec20e2.html.

FTC v. Facebook (2020, D.C. Cir., December 9). https://www.ftc.gov/system/files/ documents/cases/1910134fbcomplaint.pdf.

Gadde, V. and Beykpour, K. (2020, November 12). An Update on Our Work Around the 2020 US Elections. Twitter Company Blog. https://blog.twitter.com/en_us/topics/ company/2020/2020-election-update.html.

Gallicano, T.D., Bivens, T.H., and Cho, Y.Y. (2014). Considerations Regarding Ghost Blogging and Ghost Commenting. In M.W. DiStaso and D.S. Bortree, *Ethical Practice of Social Media in Public Relations*, pp. 21–32. New York: Routledge.

Gordon, M. (2020, November 17). Twitter, Facebook CEOs Vow Election Action; GOP Touts Curbs. *Associated Press.* https://apnews.com/article/300k-tweets-election-disinformation-244ffa8ea45ce9d79b7115d4ed044f8c.

Hayes, A.S. (2013). *Mass Media Law: The Printing Press to the Internet.* New York: Peter Lang.

Holmes, A. (2020, November 4). California Just Passed a Major Privacy Law That Will Make It Harder for Facebook and Google to Track people and Gather Data. *Business Insider.* https://www.businessinsider.com/prop-24-privacy-california-data-tracking-facebook-google-2020-11.

Hutchinson, A. (2020a, November 20). Twitter Is Looking To Re-open Its Account Verification Process, Seeks Feedback On New Process.*Social Media Today.* https://www.socialmediatoday.com/news/twitter-is-looking-to-re-open-its-account-verification-process-seeks-feedb/589681/.

Hutchinson, A. (2020b, August 20). Twitter Adds More Detail On DMs From Users You Don't Follow.*Social Media Today.* https://www.socialmediatoday.com/news/ twitter-adds-more-detail-on-dms-from-users-you-dont-follow/583917/.

IT Governance (2020). The EU GDPR Overview. https://www.itgovernance.co.uk/ data-protection-dpa-and-eu-data-protection-regulation.

Kinetz, E. (2020, December 21). Report: Social Media Manipulation Affects Even US Senators. *Associated Press.* https://apnews.com/article/media-social-media-chuck-grassley-chris-murphy-a43992f3fc8c3f4ff198a838f748a0a9.

Knight First Amendment Inst. at Columbia Univ. v. Trump (*Knight Institute I*), 302 F. Supp. 3d 541, 580 (S.D.N.Y. 2018), aff'd, 928 F.3d 226, 230 (2d Cir. 2019), reh'g **en banc** denied, 953 F.3d 216 (2d Cir. 2020).

Knight Institute II: Knight First Amendment Institute v. Trump (2020). Complaint for Declaratory and Injunctive Relief, cv-05958. https://knightcolumbia.org/ documents/ ff13289e31/2020.07.31_ECF-1-_Complaint.pdf.

Koch, T. (2017). *Ethics in Everyday Places.* Cambridge, MA: MIT Press.

Langlois, S. (2020, August 21). Navy SEAL Who Shot Bin Laden Refuses to Wear Mask – and Delta May Refuse to Let Him Fly Ever Again.*Market Watch.* https://www.marketwatch.com/story/former-navy-seal-who-shot-bin-laden-refuses-to-wear-mask-delta-may-refuse-to-ever-let-him-fly-again-2020-08-20.

Lazarus, A. (2019, December 12). Car Wrap Scam Targets College Students. *Federal Trade Commission.* https://www.consumer.ftc.gov/blog/2019/12/car-wrap-scam-targets-college-students.

Lee, S.T. (2005). SARS: The Bug That Would Not Go Away. In Phillip Patterson and Lee Wilkins, *Media Ethics, Issues and Cases,* 5th edition, pp. 54–57. Boston, MA: McGraw-Hill.

Lipschultz, J.H. (2021). *Social Media Communication: Concepts, Practices, Data, Law and Ethics,* 3rd edition. New York and London: Routledge.

Lipschultz, J.H. (2020). *Social Media Measurement and Management: Entrepreneurial Digital Analytics.* New York and London: Routledge.

Makdisi, M. and Makdisi, J. (2009). How to Write a Case Brief for Law School: Excerpt Reproduced from *Introduction to the Study of Law, Cases and Materials,* 3rd edition. LexisNexis. https://www.lexisnexis.com/en-us/lawschool/pre-law/how-to-brief-a-case.page.

Morissette v. United States, 342 US. 246 (1952).

Myers, C. (2019). The Law in Modern Society, in W. Wat Hopkins (ed.), *Communication and the Law,* pp.1–21). Northport, AL: Vision Press.

Near v. Minnesota, 283 U.S.697 (1931).

Nebraska Press v. Stuart, 427 U.S. 539 (1976).

Newton, C. and Patel, N. (2020, July 29). "'Instagram Can Hurt Us": Mark Zuckerberg Emails Outline Plan To Neutralize Competitors. *The Verge.* https://www.theverge.com/2020/7/29/21345723/facebook-instagram-documents-emails-mark-zuckerberg-kevin-systrom-hearing.

New York Times v. Sullivan, 376 U.S. 254 (1964).

NodeXL (2020, November 12). Cancel Culture. NodeXL Graph Gallery. https://nodexlgraphgallery.org/Pages/Graph.aspx?graphID=240232.

O'Neill, R.M. (2001). *The First Amendment and Civil Liability.* Bloomington, IN: Indiana University Press.

Ortutay, B. (2020, August 19). Facebook Bans Some, But Not All, QAnon Groups and Accounts. *Associated Press.* https://apnews.com/71bddeded4bfdf8f1b6efed37963768d.

Packingham v. North Carolina, 582 U.S. ___, 137 S. Ct. 1730 (2017).

Pardes, A. (2020, August 12). How Facebook and Other Sites Manipulate Your Privacy Choices, Social Media Platforms Repeatedly Use So-Called Dark Patterns to Nudge You Toward Giving Away More of Your Data. *Wired.* https://www.wired.com/story/facebook-social-media-privacy-dark-patterns/.

Patterson, P. and Wilkins, L. (2005). *Media Ethics: Issues and Cases,* 5th edition. Boston, MA: McGraw-Hill.

Pew Research (2020, August 19). Most Americans Think Social Media Sites Censor Political Viewpoints. https://www.pewresearch.org/internet/2020/08/19/most-americans-think-social-media-sites-censor-political-viewpoints.

Potter, W.J. (2008). *Media Literacy*, 4th edition. Los Angeles: SAGE.

Proposition 24 (2020, November). *Ballotpedia.* https://ballotpedia.org/California_Proposition_24,_Consumer_Personal_Information_Law_and_Agency_Initiative_(2020).

Reno v. ACLU, 521 U.S. 844 (1997).

Reuters (2020, November 9). Trump Will Lose Special Twitter Protections in January. *NBC News.* https://www.nbcnews.com/tech/tech-news/trump-will-lose-special-twitter-protections-january-rcna172.

Romm, T. (2020, December 1). Trump Threatens to Veto Major Defense Bill Unless Congress Repeals Section 230, a Legal Shield for Tech Giants. *Washington Post.* https://www.washingtonpost.com/technology/2020/12/01/trump-repeal-section-230-ndaa/.

Santa Clara Principles On Transparency and Accountability in Content Moderation (2018). https://santaclaraprinciples.org/.

Schenck v. United States, 249 U.S. 47 (1919).

Scola, N. (2020, November 20). Twitter Will Hand @POTUS To Biden On Inauguration Day, Even If Trump Doesn't Concede. *Politico.* https://www.politico.com/news/2020/11/20/twitter-trump-transition-biden-potus-438880.

Sherman, M. (2020, August 20). Trump Wants #SCOTUS OK to Block Critics on @realDonaldTrump. *Associated Press.* https://apnews.com/article/014056743890cc27d9cdd0e4be264e03.

Silverman, C. and Mac, R. (2020, December 9). The US Government Says Facebook Needs To Sell Instagram And WhatsApp.*Buzzfeed News.* https://www.buzzfeednews.com/article/craigsilverman/us-government-facebook-monopoly-sell-instagram-whatsapp.

State of New York v. Facebook (2020, D.C. Cir.). https://ag.ny.gov/sites/default/files/ facebook_complaint_12.9.2020.pdf.

Stewart, D.R. (ed.) (2017). *Social Media and the Law: A Guidebook for Communication Students and Professionals*, 2nd edition. New York and London: Routledge.

Subramanian, R. and Weare, A. (2020, June). #Notokay: Challenging Sexual Violence Through Digital Health Activism. *Critical Public Health.* https://www.tandfonline.com/doi/full/10.1080/09581596.2020.1776218.

Tatro v. University of Minnesota, 816 N.W.2d 509 (Minn. 2012).

Terry, C., Anderson, J., Wiley, S.K., and Memmel, S. (2020, Fall/Winter). Free Expression or Protected Speech? Looking for the Concept of State Action in News. *UB Journal of Media Law & Ethics*, 8(2), 102–116.

Texas v. Johnson, 491 U.S. 397 (1989).

Tinker v. Des Moines Independent Community School District, 393 U.S. 503 (1969).

United States v. O'Brien, 391 U.S. 367 (1968).

University of Texas at Austin (2020). Center for Media Engagement. Doxing in the Name of Public Health. https://mediaengagement.org/research/doxing-in-the-name-of-public-health/.

University of Wisconsin-Madison (2020). Center for Journalism Ethics. Ethics in a Nutshell, The Nature of Ethics. https://ethics.journalism.wisc.edu/ resources/ethics-in-a-nutshell/.

Whitt, R.S. (2020, December). Old School Goes Online: Exploring Fiduciary Obligations of Loyalty and Care in the Digital Platforms Era. *Santa Clara High Tech. Law Journal*, 36, 75–131.

Williams, J. (2020, August 17). Juan Williams: Social Media Dodges Blame for Spreading Hate. *The Hill*. https://thehill.com/opinion/technology/512263-juan-williams-social-media-dodges-blame-for-spreading-hate.

Xie, Q. (2020, April 14). Coronavirus: Couple Wrongly Fined £1,700 After Posting Holiday **Snaps** From Last Year Amid Lockdown. *Independent*. https://www.independent.co.uk/life-style/coronavirus-australia-lockdown-fine-holiday-photos-a9463906.html.

Student Free Speech Issues

2

> *It can hardly be argued that either students or teachers shed their constitutional rights to freedom of speech or expression at the schoolhouse gate ... In our system, state-operated schools may not be enclaves of totalitarianism. School officials do not possess absolute authority over their students.*

—U.S. Supreme Court Justice Abe Fortas,
Tinker v. Des Moines Independent Community School District, 393 U.S. 503 (1969, p. 506)

As Covid-19 impacted colleges in 2020, including more than 1,200 positive tests at the University of Alabama, campus administrators sent emails warning professors against speaking about the outbreak: "Do not tell the rest of the class," an email to the politics department read (Shugerman, 2020, para. 3). The email appeared to be an attempt to keep secret to other faculty and students that others had tested positive, but were attending class by wearing masks and practicing social distancing: "Multiple other emails from other departments reviewed by the *Daily Beast* warn teachers against telling students about a positive classmate or posting about it on social media, even in the most general terms, claiming it could constitute a HIPAA violation" (para. 4). The Health Insurance Portability and Accountability Act of 1996 Privacy Rule created national standards for protecting individual patient medical records and health information. However, attempts by public university administrators to keep students, faculty and staff from speaking also may violate First Amendment rights. Other Covid-19 outbreaks forced major universities to abandon face-to-face instruction, but Alabama continued without transparency of information:

> A ... member of the housing staff, who asked to remain anonymous for fear of losing their job, said students in quarantine had been seen congregating outside, hanging out of their windows, and screaming profanities at faculty who passed by.
>
> "There's nobody supervising these buildings, it's a complete free-for-all," this person said. "They're running wild."
>
> (paras. 17–18)

The pandemic created many academic freedom issues across the county, such as faculty rights when they desire to teach online courses rather than in-person. At Iowa Western College, faculty tried to protest by having a call-in-sick strike, but a court injunction claimed the Public Employment Relations Act (PERA) made it illegal to strike in Iowa and violators were threatened with up to six months in jail (Monroe, 2020). Amid the pandemic, faculty members also continued to be disciplined or fired for classroom speech. At Central Michigan University, for example, a tenured professor and journalism department chair lost his job for "creating a hostile environment by using the N-word in class" (Jaschik, 2020, para. 1):

> Boudreau "created a hostile learning environment through his reckless use of the n-word (and other racial and homophobic slurs) in his instruction," said a report investigating the professor. "There was no defensible reason for [Boudreau's] choice to use uncensored racial slurs. CMU will not permit such hostility to go unchecked and, as such, the employer finds separation of employment to be the appropriate sanction."
>
> (para. 2)

University administrators reportedly responded to an alumna complaint. News coverage of such cases has typically sparked social media reaction from campuses and communities.

For more than 50 years, students, faculty and staff have faced First Amendment issues within public high schools and universities the prompted U.S. Supreme Court review. As a reader of this book, you likely are a student, or have been one and can remember the experience. Students exercising a right of free speech and expression frequently face attempts by campus administrators to stifle them. In the United States, First Amendment law granted public high school, college and university students rights, but these are not absolute. The development of the Internet and social media communication on mobile phones complicated the balancing of rights.

PUBLIC HIGH SCHOOLS

Christopher Eckhardt 16, John Tinker, 15, and his sister Mary Beth, 13, were public high school students in 1965 when they planned to wear black armbands in a silent protest of the Vietnam War. Two days before they did, principals "met and adopted a policy that any student wearing an armband to school would be asked to remove it, and, if he refused, he would be suspended until he returned without the armband" (*Tinker v. Des Moines Independent Community School District*, 1969, p. 504). Decades later, we could imagine a **hypothetical** case of a silent protest staged with Instagram photographs, but the *Tinker* students did not have digital tools. After the students were sent home, they filed a complaint. The District Court upheld school suspensions as "reasonable in order to prevent disturbance of school discipline" (p. 505). A divided Eighth Circuit panel agreed, but did not write an opinion. The U.S. Supreme Court heard the case and reversed the lower courts on First Amendment grounds because, "akin to 'pure speech,'" this "does not concern aggressive, disruptive action or even group demonstrations" (p. 508). The Court noted that no evidence was provided that the wearing of black armbands interfered with instruction or student privacy on campus. "Outside the classrooms, a few students made hostile remarks to the children wearing armbands, but there were no threats or acts of violence on school premises" (p. 508). Among the apparent concerns of administrators who proactively approved the new policy was that a journalism teacher had been told that one of the students "wanted to write an article" in the school newspaper (p. 510). Students in the 1960s did not have the Internet or social media to exercise free expression on and schools could be gatekeepers of ideas by limiting what was published in the school paper. But the sweeping *Tinker* decision sought to send a message about students: "They may not be confined to the expression of those sentiments that are officially approved" (p. 511). The Court quoted Supreme Court precedent about "vigilant protection of constitutional freedoms," the classroom and the "marketplace of ideas," and "robust exchange of ideas" (p. 512, quoting *Shelton v. Tucker*, 1960, p. 487). The 7-2 *Tinker* decision stood for the interpretation that: "It can hardly be argued that either students or teachers shed their constitutional rights to freedom of speech or expression at the schoolhouse gate" (p. 506). Despite this, the Supreme Court and lower courts over the years have narrowed the impact of this important First Amendment ruling. Some of this rests on the interpretation of the *Tinker* ruling, which cited *West Virginia v. Barnett* (1943) that held that public school students may not be forced to salute the flag:

> The Fourteenth Amendment, as now applied to the States, protects the citizen against the State itself and all of its creatures – Boards of Education not excepted. These have, of course, important, delicate, and highly discretionary functions, but none that they may not perform within the limits of the **Bill of Rights**. That they are educating the young for citizenship is reason for scrupulous protection of Constitutional freedoms of the individual, if we are not to strangle the free mind at its source and teach youth to discount important principles of our government as mere platitudes.
>
> (p. 637)

The U.S. Supreme Court *Tinker* ruling, however, "emphasized the need for affirming the comprehensive authority of the States and of school officials, consistent with fundamental constitutional safeguards, to prescribe and control conduct in the schools" (p. 507). The *Tinker* court weighed a balancing test between First Amendment rights that may "collide with the rules of the school authorities" (p. 507).

COLLEGES AND UNIVERSITIES

Beyond the public high school context, college and university students continue to face First Amendment issues including campus creation of "free speech zones" based on the use of **time, place and manner restrictions** (*Uzuegbunam v. Preczewski*, 2021). There is much debate about allowing campus police powers to issue required permits for the exercise of core political free speech rights in designated areas at approved times. Public university faculty members also exercise a right of free expression and a degree of academic freedom (AAUP, 2018). At Syracuse University, however, a chemistry professor was placed on administrative leave after students complained about "derogatory language" on his syllabus (Gajjar, 2020, para. 1). Jon Zubieta reportedly used the words "Wuhan flu" and "Chinese Communist Party flu" in his notes (para. 2). University administrators stated: "The derogatory language used by a professor on his course syllabus is damaging to the learning environment for our students and offensive to Chinese, international and Asian-Americans everywhere who have experienced hate speech, rhetoric and actions since the pandemic began" (para. 3). Students using the #NotAgainSU hashtag called for dismissal. The university responded after a graduate student not in the course shared a screenshot of the course statement on his Instagram account, and others responded that they did not feel safe in a classroom with a professor using "political and racist language" (para. 9). The controversy escalated when an undergraduate, also not in the class, shared the Instagram post and an email post on Twitter. The #NotAgainSU hashtag was created a year earlier after "racial slurs against Black and Asian people were written on two floors in a Syracuse University dorm building" (para. 12). Students across the U.S.A. have demanded that classrooms be "safe spaces" for learning.

Campus policies at public and private universities, including student codes of conduct, sometimes restrict freedom of expression in the name of civility, privacy or classroom environment. Harvard Law School, for example, revised its social media policies in response to online classes during the pandemic to restrict attribution within social media posts about classroom discussion:

> Named the HLS Community Principle on Non-Attribution, the policy prohibits affiliates from publicly sharing in-class statements in a matter that would identify the speaker to anyone not present for the original discussion. Modeled after the internationally-recognized Chatham House Rule, it aims to protect students from potential widespread bullying or harassment for the opinions they express in class.
>
> (Griffin, 2020, para. 2)

Online sharing restrictions are based on the campus providing "an environment in which students feel comfortable expressing their beliefs, exploring new ideas, or asking difficult questions" (para. 3). The Harvard policy identified social media risks: "Because of the potential permanence and widespread dissemination of communications through social media and other forms of communication designed to reach members of the public, if statements made in class are quoted or described with attribution in those media, students may be reluctant to approach any question, particularly controversial ones, with the openness and vulnerability they need to grow as lawyers and to learn from one another" (para. 6). Apparently, the school policy grew from similar rules written and applied by professors within their classes. As a matter of law, the U.S. Supreme Court has ruled in series of First Amendment cases that impact only public schools. Recently, the U.S. Supreme Court voted 8-1 in favor of granting legal standing to former students suing over restrictive free speech zones (*Uzuegbunam v. Preczewski*, 2021).

KEY CASE LAW

The *Tinker* (1969) case established a strong foundation for public high school student First Amendment rights against free expression punishment, but later decisions were not as clear. The First Amendment rights of students "are frequently disturbingly similar" to those of prisoners in that "particular needs" of each setting are applied to case outcomes (Goodman, 2020, p. 115).

In *Bethel School District v. Fraser* (1986), the U.S. Supreme Court reversed the Ninth Circuit Court of Appeals and upheld a Washington state high school student's punishment over repeated use of sexual innuendo within a 1983 student government political speech in front of about 600 students, including 14-year-olds required to attend or go to study hall (p. 677). The speech included the words "firm in his pants," and "climax." The Supreme Court found the lewd speech to be unrelated to a political viewpoint and instead emphasized the school's basic educational mission. The 7-2 decision written by Chief Justice Warren Burger narrowed student speech rights. Matthew Fraser has used "an elaborate graphic, and explicit sexual metaphor" that sparked audience responses, including "gestures" that "simulated the sexual activities" (p. 678). The school's disciplinary rule prohibited obscenity, profanity and gestures. The *Hazelwood School District v. Kuhlmeir* (1988) 5-3 ruling focused on campus newspapers produced by a class. The case upheld censorship by a Missouri high school of stories about divorce and teen pregnancy. The educational context and sponsorship of school activities again was balanced against any designation of a newspaper or event as a public forum. Today, students use social media sites to express themselves on and off campus. It is more difficult for school administrators to observe communication, unless it disrupts classrooms or other school activities.

In Alaska, two decades after *Bethel* and *Hazelwood*, the Olympic Torch was passing through Juneau when Joseph Frederick and his high school friends wanted to be on television and "unfurled" a 14-feet long "Bong Hits 4 Jesus" banner (*Morse v. Frederick*, 2007, p.396). The "school-sanctioned and school-supervised event" provided a context in which the principal "reasonably" read the banner "as promoting illegal drug use" (p. 396). However, the Ninth Circuit Found a First Amendment violation and ruled that the student could sue the principal for damages. Chief Justice John Roberts delivered the opinion of the U.S Supreme Court that reversed the lower court: "Gibberish is surely a possible interpretation of the words on the banner, but it is not the only one, and dismissing the banner as meaningless ignores its undeniable reference to illegal drugs" (p. 403). Further, "Congress has declared that part of a school's job is educating students about the dangers of illegal drug use. It has provided billions of dollars to support state and local drug-prevention programs" (p. 408). "The particular concern to prevent student drug abuse at issue here, embodied in established school policy, ... extends well beyond an abstract desire to avoid controversy" (pp. 409–410). The decision backed the principal's action as a statement of "how serious the school was about the dangers of illegal drug use." Roberts wrote: "The First Amendment does not require schools to tolerate at school events student expression that contributes to those dangers" (p. 410). Justice John Paul Stevens warned in a dissenting opinion that the Supreme Court was backtracking on *Tinker* in the *Morse* ruling: "The Court's test invites stark viewpoint discrimination" (p. 437). In each case, a risk of a substantial disruption must be considered, but the *Morse* decision may have gone too far in focusing on the promotion of illegal drug activity during a school-sponsored event.

In general, schools may restrict speech that disrupts the educational mission of a high school – especially when there has been no effort to designate a public forum for free expression. In the lower courts, a high school newspaper editor in Michigan won her case against administrators trying to halt newspaper coverage about a school bus parking lot fumes lawsuit (*Dean v. Utica Community Schools*, 2004). The opinion opened with a quote from President Harry Truman: "Once a government is committed to the principle of silencing the voice of opposition, it has only one way to go, and that is down the path of increasingly repressive measures, until it becomes a source of terror to all its citizens and creates a country where everyone lives in fear" (p. 800). Katherine Dean's civil rights complaint was based on the First and Fourteenth Amendments, as unconstitutional censorship. Importantly, there had been no prior history of student newspaper censorship:

> Neither Superintendent Sergent nor anyone else from UCS administration had any involvement with the *Arrow*. The student journalists for the *Arrow* did not defer to school administrators regarding editorial or other decisions for the paper. Dean understood that she could write on whatever topic she wished if it were factually supported and relevant to the *Arrow*'s community of readers.
>
> (p. 801)

In cases where there is a history of high school press freedom, courts may find that a limited public forum exists. Less clear is how legal precedent applies to social media use on and off campus, especially when posts are not found to disrupt the classroom.

Historically, community college and public university students enjoy stronger First Amendment rights than high school students because they usually are adults living and working in a community (*Healy v. James*, 1972). During this time, the U.S. Supreme Court treated public universities as open to the marketplace of ideas, dissemination of controversial ideas, and strong enough to withstand indecent or objectionable speech (*Papish v. University of Missouri*, 1973). Barbara Papish's underground newspaper distribution on campus might be similar to what students today would post on a blog, **microblog** or social media site.

CURRENT STUDENT POLITICAL AND OTHER SPEECH

In two more recent Eighth Circuit cases, students made no specific threats, but suffered punishment for exercising First Amendment rights, and this may have had a chilling effect on future speech. The suspension in 2017 of a University of

Nebraska-Lincoln (UNL) graduate student and English lecturer without a due process hearing, and subsequent UNL administration censure in 2018 by the American Association of University Professors (AAUP), reflects a First Amendment academic freedom of speech failure that should be required at a public university (AAUP, 2018). Others, however, claimed the lecturer was trying to silence Turning Point USA conservative undergraduate Kaitlyn Mullen by shouting at her. President Donald Trump in 2019 invited Mullen and other students to an executive order signing ceremony: "Kaitlyn was approached by staff and a graduate instructor and was berated and cursed at," Trump told the audience. "If a college or university doesn't allow you to speak, we will not give them money" (Morton, 2019, paras. 3–4). Mullen, however, had also exercised First Amendment rights by taking and sharing a social media video of the protest against her and the organization.

Without clear and recent U.S. Supreme Court case law, the Eighth Circuit has been drifting away from protecting college students, faculty, staff and their public speech (*Keefe v. Adams*, 2016). One could instead reimagine core political free speech as protected under the strict scrutiny test to block high school standards from creeping into campus free speech law (Hudson, Jr., 2018). Specifically, the requirement that government provide a *compelling interest* to support action that would restrict protected speech must be understood as a primary tool for advancing the important cause of free expression at the fringes of social norms. Campus administration use of public relations (PR) and social media may weaken the practical strength of current constitutional protection. This focus applies law in two distinct cases – a suspension of a doctoral teaching assistant in Nebraska for her political speech protest of a conservative group informational table, and the removal of a Minnesota nursing student for his caustic, but nonpolitical Facebook posts. In both cases, administrators backed punishment based on vague professional and ethical standards.

Social media present new questions about what it means to be disruptive of the educational mission of a university. In *Keefe v. Adams* (2016), the U.S. Supreme Court (2017) denied review of the decision against Craig Keefe. In this case, the First Amendment did not bar administrators from concluding that the student's Facebook post was unethical and unprofessional based on a nursing code of ethics. Following complaints from other students, Keefe was removed from the nursing program at Central Lakes College in Minnesota. Court records showed that the Facebook posts other students found threatening included:

> Doesnt anyone know or have heard of mechanical pencils. Im going to take this electric pencil sharpener in this class and give someone a hemopneumothorax... with it before to long. I might need some anger management.

> LMAO [a classmate], you keep reporting my post and get me banded. I don't really care. If thats the smartest thing you can come up with than I completely understand why your going to fail out of the RN program you stupid bitch ... And quite creeping on my page. Your not a friend of mine for a reason. If you don't like what I have to say than don't come and ask...me, thats basically what creeping is isn't it. Stay off my page.
>
> (pp. 526–7)

Keefe, according to court documents, had been dismissed from the nursing program once before for poor grades, but he had been reinstated the next year. The appeals court also noted that the associate degree course catalog mentioned the American Nurses' Association ethics code, which obligated the college to "graduate students who will provide safe, competent nursing care and uphold the moral and ethical principles of the profession" (p. 529). The court rejected Keefe's blanket claim that most off-campus speech was protected:

> A serious question raised by Keefe in this case is whether the First Amendment protected his unprofessional speech from academic disadvantage because it was made in on-line, off-campus Facebook postings. On appeal, Keefe framed this contention categorically, arguing that a college student may not be punished for off-campus speech unless it is speech that is unprotected by the First Amendment, such as obscenity. We reject this categorical contention.
>
> (p. 531)

In this case, nursing confidentiality "(including any type of social media breach)" was in conflict with the First Amendment (p. 528). Unfortunately, the court applied the language of the *Hazelwood* (1988) high school case in concluding that campus administrators could exercise "legitimate pedagogical concerns" (p. 531). A dissenting judge in the appeals court case disagreed: "I think there is a genuine issue of material fact as to whether the school could constitutionally regulate Keefe's off-campus, non-academic speech" (p. 538). This also appears to be true in the high school off-campus context, as the Pennsylvania ACLU won a case for the First Amendment right of a cheerleader to post on Snapchat: "fuck school fuck softball fuck cheer fuck everything" (Baer, 2019, para. 1).

Keefe v. Adams (2016) improperly cited the *Hazelwood School District v. Kuhlmeier* (1988) high school newspaper case in which the Supreme Court upheld censorship within a journalism, school-sponsored classroom setting "reasonably related to legitimate pedagogical concerns" (p. 273). Keefe's Facebook posts clearly were outside the classroom he described. What was already bad high school First

Amendment law in terms of content regulation appeared to be extended to a "comprehensive and community technical college" and outside specific pedagogical concerns. The closest the *Keefe* (2016) case came to pedagogy was by taking seriously his post that "Im going to take this electric pencil sharpener in this class and give someone a hemopneumothorax... with it before to long." The record showed that Keefe understood the word "hemopneumothorax" to not refer to a medical procedure, but rather "a 'trauma' where the lung is punctured and air and blood flood the lung cavity" (fn. 3). Unlike the Nebraska case, the Minnesota case did not appear to produce a public opinion flap. A year later, the U.S. Supreme Court denied a request to hear the case (*Keefe v. Adams*, 2017).

President Trump's Executive Order (2019) focused on "free and open debate on college and university campuses," "this bedrock principle in their administration of student life, and "to avoid creating environments that stifle competing perspectives" (para. 3). Within the context of the rising cost of higher education, the Section 2 policy sought to: "(a) encourage institutions to foster environment that promote open, intellectually engaging, and diverse debate, including compliance with the First Amendment for public institutions and compliance with stated institutional policies regarding freedom of speech for private institutions" (para. 7). The order sought to tie public and private university research federal funding to compliance.

LAW REVIEW ANALYSES

Legal scholars have found that the *Hazelwood* high school standard has "creeped" toward a college and university application, and off-campus social media use sparks new case law (Calvert, 2017, p. 611). Wahrmann-Harry (2018) observes that:

> To date, the United States Supreme Court has consistently refused to hear cases on this issue, offering no guidance on what standard is applicable and leaving courts mired in confusion regarding off-campus speech in a university setting.
>
> (p. 426)

The "erroneous" application of student speech doctrine off-campus also fails by its **overbreadth** and lack of "narrowly tailored" standards (p. 452).

Bhagwat (2007) contends that "tiers of scrutiny" through the use of an intermediate approach over decades in the United States has led to "some sort of default standard" that Supreme Court Justice Antonin Scalia named (p. 785) – one that functions broadly and is "applicable to any governmental regulation of speech, which for whatever reason does not trigger strict scrutiny" (p. 783). While strict scrutiny was grounded in "due process and equal protection" (p. 784), Bhagwat sees a Supreme Court movement from separate and chaotic applications of symbolic conduct; time, place and manner restrictions; commercial speech and other areas *toward a unified intermediate and default standard*:

> Instead, the Supreme Court has come to emphasize … that despite somewhat differing formulations, many of the Court's new "tests" share some basic, common characteristics: … laws will be upheld so long as they serve some sort of a significant/substantial/important governmental interest and are reasonably well tailored to that purpose (i.e., not unreasonably overbroad).
>
> (p. 801)

In response, Bhagwat has called for a reversal of the reliance on intermediate scrutiny by breaking apart the "doctrinal merger" through "disaggregation" of the various distinct bodies of speech law (p. 831) and cultivate from the Supreme Court "better guidance to the lower courts" (p. 832). Specifically, it seems clear that there is a need to clarify potential differences between the meanings of significant, substantial, important, and compelling governmental interests.

Maye (2019) explored student athlete protests and found a list of First Amendment approaches: "traditional" expressive conduct, public forum time, place and manner restriction and "school-specific" (pp. 63–71). Student speech cases beginning with *Tinker* and through *Morse v. Frederick* (2007) offered more protection when public debate on political issues was in play. One additional issue is whether or not a public employee is primarily speaking "in connection with his or her job," or addressing public issues as a citizen exercising First Amendment rights (Maye, 2019, p. 79). However, it can be argued that digital and social media blur context.

Ever since *Hazelwood*, legal scholars have been troubled by the potential curtailment of First Amendment student speech rights, especially as academic freedom cases have been on the rise (Byrne, 1989). Despite rhetoric surrounding free speech, there has been a "paradox or confusion" from "inconclusive" case law applied to "the ambiguous realities of academic life (pp. 252–253). Hudson, Jr. (2018) concludes that:

> Sadly, the *Hazelwood* standard not only led to increased censorship of high school newspapers and other forms of school-sponsored student speech, but it also creeped outside of its original application in the K-12 environment and impacted First Amendment jurisprudence involving college and university campuses.
>
> (p. 492)

Courts appear to be losing their way, even in public high school cases, when it comes to defining a substantial disruption to education or distinguishing between sponsored classroom activities and a clear public forum. "College and universities are the **ideal** marketplace of ideas where First Amendment freedoms ideally should flourish" (Hudson, Jr., 2018, p. 504). This is particularly troubling within social media. Keefe should have been free to make jokes and not be removed from an academic program based on "transgression of professional boundaries" (p. 516, fn. 237). As Hudson, Jr. (2018) observed, by failing to hear and reverse his case, the Supreme Court ignored college students' fundamental rights of "mere dissemination of ideas" regardless of "good taste" (p. 517, fn. 249, quoting *Papish v. Board of Curators of University of Missouri*, 1973 p. 670).

Calvert (2017) observed that Keefe's 2-1 appellate case "ripped Hazelwood from its school-sponsored, high school speech moorings and stretched it to college students authoring decidedly independent, non-school sponsored messages" (p. 614). The combined impact of lower court case law based upon the "professional ethics standards" creep "may lurk for students studying in any field that helps prepare them for a job" (pp. 661–662). First Amendment free speech boundaries remain inconsistent when it comes to outrageous forms of expression (Calvert, 2014).

Further, when it comes to academic suspension or dismissal, "jurisprudence is murky at best" (Strasser, 2017, p. 98). Similar to Calvert, Strasser bemoans inconsistent case law, as well as lack of a clear legal standard ends with courts being "sometimes extremely deferential to university decision-making and at other times view(ing) university policies and practices with a jaundiced eye" (p. 157). Lee (2018) observed that #BlackLivesMatter campus protests, for example, are in the tradition of 18th-century student activism. He argues for on-campus "student dissent" policies covering "invited speaker interruption, unauthorized building and office occupation, and ... various forms of disruption in cyberspace" (p. 278). Shepard and Culver (2018) place these efforts within the context of culture wars and conclude that campus free expression must be protected through ideological diversity, inclusion and respect. The First Amendment protects all speakers, no matter how offensive to some. In the absence of **fighting words** or an immediate threat of violence, the First Amendment requires campuses to promote "uninhibited, robust, and wide-open" debate that may include erroneous statements (*New York Times v. Sullivan*, 1964, p. 270). The Supreme Court creep toward "proportionality," "tiers-of-scrutiny" and "a more flexible standard" (Maye, 2019, p. 91) can be viewed as backing away from *Tinker* doctrine that was essential in the protection of core political speech and other First Amendment expressive conduct. The Supreme Court *must* revisit campus speech law and reverse academic administration tendencies to protect the brand and stifle PR controversies through damage control tactics. There are social and political dangers in restriction of academic freedom and limits on robust First Amendment rights.

ETHICAL FRAMEWORKS AND ISSUES

It could be argued that in both the *Lawton* and *Keefe* cases, administrators would contend that the imposition of civility and professional norms is part of the broad educational mission. University use of social responsibility standards, as well as how the outcomes would compare with nonacademic public employee cases, remains unclear. What also remains unclear in issues of academic employee free speech within a public college or university is whether or not the long-standing expectation of **content neutral**, narrowly tailored regulation remains a First Amendment standard. Thus, the strict scrutiny model should be articulated and applied to 21st-century law.

In spite of the fact that public college student First Amendment rights are strong, increasingly these are being limited by student handbook code of conduct rules, professional standards, and other contract language between students and the university. Private college students generally enjoy weaker First Amendment rights for campus freedom of expression, but some states have included private universities in statutes designed to protect student passwords. Still, courts must interpret state "student password statutes in the context of the labyrinth of social media privacy settings" (Jebe & Park, 2019, p. 82):

> The larger question is the impact of student speech law, and the statute's attempts to protect student speech, on the university–student relationship. Since the password legislation does not protect public information on social media, students maybe loathe to question or criticize their school, courses, or instructors in any public forum. This could drive student criticism underground to those social media spheres that are password protected.
>
> (pp. 82–83)

Jebe and Park (2019) suggest that university intrusion into student online privacy could become "the status quo," as the current ambiguity fails to cultivate trust, openness and free speech (p. 83). Campuses contend they have a responsibility to protect students from "self-harm" and "potentially violent students," but student privacy also is protected under federal law (p. 83). Institutions of higher education find themselves in the middle when it comes to "liability for foreseeable harm," college students as "fully functioning adults," and adequacy of protecting students from potential harm (pp. 84–85). Beyond these difficult legal issues, public and private universities maintain student codes of conduct that may address ethical issues.

Social media sites are filled with what large numbers of users would consider unethical behavior. While social media companies write end-user agreements that attempt to restrict hate speech, bullying and other antisocial communication, individual students sometimes lack experience to make sound decisions, and they differ based on political preferences. An Arizona State University student-run radio station announcer, for example, faced pressure to resign following a tweet that offended supporters of Black Lives Matter (Stern, 2020). The campus had been dealing with racial strife. Meanwhile, on TikTok students were encouraged to participate in a potentially deadly "Benadryl Challenge" of over-dosing on the allergy medicine – the challenge coaxes "participants to take several doses" of diphenhydramine "to the point that the person trips out or hallucinates" (McGorry, 2020, paras. 1–2). In this case, the unethical urging could give rise to criminal charges against those responsible for numerous hospitalizations and deaths. New social media tools have empowered students to communice to a global audience in ways never before possible, but younger people sometimes lack experience to make the best decision about thinking before they post.

5:59

Box 2.1 Case Study: Drafting a Student Conduct Code

Amid a pandemic and rapidly changing social media uses, one Midwestern public university drafted an expansive Student Code of Conduct ("Code") that empowered university administrators to use suspension or expulsion of students for violation of state and federal laws. While most of the code does not address First Amendment issues, the following excerpted passages relate to this chapter.

Student Code of Conduct ("Code")

Students at the University of __________ are members of an academic community in which academic integrity and responsible conduct are essential for the community to function …

A. Standards of Academic Integrity

Students are expected to approach and complete their academic work with integrity. They are expected to do their own work, to be honest in the statements they make, to refrain from harming others, to refrain from improperly helping others, and to follow the rules …

Dishonesty, Falsification, and Fabrication, which includes, but is not limited to...

B. Standards of Responsible Conduct

Students are expected to conduct themselves responsibly. Students must remember that they are members not only of the University community but also of the community in which the University is located. This means that students are expected to make responsible decisions about the use of drugs and alcohol, to behave appropriately as a member of the academic community, and to refrain from conduct that threatens the safety of the community …

… *Engaging in, or attempting to engage in, behavior that may cause harm to an individual or property,* which includes, but is not limited to:

- Threatening to commit an act of violence for the purpose of terrorizing another person or persons.
- Threatening another person with imminent physical harm.

Harassing another person due to their status as a member of a protected class in a manner that is so severe, persistent, or pervasive as to limit or deny a reasonable person's ability to participate or benefit from the University's programs, activities, or employment.

Taking pictures or making recordings of another person without the person's consent in any place where a person would have a reasonable expectation of privacy, including, but not limited to: the person's bedroom; in the person's living quarters in a residence hall; in a locker room; or in a restroom.

… *Engaging in Conduct that Disrupts Classes, University Operations, Activities*, or Order, which includes, but is not limited to:

… Engaging in protests, sit-ins, or demonstrations at times or in locations where those kinds of activities are not permitted …

… *Doing Private Acts in Public*, which includes, but is not limited to:

Misusing University Computer and Network Systems, which includes, but is not limited to … Engaging in conduct prohibited by Sections 5 and 6 of the Policy for Responsible Use of University Computers and Information Systems.

Playful or humorous use of social media, such as through the use of memes, may present legal and ethical issues. Among the concerns are privacy and consent.

Box 2.2 Thought Leader Maurika Smutherman

Maurika Smutherman.

Photograph courtesy Maurika Smutherman.

Memes capture our emotions, thoughts, and behaviors in ways that impact culture and connect communities throughout the world. While memes often are considered harmless comedy, their virality has implications not only for the people who create and post them, but for those who are subjects of the memes, sometimes unbeknown to them. Sharing Internet memes may be likened to playing a game of "telephone." As the message travels farther away from its origin, it becomes muddled and may even lose its intended meaning (Phillips, 2016). The results can be disastrous as memes are often used as tools to fuel hate and degrade already marginalized groups. This essay will discuss the ethical implications of posting memes online.

THE ETHICS OF ONLINE MEMES

Shifman (2014) defines Internet memes as: "(a) A group of digital items sharing common characteristics of content, form, and/or stance, which (b) were created with awareness of each other, and (c) were circulated, imitated, and/or transformed via the Internet by many users" (p. 41). The ethical concerns associated with posting memes on the Internet are vast, but this essay focuses on the aspects of privacy and consent, hate speech and, finally, monetization.

In the online world people use their screens as shields; they forget about the people on the other side of those screens. They are more inclined to record, post, and share things they would never do or discuss in real life. This can be described as the "disinhibition effect," by which people "separate their [online] actions from their real world and identity" (Suler, 2004, para. 5). This lack of concern for the human condition causes people to create and share memes that can be harmful to others, although they do not consider that harm in the moment. They use their screens to ignore the fact that there are real people with real emotions who are impacted by these posts.

PRIVACY AND CONSENT

Millions of memes circulate on the Internet each day, but posting them presents ethical concerns about privacy and consent. Memes are not harmless; people who become subjects of them, often without their knowledge, deal with real-world effects of having their image broadcast online. Take for instance, Ghyslain Raza, a Canadian teen whose private video went **viral** in 2003 after classmates released it as a prank (Harmon, 2003). Within minutes, Raza went from being an average teen to an online sensation known as the "Star Wars Kid." Raza's image went viral without his consent, and those who originally posted the video, as well as the countless people who have recreated and reposted it, effectively invaded his privacy.

The case of Raza is a prime example of the disconnect between ethics and the posting of online memes. Raza's Internet fame had devastating effects on the teen, who eventually dropped out of school and checked into a psychiatric facility (Popkin, 2007). Today, Raza's video has been viewed more than 1 billion times. At such a critical time in his life, Raza was harassed and bullied by the leaking of his personal video (without his consent), the "Star Wars Kid" memes, and the bullying commentary that followed. His parents eventually sued the families of the three classmates who leaked the video, resulting in a settlement for an undisclosed amount (Pasternack, 2010).

HATE SPEECH

Social media memes are also sources of hate speech. Hate speech is defined as public speech that expresses hate or encourages violence toward a person or group based on something such as race, religion, sex, or sexual orientation. This type of speech, disseminated in the form of memes, is widespread online.

In 2017, Harvard University rescinded offers of admission to ten students who shared memes rooted in racist and sexual hate speech on Facebook. In a private chat generated from an official Facebook group for incoming Harvard freshmen, the students shared memes "that were racist and anti-Semitic … made light of pedophilia, among other offensive themes" (Kamenetz et al., 2017, para. 7). Harvard's decision to rescind these students' offers of admission drew controversy surrounding freedom of speech and expression. Should the students face consequences for sharing memes that fueled hate speech in a *private* online chat?

Natanson (2017) explains that, "the description for the official Facebook group for the Class of 2021 … disclaims all administrative responsibility for 'unofficial groups' and warns members their admission offers can be rescinded under specific circumstances" (para. 15). The students may have felt these memes were harmless, but sharing hate speech in an online sphere contributes to a culture of prejudice and discrimination, one that has been well-documented in the real world, particularly on the campuses of predominantly white institutions such as Harvard. The university's swift action in this case sets a standard for the student body – engaging in hate speech at Harvard has ethical consequences and will not be tolerated, in any form (Phillips & Milner, 2017).

MONETIZATION

Memes are a goldmine with many social media users profiting from creating, curating, and posting them online. But is it ethical to profit from memes, especially when the images used in them are subject to **copyright** and **fair use** claims? In 2014, Kayla Lewis, also known as Peaches Monroee, uploaded a video to the (now defunct) social media website, Vine. In the selfie video, Lewis stated that her eyebrows are "on fleek." The video was viewed more than 20 million times (BET Networks, 2018). Lewis' image became a viral meme, but when celebrities, major brands, and companies decided to monetize the phrase "on fleek," it became apparent that Lewis had missed an opportunity to **trademark** her own content. In 2017, Lewis' image and words were making money for other people, but the creator had not received a dime. The case raises an ethical question: Do our online posts belong to us? There is no clear consensus regarding memes and copyright:

> The viral spread of a meme infringes on [American copyright law] protections as the original image is modified and then displayed, distributed and reproduced when posted and reposted. However, within copyright law exists the doctrine of fair use, which allows for use of a copyrighted work in the creation of new work without permission, as long as the use fits within certain parameters.
>
> (Orlofsky, 2019, paras. 4–5)

It is up to the user to consider the source of the material used for memes: "When you see a meme going around, give a thought to the subject of that meme image, whose life may forever be changed" (Orlofsky, 2019, para. 15).

ETHICS RECONSIDERED

Memes can invade people's privacy, promote harmful hate speech and present copyright and fair use issues if used for commercial gain. However, they also may encourage us to reflect on our own ethics and apply these lessons to our daily lives. By using one's own judgment and moral compass, memes can be used for good rather than bad. The next time you are thinking about sharing a meme, consider the ethical implications of the image(s) used, its text, and the message it is sending.

Maurika Smutherman is an adjunct professor of communication and media studies at Winston-Salem State University. She received her BA in mass communications from Winston-Salem State and her MA in new media and global education from Appalachian State University. She has taught several communications and media production courses, including introduction to mass communication, law and ethics of mass communication, digital convergence and mass media management.

Sources

BET Networks. (2018, September 19). What "Eyebrows on Fleek" Creator Peaches Monroee Learned the Hard Way: I Went Viral [Video]. YouTube. https://www.youtube.com/watch?v=KbI-CXZAoNw.

Harmon, A. (2003, May 19). Compressed Data; Fame is No Laughing Matter for the "Star Wars Kid." *New York Times*. https://www.nytimes.com/2003/05/19/ business/compressed-data-fame-is-no-laughing-matter-for-the-star-wars-kid.html?pagewanted=1.

Kamenetz, A., Lattimore, K., and Depenbrock, J. (2017, June 6). Harvard Rescinds Admission of 10 Students over Obscene Facebook Messages. *NPR*. npr.org/sections/ed/2017/06/06/531591202/harvard-rescinds-admission-of-10-students-over-obscene-facebook-messages.

Natanson, H. (2017, June 5). Harvard Rescinds Acceptances for at Least Ten Students for Obscene Memes. *Harvard Crimson*. https://www.thecrimson.com/article/ 2017/6/5/2021-offers-rescinded-memes/.

Orlofsky, V.L. (2019, January 28). *Memes, Fair Use, and Privacy*. Intellectual Freedom Blog. https://www.oif.ala.org/oif/?p=16873#:~:text=Memes%20and%20Copyright& text=American%20copyright%20law%20gives%20creators,reproduced%20when%20posted%20and%20reposted.

Pasternack, A. (2010, June 1). After Lawsuits and Therapy, Star Wars Kid Is Back. https://www.vice.com/en_us/article/8qqxdv/after-lawsuits-and-therapy-star-wars-kid-is-back.

Phillips, W. (2016). The Complex Ethics of Online Memes. https://ethics.org.au/the-complex-ethics-of-online-memes/.

Phillips, W. and Milner, R.M. (2017, June 6). The Harvard Case Shows a Meme is Never "Just" a Meme. *Vice*. https://www.vice.com/en_us/article/zmen4y/the-harvard-case-shows-a-meme-is-never-just-a-meme.

Popkin, H.A.S. (2007, September 6). Survive Your Inevitable Online Humiliation: Ask Not for Whom the YouTube Video Rolls ... It's Probably You. *NBC News*. http://www.nbcnews.com/id/20611439#.X2TrU5NKjfY.

Shifman, L. (2014). *Memes in Digital Culture*. Cambridge, MA: MIT Press.

Suler, J. (2004). The Online Disinhibition Effect. *The Psychology of Cyberspace*. http://www-usr.rider.edu/~suler/psycyber/disinhibit.html.

ONLINE RESOURCES

Media Ethics Initiative (2019, January 14). One Does Not Simply Create a Meme. https://mediaethicsinitiative.org/2019/01/14/the-ethics-of-internet-memes/.

DISCUSSION QUESTIONS

1. How could a student's social media post at home on a weekend disrupt education within a classroom setting?
2. Which ethical values have helped you decide what to post or not post about teachers and other students?
3. Why should we be very careful when creating or viewing memes before reaching conclusions about the truth? How could schools build media literacy curriculum that would help?

REFERENCES

American Association of University Professors (AAUP, 2018, May). Academic Freedom and Tenure: University of Nebraska-Lincoln. *Academe, Bulletin of the American Association of University Professors*, July–August 2018, 2–12.

Baer, S.K. (2019, March 22). A Judge Ruled That a High School Cheerleader's "Fuck Cheer" Snapchat Post is Protected Speech. *BuzzFeed News*. https://www.buzzfeednews.com/article/skbaer/fuck-cheer-snapchat-free-speech-ruling.

Bethel School District v. Fraser, 478 U.S. 675 (1986).

Bhagwat, A. (2007). The Test that Ate Everything: Intermediate Scrutiny in First Amendment Jurisprudence, *University of Illinois Law Review 2007*, 783–833.

Byrne, J.P. (1989, November). Academic Freedom: A "Special Concern of the First Amendment." *Yale Law Review*, 99, 251–338.

Calvert, C. (2017, Fall). Professional Standards and the First Amendment in Higher Education: When Institutional Academic Freedom Collides with Student Speech Rights. *St. Johns Law Review*, 91, 611–662.

Calvert, C. (2014, November). Public Concern and Outrageous Speech: testing the Inconstant Boundaries of IIED and the First Amendment Three Years After *Snyder v. Phelps. University of Pennsylvania Journal of Constitutional Law 17*, 437–477.

Dean v. Utica Community Schools, 345 F. Supp. 2d 799 (E.D. Mich. 2004).

Executive Order on Improving Free Inquiry, Transparency, and Accountability at Colleges and Universities (2019, March 21). https://www.whitehouse.gov/ presidential-actions/executive-order-improving-free-inquiry-transparency-accountability-colleges-universities/.

Flaherty, C. (2018, May 10). Political Pressure in Nebraska. *Inside Higher Ed*. https://www.insidehighered.com/news/2018/05/10/aaup-nebraska-lincoln-violated-lecturers-academic-freedom-when-it-ended-her-teaching.

Foundation for Individual Rights in Education (FIRE) (2017, December 8). FIRE's 2017 Year in Review for Student and Faculty Rights On Campus. https://www.thefire.org/fires-2017-year-in-review-for-student-and-faculty-rights-on-campus/.

Gajjar, S. (2020, August 31). Syracuse Students Speak Out Against Professor's "Chinese Communist Party Flu" Syllabus Notes. *NBC News*. https://www.nbcnews.com/news/asian-america/syracuse-students-speak-out-against-professor-s-chinese-communist-party-n1238926.

Goodman, M. (2020). Regulating Student Expression, in W. Wat Hopkins, *Communication and the Law* (pp.115–120). Northport, AL: Vision Press.

Griffin, K.J. (2020, September 7). Harvard Law School Unveils Non-Attribution Policy for Social Media Posts About Classroom Discussions. *Harvard Crimson*. https://www.thecrimson.com/article/2020/9/7/harvard-law-school-non-attribution-policy/.

Hazelwood School District v. Kuhlmeier, 484 U.S. 260 (1988).

Healy v. James, 408 U.S. 169 (1972).

Hudson, Jr., D.L. (2018, Spring). Thirty Years of *Hazelwood* and its Spread to Colleges. *Howard Law Journal*, 61, 491–520.

Jaschik, S. (2020, October 1). Professor Fired for Using N-Word in Class. *Inside Higher Education*. https://insidehighered.com/quicktakes/2020/10/01/professor-fired-using-n-word-class.

Jebe, R. and Park, S. (2019, Fall/Winter). The Student–University Relationship and Access to Student Online Activity. *Connecticut Public Interest Law Journal*, 19, 45–91.

Keefe v. Adams, 840 F.3d 523 (8th Circuit, 2016), cert. denied, 137 S.Ct. 1448 (2017).

Lee, E. (2008, Winter). "Freedom of the Press 2.0," *Georgia Law Review*, 42, 309–405.

Lee, P. (2018). Student Protests and Academic Freedom in an Age of #blacklivesmatter. *Ohio State Law Journal*, 79, 223–276.

Maye, C. (2019). Public-College Student-Athletes and Game-Time Anthem Protests: Is There a Need for a Constitutional-Analytical Audible? *Communication Law & Policy*, 24, 55–99.

McGorry, A. (2020, August 31). "Benadryl Challenge" Is a Dangerous and Deadly Fad on Social Media: Medical Experts. *Fox News*. https://www.foxnews.com/health/ benadryl-challenge-dangerous-deadly-social-media.

Media Ethics Initiative (2019, January 14). One Does Not Simply Create a Meme. https://mediaethicsinitiative.org/2019/01/14/the-ethics-of-internet-memes/.

Monroe, W. (2020, August 26). Iowa Western Blocks Teacher's Call In Sick Strike, Reports 16 Coronavirus Cases in 10 Days. *KETV.* https://www.ketv.com/article/iowa-western-blocks-teachers-call-in-sick-strike-reports-16-coronavirus-cases-in-10-days/33811002.

Morse v. Frederick, 551 U.S. 393 (2007).

Morton, J. (2019, March 22). Trump Cites Incident Involving UNL Student in Signing Executive Order on Free Speech. *Omaha World-Herald.* https://www.omaha.com/news/nation/morton/trump-cites-incident-involving-unl-student-in-signing-executive-order/article_dd29e43a-2f3e-5a52-a6ff-c3105e8cdf2e.html.

Papish v. Board of Curators of the University of Missouri, 410 U.S. 667 (1973).

Shelton v. Tucker, 364 U.S. 479 (1960).

Shepard, J. and Culver, K.B. (2018, Winter). Culture Wars on Campus: Academic Freedom, the First Amendment, and Partisan Outrage in Polarized Times. *San Diego Law Review*, 55, 88–158.

Shugerman, E. (2020, August 26). University of Alabama to Profs: Don't Tell Students About COVID-Infected Classmates. *Daily Beast.* https://www.thedailybeast.com/university-of-alabama-told-profs-not-to-tell-students-about-covid-infected-classmates.

Stern, R. (2020, September 2). ASU Student Radio Journalist Won't Back Down After Jacob Blake Tweet.*New Phoenix Times.* https://www.phoenixnewtimes.com/news/asu-journalist-blaze-radio-tweet-about-jacob-blake-rape-charge-linda-raelee-klein-11491330.

Strasser, M.P. (2017, Fall). Student Dismissals from Professional Programs and the Constitution. *Case Western Reserve*, 68, 97–157.

Tinker v. Des Moines Independent Community School District, 393 U.S. 503 (1969).

Turning Point USA (2019). About. https://www.tpusa.com/aboutus/.

Uzuegbunam v. Preczewski, 592 U.S. ___ (2021).

Wahrmann-Harry, K. (2018, March). The Next Step in Student Speech Analysis? How the Eighth Circuit Further Complicates the First Amendment Rights of University Students in *Keefe v. Adams. Creighton Law Review*, 51, 425–453.

West Virginia v. Barnett, 319 U.S. 624 (1943).

3 Influencers and the Federal Trade Commission

> *In applying the First Amendment to this area, we have rejected the 'highly paternalistic' view that government has complete power to suppress or regulate commercial speech.*

—U.S. Supreme Court Justice Lewis Powell,
Central Hudson Gas and Electric Corp. v. Public Service Commission (1980, p. 562)

Celebrity social media influencer Khloé Kardashian and drug company Nurtec ODT collaborated on a paid influence campaign in 2020. Her 26.8 million @ khloekardashian followers had the potential to see this tweet:

> #Sponsored With #NurtecODT I dared to reimagine life with #migraine. From launching new businesses to spending time with family, I'm dreaming BIGGER & so are others. Ask your doctor & visit http://NURTEC.COM. Most common side effect was nausea. PI: http://nurtec.com/pi.

While Kardashian complied with Federal Trade Commission (FTC) guidelines to prominently disclose sponsorship in a hashtag, so-called "sponcon for medication" is inappropriate (Chen, 2020, paras. 1–2). She had been previously criticized for promoting weight-loss products. The tweets mentioned potential side-effects and linked to detailed scientific information, but the case is evidence that U.S. commercial free speech laws opened the door to ever-widening use of advertising and sponsorship within social media channels. In general, FTC regulation requires commercial endorsements to be truthful, lawful, not misleading and have clear and conspicuous disclosure – principles that value transparency for consumers. They should be protected from deceptive promotion of products and services. The FTC also has determined that Facebook must "clearly and prominently" disclose its data-sharing.

The rise in social media marketing has motivated large numbers of people to become authentic influencers on consumer buying, but it also created fertile ground for a rise in fake influence (Russell, 2020). A variety of leaders across many fields have used social media communication to accumulate followers who may be influenced. For example, the TikTok app offered a new space for social media influencers – sometimes outside government regulatory boundaries. During the U.S. presidential election in 2020, a BBC investigation discovered and reported that a social marketing company was behind paid posts that failed to disclose financial interests:

> The company, Bigtent Creative, funds skits and memes to persuade people to register, such as mixing rapper Cardi B's WAP song with a message from her telling people to vote … Some of the videos it has paid for are non-partisan, but others call for President Trump to be voted out of office and in none of the videos do the creators disclose that they have been paid.
>
> (Smith Galer, 2020, paras. 2–3)

The U.S. Federal Trade Commission (FTC) guidelines require paid advertising to be disclosed to consumers either by transparently describing a relationship, but frequently with the #ad or #sponsored hashtags. At the time, TikTok had a political advertising ban and removed posts. The marketers earlier had created memes supporting presidential candidate Elizabeth Warren, but then "morphed into a marketing company, working with influencers ahead of the November election" (para. 11). Funding for the TikTok campaigns reportedly came from nonpartisan and Democrat partisan organizations that are required to report spending. The U.S. Federal Election Commission (FEC) does not require disclosure of nonpartisan vote promotion efforts: "Bigtent Creative argues the material they pay for does not qualify as political advertising, but some of the creators they funded have been making anti-Trump material – which in TikTok's eyes has been deemed political advertising" (para. 14). The regulatory mix affecting social media marketing influencers contributed to this being a dynamic and interesting area of study.

Disclosure and transparency of paid posts has been an ongoing issue for years on Instagram. Beyond Federal Trade Commission (FTC) efforts, the UK Competition and Markets Authority (CMA) investigated failure to label paid advertising (BBC News, 2020). Instagram responded by promising to require influencers "to confirm whether they have received incentives to promote a product or service before they can publish their post" (para. 7). Instagram also planned to use machine learning AI to search for advertising content.

One industry study found that three-quarters (76 percent) of Instagram advertising disclosures were buried within (59 percent), at the end (24 percent), or within comments (12 percent) – much more than at the visible start of an Instagram post (5 percent) (NetImperative, 2020, para. 7). The most used hashtags were: #ad (12.8 million), #advertisement (1.8 million), #sponsored (3.3 million), #gifted (1.8 million), and #affiliate (744,000) (para. 4). The data appeared to show that most Instagram paid posts violate FTC rules requiring prominent disclosure. When influencers hide payments from followers, this presents legal and ethical issues.

At a broader level, the U.S. political system runs on financial contributions to campaigns that also may involve money exchanged for influence. For example, Kelly (2020) reported that Oracle CEO Larry Ellison donated $250,000 to the "Security is Strength" super Political Action Committee (PAC) to fund U.S. Senator Lindsey Graham's South Carolina campaign advertising, as the company "closed in on a coveted position as TikTok's US technology partner" (paras. 1–2). Graham reportedly helped convince Donald Trump to allow a U.S. company to buy into the Chinese-owned ByteDance TikTok amid concerns about data security. However, after Trump lost the presidential election, the administration appeared to back off a threat to ban it – a court had blocked the initial effort (Sonnemaker, 2020).

Commercial interests dominate social media communication, and regulation has increasingly been balanced against U.S. First Amendment rights. The Federal Communications Commission (FCC) also emphasized that Section 230 liability immunity does not shield social media companies from their responsibility to protect consumers (Kwan, 2020). FCC Chair Agit Pai had pushed ahead with FCC rulemaking to clarify the statute meaning, as it applies to social media companies: "[T]hey do not have a First Amendment right to a special immunity denied to other media outlets, such as newspapers and broadcasters" (para. 7). Concurrently, Congressional committees and the U.S. Department of Justice (2020) drafted proposed reforms to promote "transparency and open discourse" in removal of "lawful speech" (paras. 6–8). Commercial speech law and regulation is a complex and dynamic area of emerging law of First Amendment application over more than four decades.

PRINCIPLES OF COMMERCIAL SPEECH LAW

The U.S. Supreme Court initially dismissed the idea that there was any First Amendment protection for commercial speech, unanimously deciding that: "We are equally clear that the Constitution imposes no such restraint on government as respects purely commercial advertising" (*Valentine v. Christensen*, 1942, p. 54). However, *New York Times v. Sullivan* (1964) was about a political advertisement, and the decision prepared the Court for commercial speech cases.

In *Virginia State Board of Pharmacy v. Virginia Citizens Consumer Council* (1976) the U.S. Supreme Court upheld a lower court decision that state law § 54-524.35 (1974) violated both the Constitution and Fourteenth Amendment. The law banned licensed pharmacists from advertising prescription drugs and labeled the practice unprofessional conduct. The First Amendment protected consumers' right to commercial information. The 7-1 decision was consistent with a line of Supreme Court cases that established a First Amendment right of readers, viewers and listeners: "Freedom of speech presupposes a willing speaker. But where a speaker exists, as is the case here, the protection afforded is to the communication, to its source and to its recipients both" (p. 756). A year earlier, in *Bigelow v. Virginia* (1975), a Virginia newspaper publisher's misdemeanor conviction was overturned after publishing an advertisement for referral and availability of a legal abortion in New York.

Importantly, the majority in *Virginia State Board of Pharmacy v. Virginia Citizens Consumer Council* (1976) applied the First Amendment to allow for regulation of deceptive and illegal advertising:

> Obviously, much commercial speech is not provably false, or even wholly false, but only deceptive or misleading … The First Amendment, as we construe it today, does not prohibit the State from insuring that the stream of commercial information flow cleanly as well as freely … What is at issue is whether a State may completely suppress the dissemination of concededly truthful information about entirely lawful activity, fearful of that information's effect upon its disseminators and its recipients. Reserving other questions, we conclude that the answer to this one is in the negative.
> (pp. 771–773)

The Court had not completely addressed time, place and manner restriction of commercial speech, but handed down a landmark decision four years later.

Box 3.1 The *Central Hudson* (1980) Test

Cent. Hudson Gas & Elec. Corp. v. Public Serv. Comm'n, 447 U.S. 557 (1980)
Supreme Court of the United States
June 20, 1980

In *Central Hudson Gas & Electric Corp. v. Public Serv. Commission* the Supreme Court further applied the Constitution and Fourteenth Amendment to state advertising bans.

Facts. The Commission during the 1973 energy crisis had ordered utilities to stop advertising of electricity, and then later extended it. The order allowed informational advertising designed to shift demand away from peak periods.

Legal Issues. Commercial expression rights are not limited a speaker's economic interests, but also extend to consumers. Government does not have complete power to ban or regulate commercial speech. The First Amendment protects dissemination of accurate information. The Court has afforded less First Amendment protection for commercial speech, but the nature of expression and government interests must be considered.

Decision (Holding). On an 8-1 vote, the Court reversed a lower court, applied a new legal test, and ruled that a complete ban on promotional advertising violated the First Amendment.

Reasoning. "The First Amendment's concern for commercial speech is based on the informational function of advertising. *See First National Bank of Boston v. Bellotti*, 435 U.S. 765, 783 (1978) ... The government may ban forms of communication more likely to deceive the public than inform it" (p. 563). The Court reasoned that: "First, the restriction must directly advance the state interest involved; the regulation may not be sustained if it provides only ineffective or remote support for the government's purpose ... Under the first criterion, the Court has declined to uphold regulations that only indirectly advance the state interest involved" (p. 564); and "Second, if the governmental interest could be served as well by a more limited restriction on commercial speech, the excessive restrictions cannot survive ... The second criterion recognizes that the First Amendment mandates that speech restrictions be 'narrowly drawn.' ...The regulatory technique may extend only as far as the interest it serves. The State cannot regulate speech that poses no danger to the asserted state interest ... nor can it completely suppress information when narrower restrictions on expression would serve its interest as well" (p. 565). The Court then created a four-part analysis for commercial speech cases:

1. At the outset, we must determine whether the expression is protected by the First Amendment. For commercial speech to come within that provision, it at least must concern *lawful activity and not be misleading*.
2. Next, we ask whether the asserted *governmental interest is substantial*.
3. If both inquiries yield positive answers, we must determine whether *the regulation directly advances the governmental interest* asserted.
4. And, finally, whether it *is not more extensive than is necessary* to serve that interest.

(p. 566, emphasis added)

In the *Central Hudson* application of the new legal test, the Court (1) found that there was no claim of the information promoting inaccurate information or illegal activity. The Court (2) found a clear and substantial government interest in fairness and efficiency of utility rate structures. The Court (3) examined the relationship between state interest and an advertising ban: There was a tenuous link to concern over equity and efficiency, but there was a direct connection between an interest in conservation, demand for electricity and advertising. Finally, the Court (4) concluded that "more limited regulation" could serve the state's conservation interests (p. 570). "It might, for example, require that the advertisements include information about the relative efficiency and expense of the offered service, both under current conditions and for the foreseeable future ... In the absence of a showing that more limited speech regulation would be ineffective, we cannot approve the complete suppression of *Central Hudson's* advertising" (p. 570). The Court has since applied intermediate scrutiny to commercial speech cases.

The *Central Hudson* case established the right of the Federal Trade Commission (FTC) to apply narrowly tailored regulation. In the area of social media influence, the FTC could require accurate advertising of legal products or services. It also could make the case for a government interest in post transparency about sponsorship because of a relationship between **deception** and clarity of consumer information. While the FTC could not ban social media advertising, under *Central Hudson* it could develop guidelines and bring cases against deliberatively deceptive advertising through the use of social media influencers.

Sorrell v. IMS Health, Inc. (2011) clarified *Central Hudson* by emphasizing a strong consumer need for health information. The First Amendment protects speakers against viewpoint discrimination. The U.S. Supreme Court has applied scrutiny in restricting what laws Congress and states may pass without articulating a non-speech substantial interest. As we will see later, the emerging commercial speech free expression rights are in potential conflict with data privacy efforts. A legal and ethical review of the conflict should address potential consumer harm from misinformation or fraudulent disinformation.

Box 3.2 Federal Trade Commission Social Media Scam Data

Commercial speech law established a framework for the Federal Trade Commission (FTC) to regulate and event warn consumers about online scams. One report indicated that scammers use social media advertising, offers and marketing (Small, 2020): "In the first six months of 2020, people reported losing a record high of almost $117 million to scams that started on social media (para. 1). Sometimes sellers fail to send products, seek financial help, and even use romance to lure targets. Scammers use identity theft or fake profiles within virtual communities to manipulate trust. In general, the rise of social media popularity has coincided with a dramatic increase in scams that leverage social media communication (Fletcher, 2020).

Source: Fletcher, Emma (2020, October 21). Scams Starting on Social Media Proliferate in Early 2020, *Federal Trade Commission*. https://www.ftc.gov/news-events/blogs/data-spotlight/2020/10/scams-starting-social-media-proliferate-early-2020.

TRANSPARENCY OF INTERESTS

Influence on human behavior comes from a wide range of sources – individuals, organizations, social movements, politicians, employers, businesses and others. Russell (2020) suggested that there is an important distinction between traditional advertising and the rise in influencer marketing:

> Influencer marketing should be much more than a simple transaction, for everyone involved. Plenty of influencer relationships will never see cash changing hands. And, even when money *is* involved, that's not where the true value of these relationships lie.
>
> (p. 29)

Given that social media marketing posts sometimes influence audience members to respond, some employ "fake influence," either through buying questionable followers or using other techniques to deceive "clueless brands" through exaggeration and deception (pp. 156–157). Social media marketing began with **earned exposure** through **earned media**, but **eCommerce** exploits organic **electronic word-of-mouth** (eWOM) through paid and promoted advertising.

The challenge for regulators is to protect reasonable consumers from being duped by social media accounts – human or bot – that fail to be transparent in the relationship between content and original sources of information and persuasion. Unfortunately, social marketing began through attempts to attract as much **buzz** as possible to capture social media attention. Strategies and tactics designed to increase **click-through rates (CTR)** were optimized for increased sponsored content results. There is conversion economic pressure among marketers to convert social media activity into sales. Advertisers measure **cost per click (CPC)** to limit expenses required to move audience members through a series of clicks from first exposure to finalized sale. In the **C-suite**, this quickly evolved into brand strategies that were not always legal and ethical. Social media policies followed to bring some order to the chaos of a wide-open marketplace.

DECEPTION AND FTC GUIDELINES

The Federal Trade Commission (2009) applied commercial speech law to a guide for endorsement and testimonials in advertising. In 16 CFR Part 255 § 255.0 (a), the FTC applied Section 5 of the FTC Act, 15 U.S.C. 45 to testimonial advertising. Congress, through the FTC statute, granted regulatory administrative law powers to order corrective action in unlawful deception cases. Endorsements are defined as "any advertising message (including verbal statements, demonstrations, or depictions of the name, signature, likeness or other identifying personal characteristics of an individual or the name or seal of an organization) that consumers are likely to believe reflects the opinions, beliefs, findings, or experiences of a party other than the sponsoring advertiser, even if the views expressed by that party are identical to those of the sponsoring advertiser" (b). The law is broadly applied to "any product, service, company or industry" (c–d). Before social media communication, FTC regulation addressed deception in reviews, television, infomercials and other media.

Under § 255.1 (a), endorsements "must reflect the honest opinions, findings, beliefs, or experience of the endorser." Further: "An advertiser may use an endorsement of an expert or celebrity only so long as it has good reason to believe that the endorser continues to subscribe to the views presented" (b). "When the advertisement represents that the endorser uses the endorsed product, the endorser must have been a bona fide user of it at the time the endorsement was given" (c). Finally: "Advertisers are subject to liability for false or unsubstantiated statements made through endorsements, or for failing to disclose material connections between themselves and their endorsers" (d). Those influencers endorsing a product or service have liability responsibility for any statement.

Under § 255.2, the FTC guidelines also apply to endorsements made by consumers. Advertisers are responsible for the accuracy of consumer endorsements, and they "must possess and rely upon adequate substantiation, including, when appropriate, competent and reliable scientific evidence, to support such claims made through endorsements in the same manner the advertiser would be required to do if it had made the representation directly, i.e., without using endorsements" (a). Further: "an advertiser should possess and rely upon adequate substantiation for this representation" (b). If these data are not presented, then "the advertisement should clearly and conspicuously disclose the generally expected performance in the depicted circumstances" (c). In other words, endorsements must be clear about lack of scientific performance evidence. These general advertising rules, then, were a foundation for social media influence cases.

The Federal Trade Commission (2019) guides clarify that any "endorsement message should make it obvious when you have a relationship ('material connection') with a brand, including "personal, family or employment relationship" circumstances that involve payments, as well as "free or discounted products or services" (para. 2). The legal and ethical basis for transparency and lack of deception is that: "Telling your followers about these kinds of relationships is important because it helps keep your recommendations honest and truthful, and it allows people to weigh the value of your endorsements" (para. 3). FTC regulation places responsibility for transparency in the hands of social media influencers. The FTC broadly applies the guidelines to "anything of value" received by a social media influencer (para. 6). Endorsements include "tags, likes, **pins** and similar ways of showing you like a brand or product" (para. 10).

Additionally, the FTC has been tracking a growing number, thousands of social media scams, with millions of consumer dollars lost.

Facebook was among the earliest social media platforms forced to investigate scams, including one that violated site rules by deceptively posting links on user walls (Crook, 2013). *TechCrunch* reported that Facebook took Christopher Peter Tarquini to court to recover $5,000 in expenses, and banned the spammer for life.

The confusing marketing claims for consumers frequently were neither legal nor ethical, and the FTC responded by disseminating a set of endorsement guidelines that served as a warning to brands and influencers. These rules established a framework for the FTC to regulate and even fine social media campaigns that failed to be transparent.

Box 3.3 Federal Trade Commission Social Media Endorsement Guidelines

The disclosure should be placed with the endorsement message itself …

Don't mix your disclosure into a group of hashtags or links.

If your endorsement is in a *picture* on a platform like Snapchat and Instagram Stories, superimpose the disclosure over the picture and make sure viewers have enough time to notice and read it …

- Use **simple and clear** language.

  Simple explanations like "Thanks to Acme brand for the free product" are often enough if placed in a way that is hard to miss.

  So are terms like "advertisement," "ad," and "sponsored."

  On a space-limited platform like Twitter, the terms "AcmePartner" or "Acme Ambassador" (where Acme is the brand name) are also options.

  It's fine (but not necessary) to include a hashtag with the disclosure, such as #ad or #sponsored.

  Don't use vague or confusing terms like "sp," "spon," or "collab," or standalone terms like "thanks" or "ambassador," and stay away from other abbreviations and shorthand when possible ...

What Else to Know

- You can't talk about your experience with a product you haven't tried.
- If you're paid to talk about a product and thought it was terrible, you can't say it's terrific.
- You can't make up claims about a product that would require proof the advertiser doesn't have – such as scientific proof that a product can treat a health condition.

Source: Federal Trade Commission (2019, November). Disclosures 101 for Social Media Influencers. https://www.ftc.gov/tips-advice/business-center/guidance/disclosures-101-social-media-influencers.

The Federal Trade Commission (2016) approved a consent order following a complaint that Lord & Taylor department store failed to properly disclose native advertising and online advertising. The case began in 2015 with native advertising posing as news in the *Nylon* publication and its Instagram post about a new Design Lab clothing line. The social media complaint focused on the fact that "the company paid 50 online fashion 'influencers' to post Instagram pictures of themselves wearing a paisley dress from the new collection, but failed to disclose they had given each influencer the dress, as well as thousands of dollars, in exchange for their endorsement" (para. 3). The FTC consent order prohibited "Lord & Taylor from misrepresenting that paid ads are from an independent source or that an endorser is an independent or ordinary consumer" (para. 4). Lord & Taylor was also required to monitor future clear endorsement practices.

KEY CASE: *LORD & TAYLOR* (2016)

The initial Lord & Taylor complaint came from a March 2015 campaign that was developed in the fall of 2014 and included "Lord & Taylor-branded blog posts, photos, video uploads, native advertising editorials in online fashion magazines, and use of a team of fashion influencers recruited for their fashion style and extensive base of followers on social media platforms, all focused on a single article of clothing, the Design Lab Paisley Asymmetrical Dress" (*Lord & Taylor Complaint*, 2016, p. 1).

The gifting of a "Paisley Asymmetrical Dress to 50 select fashion influencers who were paid, in amounts ranging from $1,000 to $4,000, to post on the social media platform Instagram one photo of themselves wearing the Design Lab dress during a specified timeframe" included tagging @lordandtaylor and using the #DesignLab hashtag (p. 2).

Paid models failed to tell follower they worked for the company.

FTC case evidence, https://www.ftc.gov/enforcement/cases-proceedings/152-3181/lord-taylor-llc-matter

Each of the influencers signed a contract with Lord & Taylor that did not mention or require them to disclose the relationship or compensation. The campaign reached 11.4 million Instagram users and sparked 328,000 brand engagements, and the promoted dress sold out (p. 2). The FTC charged the following counts in its complaint:

COUNT I: Misrepresentations About the Design Lab Instagram Postings

COUNT II: Failure to Disclose Influencers' Material Connection to Lord & Taylor

COUNT III: Misrepresentations About the Nylon Instagram Post and the March 31, 2015 Nylon Magazine Article (p. 3)

In the *Lord & Taylor Decision and Order* (2016), the retailer agreed to a consent agreement in which it "neither admits nor denies any of the allegations in the draft complaint except as specifically stated in the consent agreement" (p. 1). The FTC ordered Lord & Taylor to "not misrepresent, in any manner, expressly or by implication, that an endorser of such product or service is an independent user or ordinary consumer of the product or service" (p. 3). In other words, it was required to follow existing law. The company was ordered to provide endorsers with clear responsibility statements, monitor disclosure practices, and immediately terminate "any with a material connection" in cases of misrepresentation and failure "to disclose clearly and conspicuously, and in close proximity, a material connection" (p. 4). While violators may face fines for misrepresentation, the case served more as a social media industry warning. Following the case, the FTC updated its online social media influence guidelines.

Commercial speech law continues to evolve. In *Sorrell v. IMS Health, Inc.* (2011), the U.S. Supreme Court clarified *Central Hudson* by ruling a Vermont law unconstitutional that regulated prescription drug data for marketing purposes. Physician prescription data were sold to pharmaceutical marketers and the Court used strict scrutiny in concluding that consumers have a strong interest in health information. The Vermont statute restricted "sale, disclosure and use of pharmacy records that reveal the prescribing practices of individual doctors" in an attempt to "safeguard medical privacy" (p. 557). The Supreme Court, however, concluded that the commercial speech of pharmaceutical marketing is protected under the First Amendment. Content and speaker restriction "disfavors marketing, that is, speech with a particular content," and "specific speakers, namely pharmaceutical manufacturers' were disfavored by the state statute (p. 564). Citing *United States v. O'Brien* (1968) the law failed the legal test because the purpose of it was to use viewpoint discrimination and "diminish the effectiveness of marketing by manufacturers of brand-name drugs" (p. 565):

> The statute imposed "a speaker- and content-based burden" on protected expression, and that circumstance is sufficient to justify application of heightened scrutiny … Under a commercial speech inquiry, it is the State's burden to justify its content-based law as consistent with the First Amendment.
>
> (p. 571).

Three justices in the case dissented, arguing that the law only stopped pharmaceutical company "data-mining," and that commercial speech law, not a "heightened" review should apply (pp. 565–566). The trio applied the *Central Hudson* test in finding "substantial" interests (p. 596), and that the statute "directly advances" objectives (p. 597). "The majority cannot point to any adequately supported, similarly effective 'more limited restriction'" (p. 599):

> The Court reaches its conclusion through the use of important First Amendment Categories – "content-based," "speaker-based," and "neutral" – but without taking full account of the regulatory context, the nature of the speech effects, the values these First Amendment categories seek to promote, and prior precedent … At best the Court opens a Pandora's Box of First Amendment challenges to many ordinary regulatory practices that may only incidentally affect a commercial message … At worst, it reawakens Lochner's pre-New Deal threat of substituting judicial for democratic decision-making where ordinary economic regulation is at issue.
>
> (pp. 602– 603)

The Court's clarification of *Central Hudson* may be read as shifting "review toward greater First Amendment protection for truthful commercial speech about legal products, even dangerous or disfavored 'vice' products" (Trager, Ross, & Reynolds, 2018, p. 542). Legal scholars have raised concern that the law could place consumer data privacy laws in conflict with commercial speech doctrine (Shah, 2020):

> The most straightforward reading of *Sorrell* is that it made no change in commercial speech doctrine at all. "Heightened scrutiny," after all, is often synonymous with "intermediate scrutiny." … Justice Kennedy faithfully applied the *Central Hudson* intermediate scrutiny standard to Vermont's Prescription Confidentiality Law … Nonetheless, numerous scholars have interpreted Justice Kennedy's use of "heightened scrutiny" to mean something else – something more stringent – than the intermediate scrutiny test promulgated in *Central Hudson*. Justice Breyer, dissenting in *Sorrell*, also

> noted that Justice Kennedy's invocation of "heightened scrutiny" suggested "a standard yet stricter than *Central Hudson*." This interpretation is more nuanced than simply looking up "heightened scrutiny" in a legal dictionary, and the arguments advanced by Justice Breyer and his supporting scholars are worth considering.
>
> (pp. 109–110)

The finer question of law is whether or not data are speech and deserve First Amendment protection within "a libertarian vision," that may open "a Pandora's Box of First Amendment challenges" (pp. 116–117). Privacy advocates, then, will need to articulate potential "harms to consumers from unfettered collection and dissemination of their personal and online data," as well as the leakage of it into "the wrong hands" that "mishandle or misuse" social and digital footprints (p. 128). Advocacy groups, such as the **Electronic Frontier Foundation** (EFF), historically promoted a free and open Internet. In the #BlackLivesMatter era, this extended to protection for protesters from police surveillance that also spills onto social media streams. In part, commercial speech laws may protect corporate power that is under social and political attacks. The broader commercial speech issues are likely to center on ambiguity about standards of scrutiny used when government acts.

Earlier, in *44 Liquormart Inc. v. Rhode Island* (1996), a state intent to reduce alcohol sales was viewed with skepticism. Likewise, the Supreme Court also struck down a state rule that prohibited lawyers from advertising because the Constitution and First Amendment protect truthful commercial speech (*Bates v. State Bar of Arizona*, 1977). In that case, lawyers for a free legal clinic placed an advertisement in the *Arizona Republic* newspaper that offered "legal services at very reasonable fees" (p. 354). They faced disciplinary action for violating a rule banning advertisements or "commercial publicity" (p. 355).

The Court found that:

> If commercial speech is to be distinguished, it "must be distinguished by its content" … Even though the speaker's interest is largely economic, the Court has protected such speech in certain contexts … The listener's interest is substantial: the consumer's concern for the free flow of commercial speech often may be far keener than his concern for urgent political dialogue. Moreover, significant societal interests are served by such speech. Advertising, though entirely commercial, may often carry information of import to significant issues of the day … And commercial speech serves to inform the public of the availability, nature, and prices of products and services, and thus performs an indispensable role in the allocation of resources in a free enterprise system.
>
> (pp. 363–364)

In more recent cases, Supreme Court justices have disagreed over application of strict scrutiny of content-based regulation versus use on lower standards when commercial speech rights clearly have been violated (*Reed v. Town of Gilbert*, 2015). The Court reversed the Ninth Circuit because the "restrictions for political, ideological, and temporary event signs apply equally no matter who sponsors them" (p. 169):

> Because "[s]peech restrictions based on the identity of the speaker are all too often simply a means to control content," [quoting *Citizens United v. Federal Election Commission*, 2010)] ... we have insisted that "laws favoring some speakers over others demand strict scrutiny when the legislature's speaker preference reflects a content preference," ... Thus, a law limiting the content of newspapers, but only newspapers, could not evade strict scrutiny simply because it could be characterized as speaker based. Likewise, a content-based law that restricted the political speech of all corporations would not become content neutral just because it singled out corporations as a class of speakers.
>
> (p. 170)

The *Citizens United* (2010) 5-4 decision freed corporations from spending limits for political advertising because they act as individuals under the law (*First National Bank of Boston v. Bellotti* (1978). The Court rejected portions of the Bipartisan Campaign Reform Act of 2002, and later also overturned individual spending limits for candidates (*McCutcheon v. Federal Election Committee*, 2014). The 5-4 decision acknowledged the right to contribute was not absolutely protected by the First Amendment, but:

> In a series of cases over the past 40 years, we have spelled out how to draw the constitutional line between the permissible goal of avoiding corruption in the political process and the impermissible desire simply to limit political speech. We have said that government regulation may not target the general gratitude a candidate may feel toward those who support him or his allies, or the political access such support may afford. "Ingratiation and access ... are not corruption." [quoting *Citizens United*, 2010] ... They embody a central feature of democracy – that constituents support candidates who share their beliefs and interests, and candidates who are elected can be expected to be responsive to those concerns.
>
> Any regulation must instead target what we have called "quid pro quo" corruption or its appearance.
>
> (p. 192)

In this view, First Amendment protection "is designed and intended to remove governmental restraints from the arena of public discussion, putting the decision as to what views shall be voiced largely into the hands of each of us, ... in the belief that no other approach would comport with the premise of individual dignity and choice upon which our political system rests" (*McCutcheon*, 2014, p. 203, quoting *Cohen v. California*, 1971). A "collective ... public interest (usually framed as an important or compelling government interest) ... may be pursued by Congress "only so long as it does not unnecessarily infringe an individual's right to freedom of speech; we do not truncate this tailoring test at the outset" (*McCutcheon*, 2014, p. 206).

The Supreme Court decision left open how future courts will apply or not apply the *Central Hudson* test to commercial speech cases. This has implications for future regulation of commercial social media platforms, the potential reach of the Federal Trade Commission (FTC) and Federal Communications Commission (FCC) to fashion new influencer and other rules, and the possibility that Congress could revise existing digital law.

ETHICAL FRAMEWORKS AND ISSUES

Regulation of social media influence, as well as the commercial speech law that frame advertising, follows ethical values of truth through information accuracy, transparency and disclosure, some independence from financial interests (or at least disclosing these), and avoidance of manipulation through explicit deception. Instead of **social naturalism**, corporate social responsibility (CSR) should advance moral values (Pompper, 2015). The philosophy of Kant focuses on a sense of duty and principles:

> Becoming a morally autonomous agent, or objective, is a central theme of **deontology** ... Self-interest alone (egoism) must be ruled out in the decision making ... as all factors are considered equally. That perspective allows bias to be minimized and decisions to be based upon the duty to uphold moral principle as a rational decision-maker.
>
> (Bowen & Stacks, 2014, p. 221)

This ethical perspective minimizes behavioral utility and passion. Within the context of social media influence, we understand that celebrity influencers have the power to effectively move followers to action. However, one should ultimately evaluate the nature of social media relationships. It is fair to conclude that those exercising influence owe a primary ethical responsibility to their social media followers instead of practicing **relativism** that sacrifices fundamental moral values. If they are beholden to employers or contracts, then the nature of these legal responsibilities must be made clear to audience members. Each reasonable follower should be given enough information to make an independent judgment about following the account and acting on persuasive communication.

Box 3.4 Thought Leader Tasha M. Davis

Tasha M. Davis.

Photograph courtesy Tasha Davis.

The introduction of social media presented one of the biggest disruptions of modern-day times for society and businesses. With the ubiquity of social media increasing over the last decade, the social media and leadership connection is vitally important. The significant use of social media and its role in our society is increasingly essential and requires organizations and their senior leaders to better understand how to engage with their constituents using this tool. I had to dig into the history of social media, its genesis from an organizational standpoint, and the contrast of the intended purpose for its use vs. how it is actually being used.

THE IMPACT OF SOCIAL MEDIA ON LEADERSHIP

Here are some insights on a few questions regarding the impact of social media on leadership. *How and why does a Fortune 500 CEO use social media to communicate with employees, customers, consumers, and other stakeholders (e.g., shareholders, Wall Street analysts, industry insiders), and what impact their use of social media has on those constituencies?*

In a study of social media use by 24 "top social CEOs," Men et al. (2018) found that the CEOs primarily used one of three strategies to engage their constituencies. The most common strategy, even among the most prolific social CEOs, was one-way informative communication. This included things such as sharing links to company websites and news resources and providing information of potential interest to followers, including product launches, financial information, major events and milestones, summaries of CEO and organizational activities and CEO announcements, statements and opinion pieces.

The second most common strategy was to establish functional dialogic (two-way) communication with stakeholders. Kent and Taylor (1998) define dialogue as any exchange of ideas and opinions in which people are willing to pursue mutual understanding and reach mutual agreements, even if they do not necessarily agree with one another. Dialogic communication is built on five key principles:

1. Mutuality (i.e., recognizing organization–public interconnectedness)
2. Propinquity (i.e., being "close" to publics and willing to engage in spontaneous interactions)
3. Empathy (i.e., being genuine and supportive of publics' needs and interests)
4. Risk (i.e., being willing to interact with publics and incorporate their perspectives)
5. Commitment (i.e., being willing to stick with a dialogic approach and let it influence the organization over the long term)

Ideally, dialogic communication is about engaging with constituencies to establish empathetic interactions, build understanding, make meaning and co-create reality (Kent & Taylor, 2002). This is the key to successful engagement online with constituents. This is what one Fortune 500 CEO has done and this is what I highly recommend for other executives. To take it a step further as it relates to electronic media (social media), Kent and Taylor recommend five dialogic internet principles:

1. Create interactive dialogic loops to solicit feedback and answer questions
2. Provide useful, relevant information of interest to constituencies
3. Generate return visitors by providing an engaging and dynamic site (posts and writing style)
4. Conserve visitors by referring them to other information provided by the organization
5. Design user-friendly, intuitive interfaces (i.e., when providing links make sure they work)

What is the perceived impact of a Fortune 500 CEO's social media use on organizational outcomes such as brand affinity, employee engagement, organizational culture, financial results, and customer satisfaction?

Building a community is part of the brand social strategy. While it takes a lot of heavy lifting to build a community, it is beneficial as a tool that can be used to rally the troops, gain trust of your constituents and better understand the culture of the organization. Building a strong social community also helps attract new employees and customers and retain existing employees and customers. Organizational outcomes are impacted by social media strategies although the social strategy isn't the only determining factor. Consistent engagement from the chief executive helped build a strong social community that lead to the company's constituents appreciating his transparency and increased customer and employee engagement and satisfaction.

This CEO has become a Twitter influencer and an online leader who is more capable than the brand of influencing other members of their industry's community. He was the textbook case for an online leader building a community of followers. He built credibility, fostered trust, communicated with passion, and increased his social capital by encouraging inclusivity and reciprocity, which, in turn, amplified his influence (Huffaker, 2010). The company soon felt the impact of this CEO taking the reins by experiencing rebounding employee morale and rising revenue which are almost always inextricably linked. Social media played an enormous role in this phase of T-Mobile's journey.

Over a period of seven years, while this CEO was at the helm, the number of awards and accolades this Fortune 500 company received increased exponentially. They were acknowledged and awarded in categories such as purchase experience, customer service, employee satisfaction, best places to work in, most military friendly, best places to work in for women, best places to work in for disability inclusion, America's best employers, employee's choice top CEO, and world's most ethical companies. All these honors came from reputable institutions and publications with long, storied histories of scrupulous research and finding the best of the best. The most recent consecutive quarterly earnings were record-breaking earnings with seven quarters in a row touting accelerated customer growth and financial performance. While the aforementioned accolades and accomplishments cannot be tied solely to the CEO's social media use, there is some perceived connection to his vision and leadership and how he chose to use social media to communicate his vision. There is a strong correlation between his presence at the helm of the company, his role as a social CEO and his pervasive acceptance in both the social media world and the corporate world. Research shows that high engagement with social media content is positively related to organizational outcomes and image (Syrdal & Briggs, 2016). The stakes are high for market share in many industries and this CEO used social media to differentiate his organization in this space and achieved record financial growth as a result.

How does a Fortune 500 CEO's social media use impact their perceived leadership style according to their constituents?

Social media served as an extension of this CEO's persona. He changed the **narrative** around what other's thought of his company and social media was his medium of choice to share his message. He used social media to amplify his organization's brand message and his commitment to change the industry for good. His authenticity and consistent presence helped increase his followership, and helped others see him as an authentic, transformational leader. Authenticity yields increased followership.

The CEO provided a macrolevel perspective of the industry and highlighted everything that was wrong with the industry in order to pivot the focus on all his organization was doing to better the industry. While his messages were full of hubris, there was a genuineness and thoughtfulness to his humorous that which makes him likeable, not villainous. The one-to-many dyadic dialogs were unique, even innovative coming from a CEO. They produced a dynamic social system of communities and individuals where everyone was welcome to contribute and the structure was not the traditional corporate structure where not every employee or stakeholder could access the CEO; it was the exact opposite structure. It was a structure that defied the norms of most organizational cultures and made every individual feel like they had immediate access to the

CEO of a Fortune 500 company. This level of access enhanced the CEO's likeability factor and was unprecedented, occurring regularly, not periodically. Legere's practice of constant, direct communication was enduring and created a sense of familiarity for his audience. His approach to creating a duality of structure in his communications brings to mind the contemporary British social theorist Anthony Giddens' structuration theory (1984). This theory states that just as an individual's autonomy is influenced by structure, structures are maintained and adapted through the exercise of individual expression largely determined by their socialization into that structure allowing for both constraint and enablement (Whittington, 2015). His leadership style was perceived as transformational and authentic according to interviewed constituents.

LEADERSHIP EVOLUTION IN PRACTICE

It is important to understand the implications for how to use this information in practice. The following are a few takeaways:

1. It's no secret you have to be an effective communicator to be a good leader but the addition of social media makes this even more essential. The notion of digital dialogic communication makes this notion that much more necessary.
2. In analyzing thousands of tweets, I uncovered how a Fortune 500's constituents generally process information from the organization's social channels. Using the Elaboration Likelihood Model (ELM), I concluded that this company's constituents process information using the "peripheral route," which means they aren't scrutinizing the message for its effectiveness, they are looking for the more interesting cues in content (video vignettes, colorful image, celebrity endorser etc.) that make it more attractive. Chief executives, please keep this in mind as you create content.
3. Leadership training should include social media management, especially for senior executives. There are many positive impacts of social media, including connecting with stakeholders and adding a social media element to this training would make it more comprehensive.

Tasha M. Davis is a Sr. Manager, Regional Marketing at T-Mobile and recently received her Ph.D. in values-driven leadership from Benedictine University in Lisle, IL. Her doctoral research focused on how social media has impacted leadership since its inception and its impact on organizational behavior. She lives in suburban Atlanta with her family.

Sources

Huffaker, D. (2010). Online Leaders and Social Influence in Online Communities. *Human Communication Research*, 36(4), 593–617. https://doi.org/10.1111/j.1468-2958.2010.01390.x.

Kent, M.L. and Taylor, M. (1998). Building Dialogic Relationships through the World Wide Web. *Public Relations Review*, 24(3), 321–334. https://doi.org/10.1016/S0363-8111(99)80143-X.

Kent, M.L. and Taylor, M. (2002). Toward a Dialogic Theory of Public Relations. *Public Relations Review*, 28(1), 21–37. https://doi.org/10.1016/S0363-8111(02)00108-X.

Men, L.R., Tsai, W.S., Chen, Z.F., and Ji, Y.G. (2018). Social Presence and Digital Dialogic Communication: Engagement Lessons from Top CEOs. *Journal of Public Relations Research*, 30(3), 83–99. https://doi.org/10.1080/1062726X.2018.1498341.

Syrdal, H.A. and Briggs, E. (2016). Developing a Positive Organizational Image: The Role of Engagement with Social Media Content. In J.G. Fowler and J. Weiser (eds.), *Proceedings of Society for Marketing Advances in Reimagining: The Power of Marketing to Create Enduring Value* (pp. 74–83). San Antonio, TX: Society for Marketing Advances.

Whittington, R. (2015). Giddens, Structuration Theory and Strategy as Practice. In D. Golsorkhi, L. Rouleau, D. Seidl, and E. Vaara (Eds.), *Cambridge Handbook of Strategy as Practice* (pp. 109–126). Cambridge: Cambridge University Press.

Concern about advertising is frequently related to social problems. The UK effort to reduce obesity has led to an effort to ban all online advertising for "junk food," which would be the "toughest digital marketing restrictions in the world" (Sweney, 2020, para. 1). Regulators planned to implement the new rules on a "stunned" ad industry that "called it indiscriminate and draconian" (para. 2). The law focuses on fat, salt and sugar levels that could be applied to restrict a wide range of online advertising. "If implemented, the ban would affect digital marketing, from ads on Facebook, to paid-search results on Google, text message promotions, and social media activity on Twitter and Instagram" (para. 7). Emerging law and regulation of advertising and digital media requires that we stay up-to-date through regular research.

ONLINE RESOURCES

Federal Trade Commission (FTC, 2021). https://www.ftc.gov/.

DISCUSSION QUESTIONS

1. What are the best ways for Instagram influencers to be transparent about financial interests within their social media posts?
2. Do you agree or disagree with the FTC guidelines? What would you do to improve them?
3. What changes need to be made to commercial speech law? Why or why not should there be limits to First Amendment freedom?

REFERENCES

44 Liquormart v. Rhode Island, 517 U.S. 484 (1996).

Bates v. State Bar of Arizona (1977).

BBC News (2020, October 16). Instagram Targets Rule-Breaking Influencers. https://www.bbc.com/news/technology-54571630.

Bigelow v. Virginia, 421 U.S. 809 (1975).

Bowen, S.A. and Stacks, D.W. (2014). Understanding the Ethical and Research Implications of Social Media. In M.W. DiStaso and D.S. Bortee (eds.), *Ethical Practice of Social Media in Public Relations.* New York and London: Routledge.

Central Hudson Gas & Electric Corp. v. Public Serv. Commission, 447 U.S. 557 (1980).

Chen, T. (2020, November 10). Khloé Kardashian's Most Recent Ad for Migraine Medication Is Raising Serious Ethical Questions About Sponcon.*BuzzFeed News.* https://www.buzzfeednews.com/article/tanyachen/khloe-kardashian-migraine-spon-controversy.

Citizens United v. Federal Election Commission, 558 U.S. 310 (2010).

Cohen v. California, 403 U.S. 15 (1971).

Crook, J. (2013, November 21). Don't Spam Facebook with Fake Bieber Porn Unless You Want to Get Sued.*TechCrunch*. http://techcrunch.com/2013/11/21/dont-spam-facebook-with-fake-bieber-porn-unless-you-want-to-get-sued/.

Federal Trade Commission (2019, November). Disclosures 101 for Social Media Influencers. https://www.ftc.gov/tips-advice/business-center/guidance/disclosures-101-social-media-influencers.

Federal Trade Commission (2016, May 23). FTC Approves Final Lord & Taylor Order Prohibiting Deceptive Advertising Techniques. https://www.ftc.gov/news-events/press-releases/2016/05/ftc-approves-final-lord-taylor-order-prohibiting-deceptive.

Federal Trade Commission (2009). Guides Concerning the Use of Endorsements and Testimonials in Advertising. 16 CFR Part 255 § 255.0, Section 5 FTC Act, 15 U.S.C. 45. https://www.ftc.gov/news-events/press-releases/2009/10/ftc-publishes-final-guides-governing-endorsements-testimonials.

First National Bank of Boston v. Bellotti, 435 U.S. 765, 783 (1978).

Fletcher, E. (2020, October 21). Scams Starting on Social Media Proliferate in Early 2020.*Federal Trade Commission*. https://www.ftc.gov/news-events/blogs/data-spotlight/2020/10/scams-starting-social-media-proliferate-early-2020.

Kelly, M. (2020, October 17). Oracle Founder Donated $250,000 To Graham PAC In Final Days of TikTok Deal. *The Verge*. https://www.theverge.com/2020/10/17/21520356/oracle-tiktok-larry-ellison-lindsey-graham-super-pac-donation-jaime-harrison.

Kwan, C. (2020, October 16). US FCC To Start Work On Reforms Of Social Media Legal Protections.*ZDNet*. https://www.zdnet.com/article/us-fcc-to-start-work-on-reforms-of-social-media-legal-protections/.

Lord & Taylor Complaint (2016, May 23). Federal Trade Commission C-4576, Exhibit B. https://www.ftc.gov/enforcement/cases-proceedings/152-3181/lord-taylor-llc-matter.

Lord & Taylor Decision and Order (2016, May 23). Federal Trade Commission C-4576. https://www.ftc.gov/enforcement/cases-proceedings/152-3181/lord-taylor-llc-matter.

McCutcheon v. Federal Election Committee, 572 U.S. 185 (2014).

NetImperative (2020, September 22). Three Quarters of Instagram Influencers Hide Their Advertisement Disclosure in Their Posts. *NetImperative*. http://www.netimperative.com/2020/09/22/three-quarters-of-instagram-influencers-hide-their-advertisement-disclosure-in-their-posts-2/.

New York Times v. Sullivan, 376 U.S. 254 (1964).

Pompper, D. (2015). *Corporate Social Responsibility, Sustainability and Public Relations: Negotiating Multiple Complex Challenges*. London: Routledge.

Reed v. Town of Gilbert, 576 U.S. 155 (2015).

Russell, K. (2020). *The Influencer Code, How To Unlock the Power of Influencer Marketing*. Hobart, NY: Hatherleigh Press.

Shah, B. (2020, Fall). Commercial Free Speech Constrains on Data Privacy Statutes After *Sorrell v. IMS Health, Columbia Journal of Law & Social Problems*, 54, 93–129.

Small, B. (2020, October 21). Scams That Start On Social Media. *Federal Trade Commission.* https://www.consumer.ftc.gov/blog/2020/10/scams-start-social-media.

Smith Galer, S. (2020, October 19).Anti-Trump TikTokkers Not Declaring Paid Content.*BBC World Service.* https://www.bbc.com/news/election-us-2020-54555798.

Sorrell v. IMS Health, Inc., 564 U.S. 552 (2011).

Sweney, M. (2020, November 10). UK to Ban All Online Junk Food Advertising to Tackle Obesity.*The Guardian.* https://www.theguardian.com/media/2020/nov/10/uk-to-ban-all-online-junk-food-advertising-to-tackle-obesity.

Trager, R., Ross, S D., and Reynolds, A. (2018). *The Law of Journalism and Mass Communication*, 6th edition. London: SAGE.

United States v. O'Brien, 391 U.S. 367 (1968).

U.S. Department of Justice (2020, September 23). The Justice Department Unveils Proposed Section 230 Legislation. https://www.justice.gov/opa/pr/justice-department-unveils-proposed-section-230-legislation.

Valentine v. Christensen, 316 U.S. 52 (1942).

Virginia State Bd. of Pharmacy v. Virginia Citizens Consumer Council, 425 U.S. 748 (1976).

Advertising, PR, and Social Marketing

4

> *In one sense, information communicated to another remains confidential whenever it is customarily kept private, or at least closely held, by the person imparting it.*

—U.S. Supreme Court Justice Neil Gorsuch,
Food Marketing Institute v. Argus Leader Media (2019, p. 2539)

Jimmy Donaldson, known on YouTube as "MrBeast" was the top creator of 2020 (Shaw & Bergen, 2020). A 2016 college dropout, Donaldson used the next four years to learn the valuable algorithm:

> Donaldson, then 18, had been posting to the site since he was 12 without amassing much of an audience. But he was convinced he was close to unlocking the secrets of YouTube's algorithm, the black box of rules and processes that determines what videos get recommended to viewers.
>
> (para. 1)

His "I COUNTED TO 100000!" viral video generated more than 21 million views (paras. 3–4). MrBeast eventually won over 48 million subscribers (para. 5). As a YouTube creator, the appeal is that, "You can practically make unlimited money" (para. 7). For Donaldson and other social media celebrities, the views translate into millions of dollars in revenue and profit, as well as lucrative deals with major advertising brands. The algorithm **tactics**, however, are only a small part of secret business practices.

The **best practices** of advertising, public relations and social media marketing typically involve working with confidential **client** information. As such, employees often are required to sign **nondisclosure agreements** (NDAs) or non-compete contracts that may extend beyond the term of employment and other exclusionary contracting.

Client relationships involve complex legal arrangements – working as a formal professional business "agency" or "an independent contract realm" (Fueroghne, 2017, pp. 103–104). The distinction lies in whether or not the individual or group is responsible as an agent of a client. Similar to attorneys, there is a fiduciary responsibility to act in the client's best interests within law and ethics. The relationship is expected to include full disclosure, accountability and protection of confidential information, such as industry trade secrets for processes and products. An agent frequently handles client money and this requires honesty and no conflicts of interests. The relationship extends "even after termination" (Fueroghne, 2017, p. 111). Contracts should specify duties of the agent and client and signing them represents knowledge, consent and potential liability for the effects from social media content and sharing. The agent or client may have "sole liability" if there is a clause in the employment contract that specifies social media work (p. 116). Alternatively, both parties to the contract may share "joint liability" (p. 117). Clients may dictate specifics of work, but independent contractors have more freedom and autonomy over process to create specific work. In both cases, agents or contractors and clients must be aware of non-speech laws that limit conduct. Internet law, for example, has developed with special provisions involving children within social media content or in the audience. Finally, a variety of business laws impact employers, clients and employees.

Some labor and public interest groups have demanded that the federal government, through the FTC, develop rules to protect workers. Employees are subject to company and social media policies that may restrict expressive conduct and free speech. At the same time, some employees have been encouraged to share corporate public relations on personal pages and social networks (Stein, 2016). In this sense, social media use falls within a larger context of workplace law that includes issues, such as hourly pay, family and medical leave, and other benefits or disciplinary action typically managed in a human resources (HR) company office.

The National Labor Relations Act (NLRA) of 1935 has been applied to emerging social media law. For example, in *Kroger Co. of Mich. v. Granger* (NLRB, 2014), a broad social media policy that restricted employee speech and required disclaimers for all posts was found to violate free speech rights. In *CVS Health* (2018), the NLRB revisited employee First Amendment rights at CVS Health and clarified a need to "differentiate" by the context of "work settings (p. 2). NLRA (1935) applies only to employee unions. A CVS Health Code of Conduct applied to all media relations, but the company expanded this to employees "who speak on social media about the company in any way" to add a disclaimer that they are "not speaking on behalf of the Company or as an official Company Representative" (p. 3). Companies generally have a right to protect their "legitimate business interest" in guarding privacy, security and lawful action (p. 11). One part of the policy found lawful by the NLRB was:

> **Use social media appropriately.** Social media is not the appropriate venue for voicing complaints about the Company or particular colleagues that could be resolved more constructively through the appropriate channels consistent with the Company's commitment to maintain a diverse and safe workplace. If CVS Health colleagues wish to use social media to voice complaints or criticisms, they must avoid posting anything that is or could be viewed as discriminatory, harassing, threatening, defamatory, or invasive of another individual's privacy. Such prohibited posts may include disparaging customers, falsely and intentionally harming someone's reputation, bullying co-workers, or otherwise creating a hostile work environment. Threats of violence, discrimination and harassment will not be tolerated.
>
> (p.11)

The NLRB found that the policy, aimed at "a safe and diverse workplace," advised "employees that if they have complaints about those issues, going through official company channels is more constructive than complaining on social media" (p. 12). NLRB also found that "employees remain free to complain or criticize on social media, but that such complaints should be made civilly" (p. 12). In other words, the policy was not a ban on all speech and the company had a right to prohibit defamatory speech that was false and intentionally harmed a person's reputation. It appeared to allow for prior restraint on workplace speech that in governmental contexts would violate the First Amendment.

Publicly held corporations have a fiduciary responsibility to protect shareholders' value. In the CVS Health Social Media Policy Colleague Handbook, there was employee protection for a "legal right to use social media to speak about your political or religious views, lifestyle and personal issues, working conditions, wages, or union-related topics or activities with others inside or outside the Company" (p. 7). CVS Health reached a settlement with the union in 2019.

Collective bargaining agreement (CBA) language is not legally binding for nonunion employees, but there is an ethical responsibility for companies to offer employees as much First Amendment freedom as possible without sacrificing confidentiality. Hirsch (2020) suggested that future workplace law will be governed by technological change:

> New technology will also transform the role of many human workers and their relationship with employers. For instance, innovations in artificial intelligence and other types of computing will interject themselves into the employer-employee relationship in ways that our current workplace laws are incapable of handling.
> (p. 890)

The reliance on technology may "magnify employers' control over workers," increase "inequality and social disruptions," and fragment workplaces that fail to develop "governance" documents (pp. 957–958).

A small group of Amazon employees, Amazonians for Employee Privacy (2020), launched a Google Sites petition against company surveillance: "We the undersigned Amazonians are concerned about your company's increasing Surveillance Obsession" (para. 1). They noted the search for an intelligence analyst who would be hired to monitor the threat of employees organizing and forming a labor union, the monitoring of private Facebook groups and the monitoring of employee email (para. 2): "The central demand of this letter is simply to stop spying on us" (para. 4). The employees claimed that the company used a "union heat map" tracking criticism over nearly 20,000 workers with the Covid-19 virus (para. 9). Apparently, this fact sparked an interest in organizing: "When Amazon discretely watches its workers, it harms are ability to do our job well, and tramples on our rights to organize and demand better from our workplace" (para. 10). As of this writing, the group had not collected 200 employee signatures needed to go forward with complaints.

Too often, managed public relations works to keep private the criticism of practices that may harm others. The best practice for PR is to offer as much truth as possible, represent clients with an eye toward social media authenticity and be guided by law and ethical behavior. Excellence theory offers an approach that emphasizes relationships and diverse stakeholders (Luttrell & Capizzo, 2019, pp. 2–3).

At the same time, Google's online advertising model has been called a monopoly by 35 state attorneys general and three territories in a lawsuit against parent company Alphabet, but the case is not scheduled for trial until September of 2023.

The claim made was that Google dominates search advertising by using tactics that squelch the competition – an antitrust violation of the Sherman Act. The action could be similar to a 1974 U.S. Department of Justice lawsuit that eventually led to the breakup of the original AT&T telephone monopoly (Slevin & Liedtke, 2020). However, Google responded that its search engine competes with others, and users may "find alternative ways to search for information on the Internet" (AP, 2020b, para. 3).

At the heart of advertising, PR, and social marketing are exploitation of user data to target consumers. In this sense, every social media communication act is represented by a private data trail that has the potential to be misused. As, artificial intelligence (AI) and natural language processing continue to spread within business, there are growing concerns about the collection, storage, management, and utilization of all forms of behavioral data.

Zoom video conferencing had a huge spike in usage during the pandemic, but the company failed to protect data privacy. The Federal Trade Commission (FTC) ultimately reached a settlement over encryption, secure recordings, cloud storage and **software** that placed Apple computers at risk:

> Though Zoom has now discontinued many of the practices challenged in the complaint, the settlement puts your security top of mind for Zoom. It requires Zoom to live up to its privacy and security promises and to put in place a comprehensive security program designed to protect your information for many years to come—or pay big fines.
>
> (Puig, 2020, para. 9)

Zoom's deceptive practices that failed to emphasize information security over about four years gave users a false sense of safety. The FTC settlement also treated this as unfair business practices and ordered Zoom to: "Design, implement, maintain, and document safeguards that control for the internal and external risks" to "security, confidentiality, and integrity" of information (*In the Matter of Zoom Communications*, 2020, p. 4).

All businesses and most organizations possess characteristics of a social media company in that they collect, maintain and analyze personal data. Commercial ventures exist to, in one way or another, monetize their customers. There are rewards and risks in using personal data and corporations must balance revenue against the potential costs from a data security breach. Social media communication presents a new business problem because of the public nature of data, as well as third-party possession of it by Facebook, Twitter, LinkedIn, and others.

After Covid-19 hit, the pandemic presented new work-from-home challenges. In spite of the availability of virtual private networks (VPN) access to company servers, there remained increasing possibilities for personal data leaks, cybercrime and other business exposure. In a world of targeted advertising, managed public relations (PR) and strategic social media marketing, companies stretched to build holistic privacy strategies, maintain consumer trust and apply ever-changing law within an ethical framework (CDO Club, 2020).

The California Consumer Privacy Act of 2018 (CCPA), state law that was amended in 2020, represents the most comprehensive attempt to codify rules than make explicit consumer rights of data privacy, at the same time as business are offered continued freedom to grow. The law focuses on collection, deletion, sale and other data uses. In the following box, key provisions of the groundbreaking law are presented in abstract form.

Box 4.1 California Consumer Privacy Act of 2018 (CCPA)

TITLE 1.81.5. California Consumer Privacy Act of 2018 [1798.100 - 1798.199]
(Title 1.81.5 added by Stats. 2018, Ch. 55, Sec. 3.)

1798.100.
(a) A consumer shall have the right to request that a business that collects a consumer's personal information disclose to that consumer the categories and specific pieces of personal information the business has collected.
(b) A business that collects a consumer's personal information shall, at or before the point of collection, inform consumers as to the categories of personal information to be collected and the purposes for which the categories of personal information shall be used ... (c) A business shall provide the information specified in subdivision (a) to a consumer only upon receipt of a verifiable consumer request. (d) A business that receives a verifiable consumer request from a consumer to access personal information shall promptly take steps to disclose and deliver, free of charge to the consumer, the personal information required by this section ... A business may provide personal information to a consumer at any time, but shall not be required to provide personal information to a consumer

more than twice in a 12-month period. (e) This section shall not require a business to retain any personal information collected for a single, one-time transaction, if such information is not sold or retained by the business or to reidentify or otherwise link information that is not maintained in a manner that would be considered personal information.
(Amended by Stats. 2019, Ch. 757, Sec. 1. (AB 1355) Effective January 1, 2020.) ...

1798.110.
(a) A consumer shall have the right to request that a business that collects personal information about the consumer disclose to the consumer the following: (1) The categories of personal information it has collected about that consumer. (2) The categories of sources from which the personal information is collected. (3) The business or commercial purpose for collecting or selling personal information. (4) The categories of third parties with whom the business shares personal information. (5) The specific pieces of personal information it has collected about that consumer ...

... Personal information includes, but is not limited to, the following if it identifies, relates to, describes, is reasonably capable of being associated with, or could be reasonably linked, directly or indirectly, with a particular consumer or household:

> (A) Identifiers such as a real name, alias, postal address, unique personal identifier, online identifier, **internet protocol** address, email address, account name, social security number, driver's license number, passport number, or other similar identifiers. (B) Any categories of personal information described in subdivision (e) of Section 1798.80. (C) Characteristics of protected classifications under California or federal **law**. (D) Commercial information, including records of personal property, products or services purchased, obtained, or considered, or other purchasing or consuming histories or tendencies. (E) Biometric information. (F) Internet or other electronic network activity information, including, but not limited to, browsing history, search history, and information regarding a consumer's interaction with an internet website, application, or advertisement. (G) Geolocation data. (H) Audio, electronic, visual, thermal, olfactory, or

similar information. (I) Professional or employment-related information. (J) Education information, defined as information that is not publicly available personally identifiable information …, (K) Inferences drawn from any of the information identified in this subdivision to create a profile about a consumer reflecting the consumer's preferences, characteristics, psychological trends, predispositions, behavior, attitudes, intelligence, abilities, and aptitudes.

1798.196.
This title is intended to supplement federal and state law, if permissible, but shall not apply if such application is preempted by, or in conflict with, federal law or the United States or California Constitution. *(Amended (as added by Stats. 2018, Ch. 55, Sec. 3) by Stats. 2018, Ch. 735, Sec. 15. (SB 1121) Effective September 23, 2018. Section operative January 1, 2020, pursuant to Section 1798.198.)…*

Source: TITLE 1.81.5. *California Consumer Privacy Act of 2018* [1798.100 - 1798.199] (Title 1.81.5 added by Stats. 2018, Ch. 55, Sec. 3.). http://leginfo.legislature.ca.gov/faces/codes_displayText.xhtml?division=3.&part=4.&lawCode=CIV&title=1.81.5

In the November, 2020 election, California voters approved Proposition 24 to limit Facebook, Google and others from selling user data, including geographic location and demographics. This trend could be important because Facebook advertising revenue models have been tied to the ability to target specific locations, demographic groups and psychographic lifestyle variables.

Social media companies, such as Facebook, have the power to regulate advertising on their sites in ways that are consistent with state and federal laws. For example, Facebook temporarily banned new political ads one week before the U.S. 2020 election to "remove posts that try to suppress or discourage voting" (Byers, 2020, para. 1). One concern was the possibility that a candidate might try to prematurely claim victory, even though mail-in voting results would not be known until days after the election. President Donald Trump's campaign quickly responded: "In the last seven days of the most important election in our history, President Trump will be banned from defending himself on the largest platform in America, …When millions of voters will be making their decisions, the President will be silenced by the Silicon Valley Mafia, who will at the same time allow corporate media to run their biased ads to swing voters in key states" (Gilbert, 2020, para. 4). Matthew Ingram wrote in a *Columbia Journalism Review* newsletter that the Facebook rules are vague and unhelpful in stopping disinformation on Facebook pages that are **organic** instead of promoted advertising.

The pandemic coincided with the holiday rush at the end of 2020. Resulting long U.S. mail delays impacted advertisers on Google, Facebook, Amazon, eBay and other sites. Delivery failures may lead to negative product and service reviews within these sites, in Google search and on Yelp (Reinstein, 2020). Small businesses fear that even a single negative review or social media comment can doom already struggling enterprises. During the Covid-19 pandemic, there were special concerns about the need to learn media literacy skills. For example, as President Trump announced on Twitter his Covid-19 test results, an enormous social media reaction followed.

Weeks before the 2020 presidential election, news that the incumbent president was going to the hospital was fertile ground for "an explosion of rumors, misinformation and conspiracy theories" spread on social media channels (Seitz & Dupuy, 2020, para. 1). The news "also ignited constant conjecture among QAnon followers, who peddle a baseless belief that Trump is a warrior against a secret network of government officials and celebrities" (para. 2). There also was an increase in so-called "copypasta" campaigns – "attempts by numerous Twitter accounts to parrot the same phrase over and over to inundate users with messaging, and they

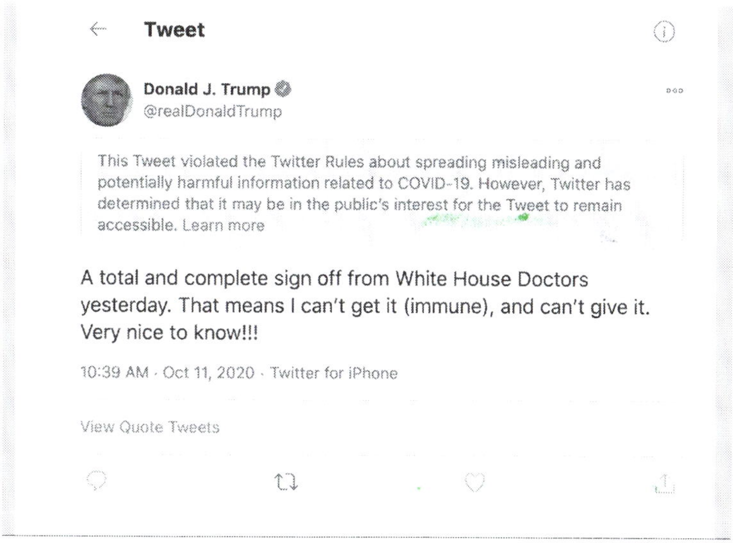

Twitter repeatedly flagged President Trumps tweets.

President Trump @realDonaldTrump used Twitter as an official government channel. https://twitter.com/realDonaldTrump.]

are sometimes signal(ing) of coordinated activity" (para. 6). Twitter has attempted to use algorithms to limit tweet views. President Trump had more than 82 million Twitter followers at the time and the first tweet quickly became his most "liked" and shared ever (Fischer, 2020). Misinformation during the president's 2020 re-election campaign was in some cases fueled by content at conservative political sites, such as Breitbart (Hsu, 2020): "The Harvard researchers described a '**propaganda** feedback loop' in right-wing media" (para. 10). The study reported that: "[P]opular news outlets, rather than social media platforms, were the main drivers of a disinformation campaign meant to sow doubts about the integrity of the election" (para. 10). On election day and as the votes were counted, Twitter labeled President Trump's tweets as "misleading" after he wrote: "We are up BIG, but they are trying to STEAL the Election" (Browning, Decker, & Silver, 2020, para. 1). *The New York Times* reported that more than 750 Twitter accounts followed with Trump's same tweet preceded by a note: "Everyone must tweet what @realDonaldTrump did before getting suppressed by Twitter" (paras. 3–4). As many as about 1,000 accounts received about 9,000 retweets with 1.5 million followers (para. 5).

Social media celebrities may wield power to influence their followers by sharing misinformation. For example, YouTube and former Disney star Jake Paul suggested that Covid-19 was a hoax and news is mostly fake. Paul and his older brother Logan Paul have millions of followers from "viral stunts" and "antics" (Stern, 2020, para, 2). Jake Paul added that "COVID cases are at less than 1 percent, and I think the disease is a hoax," and incorrectly claimed that the flu killed as many people (paras. 51–53). The example shows how misinformation spreads across social networks, making it similar to a virus that is difficult to stop once it is released. We can use **network visualization** to "see" the diffusion of untruthful posts over time. In this sense, we have new tools capable of monitoring social media law and ethics.

Box 4.2 How to Spot Misinformation or Disinformation Online: Ten Tips from the UNO Social Media Lab (@unosmlre)

1. Check the source of the social media post: Do you know and trust it as a source of truthful and reliable information?
2. Check the date: Is this a recent story, or from a long time ago?
3. Does the message seem credible to you? Is it consistent with other stories? Does it fit with your experiences?

4. Who shared the post in your newsfeed? Do you know the person? Have they always shared reliable information?
5. If there is a photograph, does it look real or could it be doctored?
6. If there is a video, does it show any possible signs of being edited?
7. Only trust experts. Now is not the time to trust this pundit or that pundit, this media celebrity or that YouTuber. If it's not coming from the CDC or WHO ..., walk away.
8. More broadly, is the language in the post boring/objective or is it exciting/subjective? Often, the way the post is written is meant to get you to click without thinking because it might align with your own beliefs.
9. A good test: right click the link or image to see what the actual URL is. If it does not come from the place that it claims to come from (look for weird letters at the end like. ru,. cn or others that just seem off), don't go to it. . com,. org,. net or. gov are typically more trustworthy. Check Snopes.com for fact-check updates.
10. Take this time to slow down and reflect on what you know. There is no need to rush to judgment before liking or sharing.

Sources

Postman, N. (2007). Bullshit and the Art of Crap-Detection. https://criticalsnips.wordpress.com/2007/07/22/neil-postman-bullshit-and-the-art-of-crap-detection/.

Poynter (2020). Covid-19 Misinformation. https://www.poynter.org/ifcn-covid-19-misinformation/page/4/.

Rheingold, H. (2013). Social Media Literacy. https://docs.google.com/document/d/1plxVqXT6EO_CoxCCD3tj9uYujVzhHzGWcYgT31LGQhc/edit.

Snopes. https://www.snopes.com/.

UNO Social Media Lab (2021). https://www.unomaha.edu/college-of-communication-fine-arts-and-media/communication/community-engagement/social-media-lab.php.

UNO Social Media Lab (2020). How To Spot Misinformation and Disinformation. https://docs.google.com/document/d/1h8pCk6yvqU0k-Bcpp7KCR2K4NT8dH51AseSix6f2GOXY/.

Facebook users also were allowed to opt out of political advertisements. The rules also limited the number of people who can receive a Messenger post. While social media platforms control communication through their user contracts, commercial speech law limits the power of government entities, such as the Federal Trade Commission (FTC) to regulate online posts.

SOCIAL MEDIA COMMERCIAL SPEECH IN ADVERTISING AND PR PROMOTION

Advertising and public relations campaigns are considered commercial speech that falls under the *O'Brien* test requiring messages for legal products and services that are not deceptive to reasonable consumers. Federal Trade Commission (FTC) and state regulation are limited by the First Amendment rights of corporations, as well as the rights of readers, listeners and viewers to receive information. While government may exercise a substantial interest in protecting consumers, regulation must be content-neutral and not discriminating against particular views.

When it comes to false or misleading advertising, the FTC has said that misrepresentation must be material, in its representation or omission, to consumer decision-making about a legal product or service. For nearly four decades, the FTC has applied a reasonable consumer standard. So-called puffery, or exaggerated claims, have limited First Amendment protection under the view that reasonable consumers recognize some claims that are not clearly deceptive.

There is a long line of precedent aimed at stopping unfair and deceptive practices and these continue to apply to social media advertising. This also applies to product labels and disclosure requirements under state and federal laws.

The European Commission (2020) uses an evidence-based policy that regulates communication within business practices. The New Consumer Agenda, for example, is a response to the Covid-19 pandemic and recovery. Business to consumer or business communication is required to recognize consumer rights.

Box 4.3 The New Consumer Agenda: Strengthening consumer resilience for sustainable recovery

1. INTRODUCTION

European consumers rightly expect to benefit fully from the single market and to be empowered to make informed choices and play an active role in the green and digital transition whenever and wherever they are in the EU. They expect to have free access to goods and services across the EU and reassurance that their rights as consumers are protected, traditional and emerging challenges notwithstanding.

The New Consumer Agenda ('the Agenda') presents a vision for EU consumer policy from 2020 to 2025, building on the 2012 Consumer Agenda (which expires in 2020) and the 2018 New Deal for Consumers. It also aims to address consumers' immediate needs in the face of the ongoing COVID-19 pandemic and to increase their resilience …

The Agenda covers five key priority areas:

1. The green transition
2. The digital transformation
3. Redress and enforcement of consumer rights
4. Specific needs of certain consumer groups
5. International cooperation

The Agenda takes a holistic approach covering various Union policies that are of particular relevance for consumers. It reflects the need to take account of consumer protection requirements in the formulation and implementation of other policies and activities. It complements other EU initiatives, such as the European Green Deal, the Circular Economy Action Plan and the Communication on Shaping Europe's digital future. It also supports relevant international frameworks, such as the United Nations' 2030 Agenda for Sustainable Development and the UN Convention on the Rights of Persons with Disabilities.

An effective response to all these priorities requires close cooperation between the EU and its member states and proper transposition, implementation and enforcement of the solid consumer protection framework developed over many years. For this reason, the Agenda puts forward priorities and key action points to be taken forward together at European and national levels …

2. CONSUMERS IN THE COVID-19 PANDEMIC

Example: Online consumer scams have surged significantly during the crisis. Fraudsters have played on consumers' fears to sell unnecessary, ineffective and potentially dangerous products on the basis of false claims as to their health benefits, for example, by marketing goods with unjustified protective characteristics, or selling masks which do not comply with the relevant requirements. The Commission and consumer authorities have reached out to platforms in order to make sure that hundreds of millions of illegal offers and advertisements were removed. Consumer rights and safety must continue to be protected, especially during a period of unprecedented uncertainty and distress.

The COVID-19 pandemic is first and foremost a health crisis ... Products and services proving essential in the crisis need to provide the consumer with full safeguards with regard to fundamental rights, medical ethics, privacy, and data protection in accordance with the General Data Protection Regulation. However, the profound social and economic disruption that has followed in its wake presents a major challenge to society ... The pandemic is also visibly changing people's consumption and mobility patterns. The confinement measures highlighted the crucial role of digital technologies in people's lives, allowing the purchase essential goods which would not otherwise be accessible and to access services despite the restrictions. Observed trends include buying more locally, booking travel less in advance, but also using online services more often. Some changes may be temporary, linked to the health situation (e.g. using public transport less) while others, notably those linked to the digital transformation (e.g. increasing online purchase of food or accessing more online streaming services at home, including for cultural and sport events) could become more structural ...

Another area of concern that has come to the fore during the pandemic is the surge in consumer scams, deceptive marketing techniques and fraud in online shopping, to which an increasing number of consumers have fallen and continue to fall victim ...

3. DIGITAL TRANSFORMATION

Example: Between 2014 and 2019, the proportion of Internet users in the EU who bought or ordered goods or services online for private use grew from 63% to 71%; in five Member States, those figures exceeded 80%. Consumers should be protected at a comparable level online as they are offline. Rules should be adapted to the connected environment to ensure that, for example, smart home devices are not subject to cybersecurity risks, and online offers of credit provide the necessary information that is easily readable and accessible on a smartphone...

This may limit effectiveness of the current rules designed to protect consumers in the digital environment, ***inter alia*** against unfair commercial practices ...

Commercial practices that disregard consumers' right to make an informed choice, abuse their behavioural biases, or distort their decision-making processes, must be tackled. These practices include the use of 'dark' patterns, certain personalisation practices often based on profiling, hidden advertising, fraud, false or misleading information and manipulated consumer reviews. Additional guidance is needed on the applicability of consumer law instruments such as the Unfair Commercial Practices Directive and Consumer Rights Directive to these practices. Ultimately, consumers should benefit from a comparable level of protection and fairness online as they enjoy offline ...

Moreover, a universally accepted public electronic identity – based on the consumers' choice, their consent and the guarantee that their privacy is fully respected in line with the General Data Protection Regulation (GDPR) – could give consumers the possibility to manage the access and use of their data in a fully controlled and secure manner. The Commission is currently reviewing such a system, taking into account the interest and protection of consumers.

To address unjustified geo-blocking, which discriminates between EU consumers to segment markets along national borders, the Commission is currently carrying out its first short term review of the geo-blocking Regulation ...

Children and minors are particularly exposed to misleading or aggressive commercial practices online. It is important to invest more in lifelong consumer education and awareness raising, for people at all stages of life from school onwards. This should also include the promotion of financial literacy as an essential skill for empowering consumers to make good decisions about their personal finances ...

4. CONCLUSION

...The Commission looks forward to a wide-ranging dialogue with all interested parties on the priorities and actions as well as the cooperation methods to promote consumer protection in the years ahead as set out in this Agenda.

Source: European Commission (2020, November 13). The New Consumer Agenda. https://ec.europa.eu/info/policies/consumers/consumer-protection/consumer-strategy_en.

CORPORATIONS AND CONTRACTS

Under national and international law, corporations act as individuals when they sign contracts with employees, clients, vendors and others. It is commonplace, for example, for employers to require employees to sign nondisclosure agreements (NDAs) that limit what can be said about proprietary client and company information. NDA's define confidential information, specify any exclusions, disclose legal obligations, length of the contract and any waivers. Any contract may be challenged in court and some NDAs have been found to violate equity law as forced compliance. Koh (2017) found that confidentiality can be "too broad" because of a "catch-all clause" (para. 11). Unreasonable language can be challenged: "There's nothing that the courts enjoy more than striking down an agreement that is unreasonably onerous or one that's too anti-competition" (para. 25). Interestingly, when "confidential information becomes public knowledge, that same piece of information would no longer be considered confidential," if the leak on social media came from someone other than the person or organization covered by the NDA (para. 35). NDAs apply only the time of the agreement, and companies may not restrict earlier or later information, careless handling or forced government disclosure. It is important to carefully read and receive legal advice before signing any contract. Written contracts, and even some oral contracts, have the force of law.

Employees may be subject to employer surveillance of their social media content, whether or not they are at work when posting:

> If the censor is a business organization targeting employee social media speech, an employee's freedom of expression is subjugated to the employer's interest in brand protection, property rights, and legal risk mitigation. Corporate social media policies

> enact this strategy by policing employees' posts and enforcing standards of online conduct, even when employees' expressive activity occurs off-duty.
>
> (Hidy, 2020, p. 349)

Companies have legitimate liability concerns over state or federal compliance in data privacy, employee discrimination, or harassment: The use of "views are my own" disclaimers "may not immunize a business organization from the legal risks attendant to the social media speech it did not authorize or condone" (Hidy, 2020, p. 357). Still, businesses also must balance social media First Amendment rights, "recalibrate their risk mitigation strategy" and recognize "unfettered access" to "the modern public square" (pp. 384–385).

ETHICAL FRAMEWORKS AND ISSUES

Web analytics have been central to social media marketing and **metrics** in Silicon Valley because of business models, capitalism and entrepreneurship (Lipschultz, 2020). Profit motives at Google, Facebook and other leading technology companies pushed aside legal and ethical concerns about data privacy boundaries. Brands seek to cultivate trust found among family and friends **word-of-mouth** communication: "The sense of raw honest is far more credible when it comes to a purchasing decision" (Gershon, 2017, p. 197). Social media brand trust has been related to voice or "the distinct personality that manifests visually and verbally, as well as volume ("how much") and vulnerability through content strategy that "foster" good feelings (Bloomstein, 2021, pp. 2–6). Brands serve an education function to consumers through "humility and transparency" that cultivates a sense of loyalty over time (p. 41). Authentic social listening can be a positive method to respond to consumers in a way that offers reciprocal loyalty, however, we should never forget that corporations have a fiduciary responsibility to shareholders to make money. Within this dynamic, hidden data collection and use may benefit social media users, but company strategic needs typically come first.

In the background are marketing research data. This has created a context of what has been called "surveillance capitalism," that forces consumers through product contract language to openly share personal data with large corporations (Zuboff, 2019, p. 7). "Surveillance capitalism unilaterally claims human experience as free raw material for translation into behavioral data" (p. 8) and the case has been made that data monetization has "become the dominant logic of accumulation" that is in conflict with data privacy (p. 14). However, this is not to say that social media advertising and promotion is universally effective, rather that dominant social media corporations must be prevented from gobbling up fresh and innovative ideas (Doctorow, 2020).

Social media marketers grasped that data allowed them to read consumers' minds through targeting, and that "the underlying technology can be used to analyze marketing materials like web sites" and "hear the voice of the marketplace" (Sterne, 2010, p. 221). Similarly, social media goals, strategies and tactics offer systematic auditing templates (Quesenberry, 2019). The aim is to trigger word-of-mouth personal influence for a "closer ... relationship" and its potential "impact on the decision-making process" (p. 253). Marketers generally lack substantive regulatory constraints and use surgical targeting. Regulators seek to balance public interests of consumers against marketplace business freedom. Within the EU, the goal is to limit how U.S. social media companies move and use personal data (Chan, 2020, para. 2). Ireland has a Data Protection Commission concerned that transatlantic data can be moved for the purpose of selling it.

The General Data Protection Regulation (GDPR) European law emphasizes lawful, fair and transparent use of data. Legitimate and accurate data processing should empower users by granting access to and control of their data. The European Court of Justice Right To Be Forgotten (RTBF) case directed data control to people and their governmental representatives as "decisive authority" (Zuboff, 2019, p. 60). These democratic powers challenge social media company manipulation through "dark patterns" or programming sequences that lead consumers to thoughtlessly give away data privacy (Pardes, 2020, para. 1). Facial recognition, for example, is framed as technological innovation that makes access to your device more secure.

Reno v. ACLU (1997) and its progeny offered early U.S. Supreme Court support for freedom to publish and limitation on government regulation. However, the Court was not fully engaged on the dangers presented by corporate powers over our digital lives. By 2020, The Federal Communications Commission (FCC) reviewed Section 230 of the Communications Decency Act of 1996 that shielded Facebook and other companies from general legal liability. Practitioners continue to use data as "fuel for multiple strategic directions" that allow them to "take full advantage of the growing appetite for accessible data" (Luttrell & Capizzo, 2019, p.123). **Return on investment** (ROI) for organic and paid social media posts depends on effective algorithm programming in terms of consumer communication behavioral optimization. Antitrust laws could be an effective legal mechanism to impose ethical marketplace competition and user data ownership (Rheingold, 2020).

The U.S. Supreme Court focus on state a national government limitation under the First Amendment presents a substantial constraint in wrestling powers from Facebook and others (*Packingham v. North Carolina*, 2017). Further, end-user terms of service (ToS) agreements empower social media companies to legally make content decisions. In extreme cases, threatening speech may rise to be found to be criminal under 18 U. S. C. §875(c) (*Elonis v. United States*, 2015). User control over content also can test government powers to block other users (*Knight First Amendment Inst. At Columbia Univ. v. Trump*, 2018; *Knight Institute, II*, 2020). Advertising and marketing that overlaps with core political speech or expression is most likely to retain First Amendment freedoms. The paradoxical framework that empowers social media companies also favors users' free expression rights, but these are not absolute when live content involves communicating about criminal acts or invading privacy of others (Stewart, 2017; Lipschultz, 2020).

The foundation for commercial speech and social media influence laws of advertising, public relations and marketing is that communication must be lawful and not deceptive (*Central Hudson v. Public Service Commission*, 1980). FTC decisions are made on a case-by-case basis with an assessment about reasonable interpretation of messages (*FTC v. Lord & Taylor*, 2016). A few large fines, however, have been levied against the worst offenders, but it is more common for financial interests to be cloaked and never acted on. The use of **key performance indicators** (KPIs) by marketers typically leads to outcome-based goals. Search **keywords**, for example, may be packed into text and hashtags in order to "game" the system of Google algorithms determining rank of **search engine result placement** (SERP). Reliance on **search engine optimization** (SEO) techniques for website-**owned media** usually is not deceptive, but it can be. While use of public relations research, planning, implementation and evaluation (**RPIE**) is a best practice that may include paid **promoted posts** and **paid search** to guarantee larger social media reach, business success can devolve into a form of ethical **nihilism**. These estimates of audience size do not equate with a **moral calculus** or **moral reasoning** of rights and wrongs. As we will see in the next chapter, use of **location-based services** (LBS) to track mobile social media users can be an effective business technique, but it also may violate privacy boundaries and expectations.

A pro-business U.S. mindset may be contrasted with the European Court of Justice's support for government regulation of network bandwidth speeds and access (Associated Press, 2020). In theory, consumers should enjoy nondiscriminatory Internet access that is not impacted by discriminatory throttling of computer and mobile site load times. The U.S. FCC sided with business marketplace freedom in rejecting network neutrality rules. The large scale of global Internet growth with billions of users in hundreds of languages translates to commercial monetization and the legal and ethical issues that follow flow of big money (Lipschultz, 2021). As national laws and cultural norms clash across global social media spaces, we should expect advertisers and marketers to be forced into social responsibility by regulators and consumers who demand trusted relationships. The blurring of personal and professional spaces during the global pandemic presents deepening theoretical and ethical concerns about social presence and activities (Sherblom, 2020). Commercial advertising and marketing, as well as PR social manipulation, may be related to human communication agency, such as over a desire to have "visual anonymity" or communication equality (p. 51). Technology and entertainment function, however, may create new cultural contexts that impact knowledge and relationships that have detachment from ethics and accountability (Postman, 1985; Postman, 1992). "Privacy," for example, may become "invisible" to Internet users (Postman, 1992, p. 48) and this can be exploited by marketers that mine personal social media communication data in order to match messages with specific demographic, psychographic and geographic groups. Similarly, PR campaigns seek ROI through effective targeting and optimization that may not reflect a **conversation** about corporate social responsibility (Lipschultz, 2018) or the nature of word-of-mouth personal influence (Katz & Lazarsfeld, 1955). Social networks may employ a transactional form of personal ethics that leverage online relationships for commercial gain (Howard, 2020), "advocacy" (Luttrell, 2016, p. 183) or influential community-building (Freberg, 2019).

Gershon (2017) concluded that social media could be reduced to "word-of-mouth advertising in its purest form" (p. 197). This serves surveillance capitalism that operates in the background of "monopoly" businesses through invasion of "privacy" (Zuboff, 2019, p. 23). Academics, too, may adhere to business practices. For this reason, there is a need to establish expanded social media research ethical standards with public relations and other fields that goes beyond early research: "The assumption is that what we see, read, hear, ask about, and respond to in social media is authentic, reliable information transmitted to the user in a clear and nondeceptive communication" (Bowen & Stacks, 2014, p. 218). An amplified social media data paradox of user consent to a lack of data protection has been in exchange for the benefits from marketed and other organic content openness.

PUBLIC RELATIONS ETHICS

The PRSA **Code of Ethics** has developed over seven decades as a statement to help practitioners maintain "their ethical responsibilities, setting out principles that uphold core values, including advocacy, honesty, expertise, independence, loyalty and fairness" (PRSA, 2020, para. 1). Additionally, the PRSA Board of Ethics and Professional Standards (BEPS) continues to develop new case studies, papers and blog posts. The PRSA code accepts a responsibility for providing "a voice in the marketplace of ideas," by utilizing "the highest standards of accuracy and truth," by balancing client loyalty and public fairness:

> We deal fairly with clients, employers, competitors, peers, vendors, the media, and the general public. We respect all opinions and support the right of free expression… [The] Core Principle Protecting and advancing the free flow of accurate and truthful information is essential to serving the public interest and contributing to informed decision making in a democratic society (PRSA Code, 2020, pp. 1–2).

The PRSA Code (2020) identifies a potential for "improper conduct" that could be applied to social media through use of "front groups," "lying by omission," failure to correct or deception (p. 4).

BEPS (2020) has developed a PRSA Ethics & Social Media position paper that states that, "unless content violates specific rules of individual social platforms and is policed by the platforms' own personnel, it is left to stand" (para. 1). It implores practitioners to "set themselves and their organizations apart through unquestioned credibility and ethical standards, ultimately building and maintaining strong reputations for the organizations those practitioners represent" (para. 3). The "interdependency" of news organizations using social media communication means that PR "practitioners must not accept on face value certain practices in the public's use of social media" (paras. 4–5). Specifically, there is concern expressed about information disclosure, confidentiality, employee First Amendment rights, potential conflicts of interests and application of PRSA Code (2020) values.

ETHICS ACROSS THE SILOS

Media ethics offers philosophies and models that cut across industries and fields of study. For example, the TARES test of ethical advertising includes:

> **Truthfulness:** the law and ethics both consider truth of words and images.
>
> **Authenticity:** this places an emphasis on sincerity of communication.
>
> **Respect:** drawing from the **virtue** of mutuality, communicators must respect audience members.
>
> **Equity:** focuses on the fairness of relational communication.
>
> **Socially responsible:** speaks to competing duties to employers, clients and targeted audiences.
>
> (Patterson & Wilkins, 2005, pp. 62–64).

Many of the challenges within social media communication have their roots in these values. For example, former president Donald Trump repeatedly tweeted challenges to the truth of news media messages – even as he spread information labeled by Twitter as disputed. We would hope that well-meaning social media users would be authentic, but there are pressures to create a celebrity brand. If we truly respect others with equity in our relational communication, then loyalties should be transparent when we use social media.

Box 4.4 Thought Leader Emily Kinsky

Emily S. Kinsky.

Photograph by Rik Andersen

While professional communicators are familiar with the legal dangers of copyright infringement, trademark violations and improper labeling of paid sponsorship for social media posts, there are issues beyond the law that also need to be considered as they use social media channels to communicate. PR practitioners' actions should not seek to merely meet minimum legal requirements; they need to go further – they need to be *ethical*.

CONSIDERING PR ETHICS WHEN MANAGING SOCIAL MEDIA

The Public Relations Society of America (PRSA) Code of Ethics offers helpful guidance on ethical PR practices, whether a practitioner is a member or not, and a valuable reminder: "The level of public trust PRSA members seek, as we serve the public good, means we have taken on a special obligation to operate ethically" (PRSA Code of Ethics, 2020, para. 2).

ETHICAL AND NON-ETHICAL BEHAVIOR

Ethical behavior on social media must be considered for both individual and organizational accounts. Problematic actions on social media include "sub-tweeting" about someone – perhaps disparaging a past client, boss, competitor, co-worker or employee or even a certain city. For example, a Ketchum executive criticized FedEx's hometown in a tweet (Edwards, 2011). Posts on an organization's or company's feed should not exaggerate claims, frame something inaccurately or share private information or photos without permission. No individual or organization should troll other accounts, neither should they anonymously post positive comments or ratings on their own. Another unethical behavior seen on company social media channels is trying to ride the popularity of a hashtag associated with a serious event in what amounts to an effort to profit while people are in pain, which is in poor taste and will not be well received. Kenneth Cole's Cairo tweet in 2011 during the Arab Spring, The Gap's tweet during Hurricane Sandy in 2012 and Epicurious' tweet related to the Boston bombing in 2013 all missed the mark.

WATCH OUT

Communicators managing social media for a client must be careful to accurately bill hours; if a practitioner becomes distracted and scrolls beyond what is needed for the client that would be unethical to bill that time to the client. Ethical behavior must be considered beyond the hours on the clock, too. Rude personal posts have shocked those who have seen them and have sometimes impacted the person's reputation, their employer's reputation and ultimately resulted in job loss. Justine Sacco was fired hours after tweeting about Africa (Ronson, 2015). If a well-known figure has a large or passionate following, that person needs to watch their own posts all the more. They are carrying an even bigger responsibility because a flippant remark can go beyond impacting their own reputation and income, they can sway markets. Elon Musk, for example, tweeted about the company's stock price being too high (Korosec, 2020). Unethical social media behavior prompted a new California law in response to egregious photos taken at Kobe Bryant's accident and shared by first responders (AP, 2020a).

PRSA VALUES

The PRSA Code of Ethics (2020) lists advocacy, honesty, expertise, independence, loyalty and fairness as "the fundamental beliefs that guide our behaviors and decision-making process. We believe our professional values are vital to the integrity of the profession as a whole" (para. 6).

These values shared in the PRSA Code of Ethics can help guide practitioners in ethical decision-making on social media. For example, to be an ethical advocate for a client via social media, public interest must be kept in mind. If a company secretly pays someone to blog about them without acknowledging that sponsorship, this goes against the value of honesty; that lack of transparency can cause a backlash for both the client and any PR practitioners/agencies involved (Siebert, 2006). To maintain expertise in social media best practices, an ethical communicator must continually seek professional development opportunities. Communication professionals need to study the specific norms and rules of each social media platform they use, as well as following general ethical principles as laid out by ethical codes of conduct. An example of unethical behavior within **Reddit**, for example, is to get a group in a subreddit to go into another subreddit and harass them, which is referred to as brigading; the mob overwhelms the moderator (Empyrealist, 2015).

To go deeper into the topic of fairness and to whom that applies, the PRSA Code says: "We deal fairly with clients, employers, competitors, peers, vendors, the media, and the general public. We respect all opinions and support the right of free expression" (para. 12). PR practitioners need to reflect on whether they are dealing fairly with others on social media, including groups they might not first think of, like their employers, competitors and the media.

LACK OF CIVILITY

Many people blame social media for allowing, or even promoting, a lack of civil discourse. PR pro Gini Dietrich (2020) has discussed ethical problems she's seen on social media: "Everything from anonymous social media posts accusing people of things that never happened and creating boycotts for companies they've never supported to downright crude and inappropriate language" (para. 27). When interacting with others online, sometimes "they seem to forget there is a human being on the other side of the computer" (Dietrich, 2020, para. 23) and use cruel words they would likely not use in person. She pointed to the broad ripples of damage some movements on social media can cause: "[W]hen we join a boycott or a movement without knowing more than what's on social media, it creates a tidal wave. People lose their jobs, their benefits, their livelihoods" (Dietrich, 2020, para. 35). An ethical communicator conducts research before taking action.

Whether it is on an individual, private account or for a client, there is a danger to blindly sharing social media posts. Dietrich (2020) recommended, "Before sharing anything—and this goes for articles, too—do your research" (para. 36) in order to keep from perpetuating what might be false information. Whether practitioners are posting on social media channels for their clients' accounts or their own, they need to treat others how they want to be treated. As the PRSA Code of Ethics reminds practitioners: "We are accountable for our actions." (para. 10).

JUST BECAUSE IT IS LEGAL

When an online rating platform allows companies to pay to remove bad ratings, it is referred to as scrubbing, and the practice is legal; however, it has been shown to damage public trust. For example, the outcries against Yelp in 2015 showed the practice of scrubbing is not a wise move (Novak, 2020). Similarly, companies and nonprofits have tried to make a bad situation disappear by removing offending posts from their social media platforms leaving a gaping hole in their timeline (Kinsky et al., 2015). In addition to considering the ethical expectations for posting on social media, there are ethical issues related to collecting data from social media profiles and tracking via cookies.

For students, instructors, or practitioners looking for more information on ethics in PR and how they connect to social media, the Arthur W. Page Center/Public Relations Ethics Training has free modules available online including one on digital ethics.

Emily S. Kinsky (Ph.D., Texas Tech University, 2008), associate professor in West Texas A&M University's Department of Communication, teaches courses related to design, public relations, new media and research. She helps advise WTAMU's student-run PR firm, 1910 PR, as well as the Public Relations Student Society of America chapter. She serves as editor-in-chief of the *Journal of Public Relations Education* and is a past head of the Public Relations Division of the Association for Education in Journalism and Mass Communication. Kinsky's research has been published in a range of journals, including *Journal of Public Relations Research*, *Public Relations Review*, *PR Journal* and *Communication Quarterly*.

Sources

Amazonians for Employee Privacy (2020, December 18). Taking a Stand Against Internal Surveillance. https://sites.google.com/view/amazonians-fr-employee-privacy/.

AP (2020a, September 29). New California Law Prompted by Crash that Killed Kobe Bryant. *Associated Press*. https://apnews.com/article/california-accidents-legislation-archive-gavin-newsom-17bc7e0b094be63e110f112f02576fe5.

AP (2020b, Google Rejects DOJ Antitrust Claims in Court Filing. *Associated Press*. https://apnews.com/article/courts-f23b7b62dc7a5c6d2bee5f77fbd11e0e.

Arthur W. Page Center (2020). Public Relations Ethics Training: 15 Ethical Guidelines for Digital Public Relations. *Arthur W. Page Center Public Relations Ethics Training*. https://pagecentertraining.psu.edu/public-relations-ethics/digital-ethics/why-digital-ethics/15-ethical-guidelines-for-digital-public-relations/.

CVS Health (2018, September 5). Advise Memorandum. National Labor Relations Board, 31-CA-210099. https://www.nlrb.gov/case/31-CA-210099.

Dietrich, G. (2020, July 23). Mea Culpa: When Things Don't Go According to Plan. *SpinSucks*. https://spinsucks.com/entrepreneur/mea-culpa-sorry/.

Edwards, J. (2011, April 22). Worst Twitter Post Ever: Ketchum Exec Insults FedEx Client on Mini-blog. *CBS News*. https://www.cbsnews.com/news/worst-twitter-post-ever-ketchum-exec-insults-fedex-client-on-mini-blog/.

Empyrealist. (2015). What Does It Mean to Brigade a Subreddit? *Reddit*. https://www.reddit.com/r/OutOfTheLoop/comments/3dc0r3/what_does_it_mean_to_brigade_a_subreddit/.

Hirsch, J.M. (2020). Future Work. *University of Illinois Law Review*, 20, 889–958.

Kinsky, E.S., Drumheller, K., Gerlich, R.N., Brock-Baskin, M.E., and Sollosy, M. (2015). The Effect of Socially Mediated Public Relations Crises on Planned Behavior: How TPB Can Help Both Corporations and Nonprofits. *Journal of Public Relations Research*, 27(2), 136–157.

Korosec, K. (2020, May 1). Tesla Shares Fall on Elon Musk "Stock Price Too High" Tweet. *TechCrunch*. https://techcrunch.com/2020/05/01/tesla-shares-fall-on-elon-musk-stock-price-too-high-tweet/.

Kroger Co. of Mich. v. Granger, NLRB. No. 07-CA-098566 (April 22, 2014).

Luttrell, R.M. and Capizzo, L.W. (2019). *Public Relations Campaigns: An Integrated Approach*. Thousand Oaks, CA: SAGE.

National Labor Relations Act of 1935 (Wagner Act). 29 U.S.C. § 151–169.

Novak, A. (2020). Yelp and Data Scrubbing. *Arthur W. Page Center Public Relations Ethics*, Digital Ethics Module 5. https://pagecentertraining.psu.edu/public-relations-ethics/digital-ethics/why-digital-ethics/yelp-and-data-scrubbing/.

PRSA Code of Ethics (2020). *Public Relations Society of America*. https://www.prsa.org/about/prsa-code-of-ethics.

Reinstein, J. (2020, December 22). Panicking Etsy Sellers Are Afraid of One-star Reviews if Postal Delays Ruin Christmas Orders, *BuzzFeed News*. https://www.buzzfeednews.com/article/juliareinstein/etsy-christmas-delivery-delays.

Ronson, J. (2015, February 12). How One Stupid Tweet Blew Up Justine Sacco's Life. *The New York Times*. https://www.nytimes.com/2015/02/15/magazine/how-one-stupid-tweet-ruined-justine-saccos-life.html.

Siebert, T. (2006, October 17). Edelman apologizes for Wal-Mart "flog." *MediaPost*. https://www.mediapost.com/publications/article/49698/edelman-apologizes-for-wal-mart-flog.html.

The application of social media ethics and corporate social responsibility also requires accountability for diversity, equity, and inclusion (DEI). Survey data suggest that most in the U.S. expect companies, brands and their leaders to say more and do more about racial justice (Olster, 2020). A major public relations theme going forward is to make decisions with racial and gender equality front-of-mind. The death of George Floyd at the hands of Minneapolis police sparked Minnesota PRSA to respond in award-winning ways with strategies that included expanding diversity opportunities and within industry internships (Brown, 2020): "Floyd's death set off a wave of emotions across the world as organizations declared their support for the movement against racial injustice" (p. 6). Social media communication was at the center of that movement. The industry increasingly will be shaped by social and economic **justice**, social media regulatory efforts and new avenues for creativity and entrepreneurship. PRSA and other professional organizations emphasized the need for action, as the fields of advertising, PR and marketing determine how to keep pace with rapid social and technological change.

ONLINE RESOURCES

BEPS (2020). PRSA Ethics & Social Media. https://www.prsa.org/about/ethics.

PRSA (2020). PRSA Code of Ethics. https://www.prsa.org/about/prsa-code-of-ethics.

PRSA Code (2020). https://www.prsa.org/docs/default-source/about/ ethics/prsa_code_of_ ethics1ee4daa82781492ab1589370d0ec198b.pdf?sfvrsn=aa659309_0.

Social Media Examiner (2020, December 23). Facebook Ads Rejected? Here's What To Do. *YouTube*. https://youtu.be/4eJf7i9kCH8.

DISCUSSION QUESTIONS

1. What is one example of a contract that you have signed? What does it require from you?
2. What strategies can help you to avoid lawsuits? Why is it important to avoid litigation?
3. How does an ethical duty to your employer sometimes have the potential to conflict with personal moral beliefs?

REFERENCES

Associated Press (2020, September 15). European Union's Top Court Supports Net Neutrality Rules. https://apnews.com/bc649983e9ddab47ac38daf0755d7700.

BEPS (2020). PRSA Ethics & Social Media. https://www.prsa.org/about/ethics.

Bloomstein, M. (2021). *Trustworthy: How the Smartest Brands Beat Cynicism and Bridge the Trust Gap.* Vancouver, BC: Canada.

Bowen, S.A. and Stacks, D.W. (2014). Understanding the Ethical and Research Implications of Social Media. In M.W. DiStaso and D. S. Bortree (eds.), *Ethical Practice of Social Media in Public Relations*, pp. 215–234. New York: Routledge.

Brown, C.F. (2020, November/December). Minnesota PRSA's Path Toward D7I Excellence. *PRSA Strategies & Tactics*, 3(10), 6. https://mydigitalpublication.com/ publication/?i=684684.

Browning, K., Decker, B., and Silver, J. (2020, November 4). Twitter Clamped Down on Trump, But Army of Accounts Spread His Message.*The New York Times*. https://www.nytimes.com/2020/11/04/technology/trump-twitter-account.html

Byers, D. (2020, September 3). Facebook Bans New Political Advertising In Week Before Election. *NBC News*. https://www.nbcnews.com/tech/tech-news/facebook-bans-new-political-ads-week-election-n1239159.

California Consumer Privacy Act of 2018, Title 1.18.5 [1798.100-1798.199]. http://leginfo.legislature.ca.gov/faces/codes_displayText.xhtml?division=3.&part=4.&lawCode=CIV&title=1.81.5

CDO Club (2020, September 16). IBM Chief Data Officer Summit Series: Data Privacy and Governance. https://cdoclub.com/ibm-cdo-summit-series-data-privacy-governance/

Central Hudson Gas and Electric Company v. Public Service Commission of New York, 447 U.S. 557 (1980).

Chan, K. (2020, September 9). Facebook May Have to Stop Moving EU User Data to US. *Associated Press*. https://apnews.com/0ae57e6d968102478046f767da4e7749.

Christians, C.G. (2019). *Media Ethics and Global Justice in the Digital Age*. Cambridge: Cambridge University Press.

Doctorow, C. (2020, August 26). How To Destroy Surveillance Capitalism, *Medium, OneZero*. https://onezero.medium.com/how-to-destroy-surveillance-capitalism-8135e6744d59.

Elonis v. United States, 575 U.S. 723 (2015).

European Commission (2020, November 13). The New Consumer Agenda. https://ec.europa.eu/info/policies/consumers/consumer-protection/consumer-strategy_en.

Fischer, S. (2020, October 2). Trump's Tweet On Positive Coronavirus Test Is His Most Shared Ever.*Axios*. https://www.axios.com/trump-tweet-coronavirus-positive-most-shared-e559d150-61a7-44fc-889a-f60ffbd5cc33.html.

Food Marketing Institute v. Argus Leader Media, 588 U. S. ____ (2019).

Freberg, K. (2019). *Social Media Strategic Communication, Creative Strategies and Research-Based Applications*. Thousand Oaks, CA: SAGE.

FTC v. Lord & Taylor (2016). https://www.ftc.gov/news-events/press-releases/2016/03/lord-taylor-settles-ftc-charges-it-deceived-consumers-through.

Fueroghne, D.K. (2017). *Law & Advertising: A Guide to Current Legal Issues, fourth edition*. Lanham, MD: Rowman & Littlefield.

Gershon, R.A. (2017) *Digital Media Innovation, Management and Decision Strategies in Communication*. Thousand Oaks, CA: SAGE.

Gilbert, B. (2020, September 3). Trump Campaign Pushes Back On Facebook's New Election Policies: "The President Will be Silenced By The Silicon Valley Mafia." *Business Insider*. https://www.businessinsider.com/trump-campaign-pushes-back-on-new-facebook-election-policies-2020-9.

Hidy, K.M. (2020). Social Media Policies, Corporate Censorship and the Right to be Forgiven: A Proposed Framework for Free Expression in an Era of Employer Social Media Monitoring. *University of Pennsylvania Journal of Business Law*, 22, 346–385.

Howard, R.A. (2020). Ethical Distinctions for Building Your Ethical Code InAli E. Abbas (ed.), *Next Generation Ethics, Engineering a Better Society* (pp. 7–16). Cambridge: Cambridge University Press.

Hsu, T. (2020, October 25). Conservative News Sites Fuel Voter Fraud Misinformation.*The New York Times*. https://www.nytimes.com/2020/10/25/business/media/voter-fraud-misinformation.html.

In the Matter of Zoom Communications (2020, November). Federal Trade Commission, Consent Order. https://www.ftc.gov/system/files/documents/cases/ 1923167zoomacco2.pdf.

Ingram, M. (2020, September 4).The Media Today. *Columbia Journalism Review*. Email newsletter.

IT Governance (2020). The EU GDPR Overview. https://www.itgovernance.co.uk/data-protection-dpa-and-eu-data protection-regulation.

Katz, E. and Lazarsfeld, P.F. (1955). *Personal Influence: The Part Played By People in the Flow of Mass Communications*. New York: Free Press.

Knight First Amendment Inst. at Columbia Univ. v. Trump (*Knight Institute I*), 302 F. Supp. 3d 541, 580 (S.D.N.Y. 2018), aff'd, 928 F.3d 226, 230 (2d Cir. 2019), reh'g en banc denied, 953 F.3d 216 (2d Cir. 2020).

Knight Institute II: Knight First Amendment Institute v. Trump (2020). Complaint for Declaratory and Injunctive Relief, cv-05958.

Koh, A. (2017, November 16). 11 Mistakes That Could Invalidate Your NDA. *EveryNDA*. https://www.everynda.com/blog/11-ways-invalidate-nda/.

Lipschultz, J.H. (2020). *Social Media Measurement and Management: Entrepreneurial Digital Analytics*. New York and London: Routledge.

Lipschultz, J.H. (2021). *Social Media Communication: Concepts, Practices, Data, Law and Ethics*, 3rd edition. New York and London: Routledge.

Lipschultz, J.H. (2018). Chapter 2: Organizations, HR, CSR and their Social Networks: "Sustainability" on Twitter In Donnalyn Pompper (ed.), *Corporate Social Responsibility, Sustainability and Public Relations: Negotiating Multiple Complex Challenges*, 2nd edition, Routledge New Directions in Public Relations & Communication Research (pp. 33–50). London: Routledge.

Luttrell, R. (2016). *Social Media: How to Engage, Share and Connect.* Lanham, MD: Rowman & Littlefield.

Luttrell, R.M. and Capizzo, L.W. (2019). *Public Relations Campaigns, An Integrated Approach.* Thousand Oaks, CA: SAGE.

Near v. Minnesota, 283 U.S.697 (1931).

New York Times v. Sullivan, 376 U.S. 254 (1964).

NodeXL (2020). NodeXL Graph Gallery, Social Media Research Foundation. http://nodexlgraphgallery.org/Pages/Default.aspx.

Olster, S. (2020, December 9). 24 Big Trends That Will Change Our World in 2021. *LinkedIn News.* https://www.linkedin.com/pulse/24-big-ideas-change-our-world-2021-scott-olster/.

Packingham v. North Carolina, 582 U.S. ___ (2017).

Pardes, A. (2020, August 12). How Facebook and Other Sites Manipulate Your Privacy Choices, Social Media Platforms Repeatedly Use So-Called Dark Patterns to Nudge You Toward Giving Away More of Your Data. *Wired.* https://www.wired.com/ story/facebook-social-media-privacy-dark-patterns/.

Patterson, P. and Wilkins, L. (2005). *Media Ethics: Issues and Cases, fifth edition.* Boston, MA: McGraw-Hill.

Postman, N. (1985). *Amusing Ourselves to Death: Public Discourse in the Age of Show Business.* New York: Penguin Books.

Postman, N. (1992). *Technolpoly: The Surrender of Culture to Technology.* New York: Alfred A. Knopf.

Potter, W.J. (2008). *Media Literacy,* 4th edition. Los Angeles: SAGE.

PRSA (2020). PRSA Code of Ethics. https://www.prsa.org/about/prsa-code-of-ethics.

Quesenberry, K.A. (2019). *Social Media Strategy: Marketing, Advertising, and Public Relations in the Consumer Revolution,* 2nd edition. Lanham, MD: Rowman & Littlefield.

Reno v. ACLU, 521 U.S. 844 (1997).

Rheingold, H. (2020, August 9). Howard Rheingold: Virtual Community in 2020. YouTube. https://www.youtube.com/watch?v=EtP6txV-aJs.

Save Journalism Project (2020, September 2, para. 3). Comment of the Department of Commerce's Section 230 Petition for Rulemaking. https://savejournalism.org/ 2020/09/02/comment-on-the-department-of-commerces-section-230-petition-for-rulemaking/.

Seitz, A. and Dupuy, B. (2020, October 2). Misinformation Spikes as Trump Confirms Covid-19 Diagnosis. *Associated Press.* https://apnews.com/article/election-2020-virus-outbreak-donald-trump-conspiracy-theories-melania-trump-50bfad6b0d2fef7ba65f54b7b8ea2a98.

Shaw, L. Bergen, M. (2020, December 22). The North Carolina Kid Who Cracked YouTube's Secret Code. *Bloomberg.* https://www.bloomberg.com/news/articles/ 2020-12-22/who-is-mrbeast-meet-youtube-s-top-creator-of-2020.

Sherblom, J.C. (2020). *Computer-Mediated Communication: Approaches and Perspectives.* San Diego, CA: Cognella.

Slevin, C. and Liedtke, M. (2020, December 19). Dozens of States File Anti-trust Lawsuit Against Google. *Associated Press.* https://apnews.com/article/technology-lawsuits-colorado-e5b26373277bcbd9234eb9682e13de18.

Sonnemaker, T. (2020, November 12). The Trump Administration Has Backed Off of its TikTok Ban, But a Federal Judge Had Already Blocked it, Citing The White House's "Hypothetical" National Security Concerns. *Business Insider.* https://www.businessinsider.com/trump-administration-wont-enforce-tiktok-ban-following-court-order-2020-11.

Stein, L. (2016, February 26). Edelman Invests in Employee Advocacy Platform Dynamic Signal. *Advertising Age.* http://adage.com/article/agency-news/edelman-invests-employee-advocacy-platform-dynamic-signal/302852/.

Stern, M. (2020, November 25). Jake Paul Believes COVID Is "a Hoax" and "98% of News Is Fake." *The Daily Beast.* https://www.thedailybeast.com/youtuber-jake-paul-believes-covid-is-a-hoaxand-i-am-fake-news.

Sterne, J. (2010). *Social Media Metrics, How to Measure and Optimize Your Marketing Investment.* Hoboken, NJ: John Wiley & Sons.

Stewart, D.R. (ed.) (2017). *Social Media and the Law: A Guidebook for Communication Students and Professionals,* 2nd edition. New York and London: Routledge.

Zuboff, S. (2019). *The Age of Surveillance Capitalism: The Fight for a Human Future at the New Frontier of Power.* New York: Hachette Book Group.

5

Intellectual Property Rights

> *The copyright is limited to those aspects of the work – termed "expression" – that display the stamp of the author's originality.*

—U.S. Supreme Court Justice Sandra Day O'Connor,
Harper & Row Publishers v. Nation Enterprises (1985, p. 547)

Social media communicators may not own an idea, but *how* the say it, or the manner of expression, is protected under copyright law. The book that you are reading, for example, does not keep other authors from publishing a social media law and ethics book, as long it is a sufficiently original presentation. Put another way, two photographers or videographers may be in about the same location and each shoot original work that they own and can sell.

The United States encourages development of intellectual property by protecting creative works through copyright law and by issuing patents. Article I of the U.S. Constitution explicitly granted Congress under the Patent and Copyright Clause the power:

> To promote the progress of science and useful arts, by securing for limited times to authors and inventors the exclusive right to their respective writings and discoveries.
> (Article I, Section 8, Clause 8)

The Supreme Court interpreted the language to mean that Congress could encourage creative progress and the Copyright Act of 1976 protected original works. Branded symbols and images also are protected under the Trademark Act of 1946, known as the Lanham Act. Social media posts have the potential to infringe copyrighted expression or show a trademarked logo and both statutes are important in a digital and social media age.

Mobile phones and social media communication have increased the number of disputes over ownership of content. User-created YouTube video, for example, sparked copyright infringement cases for use of video and music. Google and other site owners police copyright as part of their agreements with content creators. Much of what originally was in the hands of Internet service providers (ISPs) during the first digital decade shifted to social media platforms, as content sharing shifted to them. For example, some copyrighted content that has been anonymously distributed without permission is saved as files and used by people who have not paid for it. While the Supreme Court has recognized the relationship between the First Amendment and copyright, it did so in a case that limited fair use rights (*Harper & Row Publishers v. Nation Enterprises*, 1985). *Time* magazine had paid for the rights, but *The Nation* obtained and published a "scoop" with about 300 words of quotes from an unpublished memoir (p. 542). In siding with *Time*, the Court balanced the First Amendment with ownership of free expression:

> We agree with the Court of Appeals that copyright is intended to increase and not to impede the harvest of knowledge. But we believe the Second Circuit gave insufficient deference to the scheme established by the Copyright Act for fostering the original works that provide the seed and substance of this harvest. The rights conferred by copyright are designed to assure contributors to the store of knowledge a fair return for their labors.
> (pp. 545–546)

Three dissenting justices noted that *The Nation* had used "300 words from a manuscript of more than 200,000 words, and the quotes are drawn from isolated passages in disparate sections of the work" (p. 598). Following this case, a general rule of using 250 words from a book may be considered fair use. Copyright cases turn on amount and substantiality used and the brevity of social media posts means that it would not take much to steal the expression or image of another.

Copyright protects original creative content, and these are exclusive rights to copy and distribute the material. Under **first sale doctrine**, royalties from each first sale are protected. However, a buyer may resell or rent a legal copy, for example, of a textbook. In our digital world, however, uploaded files and social media posts could be considered theft. Web browsing both temporarily stores content, and also mirrors reading a library book or newsstand magazine. Infringement of copyright happens when an unauthorized copy is used for commercial purposes or is stored to avoid payment. In the late 1990s, for example, a group of national news organizations sued over website repackaging of their content. The pirating of news for profit case was settled out of court. News links to original content do not infringe copyright, but sites may not copy full text without licensing and paying rights fees for material "fixed in a tangible medium." Under threat of new media laws in Australia, Facebook, Google, and other sites have been forced to negotiate licensing of news content. For example, Facebook agreed to pay News Corp. for content:

> The three-year deal between Facebook and Australia's largest media conglomerate comes after the country's parliament amended a law requiring tech platforms to negotiate with publishers over payment for news stories. It also follows a similar deal between Google and News Corp.
>
> (Neuman, 2021, para. 2)

Earlier, Facebook blocked news stories in protest of the country's efforts to regulate social media.

The U.S. Congress had updated copyright laws through the Digital Millennium Copyright Act of 1998 to eliminate a loophole in the Digital Performance Rights in Sound Recordings Act. Webcasters must pay licensing fees negotiated through a Copyright Arbitration Royalty Panel. Further, the Supreme Court upheld the Sonny Bono Copyright Term Extension Act of 1998 as constitutional (*Eldred v. Ashcroft*, 2003). Two dissenting justices, however, worried that keeping copyrighted content out of the **public domain** for about a century limits a First Amendment right to disseminate information.

ISPs and social media platforms, such as Facebook and YouTube, also are left to police illegal pirated copies of music and videos. Supreme Court and appellate cases, however, have treated them under the precedent of **common carrier** telephone and telegraph companies that were not held liable for content. The current Section 230 debate over platform third-party immunity could alter this in the future.

The peer-to-peer Napster site was successfully sued for piracy by the Recording Industry Association of America (RIAA) in the Ninth Circuit, which found that the software was not a fair use (*A&M Records, Inc. v. Napster, Inc.*, 2001). This was a digital departure from the Supreme Court ruling that protected home video-recording device owners (*Sony Corp. v. Universal Studios, Inc.*, 1984). Court cases ultimately shifted most copyrighted music and video to paid streaming sites – Apple Music, Spotify, Netflix and others after the Supreme Court unanimously imposed copyright infringement secondary liability doctrine on sites (*MGM v. Grokster*, 2005). A rule of thumb is to follow the dollar in economic interests, but this does not always protect libraries and archives seeking to make content available. For example, Twitter allows researchers free access to collect about 18,000 tweets going backward in time for a search, but the site charges for larger historic databases. At the same time, social media change is driven by marketplace success or failure, such as when Twitter ended its separate Periscope video app (Hutchinson, 2020). When user interest declines and costs rise, the disappearance of an app usually means data also are closed to viewing. No regulation currently exists to allow users to download and save their data, but Google+ did this when the site ended operation.

COPYRIGHT INFRINGEMENT, FILE SHARING, AND FAIR USE

Social media posts that are subject to copyright law and reuse of photographs without permission continues to be a problem for freelance photographers trying to make a living through their work. They can serve notice by using the law against those violating intellectual property (Digital Theft Deterrence Act, 1999).

Social media on creative content sharing sites, such as YouTube, raise numerous important legal issues. When a user sees a posting, the computer temporarily loads the file, which might be considered illegal copying. Of course, downloading the file by taking a screen shot or saving it more clearly reflects copyright infringement under U.S. law.

The Digital Millennium Copyright Act of 1998 (DCMA, 1998) eliminated loopholes by addressing streaming media and licensing fees for music and videos (*Eldred v. Ashcroft*, 2003). The size of social media sites may make it difficult to enforce copyright and trademark law. **Digital rights management** (DRM) has been used to collect payments and control sharing, but DRM also is difficult to enforce.

Breaking news, or so-called "hot news" doctrine is another fair use issue (Ekstrand, 2015, p. 2): "Theoretically speaking, this means that I own the fact that a plane has crashed – if I have gathered that information myself – for a very (indeed VERY) short time" (pp. 2–3). News pirates may be held liable under misappropriation law, although "only the most egregious violators – those who persistently pirate fresh news, often from the same source – are the ones who are pursued in court" (p. 3).

Copyright law has become particularly important on photo sharing sites, such as Instagram and Snapchat. It turns out that, in most cases, a photographer rather than a camera owner has an intellectual property right over photos. If a user hands a **smartphone** to a friend to take a picture, technically, the friend owns rights to the photo – even though it resides on the original user's phone. This was reinforced when a crested black macaque monkey in 2014 used a photographer's tripod and camera and took a "selfie" that went viral on social media: A monkey is not a person, so a court ruled that nobody owns the photograph and "the picture is in the public domain" (*Naruto v. Slater*, 2016; Lisby, 2017, p. 265).

Over the years, DMCA (1998) has been a tool that websites have used to force users to take down content owned by others. The process often begins with rights holders sending a site takedown notices and these being forwarded to users. Both may be named in lawsuits, if they fail to comply. Twitch streamers, for example, were notified after they used copyrighted music in their livestreams and some were essentially selling requests to play songs (Slashdot, 2020; Stephen, 2020). In some cases, Twitch did not allow streamers to counterclaim before deleting their content. The streamers essentially were functioning as disc jockeys by playing music without the required licensing processes and fees.

Intellectual property law also may intersect with invasion of privacy cases. For example, **appropriation of likeness** is an area of privacy case law. In it, there may be civil liability for use of a name, image or likeness for commercial purposes without consent. Even though a smartphone photograph or video was taken in a public space, such as a sidewalk or public parking lot, written consent from the subject is normally required by lawyers to safely publish. If the social media content is gathered on private property, then commercial or noncommercial use of it may trigger an invasion of privacy case. U.S. copyright law is a piece of a global system that must be considered when posting social content.

UK AND AUSTRALIA COPYRIGHT LAW

The Copyright, Designs and Patents Act (1988) covers creative work in the United Kingdom. It covers:

1. Copyright is a property right that subsists in accordance with this part in the following descriptions of work:

    a. original literary, dramatic, musical or artistic works

    b. sound recordings, films or broadcasts

    c. the typographical arrangement of published editions

2. In this part "copyright work" means a work of any of those descriptions in which copyright subsists
3. Copyright does not subsist in a work unless the requirements of this part with respect to qualification for copyright protection are met (Chapter 1)

Copyright owners hold "exclusive right," including those of the author, the "treatment of the work," a "right to object to derogatory treatment of the work" and a "right to privacy of certain photographs and films" (Chapter 2). Under "moral rights," the author retains a right to assert ownership of creative works (pp. 77–78).

In Australia, the Copyright Act of 1968 was amended in June of 2017. It has provisions defining educational purposes and a reasonable portion of a work. It specifies infringement as:

1. ... the copyright in a literary, dramatic, musical or artistic work is infringed by a person who, not being the owner of the copyright, and without the licence of the owner of the copyright, does in Australia, or authorizes the doing in Australia of, any act comprised in the copyright

   1A In determining, for the purposes of subsection (1), whether or not a person has authorised the doing in Australia of any act comprised in the copyright in a work, without the licence of the owner of the copyright, the matters that must be taken into account include the following:

   a. the extent (if any) of the person's power to prevent the doing of the act concerned
   b. the nature of any relationship existing between the person and the person who did the act concerned
   c. whether the person took any reasonable steps to prevent or avoid the doing of the act, including whether the person complied with any relevant industry codes of practice (Division 2, 36)

The cross-national nature of intellectual property makes it a difficult area to enforce. There is a spectrum of laws – from little copyright protection to a lot – around the world. Nations depend on treaties to protect their creators and creative works. International brands also must address their trademarks when doing business in each country.

TRADEMARKS

The Trademark Act of 1946 (Lanham Act) not only protects trademarks from infringement, it also has provisions covering dilution of a trademark. The standard is whether or not a use is likely to cause confusion in the marketplace. Under

15 U.S.C. § 1125, "false descriptions, and dilution" are "forbidden." A trademark holder may sue "in connection with any goods or services, or any container for goods, uses in commerce any word, term, name, symbol, or device, or any combination thereof, or any false designation of origin, false or misleading description of fact, or false or misleading representation of fact" (§ 1125 (a)(1) if it:

A. is likely to cause confusion, or to cause mistake, or to deceive as to the affiliation, connection, or association of such person with another person, or as to the origin, sponsorship, or approval of his or her goods, services, or commercial activities by another person, or

B. in commercial advertising or promotion, misrepresents the nature, characteristics, qualities, or geographic origin of his or her or another person's goods, services, or commercial activities.

The Supreme Court, however, has recognized limits in the application of trademark law. In *Matal v. Tam* (2017) the Court ruled that the government under the First Amendment could not impose a ban on offensive ideas. The dance-rock group "The Slants" had a right to register its trademark even though some find it a derogatory term for Asians. Lead singer Simon Tam sought to "'reclaim' and 'take ownership' of stereotypes about people of Asian ethnicity" (p. 1754). The Court broadly applied viewpoint discrimination in ruling that: "Giving offense is a viewpoint" (p. 1763). Applied to the case: "The name 'The Slants' not only identifies the band but expresses a view about social issues" (p. 1764).

In an unusual case, comic artist Jeph Jacques purchased the Walmart.horse web domain, created a site and "portrayed an unexplainably funny picture of a horse in front of a Walmart store" (Mullin, 2015, para.1). Walmart sent the artist a cease-and-desist letter:

> Your use of a Domain Name that incorporates the famous Walmart mark constitutes trademark infringement and dilution of Walmart's trademark rights and unfair competition. Your use of our mark in the Domain Name is diluting use because it weakens the ability of the Walmart mark and domain name to identify a single source, namely Walmart. Further, your registration and use of the Domain Name misleads consumers into believing that some association exists between Walmart and you, which tarnishes the goodwill and reputation of Walmart's products, services, and trademarks.
>
> (Kravets, 2015, para. 3)

Clearly, the corporate retail giant did not appreciate the artist's parody. Jacques told media that he gave up on the fight and turned the domain over to Walmart.

He then posted on his Tumblr account a photograph of a horse skeleton to symbolize the outcome. The out-of-court settlement offers no insights into whether or not the artist could have won a fair use defense.

CONTENT OWNERSHIP

Intellectual property law covering one's images may intersect with a person's right of privacy. In one Wisconsin case, a hired photographer took a photo at an October 2019 homecoming dance of a student's exposed breast after her dress slipped (NBC-TV5, 2020). The company was named in a lawsuit claiming the image was of her "temporarily exposed breast" (para. 3). The student was unaware that a photo was taken and posted for sale on a public website. The lawsuit claimed members of the high school football team viewed the image and then shared it on social media. The photographer appeared to violate the **work-for-hire** agreement, as well as ethics of serving a paid client's needs: "High school students are still children, and deserve the adults involved with school events to safeguard their best interests," the student's attorney said. "There is no excuse for this lack of oversight, which literally exposed this young woman in the most humiliating way possible" (para. 7). The lawsuit also claimed that the student was "repeatedly publicly humiliated, harassed, sexually harassed and bullied, for which she sought counseling" (Peterson, 2020, para. 2). Lawyers sought at least $50,000 in damages (para. 3).

Infringement and Fair Use

Copyright infringement begins with a claim that creative works have been used without permission and sometimes payment. Intellectual property law, however, applies to humans and not animals.

Box 5.1 The Case of Naruto and His Monkey Selfie

British nature photographer David Slater objected to newspaper publication in 2011 of the monkey selfie images taken with his camera, as well as online copies. Slater claimed a copyright, but an animal rights group countered that the monkey owned the photos. Slater's claim was based on his travel to Indonesia, placement of the camera on a tripod and shutter button near the animals, as well equipment settings required to make it work. Additionally, he held the tripod steady during 30 minutes of photography. After making some money from sale of images, the photographs became very popular to share on the Internet.

Wikimedia in 2014 refused to remove the photographs because it understood the images to be in the public domain. The U.S. Copyright Office at the end of that year found that a photograph taken by an animal may not have a copyright because the law protects humans and but macaque monkeys. Animal rights groups unsuccessfully argued in a 2016 district court decision that animals should have these rights. Slater and People for the Ethical Treatment of Animals (PETA) attempted an out-of-court settlement over future shared revenues from the images, but the Court of Appeals in 2018 upheld the lower court judgment that PETA could not use "Next Friend" doctrine to represent Naruto. To date, the popular images remain in the public domain.

A court ruled animals could not hold copyrights.

Courtesy U.S. Court of Appeals, Ninth Circuit.

Photograph courtesy Naruto. https://upload.wikimedia.org/wikipedia/commons/thumb/4/4e/Macaca_nigra_self-portrait_large.jpg/440px-Macaca_nigra_self-portrait_large.jpg.

Slater has said that, after placing his camera with a wide-angle lens in position, he left the nervous monkeys to play with a camera release in order to capture the photographs while holding the tripod. The technique apparently worked because the monkeys were entertained by seeing their reflection in the lens (Wikipedia, 2020).

Under the Copyright Act, it is established law that a non-human animal cannot hold copyright because the law protects a person's creative works. Slater's technical work was indirect to the photos taken by the monkeys. The cases also address potential social media issues in which a person hands their smartphone to another person to take a photograph. The owner of the phone exercises no creativity in the process. In such a case, the phone owner could not claim copyright any more than she or he could by taking a social media screenshot and storing it. A slightly different question comes when a company issues a phone to a work-for-hire photographer and the newspaper or other business makes a claim of ownership based on contract law.

DISTRICT COURT

Naruto v. Slater, et al.,
Case No. 15-cv-04324-WHO 2016 U.S. Dist. LEXIS 11041
(N.D. Calif., Jan. 28, 2016)

Facts: Naruto, a six-year-old crested macaque, took multiple "Monkey Selfie" photos using David John Slater's camera. The People for the Ethical Treatment of Animals ("PETA") and Antje Engehardt challenged Slater and his book publisher's ownership. PETA argued that Naruto owned copyright of his selfie. Slater and his publisher argued that a monkey has neither legal standing nor a Copyright Act claim. Naruto, in Indonesia, was considered "highly intelligent" and possesses "grasping hands and opposable thumbs with the ability to move his fingers independently." Naruto lived next to a village, and was comfortable around human tourists, photographers and cameras (pp. 2–3).

On information and belief, Naruto authored the Monkey Selfies sometime in or around 2011 by "independent, autonomous action" in examining and manipulating Slater's unattended camera and "purposely pushing' the shutter release multiple times, "understanding the cause-and-effect relationship between pressing the shutter release, the noise of the shutter, and the change to his reflection in the camera lens" (p. 3).

Legal Issues: Can an animal and representatives hold intellectual property rights? Next Friends [PETA] alleged Slater repeatedly violated Naruto's copyright by selling monkey selfies. They claim Slater and his publisher violated the Copyright Act of 1975, sections 106 and 501 "by displaying, advertising, reproducing, distributing, offering for sale, and selling copies of the Monkey Selfies" (citing Copyright Act, at 43, 44), (p. 4):

1. The Federal Rule of Civil Procedure 12(b)(1) or 12(b)(6), requires that a plaintiff must allege "enough facts to state a claim to relief that is plausible on its face." ... A claim is facially plausible when the plaintiff pleads facts that "allow the court to draw the reasonable inference that the defendant is liable for the misconduct alleged" (p. 4).
2. In deciding whether the plaintiff has stated a claim upon which relief can be granted, the Court accepts the plaintiff's allegations as true and draws all reasonable inferences in favor of the plaintiff. ... However, the court is not required to accept as true "allegations that are merely conclusory, unwarranted deductions of fact, or unreasonable inferences."

5

Decision: U.S. District Judge William H. Orrick granted a motion in favor of Slater and his publisher.

The 9th Circuit rejected a photographer's claim.

U.S. Court of Appeals, 9th Circuit Panel, https://www.ca9.uscourts.gov/media/ view_video.php?pk_vid=0000011923.

Judge Orrick also denied a motion for judicial notice of exhibits:

> Naruto is not an "author" within the meaning of the Copyright Act. … The issue for me is whether Next Friends have demonstrated that the Copyright Act confers standing upon Naruto. In light of the plain language of the Copyright Act, past judicial interpretations of the Act's authorship requirement, and guidance from the Copyright Office, they have not.
>
> (p. 10)

Defendants' motions to dismiss are GRANTED…

Reasoning: The defendants argued for case dismissal "for lack of standing under Article III and the Copyright Act of 1976" (p. 5):

1. To demonstrate standing under Article III's case or controversy requirement, a plaintiff must show that: (i) it has suffered an "injury in fact" that is (a) concrete and particularized and (b) actual or imminent, not conjectural or hypothetical; (ii) the injury is "fairly traceable" to the challenged action of the defendants; and (iii) a favorable decision will be likely to redress the injury (p. 5).
2. The Ninth Circuit has stated that Article III "does not compel the conclusion that a statutorily authorized suit in the name of an animal is not a 'case or controversy'" … I need not discuss Article III standing further, because regardless of whether Naruto fulfills the requirements of Article III, he must demonstrate standing … for his claim to survive under Rule 12(b)(6), (pp. 5–6).
3. "[T]he starting point for interpreting a statute is the language of the statute itself." … The Copyright Act protects "original works of author-ship fixed in any tangible medium of expression, now known or later developed, from which they can be perceived, reproduced, or otherwise communicated, either directly or with the aid of a machine or device." 17 U.S.C. Sec. 102(a). The "fixing" of the work in the tangible medium of expression must be done "by or under the authority of the author." 17 U.S.C. Sec. 101. The Copyright Act defines neither "works of authorship" nor "author." The Ninth

Circuit has observed that the Act "purposefully left 'works of authorship' undefined to provide for some flexibility" (pp. 7–8).

4. In ... *Cetacean Community* ... the "self-appointed attorney for all of the world's whales, porpoises, and dolphins," filed suit on behalf of the Cetaceans for violations of the Endangered Species Act, the Marine Mammal Protection Act, and the National Environmental Policy Act, [and] ... the Ninth Circuit ... held that "if Congress and the President intended to take the extraordinary step of authorizing animals as well as people and legal entities to sue, they could, and should, have said so plainly" (pp. 7–8).
5. Here, the Copyright Act does not "plainly" extend the concept of authorship or statutory standing to animals. To the contrary, there is no mention of animals anywhere in the Act. The Supreme Court and Ninth Circuit have repeatedly referred to "persons" or "human beings" when analyzing authorship under the Act (pp. 8–9).
6. Moreover, the Copyright Office agrees that works created by animals are not entitled to copyright protection. It directly addressed the issue of human authorship in the Compendium of U.S. Copyright Office Practices issued in December 2014 (the "Compendium"). "When interpreting the Copyright Act, [the courts] defer to the Copyright Office's interpretations in the appropriate circumstances" (pp. 9–10).

6

COURT OF APPEALS

In *Naruto v. Slater* (2018), the Ninth Circuit Court of Appeals affirmed the District Court ruling because the monkey and, indeed, all animals lack legal statutory standing under the Copyright Act:

> We must determine whether a monkey may sue humans, corporations, and companies for damages and injunctive relief arising from claims of copyright infringement. Our court's precedent requires us to conclude that the monkey's claim has standing under Article III of the United States Constitution. Nonetheless, we conclude that this monkey—and all animals, since they are not human—lacks statutory standing under the *Copyright Act*. We therefore affirm the judgment of the district court.
>
> (p. 420)

The appellate court found that: "The Copyright Act does not expressly authorize animals to file copyright infringement suits under the stature" (p. 426). In a concurring opinion, the argument was made that there was no federal court "jurisdiction to hear this case at all" (p. 427). The opinion suggested that "PETA brought a frivolous lawsuit here" (p. 428).

Slater earned some money from initial publication of the photographs, but widespread free use of the images clearly cost him significant revenues. He was able to sell the rights to his story for a documentary about the legal dispute.

Sources

Monkey Selfie Copyright Dispute. https://en.wikipedia.org/wiki/Monkey_selfie_copyright_dispute

Naruto v. Slater, et al., 2016 U.S. Dist. LEXIS 11041 (N.D. Calif., Jan. 28, 2016).

Naruto v. Slater, 888 F.3d 418 (9th Cir., 2018); Wikipedia (2020, November 1).

COPYRIGHT SCOPE, FAIR USE, AND TRANSFORMATIVE USE

The protection of original works under copyright law including: writings; music; drama and choreography; photographs, graphics and sculptures; movies and audio-visual presentation; recordings of sound; and architecture. There is an idea-expression dichotomy under the law. Creators cannot own an idea, but their manner of expression is protected. In general, the creative expression must demonstrate some degree of originality and new aspect. To claim copyright, a work should be labeled with a ©, author name and year. Creators hold a right to derivative works. Case law supports the importance of explicit contract language when it comes to any republication rights (*New York Times v. Tasini*, 2001).

A fair use defense can be made in content when an educational or nonprofit organization uses a relatively small portion of a copyrighted work that has limited impact on the potential market for it. For example, when your professor shares a page out of a published book or shows a brief movie clip to make a point, this may be fair use. The public nature of social media can be challenging because: (1) a creator may freely share her or his content to the world; and (2) digital high-quality copies are easy to make. The safest legal and ethical course of action is to always seek consent before using content for another purpose.Mashups and sampling may be popular, but lawyers urge creators to license existing content from copyright holders. Finally, a fair use defense may include the argument that a new work is **transformative** in changing the copyrighted content. In *Campbell v. Acuff-Rose Music* (1994), the Supreme Court held that commercial character was the only element that should be considered in a fair use case. In the case, 2 Live Crew attempted a parody defense for its version of Roy Orbison's rock song "Oh Pretty Woman."

Box 5.2 Case Study: Online Photos in the EU

The European Court of Justice ruled in 2020 that a photographer's explicit permission must be obtained before an Internet user publishes an online image (Delcker, 2019). A statement read: "The posting on a website of a photograph that was freely accessible on another website with the consent of the author requires a new authorisation by that author" (para. 2).

The case began when a student in Germany downloaded a travel website photograph that was reposted without consent on a secondary school website: "The photographer who took the picture argued the school's use of his photo was a copyright infringement because he only gave the travel site permission to use it, and claimed damages amounting to €400" (para. 4). The court held that "subject to the exceptions and limitations laid down exhaustively in that directive, any use of a work by a third party without such prior consent must be regarded as infringing the copyright of that work" (para. 6). Under Germany's copyright law, the following content is protected:

1. Protected works in the literary, scientific and artistic domain include, in particular:

   a. Literary works, such as written works, speeches and computer programs
   b. Musical works
   c. Pantomimic works, including works of dance
   d. Artistic works, including works of architecture and of applied art and drafts of such works

e. Photographic works, including works produced by processes similar to photography
f. Cinematographic works, including works produced by processes similar to cinematography
g. Illustrations of a scientific or technical nature, such as drawings, plans, maps, sketches, tables and three-dimensional representations (German Copyright Act, Section 2)

The EU court also dismissed the idea that a photographer, as copyright holder, must expressly limit use of the property. "[T]he Court of Justice of the EU (CJEU) ruled upon referral by the German Federal Court of Justice (Bundesgerichtshof, BGH) that the unauthorized reposting of a copyright work that is already available online constitutes an act of communication to the public within the meaning of Art. 3(1) of the InfoSoc Directive" (Ling, 2019, para. 1). The photo of Cordoba, Spain, appeared in a student paper for Spanish class, and that led to a lawsuit against the government that operates the school: "[T]he Court stresses that the pupil's acts not only infringed the photographer's right to communication to the public, but, by creating a copy of the work on the school's server, also the right to copy (§ 16 of the German Copyright Act) ... (para. 6 6)). The Court awarded the photographer a permanent injunction, but it rejected monetary damages. An appeals court opinion read:

> If schools foresee the use of the Internet by pupils in class as part of an educational mandate to teach media competence, it is necessary to inform pupils about existing obligations and risks in connection with the use of the Internet in schools, to instruct them and to monitor compliance with the rules to the extent required.
>
> (para. 7)

German law recognizes teacher **negligence** in lawsuits against a school, but a copyright owner must sue a student to collect damages. Freelance photographers around the world frequently see their photos used without consent and payment. Their recourse is to use national copyright laws to protect intellectual property rights.

Sources

Delcker, J. (2019, April 19). Online Photos Can't Simply Be Re-published, EU Court Rules. *Politico*. https://www.politico.eu/article/ecj-photographer-permission-ruling/.

German Copyright Act (2020), Section 2. https://www.gesetze-im-internet.de/englisch_urhg/englisch_urhg.html#p0018.

IPKat. https://ipkitten.blogspot.com/2019/07/copyright-infringement-confirmed-but-no.html.

Ling, P. (2019, July 23). Copyright Infringement Confirmed, but No Damages for "Cordoba" Photographer.

LAW REVIEW ANALYSES

Ross (2020) explored the intersection of social media communication and copyright infringement and concluded that users who "merely link or share articles, pictures, or memes may actually be infringing" (p. 205). In this view, technological development is far ahead of the law. Tweeted photographs, memes and other content, for example, may be given attribution but not payment:

> As a result, some brands now attribute the source of their content to avoid infringement allegations. Although attribution may be satisfactory for some creators, others have pursued litigation to enforce their exclusive intellectual property rights against companies that use stolen content.
>
> (p. 206)

Ross (2020) noted that Jerry Media, the company posting popular FuckJerry Instagram memes, promoted the Frye Festival Bahamas scam and this drew attention to their "prolific use of stolen content on social media" (p. 207). When commercial accounts steal content and share without consent and payment to rights holders, attribution fails to account for potential lost creator revenue.

On Twitter, the platform encourages users to **retweet** creator content, but "this shared tweet is still contrary to the owner's right of distribution" (p. 209). The Twitter terms of service (ToS) promise users their retained rights at the same time the company allows others to share it and even "rewrite them under their own profile to give the **impression** that they are the originator" by "tweetdecking" it (p. 209). Similarly, screenshots of copyrighted photographs and graphics are common practices on Twitter and Instagram. When the motivation of a user is to monetize social media influence, then "it is hardly an innocent, personal use" (p. 211).

A fair use defense could be made by content aggregators, if they can prove that "the owner's dissemination of the photograph on public social media channels placed it in the public domain and created an implied license" (p. 220). A newsworthy context also could be used to launch a fair use defense. A copyright holder seeking to make a copyright claim should begin by demanding that the content be taken down before there is a lawsuit. It is common for these cases to be settled out of court, but lawmakers and the courts need to develop this area of law to fit it to social media sites.

Box 5.3 Your Professor's Social Media, Course, and Research Content

There is a long-debated legal question about intellectual property ownership of content that could extend into social media creative activity. For example, Lisby (2015) was curious about whether or not a tweet is "copyrightable" given fair use doctrine and, if so, how much of the brief content (p. 284). Professors may use Twitter and other social media sites as part of their teaching, research and service at a university.

There is a presumption that professors own their content, as employees of a college or university. Simon (1982–83), in one of the earliest analyses, suggested that without a clear precedent from the U.S. Supreme Court, a university could claim ownership of a professor's publication under a work-for-hire interpretation. Typically, professors are assigned time to research and write under an employment nine- or 12-month contract, tenured continuous appointment or other arrangement. While a paid employee, professors' social media content also may be subject to campus policies. As with any employee, social media policies and other contract language offer guidance. Likewise, Packard (2002) related the academic freedom issues to website and online course development prior to the emergence of social media communication. Under the Copyright Act of 1909 17 U.S.C. § 26 and an interpretation of it, there may have been a "teacher exception" in U.S. law (p. 282). The use of the word author included an employer in works made for hire, but the courts specified only employee works made in a regular course of employment and differently treated commissioned works. The legal distinction of employee works and those of independent contractors emerged in the law: "[I]t defined 'work made for hire' as 'a work prepared by an employee within the scope of the duties of his employment, but not including a work made on special order or commission'" (*Community for Creative Non-Violence v. Reid* (1989, pp. 744–745).

The 1976 Act and later copyright amendments and court decisions attempted to clarify emerging copyright law. Employment law can be applied to copyright and this includes a public relations function that some professors and social media managers on campus accept when using social media. Much depends on employment contract language – individual contracts or collective bargaining agreements (CBAs) – that may clarify content ownership "within the scope" of job duties. There is potential liability, for example, from a defamatory tweet. Some universities provide employees with insurance that covers possible damages.

Different rules and standards may apply for a professor developing course content, publishing research, writing for media or posting on social media. The context matters. Under fair use doctrine: "The use of copyrighted works for 'criticism, comment, news reporting, teaching (including multiple copies for classroom use), scholarship [and] research' is permitted by the rule" (Lisby, 2018, p. 270). There are four factors, including 1. "purpose and character of the use" as "a commercial nature" or "nonprofit educational purposes"; 2. "nature of the copyrighted work"; 3. "amount and substantiality" compared to the entire copyrighted work; and 4. "potential market" effect (p. 270).

In *Weinstein v. University of Illinois* (1987) the U.S. Court of Appeals, Seventh Circuit, reversed a lower court ruling and found that the university had not signed a copyright agreement and could not, therefore, claim ownership of the work. Other ways in which a professor would surrender rights would be that the university had specifically commissioned the work, or the writing was part of a job description. For example, if a professor were hired to be a social media manager, then the university may be able to claim the content of official pages. In fact, university PR offices and policies typically distinguish personal from official campus social media content. The use of professors as social media influencers, however, may create a complex context. In a study of dozens of campuses, it was common to disclaim their ownership of professors' work, as there has been a rise in respect for academic freedom (Packard, 2002). In more recent years, online course content is most likely to be of value and interest for colleges and universities:

> While new technology did not fundamentally alter the ownership question, it did raise the stakes for how that question got answered. What emerged in practice, if not policy, was a position that the college or university would only claim copyright ownership in technology-based course materials that used significant institutional resources, were commissioned by the institution, or were believed to hold considerable market value. Copyright in all other materials, including traditional scholarly work like books and articles, would lie with the faculty member who authored the work.
>
> (Rooksby, 2016, p. 206)

In *Community for Creative Non-Violence v. Reid* (1989), the U.S. Supreme Court interpreted the Copyright Act of 1976, 17 U.S.C. § 101 and congressional intent of the terms "employee," "employer" and "scope of employment" within common law of agency and the "express objective of creating national, uniform copyright law by broadly preempting state statutory" and other common law (p. 740). A group had paid an independent contractor to create a "Third World America" sculpture and this was not typical work for the organization. The artist had complete freedom over creation of the project. The Supreme Court concluded that the only way an organization could make a claim of joint authorship was if the artist and organization had "prepared the work 'with the intention that their contributions be merged into inseparable or interdependent parts of a unitary whole'" (p. 753). In other words, under 17 U.S.C. § 101, it appears that a university and professor would be required to have an explicit agreement to merge or share ownership. Employees, including professors, generally own what they have created unless the work is considered within the scope of employment, is a specifically commissioned work or is part of an employment contract or other agreement.

Lisby (2011) reminded us that individuals (and corporations) "have the right to publicize their positions about issues they believe to be important – especially political positions" as well as a "right of self-promotion and the right to make money off their likeness and activities" (p. 179). The right of publicity may also be related to work ownership:

> The Supreme Court ruled … that, unless an express contractual agreement exists to the contrary, … "free-lancers," own the copyright to works they create. Historically, corporate clients assumed they owned such works-made-for-hire because they had contracted with PR practitioners … A close look at the works-made-for-hire provisions of the Copyright Act of 1976, however, reveals that the corporation owns the finished work only if the creator is an employee acting "within the scope of his or her employment." Other works, "specifically ordered or commissioned," require an express agreement "that the work is to be considered a work-made-for-hire."
>
> (p. 193)

Employees sometimes use a disclaimer on their Twitter or other social media profiles to make clear that their views may not represent those of an employer. Beyond law and company policies, there is an ethical determination of what an employee must say when advocating on Twitter or other social media channels.

The American Library Association (ALA) and professors on some campuses have also pushed within policies for fair use of educational work and development of open educational resources (OER) that shift costs away from economically burdened students. The high library costs for academic journals were a sore point because the content of research articles was largely subsidized by universities that pay professors to do research and publish it within their promotion and tenure processes.

While a university could make a claim that it owns course content under the employment concept, it may be more interested in free access to academic curricula than external economic value. It is important to emphasize that professors, and *not* their university employers, own their research and creative work unless there is contract language that otherwise addresses intellectual property or patents.

At the same time, employees "on a frolic of their own" may be held liable for tort actions that are independent of employer assigned work (Butterworths, 2020, p. 98). For example, while an employer is responsible for employee duties and "systemic" negligence, a social media practical joke could cause harm through "casual" negligence "giving rise to vicarious liability" (p. 90). Consider a social media manager hired to represent the university. A frolic from these assigned duties would be legal cause to be fired under employment law.

Roocksby (2016) concluded that there are higher stakes now that faculty members may earn outside money for their online creative work, such as blogs, videos, mobile apps and software development "capable of generating financial return" (p. 216). In response, many universities created technology transfer arrangements in which professors and universities share revenues to avoid legal conflicts over copyright and patent ownership. It is likely that this important area of law will continue to develop, as AI and AR technologies advance.

Sources

Butterworths (2020, December 7). Division XI Employers' Liability, The Employer's Duty of Care, Vicarious Liability. *Butterworths Personal Injury Litigation Service*. Nexis Uni. https://advance-lexis-com.leo.lib.unomaha.edu/api/document?collection= analytical-materials&id=urn:contentItem:61G0-FFF1-FC6N-X0BT-00000-00&context=1516831.

Community for Creative Non-Violence v. Reid, 490 U.S. 730 (1989).

Lisby, G. (2011). Regulating Public Relations. In W. Wat Hopkins, *Communication and the Law*, pp. 179–196. Northport, AL: Vision Press.

Lisby, G. (2015). Intellectual Property. In W. Wat Hopkins, *Communication and the Law*, pp. 265–291. Northport, AL: Vision Press.

Lisby, G. (2018). Intellectual Property. In W. Wat Hopkins, *Communication and the Law*, pp. 257–286. Northport, AL: Vision Press.

Packard, A. (2002, Summer). Copyright or Copy Wrong: An Analysis of Claims To faculty Work. *Communication Law & Policy*, 7, 275–315.

Rooksby, J.H. (2016, Winter). Copyright in Higher Education: A Review of Modern Scholarship, *Duquesne Law Review*, 54, 197–221.

Simon, T.F. (1982–83). Faculty Writings: Are They "Works Made for Hire" Under the 1976 Copyright Act?, *Journal of College and University Law*, 9(4), 485–513.

Weinstein v. University of Illinois, 811 F.2d 1091 (1987).

In 2021, Congress moved toward yet another update of online copyright regulation. Legislators had added what has been called the Copyright Alternative in Small-Claims Enforcement Act (CASE Act) to a massive Covid-19 relief spending bill (Kelly, 2020). Additionally, lawmakers also included the Trademark Modernization Act, as well as a proposal that would make it a felony to steal streaming video, music or other content. The CASE Act would expand rights owners' claims by creating "a quasi-judicial tribunal of 'Copyright Claims Officers' to work on disputes, and "copyright holders could be awarded up to $30,000 if they find their creative work being shared online" (para. 3). Graphic artists have been among those creators unable to stop the use or sale of their stolen work. Questions remain about whether or not memes are transformative. However, new regulation could also be too restrictive and violate fair use. The previous DMCA, for example, led to a flurry of content takedown notices. Ethical concerns also persist within intellectual property rights about harm, honesty, integrity, fairness and respect for others. It is a common theme that digital disruption may harm existing interests at the same time that it affords entrepreneurial and innovative opportunities. This makes for a complex area of social media law and a strong need for social media ethics.

ONLINE RESOURCES

Law for the Lay (2019, March 10). Copyright & Social Media. *YouTube.* https://youtu.be/iLH5t1LzC64.

DISCUSSION QUESTIONS

1. How would you revise copyright law to account for changing technologies and social norms?
2. Copyright law in Australia and the UK is slightly different from that in the U.S.A. What should the world do to address the differences in national law that impact social media content?
3. Which ethical values do you apply to posting social media content that originates from someone else?

REFERENCES

A&M Records, Inc. v. Napster, Inc., 239 F.3d 1004 (9th Cir. 2001).

Campbell v. Acuff-Rose Music, 510 U.S. 569 (1994).

Copyright Act of 1976, 17 U.S.C. §§ 101.

Copyright Act of 1968 (Australia). Federal Register of Legislation. https://www.legislation.gov.au/Details/C2017C00180.

Copyrights, Designs and Patents Act (1988). https://www.legislation.gov.uk/ ukpga/1988/48/contents.

Delcker, J. (2019, April 19). Online Photos Can't Simply Be Re-published, EU Court Rules. *Politico*. https://www.politico.eu/article/ecj-photographer-permission-ruling/.

Digital Millennium Copyright Act (DMCA, 1998). 17 U.S.C. § 101.

Digital Theft Deterrence Act, 17 U.S.C. § 504(a), (c)(1)(1999).

Ekstrand, V.S. (2015). *Hot News in the Age of Big Data: A Legal History of the Hot News Doctrine and Implications for the Digital Age*. El Paso, TX: LFB Scholarly Publishing.

Eldred v. Ashcroft, 537 U.S. 186, reh'g denied, 538 U.S. 916 (2003).

Erlich, B. (2011, May 20). After LimeWire, the RIAA Cracks Down on Box.Net Infringers.*Mashable*, http://mashable.com/2011/05/20/riaa-boxnet/.

German Copyright Act (2020), Section 2. https://www.gesetze-im-internet.de/englisch_urhg/englisch_urhg.html#p0018.

Harper Row Publishers v. Nation Enterprises, 471 U.S. 539 (1985).

Hutchinson, A. (2020, December 15). Twitter Confirms the Shutdown of Its Separate Periscope App in March 2021.*Social Media Today*. https://www.socialmediatoday.com/news/twitter-confirms-the-shutdown-of-its-separate-periscope-app-in-march-2021/592238/.

Kelly, M. (2020, December 21). Sweeping New Copyright Measures Poised to Pass in Spending Bill. *The Verge*. https://www.theverge.com/2020/12/21/22193976/covid-relief-spending-congress-copyright-case-act-felony-streaming.

Kravets, D. (2015, March 9). Why the Long Face? Retailer Says Walmart.horse Domain Infringes Its IP.*ARS Technica*. https://arstechnica.com/tech-policy/2015/03/why-the-long-face-retailer-says-walmart-horse-domain-infringes-its-ip/.

Ling, P. (2019, July 23). Copyright Infringement Confirmed, but No Damages for "Cordoba" Photographer. *The IPKat*. https://ipkitten.blogspot.com/2019/07/copyright-infringement-confirmed-but-no.html.

Lisby, G. (2017). Intellectual Property. InW.W. Hopkins (ed.), *Communication and the Law*, pp. 259–290. Northport, AL: Vision Press.

Matal v. Tam, 582 U.S. ___, 137 S. Ct. 1744 (2017).

MGM v. Grokster, 545 U.S. 913 (2005).

Mullin, J. (2015, May 20). Walmart.horse Is Put Out Rto Pasture After retailer Starts Domain Dispute. *ARS Technica*. https://arstechnica.com/tech-policy/2015/05/ walmart-horse-is-put-out-to-pasture-after-retailer-starts-domain-dispute/.

Naruto v. Slater, et al., No, 15-cv-04324-WHO, N.D. Calif., 2016 U.S. Dist. LEXIS 11041 (N.D. Calif., Jan. 28, 2016).

Naruto v. Slater, 888 F.3d 418 (9th Cir., 2018).

NBC TV-5 (2020, October 22). Suit: Photo of Student's Breasts During Dress Slip at School Posted for Purchase. https://www.nbcchicago.com/news/local/suit-photos-of-students-breasts-during-dress-slip-at-school-dance-posted-for-purchase/2357613/.

Neuman, S. (2021, March 16). Facebook Reaches Deal with News Corp. Australia to Pay for News Content. *NPR*. https://www.npr.org/2021/03/16/977776254/facebook-reaches-deal-with-news-corp-australia-to-pay-for-news-content.

New York Times v. Tasini, 533 U.S. 483 (2001).

Packard, A. (2002, Summer). Copyright or Copy Wrong: An Analysis of Claims to Faculty Work, *Communication Law & Policy*, 7, 275–315.

Peterson, E. (2020, October 23). District 211, Photo Company Sued Over Image of Girl Exposed at Conant Dance. *Daily Herald*. https://www.dailyherald.com/ news/20201022/district-211-photo-company-sued-over-image-of-girl-exposed-at-conant-dance.

Rooksby, J.H. (2016, Winter). Copyright in Higher Education: A Review of Modern Scholarship, *Duquesne Law Review*, 54, 197–221.

Ross, C. (2020, Spring). Tweet Takers & Instagram Fakers: Social Media & Copyright Infringement, *Tulane Journal of Technology & Intellectual Property*, 22, 205–224.

Simon, T.F. (1982–83). Faculty Writings: Are They "Works Made for Hire" Under the 1976 Copyright Act?, *Journal of College and University Law*, 9(4), 485–513.

Slashdot (2020). Twitch Suddenly Mass-Deletes Thousands of Videos, Citing Copyright Claims. https://games.slashdot.org/story/20/10/24/0333233/twitch-suddenly-mass-deletes-thousands-of-videos-citing-music-copyright-claims.

Sony BMG Music et al. v. Tenenbaum, 721 F. Supp. 2d 85 (D. Mass. 2010).

Sony Corp. v. Universal Studios, Inc., 464 U.S. 417(1984).

Stephen, B. (2020, October 20). Twitch Streamers Are Getting DMCA Takedown Notices (Again). *The Verge*. https://www.theverge.com/2020/10/20/21525481/twitch-streamers-dmca-takedown-notices-riaa-copyright.

Trademark Act of 1946, 15 U.S.C. § 1051.

Weinstein v. University of Illinois, 811 F.2d 1091 (1987).

Wikipedia (2020, November 1). Monkey Selfie Copyright Dispute. https://en.wikipedia.org/wiki/Monkey_selfie_copyright_dispute.

6 Privacy, Data, and International Law

> *The growth of online platforms in recent years raises important questions about applying the ideals of the First Amendment to modern communications technology.*

—United States Magistrate Judge Laurel Beeler, quoting President Donald J. Trump, Executive Order 13925,
WeChat Users v. Trump (2020a, p. 33)

In 2016, Terry Gene Bollea, who became famous as wrestler Hulk Hogan, won an initial $140 million invasion of privacy jury award against Gawker Media, a celebrity gossip site, for its 2012 decision to post a two-minute clip (including ten seconds of explicit sexual conduct) from a 30-minute sex tape. In "Even for a Minute, Watching Hulk Hogan have Sex in a Canopy Bed is Not Safe for Work but Watch Anyway," Gawker drove audience views through the click bait. The $115 million in compensatory ($55 million economic and $60 million emotional distress) and $25 million in punitive damages was later settled for $31 million after Gawker filed for bankruptcy. The lawsuit had been partially bankrolled in a successful legal retaliation over Gawker's 2017 coverage of a billionaire's personal and professional life, the site reported at the time:

> After nearly fourteen years of operation, Gawker.com will be shutting down next week. The decision to close Gawker comes days after Univision successfully bid $135 million for Gawker Media's six other websites, and three months after the Silicon Valley billionaire Peter Thiel revealed his clandestine legal campaign against the company.
>
> (Trotter, 2016, para. 1)

Thiel's financial support falls under a growing field of **third-party litigation funding** (TPLF), also called litigation finance (Gewolb & Marra, 2019). Proposed state and federal law would align with some courts that have demanded funding transparency within all lawsuits (Pavia, 2019, paras. 6–7).

Gawker was known for its sensationalized celebrity gossip that frequently pushed the boundaries of First Amendment law and ethics. In the *Gawker* case, Bollea sent the site a cease-and-desist order to remove the video, but Gawker's editor refused. The legal case began with an unsuccessful request for an injunction to remove the 2006 video based on copyright over Bollea having "consensual" sex with the estranged wife of Florida "shock jock" radio personality Bubba "the Love Sponge" (*Bollea v. Gawker Media*, 2012, p. 1327). He apparently had recorded, labeled and saved the video, but it was unclear how Gawker obtained it. Bollea described the events on *The Howard Stern Show*, and Gawker defended its action as newsworthy under the First Amendment.

Thiel, a prominent Silicon Valley investor had been targeted by Gawker's *Valleywag* blog, which published the story that "Peter Thiel is totally gay, people" (Sorkin, 2016, para. 4). Thiel obsessively plotted to destroy Gawker and used "litigation finance" to help fund Bollea, who "didn't quite have the resources to do this alone" (para. 7). Thiel's view was that: "The way I've thought about this is that Gawker has been a singularly terrible bully" (para. 10). There has been criticism of the tactic of creating funds to pay for expensive lawsuits and Thiel's assets were protected under Florida law during Gawker bankruptcy proceedings (Thompson, 2018; *In re Gawker Media*, 2017). Thiel, a venture capitalist who cofounded PayPal, said Gawker aimed to ruin his and his friends' lives by outing him as gay. Celebrities also had made complaints about Gawker publication of nude photographs.

Invasion of privacy may rise to a criminal level, such as the case of Playboy model Dani Mathers who took a Snapchat photo and body-shamed a naked 70-year-old woman at a LA Fitness gym shower area changing room. Mathers (@missdanimathers), 29 at the time, apologized but was later charged and pleaded no contest to an invasion of privacy misdemeanor count (Chappell, 2017; Gajanan, 2016). She was later sentenced to 30 hours of community service removing graffiti, and placed on three years of probation (Columbia Global Freedom of Expression, 2017). The "If I can't unsee this then you can't either" social media post cost Mathers her job as a radio host (para. 3). She avoided up to six months in jail, however, and California lawmakers responded by increasing fines for "nude or partially nude photos" (para. 5). At this writing, Mathers' celebrity career declined after the case. The former Playmate of the Year and actress had 436,000 Instagram followers, but she had not landed any major roles since the case.

Privacy began as a right "to be let alone" from news photographers and media coverage, but it evolved with the rise of **computer-mediated communication** (CMC) in the 1990s, social networks in the decade that followed and then big data surveillance techniques: "In recent years the privacy issue has frequently arisen ... in the context of ... social media giants and their data collection and sales practices" (Terilli, Jr. & Splichal, 2020, p. 249). Social media communication technology increasingly is deploying facial recognition as an easy way to establish and maintain data security. However, rising "authoritarian" political powers also view facial recognition technologies as new tracking tools: "Unfettered deployment of this technology has particularly significant implications for privacy rights, free association, and even freedom of movement" (Cagle, 2020, para 4).

Concern over how new technologies offer the potential to invade personal privacy can be traced to late 19th-century urbanization, industrialization and mass media (Westin, 1967). U.S. state tort laws allow a harmed individual to seek damages from another under an invasion of privacy claim. Terry Bollea, for example, used Florida law to sue Gawker Media for disclosure of embarrassing private facts. Courts may judge what a reasonable person would find sensational and highly offensive, such as sexual or other intimate details of home life through words or images, published without written or oral consent (*Cohen v. Cowles Media*, 1991). Individuals experiencing emotional distress from disclosure of private information may claim an injury, but the First Amendment protects a public interest by balancing a right to legally obtained newsworthy information (*Cox Broadcasting v. Cohn*, 1975). Generally, the tort has not been extended to corporations that have a right to protect trade secrets and **confidentiality** by requiring nondisclosure agreements (NDAs).

Individual privacy may include protection from physical intrusion onto private property, as well as using technology to gather information and invade personal solitude. However, due to its massive size, Facebook may be considered a "quasi-public" place: "The public sphere almost certainly includes widely accessible Web sites, including many social networks" (Terilli, Jr. & Splichal, 2020, p. 254).

Social media privacy settings for a personal page or group could impact the outcome of an intrusion claim because an expectation of privacy may be raised in the physical world by erecting a privacy fence or closing window shades. The use of drone or Google Earth video presents thorny questions about what is considered in plain view from the sky and how much homeowners must raise privacy expectation by having patio roofs, umbrellas and other structures that obscure a view. Photographs and video are a social media content staple, so there is an increased likelihood of future legal disputes.

A visitor trespassing on private property must have permission to enter, but technologies offer tools to invade solitude that blur traditional boundaries. The use of powerful cameras and lenses extend human ability to see and hear, and privacy claims can be made when these are used to listen into conversation within zone of privacy around a private home or organization that could not otherwise be seen or heard. This can be contrasted with public sidewalks, streets, parks and other places that have no expectation of privacy. However, some privacy protection was extended to use of mobile phones on federal land (Video Voyeurism Prevention Act, 2004). A social media photograph or video could be actionable if it unwittingly includes a stranger in the background who does not wish to be included. Without implied or explicit consent, the content creator could face legal action.

There are other less common invasion of privacy claims, such as **false light** privacy that aligns with claims in defamation law. However, there must be a showing of the heightened **actual malice** standard of **reckless disregard** through serious doubts about truth (*Time, Inc. v. Hill*, 1967). Internet and social media communication sources for stories also created evolving actual malice standards that suggest the need for caution (Chow, 2013).

This may even be extended to a fictionalized account in which real names were changed on a script. In commercial content, an individual also may claim appropriation of a name, likeness, image or other identifiable **branding** without consent and payment. Celebrities, such as social media influencers, hold property to their likeness and there can be legal disputes over a right to publicity in, for example, advertising. This may extend to impersonation designed to look and sound like a celebrity in order to avoid paying them for the commercial work.

Social media celebrity influence on Instagram, TikTok and other sites is produced within a complex structure of entertainment industry agents and companies. West of Hudson Group, for example, "operates a network of content houses where many prominent young influencers live" and the "management" company claims a cut of branded content revenue in exchange for free Los Angeles mansion rent (Lorenz, Eavis, & Phillips, 2020, paras. 2–3). A newly formed Clubhouse

Media Group is selling stock (para. 8). Apparently, the houses use internal drama and conflict to pitch reality television show ideas. There is a need to examine contract law in this emerging area, as well as the ethical issues related to potential exploitation of young creative talent.

The breadth and depth of monetized social media influence is likely to spawn future case law. It also includes the recording and posting of video on social media that appropriates performance rights to a unique act (*Zacchini v. Scripps Howard Broadcasting*, 1977). It has become so difficult to enforce prohibition of concert recordings that, before the pandemic, many performers required all mobile phones to be collected and held during a show.

There is also a long history of government invasion of individual privacy rights that continues as an international problem. Al-Jazeera journalists, for example, were "targeted by advanced spyware in an attack likely linked to the governments of Saudi Arabia and the United Arab Emirates" (Debre, 2020, para. 1). The University of Toronto Citizen Lab reported that malware "that infected the personal phones of 36 journalists, producers, anchors and executives at Al-Jazeera back to the Israel-based NSO Group, which has been widely condemned for selling spyware to repressive governments" (para. 2). A so-called "zero-click vulnerability" hacking of iMessage accessed private data via "push notifications alone" (para. 3). International law attempts to protect a basic human right of privacy, but enforcement is difficult when government spyware disregards law and ethics.

HISTORY OF U.S. PRIVACY LAW

British common law expressed the view that the king could not enter a home without invitation and this was extended to the idea that U.S. law enforcement required a warrant and evidence of probable cause. For nongovernment entities, such as journalists and social media users or **nongovernmental organizations** (NGOs), philosophy advanced within the states in varying degrees. Cooley (1888) and then Warren and Brandeis (1890) advanced the privacy concept that eventually made it into American law as a right "to be let alone" (*Olmstead v. United States*, 1928, p. 478). Prosser (1960) and Bloustein (1964) debated specific privacy categories that developed into U.S. law: intrusion on seclusion or solitude; public disclosure of private facts (Stewart & Littau, 2016); false light; and appropriation of persona for commercial exploitation (Lipschultz, 1988). Courts have balanced the embarrassing nature of disclosing private facts, the newsworthiness of the information and the level of decency within new details (*Sidis v. F. R. Publishing Corp.*, 1940). Another aspect of privacy law is commercialization of a persona, and there is case law about appropriation of a right of publicity (*Virgil v. Time, Inc.*, 1975).

Surveillance and collection of data by the government is limited by a Fourth Amendment proximate zone of privacy that has been created to protect individual space (*Katz v. United States,* 1967). Federal statute law also clarifies protection of private computer data, such as health or educational records from illegal interception (Electronic Communications Privacy Act of 1986; HIPAA, 1996). Further, the post-9/11 Patriot Act relaxed government restrictions on searching emails of suspected terrorists (Terilli & Splichal, 2014, p. 315). Social media and all Internet data use a **packet switching** structure of data pieces that move quickly from a source to a destination point where the chunks are reassembled. Searches, then, involve complex tools that intercept and make sense of data.

The National Security Agency (NSA) PRISM program surveillance of online and social media communication disclosed by Wikileaks and international news media lacked safeguards to protect individual privacy because "national security" is frequently a vague and overbroad justification. Social media users disclose a vast amount of private information that is stored as data, and this further erodes personal privacy protection (Feldman, 2012), but collection and distribution by platforms is not an absolute right (*Lane v. Facebook, Inc.*, 2012; *Moreno v. Hanford Sentinel, Inc.*, 2009). A settlement in *Lane* was based on the lack of explicit consent that users had given to Facebook. Their Beacon program shared data that connected Facebook use to visits at external websites. Clearly, the business purpose of Facebook, as well as the parent company's Instagram and other apps, is to show how clicks drive traffic to commercial sites that convert sales of products and services. This use of big data continues with revised terms of service that include user consent, but the law has yet to align with rapid technological innovation and its ever-changing definition of terms (Nelson & Simek, 2013). Contextual data analysis of chatbot and human content suggest a need to develop ethical reviews that could protect personal privacy (Kollanyi, Howard, & Woolley, 2016; Neely, 2016). Commercial sale of personal data remains a concern that extends from social media sites to messaging platforms (Gibbs, 2017; Lipp, 2016). Some users incorrectly assert, for example, that they can leave Facebook and stay on Messenger to protect their privacy. To the contrary, new legal and ethical protection is needed over data collection, processing, analysis, storage and sale.

The Fourth Amendment constitutional privacy rights limit government search and seizure, including data stored on our social media pages. Historically, government collection of member lists, and telephone wiretaps, were limited under the Fourth Amendment (*Katz v. United States*, 1967; *NAACP v. Alabama*, 1958). Clearly, Facebook groups and individual site activity should be protected from warrantless search by local, state and federal law enforcement officers. While the Fourth Amendment protects individuals and corporations, individuals have more extensive personal privacy rights over their information collected by the government, but potentially publicly accessible through the Freedom of Information Act (FOIA, 1967; see also *FCC v. AT&T*, 2011). In general, the federal government has placed limits on access to personal information (Privacy Act, 1974). For example, Family Educational Privacy Act (FERPA, 1992) amendments protect student records at colleges and universities receiving federal funding, but make public campus crime records. Similarly, the Health Insurance Portability and Accountability Act (HIPAA, 2003) protects individual health record data privacy. An education or health professional posting student or patient private information in a social media post would violate federal law.

There is a patchwork of federal law since the 1980s that impacts government computer information and illegal interception of messages (Electronic Communications Privacy Act, ECPA, 1986). Personally identifiable information, such as web searches or social media clicks, may be subject to laws and regulation. Much of the current discussion about the power of Google, Facebook, Twitter and Apple to collect and monetize user data touches on the lack of respect for personal privacy.

NATIONAL AND INTERNATIONAL POLITICS

PRISM, a U.S. National Security Agency (NSA) code-named program, has scraped Internet data, including social media communication. Google and other companies were forced to turn data over to the government under Foreign Intelligence Surveillance Court (FISA, 2008) orders based on specific searches. Critics claimed that encrypted stored data should have been protected from secret government probes. The program began near the end of President George W. Bush's administration and grew under Barack Obama before the Edward Snowden leaks and news reporting in 2013 disclosed information about it. PRISM partners were apparently paid for some of the data. FISA Section 702 used national security and the threat of terrorism as justification to monitor communication, including telephone call records, in and out of the United States. For U.S. citizens, government data access requires a court-ordered **search warrant**.

In Germany and other countries with strict data privacy law, PRISM was criticized for its potential to abuse personal data for political reasons (Somaskanda, 2013). German law makes it illegal to "register and store communications data," "tap phone conversations," and broadly monitor more than 10 percent of "international communication" (para. 21). News reporting by the *Guardian* and *Washington Post* helped spark strengthening of data privacy through GDPR in the European Union (EU) and state laws in the U.S.A. (Overdorf, 2013).

In 2020, as Donald Trump widened the trade war gap between the U.S.A. and China, the president attempted to use his authority to threaten TikTok, WeChat and other apps connected to China. In the case of TikTok, he agreed to a deal with Oracle and Walmart for U.S. data management and protection, but a final agreement remained unsettled after a key deadline (Yaffe-Bellany & Banjo, 2020) was missed. The president's executive order, an injunction against enforcing it, and continuing case, however, left an uncertain future after Trump lost the election.

Box 6.1 Trump Executive Order and Legal Fallout

President Donald Trump issued Executive Order 13873 (2019) declaring a national emergency based on the threat of foreign control over information and communication technologies. That order was renewed without specific threats, but in the course of a pandemic (Federal Register, 2020).

Executive Order 13492 (2020) attempted to use the International Emergency Economic Powers Act (IEEPA), the National Emergencies Act and other statute law to block TikTok as an app from China that "continues to threaten the national security, foreign policy, and economy of the United States" (para. 2). The secretary of commerce was directed to identify transactions, and owner ByteDance was ordered to divest itself from the U.S. TikTok app.

At issue was control over personal data within a vague national security threat, but some suggested that the president was responding to anti-Trump posts weeks before the 2020 election that he ultimately lost. The U.S. Department of Commerce (2020) published prohibited transactions that included TikTok app downloads. However, TikTok won a preliminary injunction against enforcement (*Marland et al. v. Trump et al.* (2020). The district court prevented enforcement of the president's order on procedural grounds. Following the election, the Commerce Department gave notice that the administrative agency would comply with the court and continue its legal fight to enforce the order.

In *Douglas Marland et al. v. Trump Memorandum* (2020), a comedian, fashion designer and musician and two others represented millions of TikTok users and sued the president in the Eastern District of

Pennsylvania. The plaintiffs argued that First Amendment protected speech was violated, and the regulation was overbroad and not narrowly tailored. Additionally, plaintiffs cited First Amendment law to argue that the order was an impermissible prior restraint. The order had not legally applied time, place and manner restrictions, offered no procedural safeguards and infringed on the rights to express and receive information. Plaintiffs quoted the *Packingham* (2017) decision in which the U.S. Supreme Court acknowledged the importance of the Internet and social media in providing a public forum. In this sense, the case is about both data and government censorship.

Sources

Douglas Marland et al. v. Trump et al. Memorandum, No. 20-cv-4597 (2020, October 30). http://docs.dpaq.de/16978-show_temp.pl-102.pdf.

Executive Order 13492 (2020, August 6). Addressing the Threat Posed by TikTok, and Taking Additional Steps to Address the National Emergency with Respect to the Information and Communications Technology and Services Supply Chain, 85 Fed. Reg. 48,637. https://www.federalregister.gov/documents/2020/08/11/2020-17699/addressing-the-threat-posed-by-tiktok-and-taking-additional-steps-to-address-the-national-emergency.

Federal Register (2020, May 13). Continuation of the National Emergency with Respect to Securing the Information and Communications Technology and Services Supply Chain, 85 Fed. Reg. 28,321.

Marland et al. v. Trump et al., 20-4597 (E.D. Pennsylvania, 2020).

Packingham v. North Carolina, 582 U.S. ___, 137 S. Ct. 1730 (2017)

U.S. Department of Commerce (2020, November 9).15 CFR Chapter VII. https://www.commerce.gov/sites/default/files/2020-11/signedTikTok-FRNoticeofEDPaPreliminaryInjunction10302020RP.pdf.

TikTok was not the only Chinese app under attack by the Trump Administration. Chinese WeChat users went to court and won a temporary restraining order (TRO) from a judge.

Box 6.2 U.S. Magistrate WeChat Ruling

U.S. WECHAT USERS ALLIANCE, et al., Plaintiffs,
v. DONALD J. TRUMP, et al., Defendants
UNITED STATES DISTRICT COURT NORTHERN DISTRICT OF CALIFORNIA
San Francisco Division, Case No. 20-cv-05910-LB
2020 U.S. Dist. LEXIS 172816 (2020)
ORDER GRANTING MOTION FOR PRELIMINARY INJUNCTION
Re: ECF No. 17 and 48

INTRODUCTION

The plaintiffs are persons in the United States who use WeChat, a messaging, social-media, and mobile-payment app. In this lawsuit, they challenge the constitutionality of Executive Order 13943:

> The plaintiffs claim that the ban (1) violates the First Amendment to the U.S. Constitution, (2) violates the Fifth Amendment, (3) violates the Religious Freedom Restoration Act, 42 U.S.C. § 2000bb(1)(a), (4) was not a lawful exercise of the President's and the Secretary's authority under the International Economic Emergency Powers Act ("IEEPA") …
>
> … even if the prohibited transactions are content-neutral time-place-or-manner restrictions, they do not survive intermediate scrutiny because the complete ban is not narrowly tailored to address the government's significant interest in national security.
>
> The plaintiffs also contend that they are likely to succeed on the merits of their claims that, by effectively shutting down U.S. users' access to the WeChat app, (1) the President and the Secretary exceeded their authority under IEEPA, (2) the Secretary violated the APA, and (3) the Executive Order is void for **vagueness** (in part) because the government asserts conflicting interpretations of the prohibition's effect …

STATEMENT

1. WeChat

WeChat is a mobile app, developed by the Chinese company Tencent Holdings Ltd., with more than 1.2 billion users worldwide (including more than 100 million users outside of China and 19 million regular users in the

U.S.). It allows its users to send messages, make video and audio calls, and send and receive money, and it also functions as a social-media platform:

2. Executive Orders and Agency Action

2.1 Executive Order 13873 (May 15, 2019)

On May 15, 2019, the President issued an Executive Order finding that "foreign adversaries are increasingly creating and exploiting vulnerabilities in information and communications technology and services, ... in order to commit malicious cyber-enabled actions, including economic and industrial espionage against the United States and its people ..."

2.2 Executive Order 13943 (August 6, 2020)

On August 6, 2020, President Trump issued Executive Order 13943, [and] ... he said that "additional steps must be taken to deal with the national emergency ... declared in [the ICTS Executive Order]" because "the spread in the United States of mobile applications developed and owned by companies in the People's Republic of China [] continues to threaten the national security, foreign policy, and economy of the United States..."

2.3 The President's Statements Before and After the WeChat Order

The plaintiffs point to the President's anti-Chinese statements ...including his remarks about China's responsibility for the COVID-19 pandemic (including calling it the "China virus," the "China flu," and similar names), his reference to China's owning the United States if he is not reelected, and other mocking conduct that the plaintiffs characterize as showing racial animist and aimed at bolstering the President's reelection campaign ...

2.4 The Secretary of Commerce's Implementation of the WeChat Executive Order

On September 18, 2020, the Secretary issued the Identification of Prohibited Transactions, ...

3. The Government's Additional Contentions About National Security

.... the government cited reports identifying Tencent and WeChat as a growing threat and citing an Australian nonpartisan think tank's report ... discussing the attendant risks for censorship in China, the dissemination of propaganda in the Chinese the vulnerabilities that result from, for example, 5G cellular networks ...

4. Procedural History

The plaintiffs filed this lawsuit challenging the WeChat Executive Order on August 21, 2020, before the Secretary identified the prohibited transactions ...

STATUTORY SCHEME

Two statutes provide the authority for Executive Orders: (1) the NEA, 50 U.S.C. §§ 1601– 1651, and (2) the IEEPA, 50 U.S.C. §§ 1701–08:

> ... The IEEPA, enacted in 1977, authorizes the President to exercise his authority during peacetime "to deal with any unusual or extraordinary threat, which has its source in whole or substantial part outside the United States, to the national security, foreign policy, or economy of the United States, if the President declares a national emergency with respect to such threat." 50 U.S.C. § 1701(a) ...

STANDARD OF REVIEW

The standards for a TRO and a preliminary injunction are the same ... A movant must demonstrate (1) a likelihood of success on the merits, (2) a likelihood of irreparable harm that would result if an injunction were not issued, (3) the balance of equities tips in favor of the plaintiff, and (4) an injunction is in the public interest ...

ANALYSIS

The plaintiffs contend that they are likely to succeed on the merits of their claims that — by effectively shutting down the WeChat app — (1) the government violated the First Amendment, and, at least, they have raised serious questions going to the merits of the claim, (2) the President and the Secretary of Commerce exceeded their authority under the IEEPA ...

1. Likelihood of Success on the Merits: First Amendment

The plaintiffs contend that the prohibited transactions will result in shutting down WeChat, a public square for the Chinese-American and Chinese-speaking community in the U.S. that is effectively their only means of communication with their community. This, they say, is a prior restraint on their speech that does not survive strict scrutiny. Also, even if the effect of the prohibited transactions is a content-neutral time-place-or-manner restriction, it does not survive intermediate scrutiny because the effective ban on WeChat use is not narrowly tailored to address neutral restrictions are based on national-security concerns and survive intermediate scrutiny. On this record, the plaintiffs have shown serious questions going to the merits of their First Amendment claim ...

... Certainly, the government's overarching national-security interest is significant. But on this record — while the government has established that China's activities raise significant national- security concerns — it has put in scant little evidence that its effective ban of WeChat for all U.S. users addresses those concerns ...

2. Likelihood of Success on the Merits: IEEPA

The plaintiffs contend that the President and the Secretary exceeded their authority under the IEEPA because the IEEPA does not give the President authority to regulate or prohibit "any postal, telegraphic, telephonic, or other personal communication, which does not involve a transfer of anything of value ..."

3. Likelihood of Success on the Merits: APA

... On this record, the court cannot conclude that the plaintiffs are likely to succeed on their claim.

4. Likelihood of Success on the Merits: Fifth Amendment

The plaintiffs contend that the WeChat Executive Order's prohibited transactions — as identified by the Secretary — are void for vagueness because the government has provided conflicting interpretations of the effect of the prohibitions ...

5. Remaining Winter Elements

The remaining elements are a likelihood of irreparable harm if an injunction does not issue, the balance of equities tips in the plaintiff's favor, and an injunction is in the public interest ...

... Finally, at the hearing, the government cited a *Washington Post* article contending that a ban of WeChat is a net positive for human rights: "WeChat it is a closed system that keeps its 1.2 billion users in a parallel universe where they can communicate as long as they don't cross the lines, and banning it might eventually strengthen the voices of the Chinese diaspora." ... the federal government — based on its foreign-policy and national- security interests — may not want to countenance (or reward) the Chinese government's banning apps outside of the Chinese government's control and, more generally, censoring or punishing free speech in China or abroad. But as the President said recently in Executive Order 13925, Free speech is the bedrock of American democracy. Our Founding Fathers protected this sacred right with the First Amendment to the Constitution. The freedom to express and debate ideas is the foundation for all of our rights as a free people ...

6. Scope of Relief

The injunctive relief must remedy the harm ...

CONCLUSION

The court grants the plaintiffs' motion for a nationwide injunction against the implementation of Executive Order 13,943 ...

... IT IS SO ORDERED.
Dated: September 19, 2020.
LAUREL BEELER
United States Magistrate Judge
United States District Court Northern District of California

The U.S. Department of Justice, a week after this ruling to delay the Department of Commerce WeChat ban, again requested the court to stop Apple and Google app downloads while the case is being heard. An Associated Press (2020) story suggested that the 19 million daily active users and their private data in the hands of the Chinese government were a threat to national security.

Sources

Associated Press (2020, September 25). Justice Department Seeks Immediate Ban on WeChat in US, Associated Press. https://apnews.com/article/china-archive-united-states-cbf54c5fa13f2ff6dbdbb408115af7be.

U.S. WeChat Users Alliance, et al., Plaintiffs, v. Donald J. Trump, et al., Defendants (2020a, September 19). 2020 LEXIS U.S. Dist. 172816. United States District Court Northern District of California San Francisco Division. Case No. 20-cv-05910-LB. https://www.courtlistener.com/recap/gov.uscourts.cand.364733/gov.uscourts.cand.364733.59.0.pdf.

Two months later, Judge Beeler denied the government's motion to stay her order (*U.S. WeChat Users Alliance, et al., Plaintiffs, v. Donald J. Trump, et al., Defendants* (2020b). The government provided additional redacted national security information to the court, but Judge Beeler again applied First Amendment law: "The government's new evidence does not meaningfully alter its earlier submissions" (p. 25). The court accepted potential security risks, while concluding that "the government's prohibited transactions are not narrowly tailored to address the government's significant interest" (p. 25). The First Amendment rights of social media app users provide one basis for understanding emerging law. Another foundation can be found within privacy law.

UNDERSTANDING PRIVACY LAW AND ETHICS

Mobile phone data make it possible to locate a user at any moment, and government plus business collection mean that personal privacy can be continuously invaded. The collection and analysis of "Big Data" is about control and storage of it (Carter & Lee, 2016; Youm & Park, 2016). The European Union (EU) "**right to be forgotten**" (RTBF) law has empowered users to remove publicly available data through access that leads to a "right to have it rectified" (p. 275, quoting EU Charter, Art. 8(2)). The U.S.A. has maintained data surveillance for national security purposes (Stoycheff, 2016), but tracking location and movement invade privacy (Lee, 2013).

Mills (2015) made a human dignity argument about the pervasiveness in public use of personal data by the press, bloggers and social media users. At a fundamental level, the "freedom" of free expression depends on protection from pernicious surveillance of personal activities. An expectation of privacy, however, is central to the tort of invasion of privacy that allows for civil lawsuits in publication of intimate private facts and disclosure of sensitive information. A patchwork of state privacy and libel law are frequently used in tandem for cases of provably false information. A separate context is government collection of personal data that may violate the Fourth Amendment constitutional right. In this sense, privacy is one of those areas in which the First and Fourth Amendments may clash (Humbach, 2012). At the same time, national and international law have the potential to demand privacy rights based on fundamental human dignity.

Commercial sites, such as Facebook and Twitter, have fiduciary responsibilities to their stockholders and these cloud their interest in protecting user privacy within their massive pools of data (Allen, 2013). The symbiotic relationship between free social media sites and their users who are "giving away" personal data is not conducive to a "moral relationship" or "partnerships in ethical goodness" (pp. 847, 865). In the absence of a healthy paid subscriber arrangement, it falls to regulation of fairness and equity within the relationship.

The Federal Trade Commission (FTC, 2012) raised data security and sale concern over product design, consumer simplicity and clarity and company transparency (paras. 4–6). While U.S. regulators identified issues about a consumer right to delete data, the EU RTBF model has not advanced. A Facebook or Instagram user, for example, may "delete" a photograph, but the company still has it stored on its servers, and there is no transparency mechanism to view folders and files.

Class action lawsuits against Facebook, LinkedIn, and other social media companies have resulted in relatively small settlements to individual users for companies failing to adequately disclose how personal data were being used. Self-regulation comes through frequent revision of end-user agreements, pressure from U.S. state and international governments and public pressure to reform amid confusion over privacy law and ethics (Schwarz, 2015; Viera, 2015). EU privacy rules led Facebook to remove Instagram and Messenger features that automatically scanned for child abuse (Martin, 2020): "A recent change to the ePrivacy Directive, that was designed to prevent companies such as Facebook mining message content and metadata for advertising purposes, has instead resulted in the company turning a number of features off" (para. 2). The privacy rules also prompted Facebook to halt used of augmented reality (AR) filters, stickers and other features. Facebook hoped it could bring back features that balance social media use and EU privacy rules.

OTHER PERSONAL DATA

The U.S. federal government has been slow to respond, but state laws also are important. In Illinois, for example, a biometrics data privacy law allowed for a settlement with Facebook over collection and use of facial recognition data. Other states, such as California, led the way in constructing stronger data privacy frameworks. The California Consumer Privacy Act of 2018 (CCPA) offers consumers some control over data that businesses collect by making explicit a right to know, right to delete, right to opt out and right to nondiscrimination. The state attorney general and California Department of Justice interpret and enforce business disclosure of personal information and data rights.

The California Constitution was amended in 1972 to add privacy as an "inalienable" right of state residents. In 2018, the lawmakers added language to give consumers a right to opt out (but not opt in) of personal data collection. States around the U.S.A. have begun to consider passage of model legislation that makes explicit a right of data privacy, including biometric data.

Box 6.3 California Privacy Statute

TITLE 1.81.5. California Consumer Privacy Act
of 2018 [1798.100 - 1798.199]
(Title 1.81.5 added by Stats. 2018, Ch. 55, Sec. 3.)

1798.100.

- **a.** A consumer shall have the right to request that a business that collects a consumer's personal information disclose to that consumer the categories and specific pieces of personal information the business has collected.
- **b.** ...A business shall not collect additional categories of personal information or use personal information collected for additional purposes without providing the consumer with notice consistent with this section.
- **c.** A business shall provide the information specified in subdivision (a) to a consumer only upon receipt of a verifiable consumer request.
- **d.** A business that receives a verifiable consumer request from a consumer to access personal information shall promptly take steps to disclose and deliver, free of charge to the consumer, the personal information required by this section ...
- **e.** This section shall not require a business to retain any personal information collected for a single, one-time transaction, if such information is not sold or retained by the business or to reidentify or otherwise link information that is not maintained in a manner that would be considered personal information.

(Amended by Stats. 2019, Ch. 757, Sec. 1. (AB 1355) Effective *January 1, 2020.*

Source: California Consumer Privacy Act (CCPA, 2018, 2020). http://leginfo.legislature.ca.gov/faces/codes_dis.

The push for statute law to protect data privacy has led some social media companies to employ self-regulation by use of new tools, but effectiveness is always a question. Facebook Research (2020) turned to the academic community and funded five behavioral research teams:

> **Deploying visual interventions for users of varying digital literacy levels**
>
> Xinru Page (Brigham Young University), Brian Smith (Brigham Young University), Mainack Mondal (India Institute of Technology, Kharagpur), Norman Makoto Su (Indiana University Bloomington)
>
> **Empowering under-resourced parents in teens' social media privacy education**
>
> Natalie Bazarova, Dan Cosley, Ellen Wenting Zou, Leslie Park, Martha Brandt (Cornell University)
>
> **Helping people manage privacy settings using social influences**
>
> Jason Hong, Laura Dabbish (Carnegie Mellon University)
>
> **Measuring privacy across cultural, political and expressive contexts**
>
> Dmitry Epstein (Hebrew University of Jerusalem), Aysenur Dal (Bilkent University), Elizabeth Stoycheff (Wayne State University), Erik Nisbet (Northwestern University), Kelly Quinn (University of Illinois Chicago), Olga Kamenchuk (Northwestern University), Thorsten Faas (Free University of Berlin)
>
> **Privacy personas in the MENA region: A large-scale analysis of 21 countries**
>
> Bernard J. Jansen (Hamad Bin Khalifa University), Joni Salminen (Qatar Computing Research Institute), Justin D. Martin (Northwestern University in Qatar), Kareem Darwish (Qatar Computing Research Institute), Lene Nielsen (IT University of Copenhagen), Soon-gyo Jung (Qatar Computing Research Institute), Yin (David) Yang (Hamad Bin Khalifa University) (paras. 7–11)

The funded projects addressed media literacy differences across the globe. Facebook, Twitter and other sites have responded to misinformation and disinformation campaigns with labels, but how individuals manage their data and privacy also is an important concern. There is a newfound recognition that cultural, political and expressive contexts vary and may be very important within information processing and persuasion. Increasingly invasive technologies, such as biometrics and the associated personal data, present new legal and practical challenges. Part of the difficulty for lawmakers is to be able to anticipate what data Facebook and other social media companies might collect, as well as how they plan to use the personal data.

ILLINOIS BIOMETRICS DATA PROTECTION

The Illinois Biometric Information Privacy Act (BIPA) offered a unique attempt to protect consumer data, and it has spawned lawsuits at large settlements based on statutory fines imposed for each violation. There are legal questions about how the state statute applies across state lines, as well as its impact on other existing laws (Nolan, Weiner, & Sutherland, 2020). Under the Illinois law, a "biometric identifier" is defined as "a retina or iris scan, fingerprint, voiceprint, or scan of hand or face geometry." Clearly, Facebook's collection and use of facial recognition data for **tagging** and other purposes falls under the scope of the state statute.

Box 6.4 Illinois Biometrics Law

CIVIL LIABILITIES

(740 ILCS 14/) Biometric Information Privacy Act.

(740 ILCS 14/1)

Sec. 1. Short title. This Act may be cited as the Biometric Information Privacy Act.

(Source: P.A. 95-994, eff. 10-3-08.)

(740 ILCS 14/5)

Sec. 5. Legislative findings; intent. The General Assembly finds all of the following:

a. The use of biometrics is growing in the business and security screening sectors and appears to promise streamlined financial transactions and security screenings.
b. Major national corporations have selected the City of Chicago and other locations in this State as pilot testing sites for new applications of biometric-facilitated financial transactions, including finger-scan technologies at grocery stores, gas stations, and school cafeterias.
c. Biometrics are unlike other unique identifiers that are used to access finances or other sensitive information ... [they] are biologically unique to the individual; therefore, once compromised, the individual has no recourse, is at heightened risk for identity theft, and is likely to withdraw from biometric-facilitated transactions.

d. An overwhelming majority of members of the public are weary of the use of biometrics when such information is tied to finances and other personal information.
e. Despite limited State law regulating the collection, use, safeguarding, and storage of biometrics, many members of the public are deterred from partaking in biometric identifier-facilitated transactions.
f. The full ramifications of biometric technology are not fully known.
g. The public welfare, security, and safety will be served by regulating the collection, use, safeguarding, handling, storage, retention, and destruction of biometric identifiers and information.

(Source: P.A. 95-994, eff. 10-3-08.)

(740 ILCS 14/20)
Sec. 20. Right of action ... A prevailing party may recover for each violation:

1. against a private entity that negligently violates a provision of this Act, liquidated damages of $1,000 or **actual damages**, whichever is greater;
2. against a private entity that intentionally or recklessly violates a provision of this Act, liquidated damages of $5,000 or actual damages, whichever is greater;
3. reasonable attorneys' fees and costs, including expert witness fees and other litigation expenses; and
4. other relief, including an injunction, as the State or federal court may deem appropriate.

(Source: P.A. 95-994, eff. 10-3-08.)

(740 ILCS 14/25)
Sec. 25. Construction.

a. Nothing in this Act shall be construed to impact the admission or discovery of biometric identifiers and biometric information in any action of any kind in any court, or before any tribunal, board, agency, or person.

b. Nothing in this Act shall be construed to conflict with the X-Ray Retention Act, the federal Health Insurance Portability and Accountability Act of 1996 and the rules promulgated under either Act.
c. Nothing in this Act shall be deemed to apply in any manner to a financial institution or an affiliate ...
d. Nothing in this Act shall be construed to conflict with the Private Detective, Private Alarm, Private Security, Fingerprint Vendor, and Locksmith Act of 2004 and the rules promulgated thereunder.
e. Nothing in this Act shall be construed to apply to a contractor, subcontractor, or agent of a State agency or local unit of government when working for that State agency or local unit of government.

(Source: P.A. 95-994, eff. 10-3-08.)

Source: Biometric Information Privacy Act, 740 ILCS 14/1 (BIPA, 2008). https://www.ilga.gov/ legislation/ilcs/ilcs3.asp?ActID=3004&ChapterID=57.

Under Illinois law, remedies include $1,000 fines for each violation and $5,000 fines for "reckless or intentional" cases. In *Bryant v. Compass Grp. USA, Inc.* (2020), failure to follow BIPA (2008) by obtaining written consent before collecting fingerprints was found to be an invasion of privacy. The Seventh Circuit Court of Appeals found that consumer protection is based on privacy harms, such as identity theft, however, the Second Circuit found that sitting for a 15-minute face scan to use in online gaming avatars was a form of consent (*Santana v. Take-Two Interactive Software, Inc.*, 2017). Increasingly, consumers must take responsibility for reading consent forms before accepting the terms.

ETHICAL FRAMEWORKS AND ISSUES

Data privacy laws attempt to address fundamental human rights issues. Transparency, informed consent and disclosure are important ethical considerations. Employers have been sued over employee biometric data collected and stored, including through third-party vendors' systems to track worker productivity. Employee use of personal mobile phones during work breaks to access Facebook and other social media sites could be tracked. The web of companies that collect data and profile individuals also presents the concern expressed by the Illinois statute – unauthorized sale of data. While some state laws have recognized the economic value of personal data, none explicitly empowers social media users to "bank" their data – that is, deposit and withdraw it. This would lead to rigorous opt-in and opt-out rules.

Box 6.5 Thought Leader Holly Kathleen Hall

Holly Kathleen Hall

Photograph by Travis Clayton

On July 15, 2020, Twitter underwent a major security breach when hackers targeted about 130 high-profile accounts and tweeted from 45 of them including those of Joe Biden, Barack Obama, Tesla CEO Elon Musk, Bill Gates, Jeff Bezos and Apple (Lerman & Denham, 2020; Wong & Paul, 2020).

"BIT-CON"

Hackers tweeted a bitcoin deal from the accounts in which followers were informed that if they transferred cryptocurrency to the stated bitcoin wallet, they would get double the money in return:

> "I am giving back to the community. All Bitcoin sent to the address below will be sent back doubled! If you sent $1,000, I will send back $2,000. Only doing this for 30 minutes!" This was followed by the bitcoin wallet address and "Enjoy!".
>
> (Wong & Paul, 2020, para. 4)

The hackers also accessed the direct messages of 36 users and downloaded Twitter data from seven users (Kelion, 2020). As a result of the hack, there were more than 400 bitcoin transfers worth over $100,000 (Lerman & Denham, 2020).

The first account to have been compromised was Musk's around 4 pm EST. The hackers posted the bitcoin message. As those messages were deleted, however, new bitcoin scam tweets would appear (Statt, 2020). At about 5:45 pm EST, Twitter first publicly acknowledged the situation, announcing they were investigating and taking steps to remedy the situation (Statt, 2020). The majority of hacked accounts were all posting the same bitcoin wallet address (Statt, 2020).

One of the steps Twitter took included blocking new tweets from *every* verified user, whether or not they were compromised, and locking all compromised accounts (Statt, 2020). Remarkably, President Trump's Twitter account was not one that was hacked. Trump's account had special protections in place that may have kept it from becoming another victim of the bitcoin scam (Statt, 2020).

By 8:41 pm EST, most verified accounts were able to tweet again. Twitter CEO Jack Dorsey wrote:

> Tough day for us at Twitter. We all feel terrible this happened. We're diagnosing and will share everything we can when we have a more complete understanding of exactly what happened.
>
> (Statt, 2020, para. 10)

The scam was a combination of "social engineering" and "spear-phishing" targeting Twitter employees and was allegedly perpetrated by a 17-year-old Florida boy. He was aided by a 22-year-old man also from Florida and a 19-year-old from Great Britain (Satter, Paul, & Culliford, 2020).

Social engineering is a tactic that was used in 33 percent of data breaches in 2018 (Crane, 2020). Cybersecurity firm Imperva describes social engineering as "a broad range of malicious activities accomplished through human interactions. It uses psychological manipulation to trick users into making security mistakes or giving away sensitive information" (para. 1). Social engineering can be accomplished via face-to-face interactions, over the phone, SMS text messaging (known as "smishing"), email or a combination of channels. Technical expertise is not necessary. The key to successful social engineering is "exploiting a person rather than technology itself. However, using technology certainly makes pulling off these attacks a lot easier for the cybercriminals who use them" (Crane, 2020, para.10).

One of the most common digital social engineering assaults is "spear-phishing" which Imperva describes as an attack in which the aggressor chooses specific individuals or enterprises and specifically crafts their messages based on characteristics, job positions and contacts belonging to their victims. In the Twitter bitcoin hack, authorities found that Clark used social engineering to convince a Twitter employee that he was a coworker in the IT department. The employee was duped into providing credentials to access the customer service portal (Satter, Paul, & Culliford, 2020). The attack was aided by the number of employees working remotely due to the Covid-19 pandemic. The hackers directed Twitter employees to a fake virtual private network (VPN) page and took their login information in a scam targeting workers at home during the pandemic (Helms, 2020).

Phishing attacks involving internal employees are increasingly getting attention. Twitter has faced issues with internal account management in the past. In 2011, the Federal Trade Commission contended Twitter failed to guard its administrator system and, in 2017, Trump's account was temporarily disabled by an unhappy Twitter employee, which led to the special protections on his account (Geller, 2020). In 2013, hackers gained control of Twitter accounts maintained by the Associated Press and tweeted false information about explosions at the White House that had injured President Obama. Within two minutes of the tweet, the S&P 500 Index lost $136 billion (Vishnoi, Worrachate, & Golden, 2020). And in 2019, two former Twitter employees accessed thousands of users' accounts and supplied information from them to the government of Saudi Arabia (Wong & Paul, 2020).

The main hacker in this instance was arrested and faces 30 **felony** counts, including organized fraud, accessing a computer or electronic device without authority, fraudulent use of personal information and communications fraud (Lerman & Denham, 2020).

The hack uncovered vulnerabilities, especially relating to government leaders who rely on social media platforms for official communication. In addition to government and corporate leaders, government agencies such as the National Weather Service were impacted, as tornado alerts from the NWS were temporarily blocked (Geller, 2020). StopSIMCrime founder Robert Ross called this type of crime a national security risk

(Satter, Paul, & Culliford, 2020). Cybersecurity expert Marcus Hutchins noted the techniques used were simple and easy to replicate (Fischer & Bajak, 2020).

Lawmakers immediately seized on the opportunity to demand more transparency from Twitter (Statt, 2020). Senators requested briefings and more details into the breach and worries mounted regarding the future attacks that could prove vastly more devastating. Senate Intelligence Chairman Mark Warner (D-Va.) noted: "[T]he ability of bad actors to take over accounts, even fleetingly, signals a worrisome vulnerability in this media environment – exploitable not just for scams, but for more impactful efforts to cause confusion, havoc, and political mischief" (Geller, 2020, para. 13). House Intelligence Committee member Jim Himes (D-Conn.) expressed concerns about a hack producing false tweets on election day, the breaching of voter registration databases and meddling with other records (Geller, 2020).

Politicians often tweet about policies and argue with one another over Twitter. The implications of a hacker taking over a politician's or even a media outlet's account and tweeting false and/or incendiary information has the potential to generate all manner of serious global concerns from chaos to war (Helms, 2020). Investors often rely on platforms such as Twitter to glean insights on the markets. An incorrect or misleading statement on Twitter could jeopardize the financial system (Vishnoi, Worrachate, & Golden, 2020).

Social media companies must now take on their responsibilities, along with the government, to guard the public against damage done by this kind of hacking. Platforms such as Twitter will need to rethink how much access employees have to sensitive administrative tools and user accounts. Monitoring for breaches should be continuous (Young & Brown, 2020). Platforms can offer special protections for particularly vulnerable accounts. Google has an Advanced Protection Program for journalists, politicians and others (Geller, 2020). Twitter should do the same.

Imperva (2020) observed that social engineers manipulate human feelings to carry out their attacks and, therefore, recommends caution whenever an email or message creates a sense of alarm or if you are moved by an offer on a website. They offer the following strategies for avoiding falling into the social engineering trap: (1) Do not open emails or attachments from suspicious sources; (2) Use multifactor authentication; (3) Be wary of offers that sound extremely appealing; (4) Keep your antivirus software up to date (paras. 22–25).

Paul Kubler, a cyber security and digital forensics examiner, advocates supplementary training for employees utilizing at least a biannual training geared towards each user group (end-users, IT staff, managers, etc.) to keep them up to date on the latest form of social engineering attacks. In addition, employees should be put to the test by having an outside party conduct a social engineering experiment in order to keep the employees alert and aware (Lord, 2019).

Holly Kathleen Hall is a professor of Strategic Communication at Arkansas State University. She earned her law degree from UALR Bowen School of Law, a postgraduate certificate in data protection and information governance from Northumbria University, and a bachelor's degree in radio-TV news from Arkansas State. She is also accredited in public relations (APR) by the Public Relations Society of America. She is the A-State chapter advisor for Kappa Tau Alpha, a national journalism and mass communication honorary society and served as its national president (2018–2020). Before joining the faculty at A-State, Hall worked professionally in strategic communication for ten years in a variety of industries including healthcare, finance, academia and not-for-profit organizations.

Sources

Crane, C. (2020). Social Engineering Attacks: A Look at Social Engineering Examples in Action. Security Boulevard. https://securityboulevard.com/2020/04/social-engineering-attacks-a-look-at-social-engineering-examples-in-action/.

Imperva (2020). Social Engineering. https://www.imperva.com/learn/application-security/social-engineering-attack/.

Lerman, R. & Denham, H. (2020, July 31). 3 Charged in Massive Twitter Hack, Including Alleged Teenage "Mastermind." *Washington Post.* https://www.washingtonpost.com/technology/2020/07/30/twitter-hack-phone-attack/.

Lord, N. (2019, July 15). Social Engineering Attacks: Common Techniques & How to Prevent an Attack. Digital Guardian Blog. https://digitalguardian.com/blog/social-engineering-attacks-common-techniques-how-prevent-attack.

ONLINE RESOURCES

General Data Protection Regulation (GDPR). https://gdpr-info.eu/.

DISCUSSION QUESTIONS

1. Why is or is not there a need in your state to enact stronger privacy laws? Which specific areas of data privacy concern you?
2. How does the tort of invasion of privacy address emerging technologies? Which specific areas should be addressed in the courts?
3. How does GDPR in the EU go beyond the U.S. approach in terms of protecting privacy? Which approach do you favor? Why?

REFERENCES

Allen, A.L. (2013). An Ethical Duty to Protect One's Own Information Privacy?, *Alabama Law Review*, 64, 845.

Associated Press (2020, September 25). Justice Department seeks immediate ban on WeChat in US, Associated Press. https://apnews.com/article/china-archive-united-states-cbf54c5fa13f2ff6dbdbb408115af7be.

Bartnicki v. Vopper, 532 U.S. 514 (2001).

Biometric Information Privacy Act, 740 ILCS 14/1 (*BIPA*, 2008). https://www.ilga.gov/ legislation/ilcs/ilcs3.asp?ActID=3004&ChapterID=57.

Bloustein, E.J. (1964). Privacy as an Aspect of Human Dignity: An Answer to Dean Prosser, *New York Law Review*, 39, 962.

Bollea v. Gawker Media, 913 F. Supp. 1325 (2012).

Bryant v. Compass Grp. USA, Inc., 958 F.3d (Seventh Cir., 2020),

Cagle, M. (2020, September 24). Facial Recognition and Equity. High Tech Law Institute, Santa Clara University School of Law. https://law.scu.edu/event/facial-recognition-and-equity/.

California Consumer Privacy Act (CCPA, 2018, 2020). http://leginfo.legislature.ca.gov/faces/codes_dis.

Carpenter v. United States, ___ U.S. ___, 138 S. Ct. 2206 (2018).

Carter, E.L. and Lee, L.T. (2016). Information Access and Control in an Age of Big Data. *Journalism & Mass Communication Quarterly*, 93(2), 269–272.

Chappell, B. (2017, May 25). "Playboy" Model Sentenced Over Body-Shaming Woman At Gym. *NPR*. https://www.npr.org/sections/thetwo-way/2017/05/25/ 529999618/playboy-model-sentenced-over-body-shaming-woman-at-gym.

Chow, K. (2013, Fall). Handle with Care: The Evolving Actual Malice Standard and Why Journalists Should Think Twice Before Relying on Internet Sources, *N.Y.U. Journal of Intellectual Property & Entertainment Law*, 3, 53–75.

Cohen v. Cowles Media, 501 U.S. 663 (1991).

Columbia Global Freedom of Expression (2017). The Case of Dani Mathers. Columbia University. https://globalfreedomofexpression.columbia.edu/cases/dani-mathers/.

Cooley, T.M. (1888). *Cooley On Torts*, 2nd edition. p. 29.

Cox Broadcasting Co. v. Cohn, 420 U.S. 469 (1975).

Debre, I. (2020, December 21). Report: Gov't Spyware Targets Phones of Al-Jazeera Reporters. *Associated Press*. https://apnews.com/article/technology-malware-saudi-arabia-united-arab-emirates-dubai-c6cb6fc304aff092a88dd87b5c19e4fe.

Douglas Marland et al. v. Trump et al.Memorandum, No. 20-cv-4597 (2020, October 30). http://docs.dpaq.de/16978-show_temp.pl-102.pdf.

Economist, The (2016, March 26). Tracking Protest Movements, A New Kind of Weather. http://www.economist.com/news/special-report/21695192-social-media-now-play-key-role-collective-action-new-kind-weather.

Electronic Communications Privacy Act (1986). 18 U.S.C. Sec. 2510.

Executive Order 13492 (2020, August 6). https://www.federalregister.gov/documents/2020/08/11/2020-17699/addressing-the-threat-posed-by-tiktok-and-taking-additional-steps-to-address-the-national-emergency.

Facebook Research (2020, November 10). Facebook Announces Winners of the People's Expectations and Experiences With Digital Privacy Research Awards. https://research.fb.com/blog/2020/11/facebook-announces-winners-of-the-peoples-expectations-and-experiences-with-digital-privacy-research-awards/.

Feldman, M.J. (2012, February 28). Is Privacy Dead? *The Huffington Post*. www.huffingtonpost.com/miles-j-feldman/internet-privacy_b_1306701.html.

FISA (2008). Foreign Intelligence Service Act, USA PATRIOT ACT, Protect America Act of 2007. 50 U.S.C. 36 § 1801 et seq.

Fischer, D. and Bajak, F. (2020, August 1). Florida Teen Arrested as Mastermind of Twitter Hack. Associated Press. https://apnews.com/article/ap-top-news-technology-florida-bitcoin-joe-biden-54b798f49591fcea9291ada8689eb026.

FTC (2012, March 26). *FTC Issues Final Commission Report on Protecting Consumer Privacy.* Federal Trade Commission. www.ftc.gov/news-events/press-releases/2012/03/ftc-issues-final-commi ssion-report-protecting-consumer-privacy. [Full report downloaded at: FTC Report: *Protecting Consumer Privacy in an Era of Rapid Change.* www.ftc.gov/sites/default/files/documents/reports/federal-trade-commission-report-protecting-consumer-privacy-era-rapid-change-recommendations/120326privacyreport.pdf.]

Gajanan, M. (2016, November 28). Playboy Model Dani Mathers Pleads Not Guilty in Body Shaming Case. *Time.* http://time.com/4584362/playboy-dani-mathers-body-shaming/.

Galella v. Onassis, 353 F. Supp. 196 (S.D.N.Y., 1972).

Geller, E. (2020, July 16). Twitter's Security Holes are Now the Nation's Problem. Politico. https://www.politico.com/states/new-york/albany/story/2020/07/16/twitters-security-holes-are-now-the-nations-problem-1301613.

Gewolb, J. and Marra, W. (2019, November 21). Litigation Finance Glossary. *Bloomberg.* https://pro.bloomberglaw.com/litigation-finance/.

Gibbs, S. (2017, January 10). WhatsApp, Facebook and Google Face Tough New Privacy Rules Under EC Proposal. *The Guardian.* https://www.theguardian.com/ technology/2017/jan/10/whatsapp-facebook-google-privacy-rules-ec-european-directive.

Griswold v. Connecticut, 381 U.S. 479 (1975).

Guynn, J. (2013, December 12). Twitter reverses changes to blocking feature after mass protest. *Los Angeles Times.* www.latimes.com/business/technology/la-fi-tn-twitter-reverses-changesto-blocking-feature-after-mass-protest-20131212,0,1607498.story.

Helms, K. (2020, October 25). How Hackers Exploited Twitter's VPN Problems, Obtained God Mode and Took Over Accounts. Bitcoin.com. https://news.bitcoin.com/hackers-twitter-vpn-problems/.

HIPAA (1996). Health Insurance Portability and Accountability Act of 1996. 42 U.S.C.A. Sec. 1320d, 4.

Humbach, J.A. (2012). Privacy and the Right of Free Expression, *First Amendment Law Review*, 11, 16.

Hustler Magazine v. Falwell, 485 U.S. 46 (1988).

In re Gawker Media LLC, 2017 Bankruptcy 1798 (Southern District of New York, 2017).

Katz v. United States, 389 U.S. 347 (1967).

Kelion, L. (2020, July 23). Twitter Says Hackers Viewed 36 Accounts' Private Messages. *BBC News.* https://www.bbc.com/news/technology-53510574.

Kollanyi, B., Howard, P.N., and Woolley, S.C. (2016, November 17). Bots and Automation over Twitter during the U.S. Elections. *COMMPROP* Data Memo. http://politicalbots.org/.

Lane v. Facebook, 709 F.3d 791 (2013).

Lane v. Facebook, Inc., 696 F.3d 811 (9th Cir, 2012).

Lee, L.T. (2013). Privacy and Social Media. In A.B. Albarran (ed.), *The Social Media Industries*, pp. 146–165. New York: Routledge.

Lipp, K. (2016, October 25). AT&T Is Spying on Americans for Profit, New Documents Reveal. *The Daily Beast.* http://www.thedailybeast.com/articles/2016/10/25/at-t-is-spying-on-americans-for-profit.html.

Lipschultz, J.H. (1988). Mediasat and the Tort of Invasion of Privacy, *Journalism Quarterly*, 65(2), 507–511.

Lorenz, T., Eavis, P., and Phillips, M. (2020, November 20). TikTok Mansions Are Publicly Traded Now. *The New York Times*. https://www.nytimes.com/2020/11/20/ style/clubhouse-tiktok-tongji-west-of-hudson.html.

Marland et al. v. Trump et al., 20-4597 (E.D. Pennsylvania, 2020).

Martin, A. (2020, December 21). Facebook Removes Instagram and Messenger Features, Including on Child Safety, Due To EU Privacy Rules.*Sky News*. https://news.sky.com/story/facebook-removes-instagram-and-messenger-features-including-on-child-safety-due-to-eu-privacy-rules-12169332.

Mills, J.L. (2015). *Privacy in the New Media Age*. Gainsville, FL: University Press of Florida.

Moreno v. Hanford Sentinel, Inc. (2009). 172 Cal. App. 4th 1125.

Neely, J. (2016, March 2). Do You Have the Context You Need? Unlocking the Value of Big Data Marketing. *Social Media Today*. http://www.socialmediatoday.com/ marketing/do-you-have-context-you-need-unlocking-value-big-data-marketing.

Nelson, S.D. and Simek, J.W. (2013). Big Data: Big Pain or Big Gain for Lawyers? *Vermont Bar Journal & Law Digest*, 39, 33.

Nolan, F., Weiner, A., and Sutherland, E. (2020, June 26). Recent Decisions Clarify Scope of Illinois Biometric Privacy Law. *Law.Com*. https://www.law.com/legaltechnews/2020/06/26/recent-decisions-clarify-scope-of-illinois-biometric-privacy-law/.

Olmstead v. United States, 227. U.S. 438 (1928).

Overdorf, J. (2013, November 5). Germany: Privacy Protections Must Go Beyond "No-Spying Act." *MINNPOST*. www.minnpost.com/global-post/2013/11/germany-privacy-protections-must-go-beyond-no-spying-act.

Packingham v. North Carolina, 582 U.S. ___, 137 S. Ct. 1730 (2017).

Pavia, J. (2019, November 4). ANALYSIS: Transparency Wanted in Litigation Finance. *Bloomberg Law*. https://news.bloomberglaw.com/bloomberg-law-analysis/analysis-transparency-wanted-in-litigation-finance.

Prosser, D. (1960). Privacy, *California Law Review*, 48, 383.

Riley v. California, 573 U.S. 373 (2014).

Santana v. Take-Two Interactive Software, Inc., 717 Fed. Appx. 12 (Seventh Cir., 2017).

Satter, R., Paul, K., and Culliford, E. (2020, July 31). Florida Teen Accused of Masterminding Twitter Hack that Hit Biden, Musk. *Reuters*. https://www.reuters.com/ article/uk-twitter-cyber-idUKKCN24W2W5.

Schwarz, H. (2015, May 13). Millennials are a Little Confused When it Comes to Privacy. *Washington Post*. https://www.washingtonpost.com/news/the-fix/wp/2015/05/13/millenials-dont-trust-government-to-respect-their-privacy-but-they-do-trust-businesses-what/.

Sidis v. F.R. Publishing Corp. (1940) 113 F.2d 806.

Smith, M. (2014, May 3). *Mapping and Measuring Connections*. Slideshare. www.slideshare.net/Marc_A_Smith/2014-the-next-websmrfnode-xlsnasocial-media-networks.

Somaskanda, S. (2013, July 26). NSA Spying Rankles Privacy-Loving Germans. *The Atlantic.* http://www.theatlantic.com/international/archive/2013/07/nsa-spying-rankles-privacy-loving-germans/278090/.

Sorkin, A.R. (2016, May 25). Peter Thiel, Tech Billionaire, Reveals Secret War With Gawker. *New York Times.* https://www.nytimes.com/2016/05/26/ business/dealbook/peter-thiel-tech-billionaire-reveals-secret-war-with-gawker.html.

Statt, N. (2020, July 16). Twitter's Massive Attack: What We Know After Apple, Biden, Obama, Musk, and Others Tweeted a Bitcoin Scam. *The Verge.* https://www.theverge.com/2020/7/15/21326200/elon-musk-bill-gates-twitter-hack-bitcoin-scam-compromised.

Stewart, D.R. and Littau, J. (2016), Up, Periscope: Mobile Streaming Video Technologies, Privacy in Public, and the Right to Record, *Journalism & Mass Communication Quarterly,* 93(2), 312–331.

Stoycheff, E. (2016). Under Surveillance: Examining Facebook's Spiral of Silence Effects in the Wake of NSA Internet Monitoring, *Journalism & Mass Communication Quarterly,* 93(2), 296–311.

Terilli, Jr., S.A., and Splichal, S. (2020). Privacy Rights in an Open and Changing Society. In W. W. Hopkins (ed.), *Communication and the Law,* pp. 249–266. Northport, AL: Vision Press.

Thompson, D. (2018, February 23). The Most Expensive Comment in Internet History? *The Atlantic.* https://www.theatlantic.com/business/archive/2018/02/hogan-thiel-gawker-trial/554132/.

Trotter, J.K. (2016, August 18). Gawker.com To End Operations Next Week. *Gawker.* https://gawker.com/tag/gawker-media.

U.S. Department of Commerce (2020, November 9).15 CFR Chapter VII. https://www.commerce.gov/sites/default/files/2020-11/signedTikTokFR NoticeofEDPaPreliminary-Injunction10302020RP.pdf.

U.S. WeChat Users Alliance, et al., Plaintiffs, v. Donald J. Trump, et al., Defendants (2020a, September 19). 2020 LEXIS U.S. Dist. 172816. United States District Court Northern District of California San Francisco Division. Case No. 20-cv-05910-LB. https://www.courtlistener.com/recap/gov.uscourts.cand.364733/gov.uscourts.cand.364733.59.0.pdf.

U.S. WeChat Users Alliance, et al., Plaintiffs, v. Donald J. Trump, et al., Defendants (2020b, November 24). 2020 U.S. Dist. LEXIS 220797. United States District Court Northern District of California San Francisco Division. Case No. 20-cv-05910-LB.

Viera, M. (2015, April 10). Maryland Governor to Consider Student Social Media Privacy Bill. *Student Press Law Center.* http://www.huffingtonpost.com/student-press-law-center/maryland-governor-to-consider-student-social-media-privacy-bill_b_ 7042374.html.

Virgil v. Time Inc., 527 F.2d 1122 (9th Cir., 1975).

Vishnoi, A., Worrachate, A., and Golden, T. (2020, July 16). Twitter Hack Shows Risk to Social Media Obsessed Markets. Bloomberg. https://www.bloomberg.com/news/articles/2020-07-16/markets-were-spared-from-twitter-hack-but-it-s-still-a-big-risk.

Walker, A. (2016, March 16). An Algorithm Can Tell If You're Drunk Tweeting. *Gizmodo.* http://www.gizmodo.in/software/An-Algorithm-Can-Tell-If-Youre-Drunk-Tweeting/articleshow/51432774.cms

Warren, S. and Brandeis, L. (1890). The Right to Privacy, *Harvard Law Review*, 4, 193.
Westin, A.F. (1967). *Privacy and Freedom*. New York: Athenæum.
Yaffe-Bellany, D. and Banjo, S. (2020, November 25). TikTik Granted One-Week Extension of Forced Sale Deadline. *Bloomberg*. https://www.bloomberg.com/news/ articles/2020-11-25/ tiktok-granted-one-week-extension-of-forced-sale-deadline.
Youm, K.H. and Park, A. (2016). The "Right to Be Forgotten" in European Union Law: Data Protection Balanced With Free Speech?, *Journalism & Mass Communication Quarterly*, 93(2), 273–295.
Zacchini v. Scripps Howard Broadcasting, 433 U.S. 562 (1977).

7 Hate Speech, Revenge Porn, and Obscenity

> *At a minimum, prurient, patently offensive depiction or description of sexual conduct must have serious literary, artistic, political, or scientific value to merit First Amendment protection.*

—U.S. Supreme Court Chief Justice Warren E. Burger,
Miller v. California (1973, p. 26)

A suburban Chicago woman discovered nude photographs of a woman dating her husband for a decade, became angry, and allegedly posted the images on Facebook (Kenney, 2020). Ramona Martinez-Ayala, 35, found the younger woman's image files on a home computer that was shared with her husband. Following a threatening private message, a state attorney in Elgin, Illinois, said: "Martinez-Ayala carried out the threat by sharing the messages and three nude photos of the woman on her Facebook timeline," and "included the victim's name and profile picture on the post" (para. 4). After the victim saw the public post, Facebook removed it as a terms of service violation. Under Illinois law, Martinez-Ayala could be convicted of a criminal felony "non-consensual dissemination of private sexual images" charge.

Box 7.1 Illinois Chapter 720. Criminal Offenses §-23.5

§ 11-23.5. Non-consensual dissemination of private sexual images.

a. Definitions. For the purposes of this Section:
"Computer", "computer program", and "data" have the meanings ascribed to them in Section 17-0.5 of this Code.

"Image" includes a photograph, film, videotape, digital recording, or other depiction or portrayal of an object, including a human body.

"Intimate parts" means the fully unclothed, partially unclothed or transparently clothed genitals, pubic area, anus, or if the person is female, a partially or fully exposed nipple, including exposure through transparent clothing.

"Sexual act" means sexual penetration, masturbation, or sexual activity.

"Sexual activity" means any:

1. knowing touching or fondling by the victim or another person or animal, either directly or through clothing, of the sex organs, anus, or breast of the victim or another person or animal for the purpose of sexual gratification or arousal; or
2. any transfer or transmission of semen upon any part of the clothed or unclothed body of the victim, for the purpose of sexual gratification or arousal of the victim or another; or
3. an act of urination within a sexual context; or
4. any bondage, fetter, or sadism masochism; or
5. sadomasochism abuse in any sexual context.

b. A person commits non-consensual dissemination of private sexual images when he or she:

1. intentionally disseminates an image of another person:

A. who is at least 18 years of age; and
B. who is identifiable from the image itself or information displayed in connection with the image; and

C. who is engaged in a sexual act or whose intimate parts are exposed, in whole or in part; and

2. obtains the image under circumstances in which a reasonable person would know or understand that the image was to remain private; and
3. knows or should have known that the person in the image has not consented to the dissemination.

c. The following activities are exempt from the provisions of this Section:

1. The intentional dissemination of an image of another identifiable person who is engaged in a sexual act or whose intimate parts are exposed when the dissemination is made for the purpose of a criminal investigation that is otherwise lawful.
2. The intentional dissemination of an image of another identifiable person who is engaged in a sexual act or whose intimate parts are exposed when the dissemination is for the purpose of, or in connection with, the reporting of unlawful conduct.
3. The intentional dissemination of an image of another identifiable person who is engaged in a sexual act or whose intimate parts are exposed when the images involve voluntary exposure in public or commercial settings.
4. The intentional dissemination of an image of another identifiable person who is engaged in a sexual act or whose intimate parts are exposed when the dissemination serves a lawful public purpose ...

Source: FindLaw (2021). Illinois Statutes Chapter 720. Criminal Offenses §-23.5. Non-consensual dissemination of private sexual images, https://codes.findlaw.com/il/chapter-720-criminal-offenses/il-st-sect-720-5-11-23-5.html.

Under the Illinois statute a "reasonable person" standard is applied to the privacy of an image (C)(2). Photographs or video that include nudity or sexual behavior may fall under the law.

Revenge porn – posting graphic sexual images to retaliate in a domestic dispute – includes obscene content with no First Amendment protection, or non-obscene content that could have some legal free expression protection. A variety of statute laws regulate **pornography**, but revenge porn cases are a relatively new area of law. The earliest cases involved magazine photographs prior to the development of social media sites. As Facebook became popular, a woman's ex-boyfriend from a distance relationship had saved explicit photos and a video shared that were posted on her "wall" and emails in 2009 (Miller, 2013). In 2012, the alleged source of the Facebook posts faced criminal charges. The ex-boyfriend countered that the victim bullied him by spreading the story and his name: "She has ruined my life" (para. 8). County prosecutors eventually dropped the charges in the case because, at the time, Florida did not have a revenge porn state law.

"Revenge pornography" may be traced to IsAnyoneUp.com, a website that focused on victim responses to "the consequences of having their sexually explicit images spread across the Internet" (Sanders, 2017, p. 182). Hunter Moore served prison time and faced fines for "unauthorized access to a private computer and aggregated identity theft" (p. 191). The site had been launched in 2010 and included its social media profile alongside the photograph, which ensured the pictures "would emerge upon a Google search" (Bustamante, 2017, p. 363). Moore had called himself a "professional life ruiner," and "taunted victims" with claims that his viewers were laughing and masturbating to the images (p. 363). Facebook banned Moore's account and content, but the monetized website did not close until 2012.

Revenge porn is part of a larger area that also may include cyberbullying through criminal threats and illegal obscenity (Sanders, 2017). Obscenity has "scant" legal protection, but non-obscene erotica can be regulated under criminal threats laws (Watson, 2021, p. 74). Invasion of privacy also may be claimed based on "colloquial linking of the suffix 'porn' to some socially and politically unacceptable" social media posts:

> For example, the term "revenge porn" refers to depictions of intimate situations that are not necessarily overtly sexual, but usually include nudity in an apparently private circumstance. The term "animal crush porn" has been applied to depictions of the killing of small animals … [a]nd "war porn" is the … label for videos of graphic violent military or terrorist attacks.
>
> (p. 68)

"Victims have tried to pursue civil litigation based on a theory of invasion of privacy, but that approach has been largely unsuccessful in the courts" (Sanders, 2017,

p. 190). Feminists have been battling pornography since the 1970s in advocating for laws that "reduce gender oppression, creating social change that would allow women to claim real sexual freedom" (Bronstein, 2011, p. 335). The critique applied to traditional media also is relevant when social media content promotes patriarchy through revenge porn or other means.

Victims also could approach a case from contract or intellectual property law, depending on the facts of a case. For example, a social media selfie photo or video could be owned by a victim and any commercial use of their likeness would be protected. Still, a case also turns on the definition of pornography. The word "porn" has been vaguely applied to content that would not be found illegally obscene under case law. This explains why other forms of law have been applied to offensive content.

Obscenity around the world is frequently among the categories of unprotected speech, such as social media rules in Pakistan that "prohibit live-streaming ... for the ISPs ... by deploying [an] online mechanism, related to terrorism, extremism, hate speech, pornographic, incitement to violence and detrimental to national security" (*Tribune India*, 2020, para. 9). The Ministry of Information Technology applied the Prevention of Electronic Crimes Act (PECA, 2016) in Pakistan to all large Internet service providers and social media sites under Removal of Unlawful Online Content (RBUOC) oversight regulation. Similar to other countries, all companies are required to appoint a person responsible for compliance. Penalties include fines under the rules that mat may be challenged in court by the Internet Service Providers of Pakistan (ISPAK). The Nighat Dad of Digital Rights Foundation has called it "a draconian law" that imposes "too much government in the affairs of social media" (para. 15). Associated Press (2020a) also reported that the Asia Internet Coalition's members were "alarmed by the scope" of the law, "the government's opaque process," and suffocating rules that led some companies to threaten to leave the country (para. 3). Meanwhile, social media companies operating in the UK could be fined large amounts under the Online Safety Bill, if they fail to "remove and limit the spread of harmful content" (Chan, 2020, para. 1). The new proposal targeted terrorism and child sexual abuse with fines of up to 10 percent of annual global revenue (para. 3):

> These companies will face special requirements to assess whether there's a "reasonably foreseeable risk" that content or activity that they host will cause "significant physical or psychological harm to adults," such as false information about coronavirus vaccines. They'll have to clarify what is allowed and how they will handle it.
>
> (para. 4)

The legislative threat came as the European Union (EU) rolled out a digital regulation update to address hate speech, and Ireland fined Twitter for a data breach. At the same time, however, Twitter and other social network sites (SNSs) control storage data servers, and they have exercised the power to block governments from using snooping tools (Gilmer, 2016).

Sometimes, the lack of government rules leaves content regulation to online platforms. The Pornhub website announced that it was making safety changes after *The New York Times*' Nicholas Kristof alleged in an opinion piece that the site contained "rape videos" and illegal child pornography (Jibillian, 2020, para. 1). The company responded that: "Our core values such as inclusivity, freedom of expression and privacy are only possible when our platform is trusted by our users" (para. 2). Kristof's (2020) "The Children of Pornhub" article found that Pornhub may be the tenth most visited site – its 3.5 billion visitors *monthly* is more than Netflix or Amazon (para. 2):

> Its site is infested with rape videos. It monetizes child rapes, revenge pornography, spy cam videos of women showering, racist and misogynist content, and footage of women being asphyxiated in plastic bags. A search for "girls under18" (no space) or "14yo" leads in each case to more than 100,000 videos. Most aren't of children being assaulted, but too many are.
>
> (para. 3)

Kristof has long written about global child exploitation in a wide range of businesses and products. Pornhub videos may be downloaded: "So even if a rape video is removed at the request of the authorities, it may already be too late: The video lives on as it is shared with others or uploaded again and again" (para. 8). Kristof documented individual cases in which missing children had been found through their participation in violent sexual videos. In spite of Pornhub's attempts to use community policies to regulate content, it can be found through Google searches that showed nearly 1 billion such videos existed.

In the U.S.A., regulation of social media user behavior is primarily governed by terms of service end-user contract law and state data privacy statutes. YouTube is among those platforms that regularly update policies in an attempt to protect users: "Harassment hurts our community by making people less inclined to share their opinions and engage with each other" (Halprin, 2019, para. 2). While some are most concerned about online bullying, others express concerns about restriction of free expression, particularly within political communication. YouTube said it values "openness" and "spirited debate and a vigorous exchange of ideas" (para. 3) "However, we will not tolerate harassment and we believe the steps outlined below will contribute to our mission by making YouTube a better place for anyone to share their story or opinion" (para. 3). In 2019, Google's YouTube emphasized:

- A stronger stance against threats and personal attacks
- Consequences for a pattern of harassing behavior
- Addressing toxic comments (paras. 4–7)

Harassment and online bullying may be seen in some forms as related to the use of "revenge porn" pornography – some of which could be found to be illegal obscenity under U.S. law. Other forms of bullying are related to threats of violence. For example, Facebook banned a 350,000-member "Stop the Steal" group after the 2020 presidential election (Ortutay & Klepper, 2020, para. 2). Facebook, based on a "period of heightened tension," took "exceptional measures" to ban the largest group that "organized around the delegitimization of the election process" because "some members" called for violence (para. 3). Facebook failed to single out those group members, and the company allowed smaller groups aiming to stop vote counting and certification in swing states to remain. A new "Stop the Steal" group quickly amassed 13,000 members by sharing threats (para. 4): "Neither side is going to concede. Time to clean the guns, time to hit the streets" (para. 5). Critics claimed Facebook suffers from "a systematic issue" in exploitation of groups "by people spreading misinformation, hate and inciting violence" (para. 10). Donald Trump also was eventually banned from Facebook amid the Capitol siege that followed.

Facebook also has difficulty in enforcing rules against individuals who target others with revenge porn or other forms of bullying. Facebook Community Standards efforts include more than 4,500 people reviewing complaints and hundreds of thousands of posts are deleted each month. Hate speech is defined as attacks against "protected characteristics, under the terms of service – 'race, ethnicity, national origin, religious affiliation, sexual orientation, sex, gender, gender identity, or serious disability or disease.'" As a global corporation, Facebook must be responsive to, for example, German law that bans "incitement to hatred" and "blasphemy," which are areas that may be protected elsewhere. Facebook employees and AI software evaluate context and intent that may be protected speech, such as satire. AI tools may be used to filter content for keywords, such as "bullying."

The Center for Countering Digital Hate (2020) places social media communication within a larger targeting of identity-based hate groups that thrive on violent speech. The Washington, DC Council may be leading a trend by extending its Human Rights Act public accommodations protection to social media sites. The Lawyers' Committee for Civil Rights Under Law said the "new law also strengthens the District's hate crimes protections for LGBTQ persons and gives new anti-discrimination enforcement powers to the D.C. attorney general" (Weiner, 2020, para. 2). The law makes service denial illegal when based on sexual orientation, race, religion, gender and other protected categories and it targets disproportional harm to specific groups.

A lot of hate speech falls under the umbrella of protected free expression and some targets authority. Prince Charles and Duchess Camilla, for example, disabled Twitter replies on a post to avoid hateful comments about them:

> "The Duchess of Cornwall, Patron of @EmmausUK, recently joined a video call with staff and formerly homeless residents of @EmmausBrighton, known as companions, to discuss the challenges faced by the charity as a result of the coronavirus crisis," the message read. Only users who the Clarence House account follows are able to reply to the tweet.
>
> (Longeretta, 2020, para. 2)

The couple had been "flooded with comments," including "hateful messages," following the fourth season of *The Crown* on Netflix that chronicled the late Princess Diana's eating disorder and Charles' ongoing affair with Camilla (para. 4). Blocked Twitter users may still tweet about the television series to their followers.

Platform regulation of end-user agreements are regularly updated to address new problems and issues. At the same time, corporations claim important and valuable rights. Instagram, for example, claims a free license to all user content and they force users to waive class-action lawsuit and jury trial rights in disputes with the company. The contract law also addresses Instagram's desire to maintain a "positive, inclusive and safe" community.

Box 7.2 Updated Instagram Terms of Service

Instagram updated its user agreement with Facebook, Inc. in late 2020. The "Terms of Use." In all-caps, the service forced disputes into arbitration instead of expensive class action lawsuits:

> ARBITRATION NOTICE: YOU AGREE THAT DISPUTES BETWEEN YOU AND US WILL BE RESOLVED BY BINDING, INDIVIDUAL ARBITRATION AND YOU WAIVE YOUR RIGHT TO PARTICIPATE IN A CLASS ACTION LAWSUIT OR CLASS-WIDE ARBITRATION …

Instagram promoted "a positive, inclusive and safe environment" that responded to "harmful and deceptive behavior. It reserved the right to conduct research for its relationships with brands. Instagram also reminded users that advertising pays for the service.

Users are not allowed to "sell, license, or purchase any account data obtained." Importantly, users license their photos and other content to Instagram:

> We do not claim ownership of your content, but you grant us a license to use it... When you share, post, or upload content that is covered by intellectual property rights (like photos or videos) on or in connection with our Service, you hereby grant to us a non-exclusive, royalty-free, transferable, sub-licensable, worldwide license to host, use, distribute, modify, run, copy, publicly perform or display, translate, and create derivative works of your content (consistent with your privacy and application settings). This license will end when your content is deleted from our systems ...

Instagram may remove content for violation of the rules. In disputes, Instagram says "you and we agree that any **cause of action**, legal claim, or dispute between you and us arising out of or related to these Terms or Instagram ("claim(s)") must be resolved by arbitration on an individual basis. Class actions and class arbitrations are not permitted; you and we may bring a claim only on your own behalf and cannot seek relief that would affect other Instagram users ..." For small claims, users and Instagram "expressly waive a trial by jury."

Source: Instagram Terms of Service (2020, December 20). https://help.instagram.com/1215086795543252

REVENGE PORN, CYBERBULLYING, AND OBSCENITY

Revenge porn has emerged as a feminist issue because U.S. law "fails to adequately provide redress for victims of nonconsensual pornography" (Gabriel, 2020, p. 849). At least 46 U.S. states and the District of Columbia enacted laws addressing the revenge porn problem (pp. 849-850). Still, the law is considered to be difficult to apply:

> The terms *nonconsensual pornography* and *revenge pornography* are often used interchangeably. Both terms refer to the dissemination of explicit material without the consent of the subject. The key difference between the two terms, however, "is one of motive, not effect: revenge porn is often intended to harass the victim, while any image that is circulated without the agreement of the subject is nonconsensual porn. Both can result in public degradation, social isolation, and professional humiliation for the victims."
>
> (p. 852)

Women who are active online frequently have been the targets of bullying and harassment central to revenge porn communication behavior. One possible solution builds upon Facebook and other social media monitoring systems to construct a "comprehensive system" with "a preventative measure that aims to proactively" offer "alerts to victims or blocking user uploads of pre-registered nonconsensual pornography" (p. 892).

Under Florida law, for example, lawmakers compromised on a statute that recognized harm from nonconsensual photography (Bustamante, 2017). The law "required a showing of intent to harass the victim," and not other motives, such as entertainment or financial gain (p. 381). The **misdemeanor** penalties aligned with an approach in California, but were much weaker than New Jersey felony law that might serve as an "effective deterrent" (p. 382). State laws also vary in application to, for example, email distribution. The lack of consistent federal revenge porn law is partially based upon First Amendment concerns about restricting non-obscene content.

Box 7.3 Cyberbullies and #MoreThanMean

Although the #MoreThanMean YouTube video was nearly five years old at this writing, it continues to receive fresh views that add to its total of more than 4.5 million, including 3.7 million in its first six months. Women in Chicago fought online harassment with a hashtag campaign. Former Chicago Sportswriter Julie DiCaro (@JulieDiCaro) had more than 36 thousand Twitter followers. As senior writer and editor for *Deadspin*, former 670 The Score sports radio host, lawyer and author of the book *Sidelined: Sports, Culture, and Being A Woman in America* (2021), DiCaro champions a continuing fight against online bullies on Twitter and elsewhere across social media channels.

DiCaro was an **early adopter** of Twitter in 2009, but she found it necessary to block accounts that attack her for having opinions about sports. While Twitter makes it so easy to connect, in sports media women get "constant trolling harassment," and "a stream of sexism and misogyny and threats."

There apparently are many different motivations – wanting attention, seeking "perverse pleasure out of getting under someone's skin," and even "trolls" trying to force women sportscasters and writers out of the business and offline, DiCaro says: "They're basically out to ruin my reputation." Some days the problem is so large that DiCaro says she spends hours blocking new and anonymous Twitter accounts. She is thankful for allies rushing to her defense, even though they also are sometimes attacked. Exposing online harassment is one way to fight back.

The #MoreThanMean project organically began with a piece DiCaro wrote for *Sports Illustrated* about women in sports media and on social media. The online harassment, though, continued through the winter. The idea for the YouTube video followed, and DiCaro was one of only two women agreeing to participate among as many as 20 asked.

Most of the women were afraid of the backlash, DiCaro says. She agrees that what women in sports see is part of a larger cultural problem of not placing value on what women say. During the 2016 election, for example, there was a noticeable lack of kindness, civility, and compassion. "I think that it's all part of the same thing," DiCaro says.

The actual offenders did not read the mean tweets in the Youtube video, so it is difficult to measure project impact on changing attitudes and behaviors. Still, there is "something about hearing out loud and viscerally, and then having to look in someone's eyes and those things that seem to change people and sort of hit home," DiCaro says. She does her best to accept "what they throw at me," but DiCaro says sometimes the insults are overwhelming:

> In fact, there are some days when I don't deal with it well, and you can ask my husband. He'd be happy to tell you about all the days when … someone will say something… he'll find me like a heap of tears on the bed because they do hurt … I don't know if there's any way to really prepare someone for this. I think you have to believe in what you're doing, and why I feel that violence against women is something that has been remarkably under-reported in sports media.

DiCaro is on a mission to change this.

A community of sports women has developed, and they support each other. "I really lean on other women in the industry to help me get through it because we're all going through it," DiCaro says.

While cyberbullies can be found across the Internet, Twitter is instantaneous. DiCaro says the ease of creating new and quasi-anonymous accounts means that Twitter is "so much worse."

Media people must "develop a very thick skin," DiCaro says. "I think that whatever you can do to prepare yourself mentally ... you need to do." DiCaro has considered leaving Twitter, but for now she continues to engage and "out" the online attackers. Twitter also continues to work on the troll problem. Victims may now report a series of tweets that personally attack and reflect a pattern, but it remains difficult to keep individuals from creating new accounts.

Filter and blocking tools also may help.

We need to remain true to our First Amendment free speech values, but also challenge speech that hurts people. Look for the problem of online harassment to continue to be addressed, as social media platforms mature and evolve.

Sources

Lipschultz, J. H. (2016, November 11). Dealing with Social Media Bullies. LinkedIn Articles. https://www.linkedin.com/pulse/dealing-social-media-bullies-jeremy-harris-lipschultz/.

#MoreThanMean (2016, April 26). Women in Sports 'Face' Harassment, *YouTube*. https://youtu.be/9tU-D-m2JY8.

Cyberbullying is a personal attack, but there are ways for responding. After a 15-year-old girl took her life because of bullying, a 17-year-old from Bangladesh, Sadat Rahman, built an app and won the International Children's Peace Prize for it: "The fight against cyberbullying is like a war, and in this war I am a warrior" (Associated Press, 2020b, para. 2). Cyberbullying can be viewed as a human rights violation, but national and international law remains a developing area.

Employees of major companies have been punished and even fired in connection with social media communication behavior. Delta airlines flight attendant Kiersten Bak, for example, lost her job for violating company social media policies in her response to harassment from online trolls (Reinstein, 2020). Bak, 26, had a Shopify and Facebook Marketplace businesses called "That Fucking Feminist" that attracted men opposed to her "cheeky feminist merchandise" (para. 2). After being called "dumb," she responded:

> "Imagine having the ego of a white man in America □ □," Bak captioned the screenshot. "(no idea who this guy is. just some random snowflake who messaged me and immediately blocked me so I couldn't respond 😂)."
>
> (para. 4)

Bak claimed that Delta managers called her "racist" toward men (para. 5). Delta responded that "our employees know and understand that they are representatives of our brand at work and through their conduct in social media and other public forums" (para. 11). As a matter of law, companies are free to fairly enforce social media policies. Ethical issues would explore the duty of an employee to represent her or his company, potential harm to the brand or others, and what corporate social responsibility (CSR) exists inside and outside the workplace.

KEY CASES

Revenge pornography law was on the U.S. Supreme Court docket in *Austin v. Illinois* (2020) on appeal from the Illinois Supreme Court. That court had applied intermediate scrutiny to uphold the constitutionality of a state law based upon, among other points, lack of consent and privacy law (*People v. Austin*, 2019). The court voted 5 to 2 to overturn a lower court case that suggested a First Amendment defense in criminal cases (Mansur and Reiland, 2019). Bethany Austin had found that her fiancé stored nude photographs of another woman on an iPad using a shared iCloud account. After the fiancé claimed he and Austin ended their relationship for other reasons, she shared text messages and the nude photos with a family member. Austin was charged with sharing the content without consent of her former fiancé and the woman in the nude photos. The Illinois Supreme Court majority found that the state revenge porn law regulated distribution of private information. Two dissenting justices would have applied strict scrutiny based upon the lack of narrowly tailored content restriction within the statute. The First Amendment argument is that the law passed in 2015 essentially created a new classification of unprotected speech that includes nude or sexually explicit images. The Illinois Supreme Court, however, distinguished the facts in the case as criminally liable under the state law because Austin used the iCloud files to distribute the images without consent. Despite the First Amendment implication of defining and restricting private revenge pornography, the U.S. Supreme Court considered filings and then denied full review of the case (U.S. Supreme Court, 2020). Austin, as a third-party, could face a criminal trial on charges of not having consent to distribute the images sent from the victim to her ex-fiancé as part of *their* personal relationship. Austin could be fined and be sentenced to prison time.

Box 7.4 U.S. Supreme Court Denied Certiorari in *Illinois v. Austin* (2019)

2019 IL 123910
IN THE SUPREME COURT
OF THE STATE OF ILLINOIS
(Docket No. 123910)

THE PEOPLE OF THE STATE OF ILLINOIS, Appellant, v. BETHANY AUSTIN, Appellee.

Opinion filed October 18, 2019.

OPINION

Defendant Bethany Austin was charged with violating section 11-23.5(b) of the Criminal Code of 2012 ..., which criminalizes the nonconsensual dissemination of private sexual images ...

I. Background

Defendant shared an iCloud account with Matthew, and all data sent to or from Matthew's iPhone went to their shared iCloud account, which was connected to defendant's iPad... Matthew was aware of this data sharing arrangement but took no action to disable it.

While Matthew and defendant were engaged and living together, text messages between Matthew and the victim, who was a neighbor, appeared on defendant's iPad. Some of the text messages included nude photographs of the victim. Both Matthew and the victim were aware that defendant had received the pictures and text messages on her iPad. Three days later, Matthew and the victim again exchanged several text messages...

Defendant and Matthew cancelled their wedding plans and subsequently broke up. Thereafter, Matthew began telling family and friends that their relationship had ended because defendant was crazy and no longer cooked or did household chores.

In response, defendant wrote a letter detailing her version of events. As support, she attached to the letter four of the naked pictures of the victim and copies of the text messages between the victim and Matthew. When Matthew's cousin received the letter along with the text messages and pictures, he informed Matthew. Upon learning of the letter and its enclosures, Matthew contacted the police ...

The victim acknowledged that she was aware that Matthew had shared an iCloud account with defendant, but she thought it had been deactivated when she sent him the nude photographs.

Defendant was charged by indictment with one count of nonconsensual dissemination of private sexual images ... She moved to dismiss the charge, asserting, *inter alia*, that the statute is facially unconstitutional because it is a content-based restriction of speech that is not narrowly tailored to serve a compelling government interest, in violation of the federal and state constitutions ...

The State opposed defendant's motion, arguing that the type of speech restricted by the statute is not constitutionally protected and that the statute is narrowly tailored to serve a compelling government interest.

The circuit court agreed with defendant ...

II. Analysis

... Defendant responds by contending that the circuit court correctly found the statute to be unconstitutional ... She further argues that the distribution of nude images that have been disclosed to another person is constitutionally protected because such images are not truly private facts as the State contends.

All statutes are presumed to be constitutional, and the party challenging a statute's constitutionality bears the burden of clearly establishing its invalidity ... In addition, a court must construe a statute so as to uphold its constitutionality, if reasonably possible ...

A. The Necessity for the Law

Section 11-23.5 addresses the problem of nonconsensual dissemination of private sexual images, which is colloquially referred to as "revenge porn." Generally, the crime involves images originally obtained without consent, ... and images originally obtained with consent, usually within the context of a private or confidential relationship ...

... Indeed, the term "revenge porn," though commonly used, is misleading in two respects. First, "revenge" connotes personal vengeance. However, perpetrators may be motivated by a desire for profit, notoriety, entertainment, or for no specific reason at all. The only common factor is that they act without the consent of the person depicted. Second, "porn" misleadingly suggests that visual depictions of nudity or sexual activity are inherently pornographic ...

Because the nonconsensual dissemination of private sexual images "so often involves the Internet and social media, the public, law enforcement, and the judiciary sometimes struggle to understand the mechanics of the conduct and the devastation it can cause ..."

Consent is contextual. "The consent to create and send a photo or the consent to be photographed by another is one act of consent that cannot be equated with consenting to distribute that photo to others outside of the private relationship ... The nonconsensual dissemination of private sexual images "is not wrong because nudity is shameful or because the act of recording sexual activity is inherently immoral. It is wrong because exposing a person's body against her will fundamentally deprives that person of her right to privacy" ...

B. The General Assembly's Solution

... Section 11-23.5(b) provides as follows:

"(b) A person commits non-consensual dissemination of private sexual images when he or she:

1. intentionally disseminates an image of another person:
   - **A.** who is at least 18 years of age; and
   - **B.** who is identifiable from the image itself or information displayed in connection with the image; and
   - **C.** who is engaged in a sexual act or whose intimate parts are exposed, in whole or in part; and
2. obtains the image under circumstances in which a reasonable person would know or understand that the image was to remain private; and
3. knows or should have known that the person in the image has not consented to the dissemination ..."

C. Preliminary Findings

We observe that we cannot avoid addressing the constitutionality of section 11-23.5(b) ...

D. First Amendment

The first amendment, which applies to the states through the fourteenth amendment, provides that government "shall make no law *** abridging freedom of speech" ...

1. No Categorical Exception

... In this case, the circuit court found that the targeted speech did not fit into any categorical first amendment exception. Before this court, the State argues that "state laws protecting individual privacy rights have long been established." According to the State, "history supports the conclusion that States may regulate speech that invades privacy without violating the First Amendment."

We decline the State's invitation to identify a new category of speech that falls outside of first amendment protection ... We acknowledge, as did the Vermont Supreme Court, that the nonconsensual dissemination of private sexual images "seems to be a strong candidate for categorical exclusion from full First Amendment protections" based on "[t]he broad development across the country of invasion of privacy torts, and the long-standing historical pedigree of laws protecting the privacy of non-**public figures** with respect to matters of only private interest without any established First Amendment limitations ..."

2. Degree of Scrutiny

The United States Supreme Court has long held "[c]ontent-based prohibitions, enforced by severe criminal penalties, have the constant potential to be a repressive force in the lives and thoughts of a free people. To guard against that threat the Constitution demands that content-based restrictions on speech be presumed invalid ..."

Accordingly, courts "apply the most exacting scrutiny to regulations that suppress, disadvantage, or impose differential burdens upon speech because of its content ..." A content-based law is justified only if it survives strict scrutiny, which requires the government to demonstrate that the law is narrowly tailored to serve a compelling state interest ...

In the case at bar, the circuit court found that section 11-23.5(b) "is a content- based speech restriction because it doesn't target all pictures, videos, depictions, and portrayals, but only those showing nudity or sexual activity ..."

However, because this is a first amendment case, we, as a court of review, must decide independently "whether a given course of conduct falls on the near or far side of the line of constitutional protection ..."

a. Time, Place, and Manner

It is generally understood "that the First Amendment does not guarantee the right to communicate one's views at all times and places or in any manner that may be desired." ... Laws that "impose burdens on speech without reference to the ideas or views expressed are in most instances content neutral." ... "The principal inquiry in determining content neutrality, in speech cases generally and in time, place, or manner cases in particular, is whether the government has adopted a regulation of speech because of disagreement with the message it conveys." ...

Content-neutral laws are subject to an intermediate level of scrutiny because they generally present a less substantial risk of excising certain ideas or viewpoints from the public dialogue ...

b. Purely Private Matter

We conclude that section 11-23.5(b) is subject to an intermediate level of scrutiny also because the statute regulates a purely private matter. Speech on matters of public concern lies at the heart of first amendment protection. The first amendment reflects a national commitment to the principle that debate on public issues should be robust and uninhibited. Accordingly, speech on public issues occupies the highest position of the hierarchy of first amendment values and is entitled to special protection ...

However, first amendment protections are less rigorous where matters of purely private significance are at issue: ...

The Supreme Court has articulated some guiding factors:

"Speech deals with matters of public concern when it can be fairly considered as relating to any matter of political, social, or other concern to the community [citation], or when it is a subject of legitimate news interest; that is, a subject of general interest and of value and concern to the public [citation] ...

Applying these principles to the instant case, we have no difficulty in concluding that the nonconsensual dissemination of the victim's private sexual images was not an issue of public concern. Matthew was telling his and defendant's families and friends that it was defendant's **fault** that their relationship ended. Defendant responded with a letter, in which she explained her version of events. ... The victim's private sexual images, in context with her and Matthew's text messages, were never in the public domain. They do not relate to any broad issue of interest to society at large. The message they convey is not a matter of public import ...

3. Applying Intermediate Scrutiny

... Generally, to survive intermediate scrutiny, the law must serve an important or substantial governmental interest unrelated to the suppression of free speech and must not burden substantially more speech than necessary to further that interest or, in other words, must be narrowly tailored to serve that interest without unnecessarily interfering with first amendment freedoms, which include allowing reasonable alternative avenues of communication...

Accordingly, in the context of the first amendment, fit matters. Even when the Supreme Court is not applying strict scrutiny, the court still requires a fit that is not necessarily perfect but reasonable, a fit that represents not necessarily the single best disposition but one whose scope is in proportion to the interest served, a fit that employs not necessarily the least restrictive means but a means narrowly tailored to achieve the desired objective ...

In the case at bar, we conclude that section 11-23.5 serves a substantial government interest. "It is a traditional exercise of the States' police powers to protect the health and safety of their citizens." ...

Based on the statutory terms set forth above, section 11-23.5 is narrowly tailored to further the important governmental interest identified by the legislature. Accordingly, we conclude the statute does not burden substantially more speech than necessary ...

E. First Amendment Overbreadth

We have concluded that section 11-23.5 does not improperly restrict defendant's freedom of speech as guaranteed by the first amendment. However, in support of the circuit court's order, defendant alternatively contends that section 11-23.5(b) is facially unconstitutional because it is overbroad. We do not agree ...

We recognize that most state laws prohibiting the nonconsensual dissemination of private sexual images expressly require some form of malicious purpose or illicit motive as a distinct element of the offense... Most of these states provide elaborate descriptions of malice, such as "the intent to harass, intimidate, threaten, humiliate, embarrass, or coerce" ... or "the intent to annoy, terrify, threaten, intimidate, harass, offend, humiliate or degrade" ... or "the intent to harass, intimidate, or coerce" ...

F. Constitutional Vagueness

...A vagueness claim based on due process is analytically distinct from a first amendment overbreadth claim and does not depend upon whether a law applies to a substantial amount of protected speech ... A facial challenge to a statute that is premised on due process vagueness grounds can succeed "only if the enactment is impermissibly vague in all of its applications. A [litigant] who engages in some conduct that is clearly proscribed cannot complain of the vagueness of the law as applied to the conduct of others." ...

III. Conclusion

For the foregoing reasons, the judgment of the circuit court of McHenry County is reversed, and the cause is remanded to the circuit court for further proceedings.

Reversed.
Cause remanded.

JUSTICE GARMAN, dissenting:

Even though both parties agree a strict scrutiny analysis applies in this case, the majority concludes an intermediate level of scrutiny is the appropriate standard...

... I, however, would find the statute criminalizes the dissemination of images based on their content — "private sexual images"— and thus strict scrutiny applies. Moreover, in applying strict scrutiny, I would find the statute is neither narrowly tailored nor the least restrictive means of dealing with the nonconsensual dissemination of private sexual images. Accordingly, I respectfully dissent ...

'[T]he First Amendment means that government has no power to restrict expression because of its message, its ideas, its subject matter, or its content.'" *United States v. Alvarez*, 567 U.S. 709, 716 (2012) (quoting *Ashcroft v. American Civil Liberties Union*, 535 U.S. 564, 573 (2002)). "Content-based laws—those that target speech based on its communicative content—are presumptively unconstitutional and may be justified only if the government proves that they are narrowly tailored to serve compelling state interests." ...

Laws burdening speech based on its content are subjected to "the most exacting scrutiny." ...Here, the statute cannot withstand strict scrutiny, as it is not narrowly tailored to serve the State's interests and less restrictive alternatives are available. Thus, I would find the statute unconstitutional and affirm the circuit court's judgment.

JUSTICE THEIS joins in this dissent.

Sources

People v. Austin, 2019 IL 123910 (2019). http://illinoiscourts.gov/Opinions/SupremeCourt/2019/123910.pdf

U.S. Supreme Court (2020, October 5). Docket No. 19-1029. Petition DENIED. https://www.supremecourt.gov/docket/docketfiles/html/public/19-1029.html

In the U.S. Supreme Court filings for the *Austin* case, she was supported in a friend of the court brief by the First Amendment Lawyers Association and the Marion B. Brechner First Amendment Project at the University of Florida (First Amendment Lawyers Association, 2020). First Amendment lawyers argued that the Illinois "… court below effectively identified two categories of speech as falling outside the First Amendment's usual requirement that strict scrutiny be applied to content-based laws like the one squarely at issue in *Austin*: *speech with secondary effects on privacy interests*; and *speech on purely private matters*" (pp. 3–4). Their U.S. Supreme Court brief contended that: A) "A content-based restriction's justification does not render it content neutral;" and B) "A content-based restriction is no more valid because it restricts speech involving purely private matters;" (pp. 4–12). They cited four precedents – *Stevens, Alvarez, Brown* and *Reed* – in which the U.S. Supreme Court "… meant what it said: speech outside of a few narrow categories of historically unprotected speech is protected, and a facially content-based restriction on protected speech is void unless it survives strict scrutiny, not some lesser standard of review" (p. 13). The Court, however, saved for a future case to elaborate on legal restriction of online speech.

ETHICAL FRAMEWORKS AND ISSUES

Social media content moderation falls within contract law between sites and users that makes possible the application of rules …

Box 7.5 Case Study: Social Media Moderators

Social media platforms, such as YouTube and Facebook, have a daunting task to filter video and other content that does not meet site standards. A former YouTube moderator sued parent company Google "accusing it of failing to protect workers" from having to "watch murders, abortions, child rape, animal mutilation, and suicides" (Elias, 2020, paras. 1-2). Google had hired moderators from a contractor, Collebera, and the lawsuit claimed that moderators paid for their own mental health treatment because "wellness coaches" were unavailable during evening and weekend shifts. Facebook faced similar challenges with the use of human coders after artificial intelligence software lacked accuracy and blocked too much content.

Jane Doe v. YouTube, Inc. (2020) was filed as a class action **civil case** in San Mateo, California, and it claimed that YouTube failed "to provide a safe workplace for the thousands of contractors that scrub YouTube's platform of disturbing content" (p. 1). The lawsuit alleged that the contractor system was designed to "maintain a sanitized platform" needed to maximize profits (p. 1). YouTube used a Single Review Tool (SRT), and the lawsuit claimed that moderators were forced to sign a consent form and use "robust and mandatory counseling and mental health support" (p. 2).

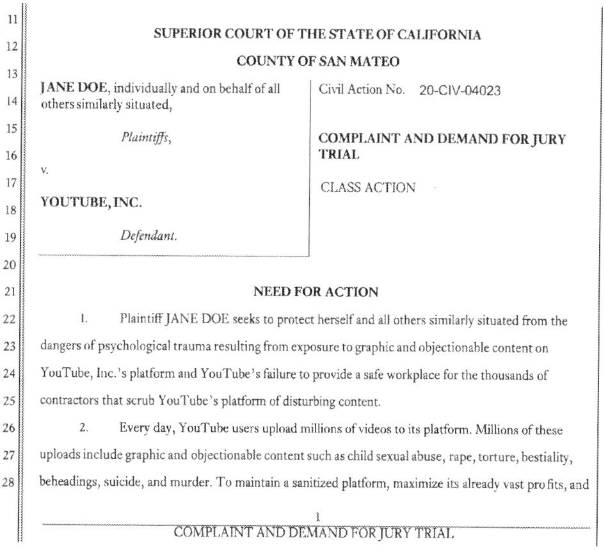
SUPERIOR COURT OF THE STATE OF CALIFORNIA

COUNTY OF SAN MATEO

JANE DOE, individually and on behalf of all others similarly situated,

Plaintiffs,

v.

YOUTUBE, INC.

Defendant.

Civil Action No. 20-CIV-04023

COMPLAINT AND DEMAND FOR JURY TRIAL

CLASS ACTION

NEED FOR ACTION

1. Plaintiff JANE DOE seeks to protect herself and all others similarly situated from the dangers of psychological trauma resulting from exposure to graphic and objectionable content on YouTube, Inc.'s platform and YouTube's failure to provide a safe workplace for the thousands of contractors that scrub YouTube's platform of disturbing content.

2. Every day, YouTube users upload millions of videos to its platform. Millions of these uploads include graphic and objectionable content such as child sexual abuse, rape, torture, bestiality, beheadings, suicide, and murder. To maintain a sanitized platform, maximize its already vast profits, and

1

COMPLAINT AND DEMAND FOR JURY TRIAL

Doe v. YouTube (2020).

Courtesy Superior Court of the State of California. https://www.pacermonitor.com/public/case/36840848/Doe_v_YouTube,_Inc.

The lawsuit claimed that Google wrote workplace safety standards that acknowledge psychological effects of moderating abusive content, but constant viewing could lead to posttraumatic stress disorder (PTSD), anxiety and depression.

The unnamed plaintiff, "Jane Doe," sought compensation for being exposed to "graphic and objectionable content," mental health support and screening (p. 3). She worked for the Google contractor in 2018 and 2019, at a time when the company reported more than $175 billion earnings. Among other factual allegations in the lawsuit:

- YouTube and Google had combined advertising revenue of $150 in 2019
- YouTube users upload 500 hours of video per minute
- YouTube flagged content queues included: "Violent Extremism" (VE), "Adult," "Hate and Harassment," "Child Sexual Abuse Imagery" (CSAI), "Redshift," "Flagged," and "Sexual Activity and Nudity" (pp. 5–6)

Google was a member of the "Technology Coalition" that was created "to develop technology solutions to disrupt the ability to use the Internet to exploit children or distribute child pornography (p. 7). That group published *Employee Resilience Guidebook for Handling Child Sexual Abuse Images* (2015), and suggested that employers create formal programs (pp. 7–8). The guide suggested limiting the amount of time employees are exposed to these harmful images. The *Doe* lawsuit alleged that YouTube failed to implement the industry guidelines and standards (pp. 10–11). "Despite these complex Community Guidelines, YouTube imposed strict quantity quotas on Content Moderators ... [and they were] required to review between 100 and 300 pieces of content per day with an error rate of two to five percent" (p. 13).

The moderators allegedly were required to also sign nondisclosure agreements (NDAs) and attend "confidentiality trainings" provided by the YouTube contractor (p. 21). The lawsuit alleged that YouTube failed to comply with California state law that requires "safe and healthful" workplaces (p. 25).

Sources

Elias, Jennifer (2020, September 22). Former YouTube Content Moderator Describes Horrors of the Job in New Lawsuit. *CNBC*. https://www.nbcnews.com/tech/tech-news/former-youtube-content-moderator-describes-horrors-job-new-lawsuit-rcna134.

Jane Doe v. YouTube. https://www.scribd.com/document/476939218/Moderator-complaint-against-YouTube#download.

Social media bullies present a challenge to maintaining civility because they sometimes hide their identities. "The Science Femme" on Twitter, for example, turned out to be a white male assistant professor of chemistry at the University of New Hampshire (Weill, 2020). After claiming to derail a departmental statement condemning racism and then being attacked on Twitter, the account allegedly run by Craig Chapman responded that she was "a woman of color herself – and an immigrant to boot" (paras. 1–2). The university investigated complaints and a @piney_ the account was closed. Other professors and graduate students have faked racial or ethnic identities for career advancement, but this was a cover for political views, as the account shared an Elizabeth Warren meme that was captioned "growing up Chinese in South Detroit I struggled as an African American Jewish Boy" (paras. 22–24).

In another case, viral two-minute video of a "racist white man being smacked in the head with a can" of "Twisted Tea" also "spawned" a large number of memes (Lock, 2020, para. 1). The convenience store video had millions of views and social media shares:

> The altercation, first shared to Reddit alongside the title "Drunk guy yells N Word and gets SMACKED with Twisted Tea Can," shows two men embroiled in an exchange at the register.
>
> (para. 3)

At the start of the video, a white man used profanity and sexual threats against the black man's mother. The "seemingly inebriated white man" appeared to be drunk and was buying beer, as he claimed to live "two blocks away" (paras. 5–6). One could argue that, under the law, the use of the N-word and other threats are fighting words. The altercation escalated before the tea was tossed. The social media attraction of the viral video raises important social questions about the popularity of the video.

Box 7.6 Facebook Mental Health Resources

In 2020, Facebook appeared to acknowledge the negative impact social media can have on mental health. Social media addiction, fear of missing out (FOMO), online harassment, suicide and other issues should be reason for sites and users to exercise ethical responses. Facebook collaborated with mental health experts, as it used the Covid-19 pandemic as an impetus to support "struggling" users through its emotional resource center:

> We've been working with leading authorities around the world – like NAMI, Kids Help Phone and It's OK to Talk – to invest in the critical areas of mental health support, including handling financial stress, parenting support, coping with loss and grief, managing substance use and taking care of overall emotional health … The resource will be available globally, with locally relevant information from mental health officials. Over time we will build on the features and topic areas based on the guidance of our global and national partners.
>
> (para. 2)

Facebook developed a separate app designed to connect people with mental health professionals. It also used the World Health Organization (WHO) Digital Stress Management Guide and integrated a WhatsApp WHO Health Alert chatbot.

Source: Facebook (2020, October 5). Connecting People to Mental Health Resources Around the World. https://about.fb.com/news/2020/10/connecting-people-to-mental-health-resources/.

Even as most states passed laws to create misdemeanor or felony penalties for use of revenge porn on social media or other Internet communication, technology presents a new issue. "Deep fake" videos could be created that place a person's head on another body through artificial intelligence (AI) manipulation (Gieseke, 2020):

> Consider this technology to represent the next iteration of revenge pornography: instead of leaking a nude image initially shared privately, the perpetrator can create – or request the creation of – a pornographic video starring any woman who has shared images of herself, clothed or not, on social media.
>
> (p. 1481)

The AI application may be difficult to stop because sites hosting the video have "hyper-immunity" under Section 230 statute law since the late 1990s (p. 1493). Beyond this, it is not clear that civil privacy tort cases would be effective in stopping the posts and punishing the creators. Likewise, creators could use a transformative content argument as a defense in a copyright case. State, federal, and international law currently are not strong enough to fully protect "sexual privacy" from "weaponized" video manipulation designed to deceive viewers and harm victims (pp. 1514–1515). At the same time, revenge porn continues to create thorny First Amendment issues when content is otherwise protected free expression.

Box 7.7 Thought Leader William R. Davie

William R. Davie.

Photograph by Yuling Huang-Davie.

Social media have become a virtual battleground for some, where the rules of engagement are not always clear. This fog of war helps those who stage attacks anonymously, but former president Donald Trump preferred to attack his foes in full view of the world with tweets squarely aimed between the eyes of journalists.

TAKING THE STING OUT OF SOCIAL MEDIA SLURS

In 2019, after turning down a banquet invitation from the White House Correspondents' Association (WHCA), the president tweeted how the press had worked against his Make America Great (MAGA) catchphrase and hurled an epithet in all caps coined by playwright Henrik Ibsen (Samuels, 2019):

> The press is doing everything within their power to fight the magnificence of the phrase, MAKE AMERICA GREAT AGAIN!" They can't stand the fact that this Administration has done more than virtually any other Administration in its first 2yrs. They are truly the ENEMY OF THE PEOPLE!
>
> (@realDonaldTrump)

This presidential tweet and similar ones generated much attention from their intended target, the news media that dutifully reported both Trump's attacks and the public reaction to them. By then the president's stock in trade was familiar to all since his list of insults had grown longer and stronger: "clown," "dummy," "phony," "lightweight," "wacko," "nasty," "slimeball," "obnoxious," "crooked," "little," and "lying," to quote but a few of his so-called nicknames (Lee & Quealy, 2019).

In her *New York Post* column titled, "Why I swore off social-media name calling," Karol Markowicz explained the president's tweets were actually a part of his New York-ness, although she preferred a different principle for social media replies: "Never argue with a fool; onlookers may not be able to tell the difference" (Markowicz, 2017, para. 12). The president's style of name calling raised pertinent questions about what might be done to curb *anti*-social media abuse.

One key concern was how the online conversation that descended into name calling could deteriorate into *hate speech* once the insults began to stereotype participants based on their gender, race, ethnicity, sexual identity, religion, disability, age, or national origin. Facebook's public policy official, Richard Allan, determined that online messaging could turn into a hateful label without even naming a specific person. When a social media post, for example, labels a certain race as *violent animals* or describes a sexual orientation as *disgusting*, it enters the realm of dangerous hate speech (Allan, 2017).

When such insults are repeated and reinforced it can become worthy of criminal prosecution in the United States. Forty-four states have enacted cyberbullying laws designed to prevent *willful and repeated harm inflicted through the use of digital and mobile devices*. In Louisiana, the crime covers "transmission of any electronic textual, visual, written, or oral communication with the willful intent to coerce, abuse, torment, or intimidate a person under the age of eighteen" (Louisiana Laws, 2011).

These laws tend to protect minors but online exchanges causing *anti*-social abuse between adults are unfettered even if the debate devolves into a vindictive and vulgar war of words. British scholar and programmer Paul Graham's Hierarchy of Disagreement classified online name calling as the lowest form of argument. The verbal abuse can use insulting or demeaning labels directed at an individual or group (2008). Graham places it lower even than ad hominem attacks, where the authority of the opponent is challenged without addressing the points of their argument. Presiding at the top of Graham's hierarchy is refuting the main points of the adversary's case. Name calling, in contrast, fosters an atmosphere of disrespect and intimidation discouraging to those who seek to be enlightened by the discussion and not just enflamed.

Papacharissi (2004) studied civility in political discussions and found how anonymity emboldened some, but when speakers were "focused on structuring a valid argument, they were seldom impolite and rarely uncivil" (p. 278). "The lack of face-to-face interaction may make some less mindful of their manners," she noted pointing to the cowardice, "frequent instances of flaming between participants who did not seem to know each other virtually as well attest to the influence of anonymity in online interaction" (p. 277).

If the controversial discussion online produces a toxic interplay of exclusion and intimidation, social media name calling can reach the point of real-world peril. Legal scholar Susan Benesch coined the term "dangerous speech" to describe how fear-inducing, divisive attacks historically inflamed mass violence whether the country was Nazi Germany or Rwanda, Africa. In identifying the causes of such attacks, she defined the dehumanizing attacks as "referring to people as insects, despised animals, bacteria, or cancer" (Dangerous Speech Project, 2020, para. 1). Such a verbal attack might make the violence seem reasonable and acceptable because it is not actually human beings but another form of life, such as a rodent or vermin that should be exterminated.

There are other hallmarks to dangerous tactics that turn civilians into aggressors. Benesch and Buerger described one as the *accusation in a mirror*, when the dangerous speaker projects a threatened activity on an enemy when, in fact, the speaker is planning to commit the offense on their own. The proper response is to use *counter-speech*, which has the positive impact of convincing the abusive speaker to stop speaking dangerously. Two types of counter-speech are described as counter-messaging campaigns and spontaneous responses (Dangerous Speech Project, Counter-speech, para. 2). Benesch and Buerger encourage *counter-speech* to respond directly to refute or undermine such assaults.

Finally, the question becomes how effective counter-speech can be in turning back an online aggressor who is committed to belittling and demeaning opposing social media speakers. It is reasonable to assume counter-speech would provoke and escalate name calling to an even more onerous exchange. Such offenders are not easily disarmed by ethical rebuttals since they relish their role of rule breaker and are well practiced at ignoring codes of rights and responsibilities. A better solution is to forcibly disarm the abusers by identifying them by name; then placing their names in a type of "rogue's gallery" of social media, where their punishment will be a permanent exodus from the forum of online conversation. Only then can social media channels return to a state of peaceful conversation and civil discussion. The alternative is to stand by idly while such spaces are further marred by vicious attacks as a prelude to violence.

William R. Davie heads the Mass Communication/Broadcasting program for the University of Louisiana at Lafayette. He is the holder of the Board of Regents Support Fund professorship and has served as the acting head of his department and coordinator of the graduate program. He was a Fulbright teaching scholar in China and is a frequent presenter at conferences of the Broadcast Education Association (BEA), the International Communication Association (ICA) and Association of Education of Journalism and Mass Communication (AEJMC). Professor Davie received the Edward L. Bliss Award for his contributions to journalism education from the Association of Education in Journalism and Mass Communication (AEJMC) and was listed among News Pro's Top Ten Outstanding Journalism Educators in 2018. He is a coauthor of textbooks in media law and ethics and has contributed to other edited volumes, journal articles, encyclopedias, book reviews and research papers.

Sources

Allan, R. (2017, June 27). Hard Questions: Who Should Decide What is Hate Speech in an Online Global Community. *Facebook*. https://about.fb.com/news/2017/06/hard-questions-hate-speech/.

Benesch, S. & Buerger, C. (2018, December). Dangerous Speech: A Practical Guide. *ResearchGate.* https://dangerousspeech.org/guide/.

Dangerous Speech Project (2020). What is Dangerous Speech? https://dangerousspeech.org/about-dangerous-speech/.

Dangerous Speech Project (2020). CounterSpeech. https://dangerousspeech.org/counterspeech/.

Louisiana Laws (2011). Cyberbullying, Title 14, Criminal Law RS 14:40.7. https://law.justia.com/codes/louisiana/2009/rs/title14/rs14-40.7.html.

Graham, P. (2008, March). How to Disagree. http://www.paulgraham.com/disagree.html.

Lee, J.C. and Quealy, K. (2019, May 24). The 598 People, Places and Things Donald Trump Has Insulted on Twitter: A Complete List. *New York Times*. https://www.nytimes.com/interactive/2016/01/28/upshot/donald-trump-twitter-insults.html.

Markowicz, K. (2017, Dec. 3). Why I Swore Off Social-media Name Calling. *New York Post*. https://www.nypost.com/2017/12/03/why-i-swore-off-social-media-name-calling/amp/.

Papacharissi, Z. (2004) Democracy Online: Civility, Politeness, and the Democratic Potential of Online Political Discussion Groups, *new media & society*, 6(2), 259–283.

Samuels, B. (2019, April 5). Trump Ramps Up Rhetoric on Media, Calls Press 'The Enemy of the People.' *The Hill.* https://www.amp/s/thehill.com/homenews/.administration/437610-trump-calls-press-the-enemy-of-the-people%3famp.

Trump, D. J. (2019, April 5). Tweet @realDonald Trump.

ONLINE RESOURCES

FindLaw (2020, January 13). State Revenge Porn Laws. https://criminal.findlaw.com/ criminal-charges/revenge-porn-laws-by-state.html.

Center for Countering Digital Hate (2020). Strengthening Communities and Democracy by Disrupting Identity-based Hate and Dangerous Misinformation in Digital Spaces. https://www.counterhate.co.uk/.

DISCUSSION QUESTIONS

1. Why or why not should the First Amendment protect speakers against state revenge porn laws?
2. What protection under the law should victims of revenge porn have to fight back? Should criminal or civil law be used after nude photographs are distributed without a victim's consent?
3. What specific legal remedies are there for cyberbullying? Beyond law, which ethical values can be used to fight it?

REFERENCES

Associated Press (2020a, November 20). Global Tech Giants Threaten to leave Pakistan Over New Rules. https://apnews.com/article/technology-pakistan-media-social-media-asia-2d9071247273bf0f1a9758aaaa1efe85.

Associated Press (2020b, November 13). Bangladeshi Wins Children's Prize for Fighting Cyberbullying. https://apnews.com/article/parkland-florida-school-shooting-netherlands-the-hague-52ead1bffe399dcd66b5fd96b9b6f624.

Bronstein, C. (2011). *Battling Pornography: The American Feminist Anti-Pornography Movement, 1976–1986*. New York: Cambridge University Press.

Bustamante, D. (2017, Spring). Florida Joins the Fight Against Revenge Porn: Analysis of Florida's New Anti-Revenge Porn Law, *Florida International University Law Review*, 12, 357–389.

Center for Countering Digital Hate (2020). Strengthening Communities and Democracy by Disrupting Identity-based Hate and Dangerous Misinformation in Digital Spaces. https://www.counterhate.co.uk/.

Chan, K. (2020, December 15). UK Plans Big Fines for Online Companies Over Harmful Content. *Associated Press*. https://apnews.com/article/business-media-bills-social-media-19038a8f0a68448ce6037308930a5efc.

Elias, J. (2020, September 22). Former YouTube Content Moderator Describes Horrors of the Job in New Lawsuit.*CNBC*. https://www.nbcnews.com/tech/tech-news/former-youtube-content-moderator-describes-horrors-job-new-lawsuit-rcna134.

Facebook (2020, October 5). Connecting People to Mental Health Resources Around the World. https://about.fb.com/news/2020/10/connecting-people-to-mental-health-resources/.

FindLaw (2020, January 13). State Revenge Porn Laws. https://criminal.findlaw.com/ criminal-charges/revenge-porn-laws-by-state.html.

First Amendment Lawyers Association (2020, March 20). Brief amici curiae of First Amendment Lawyers Association and the Marion B. Brechner First Amendment Project filed. U.S. Supreme Court Docket No. 19-1029. https://www.supremecourt.gov/docket/docketfiles/html/public/19-1029.html.

Gabriel, K. (2020, Summer). Feminist Revenge: Seeking Justice for Nonconsensual Pornography Through "Revenge Porn" Reform, *Vermont Law Review*, 44, 849–892.

Gieseke, A.P. (2020, October). "The New Weapon of Choice": Law's Current Inability to Properly Address Deepfake Pornography, *Vanderbilt Law Review*, 73, 1479–1515.

Gilmer, M. (2016, May 8). Twitter Blocks U.S. Intelligence Agency Access to Social Media Tool, Report Says. *Mashable*. http://mashable.com/2016/05/08/twitter-blocks-dataminr-access/.

Halprin, M. (2019, December 11). An Update to Our Harassment Policy. *YouTube Official Blog*. https://blog.youtube/news-and-events/an-update-to-our-harassment-policy.

Instagram Terms of Service (2020, December 20). https://help.instagram.com/1215086795543252.

Jane Doe v. YouTube, Inc. (2020, September 21). 20-CV-04023, California Superior Court, San Mateo. https://www.scribd.com/document/476939218/Moderator-complaint-against-YouTube#download.

Jibillian, I. (2020, December 8). *Business Insider*. https://www.businessinsider.com/pornhub-visa-mastercard-major-changes-platform-rules-revenge-porn-2020-12.

Kenney, M. (2020, November 23). Elgin Woman Accused of Posting Nude Photos of Husband's Mistress on Facebook. *Chicago Sun-Times*. https://chicago.suntimes.com/crime/2020/11/23/21595019/elgin-woman-accused-posting-nude-photos-husbands-mistress-facebook.

Kristof, N. (2020, December 4). The Children of Pornhub. *New York Times.* https://www.nytimes.com/2020/12/04/opinion/sunday/pornhub-rape-trafficking.html.

Lock, S. (2020, December 29). "Twisted Tea" Video Viewed Over 1 Million Times, Inspires Wave of Memes. *Newsweek.* https://www.newsweek.com/twisted-tea-video-1-million-times-memes-1557664.

Logeretta, E. (2020, November 25). Prince Charles and Duchess Camilla Disable Twitter Replies After Receiving Backlash from "The Crown." *Us Magazine.* https://www.usmagazine.com/celebrity-news/news/prince-charles-camilla-disable-twitter-replies-amid-the-crown/.

Mansur, S. and Reiland, J. (2019, October 25). State High Court: "Revenge Porn" is Constitutional. *Chicago Daily Law Bulletin.* https://www.chicagolawbulletin.com/illinois-revenge-porn-law-survives-high-court-challenge-20191019.

Miller, M.M. (2013, October 17). Revenge Porn Victim Holly Jacobs "Ruined My Life," Ex Says. *Miami New Times.* https://www.miaminewtimes.com/news/revenge-porn-victim-holly-jacobs-ruined-my-life-ex-says-6393654.

Ortutay, B. and Klepper, D. (2020, November 5). Facebook Bans Big "Stop the Steal" Group for Sowing Violence. *Associated Press.* https://apnews.com/article/election-2020-donald-trump-misinformation-violence-elections-d5c9bd5fe6a799fd627c50521b6cbb36.

People v. Austin, 2019 IL 123910 (2019). http://illinoiscourts.gov/Opinions/SupremeCourt/2019/123910.pdf.

Reinstein, J. (2020, November 25). Delta Fired A White Flight Attendant After Asking Whether She Was "Racist" Toward White Men. *BuzzfFeed News.* https://www.buzzfeednews.com/article/juliareinstein/delta-fires-flight-attendant-feminist-facebook-trolls.

Sanders, A.K. (2017). Obscenity, Revenge Pornography, and Cyberbullying. In Daxton R. Stewart, *Social Media and the Law, A Guidebook for Communication Students and Professionals,* 2nd edition, pp. 182–202. New York and London: Routledge.

Tribune India (2020, November 19). Pakistan's New Social Media Rules Draw Criticism. https://www.tribuneindia.com/news/world/pakistans-new-social-media-rules-draw-criticism-172721.

U.S. Supreme Court (2020, October 5). Docket No. 19-1029. Petition DENIED. https://www.supremecourt.gov/docket/docketfiles/html/public/19-1029.html.

Watson, J.C. (2021). Regulating Pornography. In W. Wat Hopkins, *Communication and the Law,* pp. 67–80. Northport, AL: Vision Press.

Weill, K. (2020, October 6). White Male Professor Allegedly Posed as Woman of Color to Bully Women. *Daily Beast.* https://www.thedailybeast.com/the-science-femme-was-allegedly-a-white-male-professor-who-posed-as-woman-of-color-and-bullied-women.

Weiner, I. (2020, December 15). Washington, DC Passes Landmark Civil Rights Legislation, Prohibiting Discrimination by Websites and Online Services. *Lawyers' Committee for Civil Rights Under Law.* https://www.lawyerscommittee.org/washington-d-c-passes-landmark-civil-rights-legislation-prohibits-discrimination-by-websites-and-other-online-services/.

Defamation

8

> *The common law of defamation is an oddity of tort law, for it allows recovery of purportedly compensatory damages without evidence of actual loss ...*
>
> *The largely uncontrolled discretion of juries to award damages where there is no loss unnecessarily compounds the potential of any system of liability for defamatory falsehood to inhibit the vigorous exercise of* First Amendment *freedoms. Additionally, the doctrine of presumed damages invites juries to punish unpopular opinion rather than to compensate individuals for injury sustained by the publication of a false fact.*

—U.S. Supreme Court Justice Lewis F. Powell,
Gertz v. Robert Welch (1974, p. 349)

Within a social media communication context, "exaggerated, loose, figurative language, rhetorical hyperbole and parody," and opinions "incapable of being proven true or false" have First Amendment protection (p. 44). However, if a social media user posts provably false statements as fact, a lawsuit could follow. Even when no individual is named within an attack on reputation of a few individuals, **group libel** law allows them to sue for damages under the theory that they may be identifiable in context of a story.

The U.S. Supreme Court has yet to clarify a lower court issue with the protection of media and non-media defendants in libel cases (*Gertz v. Welch*, 1974). Civil subsequent punishment lawsuits arise from defamatory statements that frequently happen within Internet communication and its limited government regulation (*Reno v. ACLU*, 1997). Online speech grew at a time when libel and privacy lawsuits against media were rising (Sanford, 1991).

In 2020, for example, former Liberty University president, Jerry Falwell, Jr., sued for defamation and breach of contract in Lynchburg, Virginia Circuit Court. The case was related to a sex scandal, inappropriate behavior and statements made by university officials before his resignation (Burke, 2020). Online content about Falwell was widely spread across social media channels, including an Instagram photo with his arm around a woman and both wearing unzipped pants during a "costume party" (para. 21). Earlier in the year, Falwell was criticized for the photo he tweeted (and later deleted) of a man in blackface and another wearing a Ku Klux Klan robe. Officials said: "[W]e have learned enough about the past to know that we had no choice but to take the leadership of Liberty University in a new direction" (para. 19). Falwell, a lawyer, real estate developer and son of the university's Moral Majority cofounder, responded in a radio interview that he grew the university while not being Liberty's "moral leader" (para. 23). The lawsuit claimed:

> When Mr. Falwell and his family became the targets of a malicious smear campaign incited by anti-evangelical forces, Liberty University not only accepted the salacious and baseless accusations against the Falwells at face value, but directly participated in the defamation. This action seeks redress for the damage Liberty has caused to the reputation of Mr. Falwell and his family.
>
> (Rankin & Schor, 2020, para. 3)

The lawsuit denied allegations about Falwell's "involvement in an extramarital affair between his wife and a business partner" and claimed Liberty University instead accepted them "and 'moved quickly' to destroy his reputation" (para. 2). His father, Jerry Falwell, known for his conservative politics when Liberty University was established in 1971, was also a party in a landmark Supreme Court First Amendment case involving a magazine advertisement parody (*Hustler Magazine v. Falwell*, 1988). Falwell had sued *Hustler* and publisher Larry Flynt and initially won for libel, **slander** and intentional infliction of emotional distress for a caricature of him, but the judgment was overturned by the Supreme Court because he was a public figure, and the actual malice evidence standard had not been proved. *Hustler Magazine*'s November 1983 issue inside front cover featured a parody of a Campari Liqueur ad titled "Jerry Falwell talks about his first time" and claimed "his 'first time' was during a drunken incestuous rendezvous with his mother in an outhouse" (p. 48). The parody ad portrayed Falwell as "a hypocrite who preaches only when he is drunk" and, in small print at the bottom of the page, the ad contains the disclaimer "ad parody – not to be taken seriously" (p. 48). The lawsuit also originally made a claim of invasion of privacy and the libel claim survived with a jury finding "that the ad parody could not 'reasonably be understood as describing actual facts about [respondent] or actual events in which [he] participated'" (p. 49). The 8-0 Supreme Court decision relied on established precedent in U.S. defamation law and reversed the Fourth Circuit that had "interpreted the jury's finding to be that the ad parody 'was not reasonably believable'" (p. 57). Public figures and officials, under the tort of intentional infliction of emotional distress, must show that a publication "contains a false statement of fact which was made with 'actual malice,' i.e., with knowledge that the statement was false or with reckless disregard as to whether or not it was true" – central to the "adequate 'breathing space' to the freedoms protected by the First Amendment" (p. 56).

Defamation law in the United States is divided into libel and slander. These legal torts address publication and speech that may harm the reputation of someone or organization within the collective eye of the public. Damage to reputation, then, may come in the form of publishing in a written form (libel) or an oral expression (slander). State law is in disagreement over the libel and slander distinction – especially as it relates to broadcast news in which written scripts are read. Libel cases apply state laws and the U.S. Supreme Court has repeatedly supported the idea that a reputation can be damaged by free expression. In *Milkovich v. Lorrain Journal* (1990), a high school wrestling coach in Ohio had been sanctioned after the team fought with opponents. Parents won a restraining order against team punishment because the coach may have incited the brawl. A sports columnist claimed in 1974 that this was a "big lie" and that the coach lied at a hearing. Following 15 years of litigation, the Ohio Court of Appeals found that the newspaper column was constitutionally protected speech. On appeal, the U.S. Supreme Court reversed the decision, noting that the Constitution protects some false statements, but there is not a complete exemption for labeled opinion. The *Milkovich* court quoted Restatement of Torts, §§ 565–567:

> Under the law of defamation, an expression of opinion could be defamatory if the expression was sufficiently derogatory of another as to cause harm to his reputation, so as to lower him in the estimation of the community or to deter third persons from associating or dealing with him … The expression of opinion was also actionable in a suit for defamation, despite the normal requirement that the communication be false as well as defamatory … This position was maintained even though the truth or falsity of an opinion – as distinguished from a statement of fact – is not a matter that can be objectively determined and truth is a complete defense to a suit for defamation.
>
> (*Milkovich*, 1990, pp. 16–17)

Applied to our social media era, this case should serve as a warning to those believing they can offer any online opinion without liability. In this regard, social media users should be careful to avoid "red flag" words and phrases identified by Sanford (2020) in his analyses of defamation litigation over several decades.

Box 8.1 Sanford's "Red Flag" Words

Noted First Amendment scholar Bruce W. Sanford (1991) has listed words that courts in libel cases interpret as actionable. There are dozens of words and phrases, but here are some that could be problematic when used in social media posts:

- Adultery
- Bribery
- Child abuse
- Deadbeat
- Ex-convict
- Fraud
- Gangster
- Hypocrite
- Incompetent
- Ku Klux Klan

- Mental illness
- Nazi
- Plagiarist
- Rapist
- Slacker
- Thief
- Unethical
- Villain

Sources

Sanford, B.W. (1991). *Sanford's Synopsis of Libel & Privacy*, 4th edition. Mahwah, NJ: World Almanac Books, pp. 32–33.

Sanford, B.W. (2020). *Libel and Privacy*, 2nd edition, Section 4. South Holland, Netherlands: Wolters Kluwer. https://lrus.wolterskluwer.com/store/product/libel-and-privacy-second-edition/.

Sanford (1991) also has urged that journalists and other speakers avoid libel and privacy lawsuits by avoiding carelessness, adhering to the truth, being cautious about any statement that "reasonably implies false facts about someone," watching out for the "routine," examining all sides, accurately quoting, avoiding "sly or cute innuendo," obtaining consent for images and correcting errors (pp. 3–4). Under the law, "false-light" invasion of privacy cases are "closely akin to libel" because of "the element of falsity" (p. 28).

U.S. law limits government from blocking most speech ahead of publication but civil and criminal cases may follow. In the area of libel law, individuals and organizations may sue a speaker by making a claim that free expression harmed reputation. International legal scholar Kyu Ho Youm (2020) concludes that there is a considerable amount of balancing of interests in this area of law:

> The libel law of a society indicates to a large extent how the society balances the importance of reputational interests with freedom of speech. Harm to reputation has been a criminal offense or a civil wrong since civilization's earliest days, but the social and cultural approach to reputation as a value varies from society to society.
>
> (p. 79)

Historically, journalists and other speakers have been the target of a majority of libel lawsuits, but the blunt nature of social media communication on Twitter and other platforms creates a complex social and legal context. Many lawyers have suggested that bloggers and other professionals should purchase libel insurance to protect personal assets from multi-million-dollar cases. The chilling effect on speech has been amplified because some courts are treating bloggers as no different from professional journalists: "We hold that liability for a defamatory blog post involving a matter of public concern cannot be imposed without proof of fault and actual damages" (*Obsidian Finance Group v. Cox*, 2014, p. 1287).

Libel, as well as privacy law, can be traced to English common law of the 15th and 16th centuries. Even before this, "false news or tales" that sparked "discord" between people and the king were punishable as early as 1275. Prior restraints were the norm for hundreds of years in the form of press licensing through the Stationer's Company, prosecution in the Court of High Commission and the secret Star Chamber and other means. Under **seditious libel** law, criminal prosecution did not allow for truth as defense under the theory that harm to the government was greater for truthful claims. By the time of the U.S. colonies, however, a degree of partisan speech had emerged. The Constitution, First Amendment and the Bill of Rights were not immediately a protection against state seditious libel prosecution. The 20th-century acceptance by the Court of a marketplace of ideas philosophy was strengthened by *Near v. Minnesota* (1931) and the limiting of government prior restraint, as well as acceptance that claims against **public officials** create scandal. **Private libel** cases became more frequent concerns.

In *New York Times v. Sullivan* (1964), the U.S. Supreme Court constitutionalized libel law in a way that made it more difficult for officials to successfully sue for defamation. In that landmark case, the Court was required "to determine for the first time the extent to which the constitutional protections for speech and press limit a State's power to award damages in a libel action brought by a public official against critics of his official conduct" (p. 256):

> Thus we consider this case against the background of a profound national commitment to the principle that debate on public issues should be uninhibited, robust, and wide-open, and that it may well include vehement, caustic, and sometimes unpleasantly sharp attacks on government and public officials … The present advertisement, as an expression of grievance and protest on one of the major public issues of our time, would seem clearly to qualify for the constitutional protection. The question is whether it forfeits that protection by the falsity of some of its factual statements and by its alleged defamation of respondent.
>
> (pp. 270–271)

While a private individual under state law generally must only prove that speech was negligent or sloppy, a public figure or official must show actual malice – that the speaker entertained serious doubts and recklessly disregarded the truth (*Garrison v. Louisiana*, 1964). Under these rules, the plaintiff in a libel suit must first show:

1. **Publication** – the information was shared with the public
2. **Identification** – the defamatory statement either named the plaintiff or was clearly about the person
3. **Falsity** – a plaintiff must prove that a statement was false
4. **Defamation** – the expression must ridicule, disparage or otherwise damage reputation
5. **Fault** – a plaintiff must prove negligence or actual malice
6. **Damages** – there must be actual (compensatory) and/or punitive damages

Defamation may be libel per se in that on face the statements are defamatory. For example, if a social media post accuses someone of a crime, disparages professional performance, claims a terrible disease or suggests illicit sexual behavior, then a statement is more obviously defamatory. A libel otherwise may be per quod, which is in context. Some states use an innocent construction rule that protects statements that reasonably can be innocently construed.

At the end of a plaintiff's case, a speaker's lawyer would ask for summary judgment, ending the case, if the above are not proved. If there is enough evidence to continue, then a media or social media defendant must respond by showing:

1. **Truth** – the story or post had substantial truth and the gist of it was correct
2. **Libel-proof** – a reputation already in tatters may not be further damaged
3. **Fair reporting** – public meetings and records fairly described may be protected
4. **Neutral reporting** – a fair summary of conflict may be protected
5. **Opinion privilege** – conclusions that offer readers enough factual information to make their own conclusions may be protected

In tweets, blog posts and other social media communication, it is essential that site users think before they post about the potential legal ramification of reputational harm. Time-consuming and costly litigation is personally and professionally dangerous. While large media corporations have First Amendment lawyers ready to respond, bloggers and social media commentators may have no protection against litigation for making a false statement of fact.

FALSE STATEMENTS

In *Susan B. Anthony List v. Driehaus* (2014), the U.S. Supreme Court reversed and remanded an Ohio case involving a state law that prohibited specific "false statements" during a political campaign (p. 151). The Susan B. Anthony List "pro-life" group in 2010 criticized members of Congress who voted for the Patient Protection and Affordable Care Act (ACA), also known as "Obama Care" (p. 154). At issue was the statement that Steve Driehaus had "voted FOR taxpayer-funded abortion" (p. 154). He lost the election and entered the Peace Corps in Africa. Justice Clarence Thomas, writing for the Court for a "credibility of threat," implies that:

> ... the false statement statute allows "any person" with knowledge of the purported violation to file a complaint ... Because the universe of potential complainants is not restricted to state officials who are constrained by explicit guidelines or ethical obligations, there is a real risk of complaints from, for example, political opponents ... And **petitioners**, who intend to criticize candidates for political office, are easy targets.
>
> (p. 164)

State laws and a commission could pose substantial First Amendment chilling effects on individuals and organizations posting social media candidate criticism during an election.

Applied to social media communication, any statement that could injure a reputation under the civil tort of defamation could result in a libel or slander lawsuit. Under the law, a prima facie defamation case rests on a false statement of fact that is published on a social media site in a negligent manner in which harm can be remedied through monetary damages. State laws determine how a private person proves negligence. Under *the New York Times v. Sullivan* (1964) actual malice standard, a public figure or official must prove reckless disregard for the truth via provable falsehoods.

GLOBAL APPROACHES

Civil and **criminal libel** laws vary from nation to nation and the global nature of social media communication and the Internet makes it difficult to generalize. The International Press Institute (2020) advocates for "international standards of freedom of expression and the protection of reputation" (para. 1). A group of human rights organizations are at the forefront of confronting national governments and leaders:

- U.N. Human Rights Committee
- European Court of Human Rights
- African Commission on Human and Peoples' Rights (ACHPR). (paras. 1–3)

The U.N. Human Rights Committee (2011) General Comment No. 34, for example, addresses Article 19, freedoms of opinion and expression:

> Freedom of opinion and freedom of expression are indispensable conditions for the full development of the person. They are essential for any society. They constitute the foundation stone for every free and democratic society. The two freedoms are closely related, with freedom of expression providing the vehicle for the exchange and development of opinions.
>
> (p. 1)

Free expression is considered an essential element of transparency and accountability in government: "The obligation to respect freedoms of opinion and expression is binding on every State party as a whole" (p. 2). The approach informs emerging international defamation law to avoid stifling free expression and to treat truth as a defense:

> At least with regard to comments about public figures, consideration should be given to avoiding penalizing or otherwise rendering unlawful untrue statements that have been published in error but without malice ... Care should be taken by States parties to avoid excessively punitive measures and penalties. Where relevant, States parties should place reasonable limits on the requirement for a defendant to reimburse the expenses of the successful party ... It is impermissible for a State party to indict a person for criminal defamation but then not to proceed to trial expeditiously – such a practice has a chilling effect that may unduly restrict the exercise of freedom of expression of the person.
>
> (p. 12)

Criminal defamation laws have been identified as primary threats to free expression. The Council of Europe passed a resolution in 2007 that called for definition clarity of defamation, if not decriminalization. The European Court of Human Rights expressed concern that journalists have been arrested, convicted and imprisoned for criminal libel and this in itself is a violation of international human rights. The U.S. Supreme Court has gone further than international law in ruling against criminal libel prosecution (*Garrison v. Louisiana*, 1964):

> At the outset, we must decide whether, in view of the differing history and purposes of criminal libel, the *New York Times* rule also limits state power to impose criminal sanctions for criticism of the official conduct of public officials. We hold that it does.
>
> (p. 67)

The U.S. Supreme Court appeared to favor use of civil libel law when a "calculated falsehood" is published against a public figure or official: "Although honest utterance, even if inaccurate, may further the fruitful exercise of the right of free speech, it does not follow that the lie, knowingly and deliberately published about a public official, should enjoy a like immunity" (p. 75). In such cases: "The test which we laid down in *New York Times* is not keyed to ordinary care; defeasance of the privilege is conditioned, not on mere negligence, but on reckless disregard for the truth" (p. 79). While the Court has not explicitly rejected criminal libel, it also has not upheld a narrowly tailored law in this area. Thus, it is much more likely to see a public figure or official sue under civil defamation law over the content of a social media post.

ETHICAL FRAMEWORKS AND ISSUES

Lawyers who make false and defamatory statements are not as common an issue as, for example, following state bar rules about maintaining client confidentiality, including within anonymous social media posts:

> Depending on your goals and use of social media, privacy settings may be beneficial. While a private profile may help separate your personal and professional online presence, it is not an automatic fix. Most states' professional conduct rules also extend to personal social media posts and profiles, making it imperative that attorneys remain mindful of the possible professional consequences for personal posts.
>
> (Saruya, 2020, para. 6)

One could imagine an anonymous post on Twitter that could lead to a defamation lawsuit, once the identity of the account came to light.

Harper (1926) focused on "the ethical canon of the speaker," a set of "moral principles" and what he called "the highest moral doctrine of the time and place" (p. 63). Legal and moral methods diverge, but the law historically made a connection: "To falsely accuse one of crime has always been regarded as a wrong which the law would redress with proof of naught but the defamatory words" (p. 65). The condemnation of gossip, for example, can be made by "critical moralists" and also be found defamatory under the law of falsity (p. 69). As an ethical issue, one must consider public interest in applying this to social media content. By disclosing that someone near you had Covid-19 and posting the information on Facebook or another site, this could be provably true or false and the subject of a libel suit. The legal questions would be about proof of falsity and whether negligence or actual malice would apply. As an ethics issue, however, we would apply fundamental values. As Ward suggested in Chapter 1, society-wide measures of responsibility would require common social values. Open ethics systems and structures may function better within social media communication (Ward & Wasserman, 2010).

For any social media post, we might consider the degree of integrity, honesty, fairness, loyalty, compassion, trustworthiness, restraint and other values (Murdough Center, 2020). In this sense, social media ethically require professional values to be applied even to our private or personal content and posts. While journalism professional norms empowered traditional media gatekeepers to consider fairness in search of truths (Mathewson, 2014), social media communication explores "meaning creation" and "plurality of meaning" (Caldiero, 2016, p. 34). If we lack agreement on objective truths, then legal constructs of defamation and privacy wade in muddy waters.

Box 8.2 Case Study: *Kogan v. Facebook, Inc.* (2020)

Facts. Aleksandr Kogan filed a complaint in New York in 2019 that Facebook executives had defamed him in 2018 as one of the data scientists who developed Cambridge Analytica software used to collect personal data from 80 million users.

Issues. Under federal rules of civil procedure, a defendant must be served within 90 days of a complaint filing, unless the plaintiff can show "good cause for the failure" and a need to extend time (p. 7). News reports claimed Kogan agreed to drop his lawsuit against

Facebook in early July of 2019, but "Kogan disputes that he told a reporter that he was 'dropping' the suit; he states that he instead indicated that he 'did not at the time see how [he] could, given [his] circumstances' (fn. 5).

Holding. District Judge Paul A. Engelmayer wrote the opinion for the court that dismissed the complaint against Facebook.

Reasoning. "Here, Kogan has not come forward with any coherent, substantiated excuse for his failure to effect timely service. And any excuse would have to take into account the extent of Kogan's lapse. Far from having effected service 'slightly late,' Kogan did not even request leave to file a waiver of service or an extension of time to serve defendants until six months after the *Rule 4(m)* deadline and nine months after the filing of his original Complaint" (p. 16).

Source: *Kogan v. Facebook, Inc.*, U.S. Dist. LEXIS 19464 (2020).

ONLINE RESOURCES

Legal Information Institute, Cornell Law School. Defamation. https://www.law.cornell.edu/ wex/defamation.

DISCUSSION QUESTIONS

1. Why should bloggers and micro-bloggers on Twitter be careful in the choice of words used to describe private people?
2. Why does the context of a political campaign or debate over public issues offer broader freedom to have "robust" social media exchanges with opponents?
3. If you could change U.S. defamation law, what would you propose? Why?

REFERENCES

Burke, D. (2020, October 29). Jerry Falwell, Jr. Sues Liberty University for Defamation. *CNN*. https://www.cnn.com/2020/10/29/us/falwell-liberty-university-lawsuit-defamation/index.html.

Caldiero, C. (2016). *Neo-PR, Public Relations in a Postmodern World.* New York: Peter Lang.
Food Lion, Inc. v. Capital Cities/ABC, 184 F.3d 505 (4th Cir. 1999).
Garrison v. Louisiana, 379 U.S. 64 (1964).
Gertz v. Robert Welch, Inc., 418 U.S. 323 (1974).
Harper, F.V. (1926). Ethical Basis of the Law of Defamation, *Dickinson Law Review,* 31(3), 63–78.
Hustler Magazine v. Falwell, 485 U.S. 46 (1988).
International Press Institute (2020). International Standards on Criminal and Civil Defamation Laws. *Media Laws Database.* http://legaldb.freemedia.at/international-standards/.
Kogan v. Facebook, Inc., U.S. Dist. LEXIS 19464 (2020).
Mathewson, J. (2014). *Law and Ethics for Today's Journalist: A Concise Guide.* Armonk, NY: M.E. Sharpe.
Milkovich v. Lorain Journal, 497 U.S. 1 (1990).
Murdough Center for Engineering Professionalism (2020). Recommended Core Ethical Values. http://www.depts.ttu.edu/murdoughcenter/products/resources/recommended-core-ethical-values.php.
New York Times v. Sullivan, 376 U.S. 254 (1964).
Obsidian Finance Group v. Cox, 740 F.3d 1284 (2014).
Rankin, S. and Schor, E. (2020, October 29). Falwell Sues Liberty, Saying School Damaged His Reputation. *Associated Press.* https://apnews.com/article/jerry-falwell-lawsuits-lynchburg-45e11f1455980d0bed7961bf9c03daaf.
Reno v. ACLU, 521 U.S. 844 (1997).
Sanford, B.W. (2020). *Libel and Privacy,* 2nd edition, Section 4. South Holland, Netherlands: Wolters Kluwer. https://lrus.wolterskluwer.com/store/product/libel-and-privacy-second-edition/.
Sanford, B.W. (1991). *Sanford's Synopsis of Libel & Privacy,* 4th edition. Mahwah, NJ: World Almanac Books.
Saruya, J.M. (2020, August 10). Legal and Ethical Considerations for Utilizing Social Media. *The Legal Intelligencer.* https://www.law.com/thelegalintelligencer/ 2020/08/10/legal-and-ethical-considerations-for-utilizing-social-media/.
Susan B. Anthony List v. Driehaus, 573 U.S. 149 (2014).
U.N. Human Rights Committee (2011, July). General Comment No. 34, International Covenant on Civil and Political Rights. 102nd Session. http://www2.ohchr.org/ english/bodies/hrc/docs/GC34.pdf.
Ward, S.J.A. and Wasserman, H. (2010). Towards an Open Ethics: Implications of New Media Platforms for Global Ethics Discourse, *Journal of Mass Media Ethics,* 25, 275–292.
Youm, K.H. (2020). Defamation. In W. Wat Hopkins (ed)., *Communication and the Law.* Northport, AL: Vision Press, pp. 79–113.

9 Government Censorship

> *The Court has interpreted these guarantees to afford special protection against orders that prohibit the publication or broadcast of particular information or commentary – orders that impose a "previous" or "prior" restraint on speech.*

—U.S. Supreme Court Chief Justice Warren E. Burger,
Nebraska Press Assn. v. Stuart (1976, p. 556)

Jacob Blake was shot by police in Kenosha, Wisconsin, and social media video sparked more than a week of #Kenosha protests. When antigovernment groups posted encrypted updates from the scene, the extremist speech was connected to the deadly shootings of two others (Kunzelman, 2020). One group had been banned by a site called Discord and some "migrated" to the Keybase messaging app (para. 3). Facebook has been among the social media sites trying to use its community policies to ban political extremists, but a computer science professor concluded that:

> The whole landscape is too big and each individual player is very big … The number of people you would need to truly police this on the platforms is inadequate right now. The resources just aren't there.
>
> (para. 6)

Among the anarchists was a group called "Boogaloo" that advocated a second U.S. civil war, showed up at events wearing body armor and created large private Facebook groups with "innocuous sounding names," such as. "CNN Journalist Support Group" (paras. 13–15). While social media sites are slow to use their powers to ban violent, hateful and other offensive speech under contract law based on user agreements, the U.S. First Amendment limits government power as state action to censor speech before violence happens.

In *Brandenburg v. Ohio* (1969), a Ku Klux Klan leader was convicted under a state criminal statute of advocating violence during a speech recorded by a local television station. The U.S. Supreme Court reversed a criminal conviction based on a jury instruction that failed to address "the statute's bald definition of the crime in terms of mere advocacy not distinguished from incitement to imminent lawless action (pp. 448–449). The Court found that the statute violated the First and Fourteenth Amendments by overruling the *Whitney v. California* (1927) precedent. While Justice William O. Douglas concurred with the decision, the absolutist more clearly divided protected speech from dangerous acts that could be prosecuted. He returned to the "clear and present danger test" found in *Schenck v. United States* (1919): "The question in every case is whether the words are used in such circumstances and are of such a nature as to create a clear and present danger that they will bring about substantive evils that Congress has a right to prevent. It is a question of proximity and degree" (p. 47). However, in *Brandenburg,* Douglas found that Holmes was "rejecting" a First Amendment defense (p. 450). In a companion World War I case, *Abrams v. United States* (1919), a dissent concluded that: "Congress certainly cannot forbid all effort to change the mind of the country" (p. 628). In *Brandenburg,* Justice Douglas used this point to conclude: "Though I doubt if the 'clear and present danger' test is congenial to the First Amendment in time of a declared war, I am certain it is not reconcilable with the First Amendment in days of peace" (p. 452). He quoted Justice Holmes' later views that: "Every idea is an incitement" (*Gitlow v. United States,* 1925, p. 673). Returning to *Brandenburg,* Holmes rejected the "clear and present danger test" – "whether strict and tight ... or free-wheeling" (p. 454). Too often, he wrote, "threats were often loud but always puny" and "part and parcel of the cold war that has eroded substantial parts of the First Amendment" (p. 454). As the Supreme Court later explained in *Texas v. Johnson* (1988), action, such as the burning of an American flag, may have First Amendment protection *if* it has the meaning of political expression. Justice Douglas' First Amendment absolutism in *Brandenburg* was founded on a deeper treatment of beliefs as "sanctuaries" and a desire to prohibit government from any "power to invade that sanctuary of belief and conscience" (pp. 456–457).

When it comes to applying First Amendment law to social media communication, it is messy because of what has been called "private censorship" within this context:

> Much of the censorship on social media does not emanate directly from the government. Often, the censorship comes from social media companies that police content pursuant to their own terms-of-service agreements. Outcries of political censorship abound. Recent controversies include radio show provocateur Alex Jones being removed from Facebook, YouTube and Apple for engaging in hateful speech; Facebook at least temporarily removing a newspaper's online postings of sections of the Declaration of Independence; and uneven or inconsistent application of hate speech removal policies.
>
> (Hudson, Jr., 2019, para. 16)

Hudson, Jr. (2019) reminded readers that retired Justice Anthony's Kennedy's public forum argument in *Packingham v. North Carolina* (2017) was plainly rejected by Justice Samuel A. Alito as "undisciplined dicta" and "unnecessary rhetoric" (para. 2). Further, an eleventh circuit recent case, *United States of America v. Bobal* (2020), applied a narrow reading of *Packingham* to criminal cases involving digital technology use. Setting aside criminal law, social media companies continue to exercise protected editorial powers over content.

Social media speakers trade the promise of large audiences for checking a box that agrees to site regulation of content in a way that would never be found as a constitutional act of governmental power. The public appears to recognize the distinction by, on the one hand having comfort with Facebook controls over content management and, on the other, supporting limited government interference with free speech and protest rights. Public opinion data, however, suggest that there is a partisan divide over the democratic right to peacefully protest in the streets (Pew, 2020).

During two years, there appeared to be a significant decline among Democrats agreeing with the statement that, "people are free to peacefully protest" (para. 2):

> Among the public overall, 68% say it is very important for the country that people are free to peacefully protest, down from 74% two years ago. In this case, the decline has come entirely among Republicans. Only about half of Republicans and Republican-leaning independents (53%) say it is *very* important for the country that people are free to peacefully protest, while 33% say this is somewhat important; 13% say it is not too or not at all important. Two years ago, 64% of Republicans said that it was very important that people are free to protest peacefully.
>
> (para. 6)

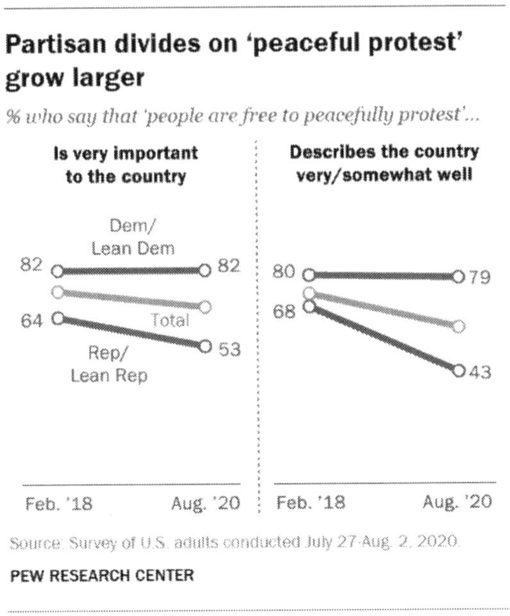

Partisan Divide Data.

Courtesy Pew Internet Research Center. https://www.pewresearch.org/politics/2020/09/02/in-views-of-u-s-democracy-widening-partisan-divides-over-freedom-to-peacefully-protest/.

In contrast, Democrats' data were unchanged, with 82 percent strongly supporting a right to protest (para. 7). This view aligns with the precedent in U.S. Supreme Court case law.

Traditional First Amendment law offered protection of individuals from government action that amounted to censorship of free speech through use of criminal libel or defamation prosecutions, as well as other attempts to stop speech. In *Garrison v. Louisiana* (1964), the U.S. Supreme Court limited states from prosecuting cases that involved public official conduct and this was consistent with the *New York Times v. Sullivan* (1964) defamation ruling applied to civil lawsuits. New Orleans District Attorney Jim Garrison had been tried and convicted under a state statute for calling parish judges lazy, inefficient and the cause of a case backlog. The 9-0 unanimous U.S. Supreme Court applied the *Sullivan* actual malice standard of knowing falsehoods in reckless disregard of the truth to strike down the state law as unconstitutionally broad under the First Amendment. Truth became an absolute defense for criticism related to official conduct and public business. Pritchard (2009), however, found that online "relationship-related revenge" posts in email or on websites sometimes led to criminal prosecution and about 15 percent of those cases in Wisconsin offered a First Amendment defense (p. 318). A criminal conviction sometimes led to jail time and fines. The cases frequently ended with charges dropped or in plea agreements rather than going to trial. The cases under study sometimes predated creation of state revenge porn laws.

PRIOR RESTRAINTS

The First Amendment of the U.S Constitution prevents most government censorship of free speech unrelated to broadly defined national security issues (*Near v. Minnesota,* 1931). In general, halting non-obscene speech or banning publication violates the First Amendment. Outside the U.S.A., however, it is much more likely to see governments act to stifle free speech. For example, Facebook was forced to block the "Royalist Marketplace" group to users within Thailand (Associated Press, 2020). The group focused on the Thai monarchy in Bangkok, which "is staunchly protected from criticism by strict laws" (para. 1). The social media giant explained in a statement that: "After careful review, Facebook has determined that we are compelled to restrict access to content which the Thai government has deemed to be illegal" (para. 3). The Facebook group remained open outside Thailand. The academic living in exile in Japan who created the group of more than 1 million opened a new one and Facebook also vowed to fight government action:

> The monarchy is considered sacrosanct in Thailand and any criticism is normally kept private. A lese majeste law calls for a prison sentence of up to 15 years for anyone found guilty of defaming the king.
>
> (para. 14)

Criminal libel laws popular hundreds of years ago in England under common law faded from U.S. precedent with the *New York Times v. Sullivan* (1964). It applied the First Amendment to defamation cases. Despite existing law, ByteDance, Chinese owner of the popular TikTok app, was forced to sue President Donald Trump over his executive order citing national security in the proposed ban on foreign ownership (Arbel, 2020). ByteDance claimed in a 129-point complaint that the first of two orders were about "the president's anti-China political campaign" (para. 2). The federal lawsuit, filed in California, named Trump and Commerce Secretary Wilbur Ross. In *TikTok v. Trump* (2020), ByteDance sought "to prevent the government from impermissibly banning TikTok" through emergency economic powers (p. 2). Presidents previously used the International Emergency Economic Powers Act (IEEPA) to fight terrorism and weapons of mass destruction, but TikTok earlier had created a U.S. company based in Los Angeles. TikTok claimed to store U.S. users' data on servers located in the United States and Singapore "to protect privacy and security" (p. 3). There also had been a national security review of ByteDance's 2017 purchase of Musical.ly. The lawsuit alleged violation of Fifth Amendment due process and "not based on a bona fide national emergency" (p. 4). By preventing TikTok Inc. from operating in the United States, the executive order violates TikTok Inc.'s First Amendment Rights in its code, an expressive means of communication" (pp. 4–5). TikTok also claimed free speech rights through its political content, including the death of George Floyd, Covid-19 and LGBTQ awareness (p. 8). The hashtag #Juneteenth had more than 230 million views (p. 8). TikTok was frequently at the center of anti-Trump activities, including a movement to obtain and block tickets for a Tulsa, Oklahoma rally during a peak of the pandemic:

> At his Tulsa campaign rally on June 20, 2020 ... the President deployed the term "Kung Flu" in discussing COVID-19, and added: "China sent us the plague, thank you very much." On July 14, 2020, the President returned to the theme, stating that "[n]o administration has been tougher on China than this administration," including by "hold[ing] China fully responsible for concealing the virus and unleashing it upon the world."
>
> (p. 23)

TikTok did not fight a second presidential order that specifically banned foreign ownership. Microsoft and Twitter were among U.S. companies offering to buy TikTok. At the same time, however, TikTok users successfully sued and obtained a preliminary injunction against the U.S. Department of Commerce (2020) to enforce Executive Order 13942 (2020). In *Marland et al. v. Trump et al.* (2020), an injunction was issued on procedural grounds without considering First Amendment issues. The plaintiffs claimed that the president's proposed ban was overbroad and violated the First Amendment right of expression and access to information (*Douglas Marland et al. v. Trump et al. Memorandum*, 2020). It failed to apply time, place and manner restrictions. In short, a ban on a popular social media app would be government censorship cloaked in a national security argument. As discussed in more detail earlier in this book, the U.S. Supreme Court in *Packingham v. North Carolina* (2017) and earlier case law has articulated the importance of social media communication in providing a public forum for political communication.

Around the world, government censorship of social media communication is a growing problem. In Thailand, for example, strict defamation laws can easily land speakers exercising free expression in prison. U.S. citizen Wesley Barnes' critical travel review of the Sea View Koh Chang resort sparked the threat of prosecution under criminal libel law in that country. After two days in jail, Barnes "publicly apologized" in exchange for the resort dropping its defamation charges against him (Paddock, 2020, para. 2). The strongly worded apology was clearly forced:

> All of the statements that I made are completely untrue ... These reviews and comments were written out of anger and malice. Now, I, Mr. Barnes, have regretted my actions and would like to apologize to Sea View Koh Chang, and its staff.
>
> (para. 6)

Sea View also "has been excoriated online" and faced a backlash for using defamation laws to jail the reviewer (para. 4).

LAW REVIEW ANALYSES

The key to understanding strict scrutiny is that it applies when government, such as public university administrators and their PR staff, attempt to "prohibit the expression of an idea simply because society finds the idea itself offensive or disagreeable" (Olson, 2019, p. 33, quoting *Texas v. Johnson,* 1989, p. 414). The focus is on regulation of expressive conduct, as opposed to a balancing of other interests. In the absence of public safety or national security threats (as opposed to *fears* about possible violence) that would compel a legal restriction, speech must be protected: "The reason, in fact, must be so compelling it requires free expression to take a subordinate role" (Olson, 2019, p. 33). The value of free expression has long been understood as a vital tool of democracy (Lee, 2008). By the 1774 Continental Congress address in Quebec, for example, freedom's value was found: "[I]n its **diffusion** of liberal sentiments on the administration of Government, its ready communication of thoughts between subjects, and its consequential promotion of union among them, whereby oppressive officers are shamed or intimidated, into more honourable and just modes of conducting affairs" (p. 343). Hopkins (2019) distinguishes conduct as having one of three attributes: without "communicative value," "purely communicative" or "a mix" (p. 38). Two key questions for a court to answer are: Is there an intent to express a message? Is there a likelihood the message will be understood by a witness? (p. 33).

The *Texas v. Johnson* (1989) flag-burning case stands as the clearest U.S. Supreme Court protection for intentionally political speech. It is a foundation for requiring that a governmental entity demonstrate a compelling interest and then apply a narrowly tailored restriction. *Texas v. Johnson* (1989) is exemplar of the strict scrutiny test about expressive conduct. The case first surfaced amid the 1984 Republican National Convention in Dallas. A U.S. flag was burned while chanting against the policies of the incumbent president and corporations in a nonviolent march. Gregory Lee Johnson, convicted of violating a Texas statute prohibiting flag desecration, had won before the Texas Court of Criminal Appeals his appeal of a fine and imprisonment. U.S. Supreme Court Justice William Brennan wrote: "This case presents the question whether his conviction is consistent with the First Amendment. We hold that it is not" (p. 399). In the case, the Court explained the complicated determination of applying an appropriate standard:

> We must first determine whether Johnson's burning of the flag constituted expressive conduct … we next decide whether the State's regulation is related to the suppression of free expression … If the State's regulation is not related to expression, then the less stringent standard we announced in *United States v. O'Brien* for regulations of noncommunicative conduct controls.
>
> (pp. 403–404)

The Court identified several important First Amendment concerns:

1. Is the behavior expressive conduct? If it is, then the First Amendment may be utilized as protection against government action. This is perhaps the most valuable aspect of strict scrutiny because it isolates the core value of expression, as well as expressive behavior. For communicators and artists alike, the shield of the First Amendment is available to protect speech and some behavior against the blunt power of repressive, tyrannical and squelching governments and their officers.
2. Is the state regulation related to suppressing freedom of expression? If not, the intermediate scrutiny *O'Brien* test may apply. If it is, then the *more demanding* strict scrutiny approach comes into play. Thus, the courts must deduce from the available evidence the motivation of restrictive and regulatory forces.
3. An overriding concern, further, is whether or not the state has an interest based upon facts in a particular case. Unfortunately, state intervention in cases is fairly commonplace – even when it is not entirely clear that there is a larger public interest, as opposed to a narrow political, religious, social or economic value.

Thus, any state action limiting expression or expressive conduct that has the effect of suppression of free expression requires a careful examination by the court. While the "government generally has a freer hand in restricting expressive conduct than it has in restricting the written or spoken word" (*Texas v. Johnson*, 1989, p. 406):

> "[A] law directed at the communicative nature of conduct must, like a law directed at speech itself, be justified by the substantial showing of need that the First Amendment requires" ... It is, in short, not simply the verbal or nonverbal nature of the expression, but the governmental interest at stake, that helps to determine whether a restriction on that expression is valid.
>
> (pp. 406–407)

In the *Texas v. Johnson* case, the Court concluded that the state's main interest seemed to be preventing disturbing the peace, but the law gives higher weight to the value of free expression:

> Our precedents ... recognize that a principal "function of free speech under our system of government is to invite dispute. It may indeed best serve its high purpose when it induces a condition of unrest, creates dissatisfaction with conditions as they are, or even stirs people to anger"... It would be odd indeed to conclude both that "if it is the speaker's opinion that gives offense, that consequence is a reason for according it constitutional protection" ... and that the government may ban the expression of certain disagreeable ideas on the unsupported presumption that their very disagreeableness will provoke violence.
>
> (pp. 408–409)

Disagreeable or objectionable expression cannot be the sole basis for establishing a substantial government interest that would overcome the strict scrutiny test and allow for restriction of free expression. However, campus administrators are prone to focus on speech content and their PR operatives may apply crisis communication models in order to shape media coverage and subsequent public opinion.

In the *Texas v. Johnson* (1989) case, the Court subjected the state's "interest in preserving the special symbolic character of the flag to 'the most exacting scrutiny'" (p. 412). The court's conclusion was crystal clear: "If there is a bedrock principle underlying the First Amendment, it is that the government may not prohibit the expression of an idea simply because society finds the idea itself offensive or disagreeable" (p. 414). Yet, in spite of this seeming clarity, other government interests beyond the speech itself, such as the aforementioned desire to protect administrator and campus branding, have survived constitutional challenge that fails to employ the strict scrutiny test. Still, offensiveness cannot be the sole basis for restriction of expression. In the *Texas v. Johnson* case, an emerging counter argument surfaced when Chief Justice William Rehnquist (1986–2005) wrote for three dissenters that free expression "is not absolute," and quoted a unanimous court in *Chaplinsky v. New Hampshire* (1942):

> Allowing the broadest scope to the language and purpose of the Fourteenth Amendment, it is well understood that the right of free speech is not absolute at all times and under all circumstances. There are certain well-defined and narrowly limited classes of speech, the prevention and punishment of which have never been thought to raise any Constitutional problem. These include the lewd and obscene, the profane, the libelous, and the insulting or "fighting" words – those which by their very utterance inflict injury or tend to incite an immediate breach of the peace. It has been well observed that such utterances are no essential part of any exposition of ideas, and are of such slight social value as a step to truth that any benefit that may be derived from them is clearly outweighed by the social interest in order and morality.
>
> (*Texas v. Johnson*, 1989, p. 430)

The fighting words doctrine is central to any application of campus speech freedom because administrators, PR practitioners and campus police or safety officers should determine if the speech in question inflicts injury or tends to incite *immediate* disturbance of the peace. For strict scrutiny to become a useful tool in protecting free expression, the courts would need to be able to define "injury" and articulate what constitutes "compelling government interest" and "necessary and narrowly tailored" regulation. More often, balancing interests have been applied and not always to protect First Amendment rights.

Hopkins (2019) refers to the *O'Brien* test as "intermediate scrutiny" that may "justify incidental limitations of First Amendment freedoms" (pp. 40–41). When David Paul O'Brien and three others burned draft cards on South Boston Courthouse steps in 1966, O'Brien knew he was breaking a federal law, yet he also sought to persuade others "so that other people would reevaluate their positions with Selective Service, with the armed forces, and reevaluate their place in the culture of today, to hopefully consider my position" (*United States v. O'Brien*, 1968, p. 370). At issue, then, was whether or not a free expression argument could overcome other illegal behavior and the key to understanding intermediate scrutiny is the combination of speech with non-speech behavior. It is within this specialized context that the *O'Brien* four-part test emerged:

> We cannot accept the view that an apparently limitless variety of conduct can be labeled "speech" … To characterize the quality of the governmental interest which must appear, the Court has employed a variety of descriptive terms: compelling;

> substantial; subordinating; paramount; cogent; strong. Whatever imprecision inheres in these terms, we think it clear that a government regulation is sufficiently justified if it is within the constitutional power of the Government; if it furthers an important or substantial governmental interest; if the governmental interest is unrelated to the suppression of free expression; and if the incidental restriction on alleged First Amendment freedoms is no greater than is essential to the furtherance of that interest.
>
> (pp. 376–377)

INTERNATIONAL CONSIDERATION OF LAW AND ETHICS

The Austrian Supreme Court has ruled that Facebook must remove a post that insulted a former Green Party leader and this raised concern over the global censorship impact of EU rulings (Daskal, 2020). The defamation case began with a post in 2016 that used defamatory words, such as "lousy traitor" and "corrupt oaf" (para. 2). Facebook had used geo-blocking within Austria and "it argued that the order violated the applicable EU's e-Commerce Directive, which prohibits EU member states from imposing general monitoring obligations on tech companies like Facebook" (para. 3). The European Court of Justice (CJEU) sided with Facebook. Free expression is an international human right, however, "the specific contours of international human rights are themselves highly contested" (para. 7). In the short term, nation states continue to apply their law, but Facebook may be forced to comply with other countries through additional geo-blocking of content found libelous by those jurisdictions. That would include, for example, criminal libel, hate speech, privacy and other unsettled law in the U.S.A.

Box 9.1 Thought Leaders Donnalyn Pompper and Molly Schwartz

When social media emerged in 1997, few could have predicted the significance of them. Putting the power of public shaming and a 24-hour news cycle into the hands of people who seek to sound off directly to public figures and to others *about* those public figures is a phenomenon shaping the third millennium. The effects of our typed words and videos to hold people accountable via social media platforms, such as Twitter and Instagram, have deep and lasting ethical implications.

Donnalyn Pompper

Photograph by Jules Portrait Design

Molly Schwartz

Photograph by Daniel Desmet

The viral nature of hashtag content reach includes **hashjacking** existing threads for ulterior motives, paid and "sticky" use of a **hashflag** and other strategies and tactics that may or may not be ethical. These externalities of the social media landscape may supplant individual autonomy in what ethics label **heteronomy**. The massive size of social media potential audiences may explode into crisis communication for a brand or individual.

CANCEL CULTURE IN THE THIRD MILLENNIUM

While many celebrate the opportunity to tell musicians, actors, politicians and others exactly what they think about their performances and products, there is a dark side. Controversy plus free speech has given birth to what's become known as *cancel culture*. Don't like what a celebrity has done? Chastise them online and inspire others to do the same. #Canceled. Cancelling offers a means "for marginalized communities to publicly assert their value systems through popular culture" (Ibrahim, 2019, para. 8). Women, in particular, endure greater amounts of online hate (Khrosavinik & Esposito, 2018). When Barack Obama spoke out about cancel culture, Rueb and Taylor (2019) characterized it in the *New York Times* coverage as:

> .[M]uch remarked upon, but still nebulously defined. It tends to refer to behavior that mostly plays out on the Internet when someone has said or done something to which others object. That person is then condemned in a

> flurry of social media posts. Such people are often referred to as "canceled," a way of saying that many others (and perhaps the places at which they work) are fed up with them and will have no more to do with them.
>
> (para. 5)

Cancel culture may be likened to the 21st-century's version of what George Orwell (1949) prophesied as creating an *unperson*. In Orwell's visionary book, *Nineteen Eighty-Four*, an unperson is someone who is secretly murdered and erased from society and memory. Orwell was no doubt inspired by the mid-20th-century Stalinist Soviet Party, which erased real people from photographs after their death. In *Nineteen Eighty-Four*'s fictional account, the unperson offends the government party and all record or evidence of their existence is eliminated. Today, the public or "cybermob" (Citron, 2009) mobilizes online. When a celebrity is deemed offensive or otherwise wrong, former fans use social media platforms to cancel them by diminishing their power, effectiveness and validity – weakening a celebrity's economic viability and reputation. DeBos (2019) called cancel culture "a breeding ground for toxicity that hides behind a façade of moral righteousness' (para. 7). This may be especially true for celebrities who owe a large part of their success *to* social media.

Over the past few years, online actions aimed at cancelling has impacted a number of celebrities, including R. Kelly, Roseanne Barr, Michael Jackson, Louis CK, Kevin Spacey, Woody Allen, Lena Dunham, Jess Hilarious, Kanye West, Taylor Swift, Mel Gibson, Chris Brown, Kevin Hart, Shane Gillis, Johnny Depp, Nick Cannon and Caroline Flack. Reasons for cancellation have included allegations/charges of sexual assault, homophobia, xenophobia, pedophilia, racism, anti-Semitism, domestic abuse and other violence. When social media users launch campaigns to cancel celebrities for what they've done (or are accused of) by boycotting their music, films, shows and amplifying all on social media, bouncing back for the celebrity is not simple or straightforward. Some have been able to weather the storm – like Nick Cannon, who educated himself by publicly visiting the Holocaust Museum, pledging a donation and inviting a rabbi to guest on his YouTube show (Spiro & Weiss, 2020).

Celebrities such as Kanye West and Taylor Swift may be considered "too big" to cancel (Asmelash, 2019, para. 16), but the experience proves too painful for others. At the extreme end of the continuum, British television presenter Caroline Flack took her life on February 15, 2020 after being cancelled on social media once she was arrested for hitting her boyfriend over the head with a lamp. She had found evidence that he was cheating on her. The high level of online hate was too much for Flack to bear.

The public apology, as a form of discourse, is here to stay. Some say that cancel culture does not work. Some say it is necessary. Cancelled celebrities hope to return to good standing with audiences and use social media and public relations consultants to repair the reputational damage created by their bad behavior. Battistella (2014) explained that hollow apologies or simply saying "I was misunderstood," "I was only kidding" or "this is a private matter, let's move on" may not be enough and people will continue to use their social media pulpit to demand a genuine apology and/or behavior change (Ibrahim, 2019, para. 8). The timeline depends on the gravity of the offense, industry standards, expectations and social rhythms (Ibrahim, 2019).

The cancel culture phenomenon raises many questions and also carries **opportunity costs** of social attention on a long list of important news agenda items – public health care, global climate change, education, media literacy and others. The social value of cancel culture, however, may be a need to examine the dynamics of free speech colliding with ethics in social media contexts where dialog sometimes inspires more questions than it answers. First, cancelling someone does not undo the harm they've done – such as the physical and mental bruises Rihanna experienced in 2009 – but cancel culture may offer victims a personal catharsis. Second, legends including Michael Jackson are so engrained in popular culture that cancelling such an omnipresent figure may prove impossible. Third – and more central to the point of this "Thought Leader" essay, is the question of whether or not cancel culture's justification in forcing celebrities to face repercussions of their actions ethically measures up to negative outcomes like getting someone fired or irrevocably wounding someone emotionally to the degree that they are driven to suicide? Social media posts are instant and how often do we rush to judge someone before all of the facts are in and the legal system has the necessary time to follow its course? Is the next phase of cancel culture more about holding celebrities accountable to embracing their mistakes and atoning with better behavior – without bullying or getting them fired, but by giving them a second chance? Lipschultz (2018) offered media literacy as one (audience-based) solution model when considering philosophical debates about truth seeking.

This essay explores one specific way the online world has transformed the concept of mob mentality via social media used to dehumanize individuals when critique and commentary about accountability turns into hate speech. It is an ethics versus free speech quagmire. The court of public opinion in a social media world where no one is perfect can be pretty rough.

Donnalyn Pompper, Ph.D., APR is professor and endowed chair in public relations, School of Journalism & Communication, University of Oregon. Dr. Pompper (Ph.D., Media & Communication, Temple University) teaches courses in and researches public relations, corporate social responsibility and social identity. Overall, her research provides routes for enabling people, globally, to achieve their maximum potential at work, to embrace their intersecting social identity dimensions (e.g., age, ethnicity gender) and to critically examine these issues across mass media representations.

Molly Schwartz, undergraduate bachelor's degree journalism major, University of Oregon, was born and raised in Los Angeles, CA. Schwartz served as a staff writer and managing editor for *Ethos Magazine*. In her spare time, she is a songwriter and performs with a band based in Eugene, OR.

Sources

Asmelash, L. (2019, September 21). Why Cancel Culture Doesn't Always Work. *CNN*. https://www.cnn.com/2019/09/21/entertainment/cancel-culture-explainer-trnd/index.html.

Battistella, E.L. (2014). *Sorry About That: The Language of Public Apology*. New York: Oxford University Press.

Citron, J. (2009). Cyber Civil Rights, *Boston University Law Review*, 89, 61–125.

DeBos, C. (2019). The Problem with Cancel Culture and Why It Needs to Stop. *The Burn-In*. https://www.theburnin.com/thought-leadership/problem-with-cancel-culture-why-it-needs-to-stop-2019-11/.

Ibrahim, S. (2019, April 4). In Defense of Cancel Culture. *VICE*. https://www.vice.com/en/article/vbw9pa/what-is-cancel-culture-twitter-extremely-online.

Khrosavinik, M. and Esposito, E. (2018). Online Hate, Digital Discourse and Critique: Exploring Digitally-mediated Discursive Practices of Gender-based Hostility, *Lodz Papers in Pragmatics*, 14(1), 45–68.

Lipschultz, J.H. (2018). New Mobile Media Technologies, Innovation and Investment. In *Social Media Communication: Concepts, Practices, Data, Law and Ethics*. New York: Routledge, pp. 183–206.

Orwell, G. (1949). *Nineteen Eighty-four*. New York: Signet Classics.

Rueb, E.S. and Taylor, D.B. (2019, October 31). Obama On Call-out Culture: "That's not activism." *The New York Times*. https://www.nytimes.com/2019/10/31/us/politics/obama-woke-cancel-culture.html.

Spiro, A. and Weiss, M. (2020, July 22). Nick Cannon Visits Holocaust Museum, Pledges Donation. *Jewish Insider*. https://jewishinsider.com/2020/07/nick-cannon-visits-holocaust-museum-pledges-donation/.

The chilling effect of censorship effects journalists and the public in many ways – from access to confidential information to protection of sources. Journalists use the Freedom of Information Act (FOIA) and state public records "sunshine laws" to search public records, but there are many exemptions. Additionally, access to public meetings usually is protected under the First Amendment, but unethical public officials sometimes hold secret meetings. In an era of citizen journalism and social media communication, these contexts potentially impact the information that is disclosed and shared.

In an early case, a Lousiville *Courier-Journal* newspaper reporter sought protection from the Kentucky shield law statute to refuse to testify before a grand jury (*Branzburg v. Hayes*, 1972). The U.S. Supreme Court sided with the government that information about serious crimes must be disclosed:

> It is apparent from this statute, as well as from our history and that of England, that concealment of crime and agreements to do so are not looked upon with favor. Such conduct deserves no encomium, and we decline now to afford it First Amendment protection by denigrating the duty of a citizen, whether reporter or informer, to respond to grand jury subpoena and answer relevant questions put to him.
>
> (p. 697)

Journalists were concerned that sources might not disclose information without attribution, if there was a possibility that a news reporter may be forced to name them later.

The current issues involve the difficulty in protecting private digital conversation. The National Security Agency PRISM case revealed government backdoor access to private data. Counterterrorism national security surveillance programs may not be justifiable reason to spy on U.S. citizens. Our use of smartphones, however, makes it easier for government and others to spy on personal communication, use **location-based services** (LBS) movement tracking and learn more about the editorial process of creating social media content. Cloud servers store big data and use of Google Drive or Apple Cloud increase the likelihood that government may be looking at data – in violation of international human dignity legal principles. There is a lack of transparency, but China has pressured manufacturers to preinstall filtering software on Internet devices. Some have said that "information wants to be free" and social media allow for greater sharing. At the same time, government, corporate and other centers of power frequently work to limit access to information and stop its release. Facebook and other social media companies have their own corporate interests that may seek to stop information flow that could be damaging to individual or group interests. In the end, ethical social media always should favor a public interest in truth, honesty and transparency that causes no danger to safety and security. Harm is sometimes difficult to assess because personnel information, for example, is kept private to protect individual privacy. Conflicting information goals leave open the need for litigation in balancing interests and deciding fair outcomes.

ONLINE RESOURCES

Hudson, Jr., D.L. (2019, April 1). Free Speech or Censorship? Social Media Litigation Is a Hot Legal Battleground. *ABA Journal*. https://www.abajournal.com/magazine/article/social-clashes-digital-free-speech.

DISCUSSION QUESTIONS

1. What are the practical differences between government censorship and social media company site management?
2. Which specific ethical frameworks and values should be applied to a case in which the government attempts to sustain a prior restraint of publication?
3. Why or why not does a social media company based in China, such as ByteDance's TikTok, present any legitimate national security threats? Did TikTok's U.S. company based in Los Angeles effectively protect user privacy and security?

REFERENCES

Abrams v. United States, 250 U.S. 616 (1919).
Arbel, T. (2020, August 24). TikTok Sues Trump Over His Pending Order To Ban Its App. *Associated Press*. https://apnews.com/b5b90af034c4911dd0bf1bfdb7f23f64.
Associated Press (2020, August 25). Facebook Blocks Group That Discusses Thai Monarchy. https://apnews.com/849386fbf5291ca6ba6e72210c9cfa03.
Brandenburg v. Ohio, 395 U.S. 444 (1969).
Branzburg v. Hayes, 408 U.S. 665 (1972).
Chaplinsky v. New Hampshire, 315 U.S. 568 (1942).
Daskal, J. (2020, November 13). A Court Ruling in Austria Could Censor the Internet Worldwide. *Slate*. https://slate-com.cdn.ampproject.org/c/s/slate.com/ technology/2020/11/austria-facebook-eva-glawischnig-piesczek-censorship.amp.
Douglas Marland et al. v. Trump et al.Memorandum, No. 20-cv-4597 (E.D. Pennsylvania 2020, October 30). http://docs.dpaq.de/16978-show_temp.pl-102.pdf.
Executive Order 13492 (2020, August 6). https://www.federalregister.gov/documents/2020/08/11/2020-17699/addressing-the-threat-posed-by-tiktok-and-taking-additional-steps-to-address-the-national-emergency.
Garrison v. Louisiana, 379 U.S. 64 (1964).
Gitlow v. United States, 268 U. S. 652 (1925).
Hopkins, W.W. (2019). Conduct and Speech. InW. Wat Hopkins (ed.), *Communication and the Law*. Northport, AL: Vision Press, pp. 37–48).

Hudson, Jr., D.L. (2019, April 1). Free Speech or Censorship? Social Media Litigation Is a Hot Legal Battleground. *ABA Journal.* https://www.abajournal.com/magazine/ article/social-clashes-digital-free-speech.

International Emergency Economic Powers Act (IEEPA), 50 U.S.C. §1701-1706. https://www.law.cornell.edu/uscode/text/50/chapter-35.

Kunzelman, M. (2020, September 4). Online Bans Fail To Silence US Extremists Drawn To protests. *Associated Press.* https://apnews.com/26a50d7d3c92045bb67d87d5c6de580a.

Lee, E. (2008, Winter). "Freedom of the Press 2.0," *Georgia Law Review*, 42, 309–405.

Marland et. al. v. Trump et al., 20-4597 (E.D. Pennsylvania, 2020).

Near v. Minnesota, 283 U.S. 697 (1931).

Nebraska Press Assn. v. Stuart, 427 U.S. 539 (1976).

New York Times v. Sullivan, 376 U.S. 254 (1964).

Olson, K.K. (2019). The First Amendment in Theory and Practice. In W. Wat Hopkins (ed.), *Communication and the Law.* Northport, AL: Vision Press, pp. 23–35.

Packingham v. North Carolina, 582 U.S. ___, 137 S. Ct. 1730 (2017).

Paddock, R.C. (2020, October 9). He's Sorry for His Bad Reviews. He May Now Avoid Prison. *New York Times.* https://www.nytimes.com/2020/10/09/world/asia/ thailand-review-american-apology.html.

Pew (2020, September 2). In Views of U.S. Democracy, Widening Partisan Divides Over Freedom to Peacefully Protest.*Pew Research Center.* https://www.pewresearch.org/politics/2020/09/02/in-views-of-u-s-democracy-widening-partisan-divides-over-freedom-to-peacefully-protest/.

Pritchard, D. (2009). Rethinking Criminal Libel: An Empirical Study, *Communication Law and Policy*, 14, 303–339.

Shepard, J. and Culver, K.B. (2018, Winter). Culture Wars on Campus: Academic Freedom, the First Amendment, and Partisan Outrage in Polarized Times, *San Diego Law Review*, 55, 88–158.

Strasser, M.P. (2017, Fall). Student Dismissals from Professional Programs and the Constitution, *Case Western Reserve*, 68, 97–157.

Texas v. Johnson, 419 U.S. 397 (1989).

TikTok v. Trump, 2:20-cv-7672, Central Dist. of Cal. Western Div. (2020, August 24). https://www.documentcloud.org/documents/7043072-TikTok-v-Trump-administration-complaint.html.

United States v. O'Brien, 391 U.S. 367 (1968).

United States of Amercia v. Peter Robert Bobal, 19-10678 (11th Cir. 2020, November 30).

U.S. Department of Commerce (2020, November 9).15 CFR Chapter VII. https://www.commerce.gov/sites/default/files/2020-11/ signedTikTokFRNoticeofEDPaPreliminary-Injunction10302020RP.pdf.

Whitney v. California, 274 U.S. 357 (1927).

Theories and Practices

Everyone has the right to freedom of opinion and expression; this right includes freedom to hold opinions without interference and to seek, receive and impart information and ideas through any media and regardless of frontiers.

—United Nations (1948, para. 27)

Public relations marketer Peter Shankman (@Shankman) was reacting to the dramatic business shift during the pandemic in 2020 when he tweeted that there was a lack of rules that allowed entrepreneurs to "just start over with something else." In truth, however, we have seen in this book that there are legal rules, and there should be ethical ones. For example, early in the crisis there were calls for ethical leadership practices, including the need to model practices for followers:

> The cornerstone of an ethical leadership practice is the character of individual leaders and the model they provide others for expected behavior. Followers want a clear understanding of leaders' values and a belief that the leader will put the interest of follower's ahead of the leader's own interests. Officials in elected and appointed office who are self-quarantining following exposure are one example of

> model behavior, of placing the public's interests above their personal freedom for a period of time. Leaders that move quickly and decisively to serve the public over private or organizational goals are another. Adam Silver's decision to suspend the NBA season once a player tested positive for the virus was one such example.
>
> (Skeet, 2020, para. 3)

Online communities can be important spaces for the public to learn in and engage within social media communication, cultivate "a sense of connection," utilize relational communication that demonstrates "mutual respect" as "a marker of organizational and community health" (para. 4). A context of authenticity and trust should already exist. In cases where ambiguous information is spread across social media and facts are replaced by misinformation and disinformation, applied ethics demands that we bring clarity, honesty and transparency to our content.

Social sharing of breaking news content is one example of how ethics may be lost in the fog of real-time events. For example, KABC-TV (2020), Los Angeles, reported in a headline: "Rapper Offset briefly detained while live on Instagram, later released." He was live when police arrived at a Beverly Hills location: "The Migos rapper and husband to Cardi B, was recording himself live from inside a car as officers approached the vehicle and asked him to remove his hands from the steering wheel" (para. 2). The video received an estimated 30,000 views before being taken down. While there were some facts from the live video, the breaking news story lacked broader context: "The rapper was detained near a demonstration of Trump supporters but police did not say whether the two incidents were related" (para. 9). The rush to report news and share it on social channels follows First Amendment law, but live video and breaking news present some of the most difficult ethical challenges. Celebrities tend to be newsworthy, and clearly the Instagram video attracted a lot of attention during an otherwise quiet weekend. There is a tendency to share content that attracts attention, whether or not there was long-term social value. Live news events frequently lack a larger context that helps explain what happened.

SPEECH AND PRESS FIRST AMENDMENT LAW

Over decades, legal scholars have published law reviews that attempt to develop meaningful and coherent free expression theories. The law tends to focus "on the original act of expression, and on the individual's freedom to engage in the isolated intellectual act of formulating a message (Bezanson, 2003, p. 987). Alternatively, it is possible to consider manner and medium of expression context of "selection judgments" (p. 987): "In other words, we lack a fundamental definition of First

Amendment expression" (p. 988). In terms of the speech itself, Bezanson applied several communication theories including James Carey's treatment of communication from a "cultural perspective" (p. 1008). If Carey were here to comment about social media communication, he might emphasize symbolic cultural reproduction, social construction of reality through words, "semi-stabilized" and "shared meaning" and "ritualized communication practices" (p. 1009): "Carey's radically 'public' theory of communication [is that it] ... is always public because it relies on a publicly shared stock of symbols" (p. 1014). Bezanson's point seems to be that once we divorce the speaker from a message, it is impossible to separate many forms of speech from conduct:

> Only if individuals are free agents of speech, deciding individually and privately what they choose to enter into the marketplace for others to hear or read or see, will a completely open and unrestricted range of opinion and information be assured in the long run. Protecting individuals' liberty to speak has the necessary consequence of protecting the speech those individuals have communicated from being altered or extinguished by government. In contrast, protecting speech first, and the individual's liberty second, warrants government action that sacrifices individual freedom to speak in the name of other interests, such as equality, fairness, truth, and the relative importance or value of speech's content.
>
> (pp. 1108–1109)

It may be possible, then, to construct and apply social-legal theory that conceptualizes the importance of liberty within a free expression context. Computer-mediated communication and social media theories, such as diffusion of innovation for example, could be used to develop conceptual research questions that apply to law and ethics.

We begin with a simple statement about the value in "liberty of thought and discussion" that should limit the "power of coercion" by government (Mill, 1859, 1956, pp. 19–20): "To refuse a hearing to an opinion because they are sure that it is false is to assume that *their* certainty is the same thing as *absolute* certainty" (p. 21). Yet, society also has an interest in "damage, or probability of damage," "fraud or treachery" and other "crimes" (pp. 114–116). In the social media context, a legal structure must "provide ... in protecting individuals or groups from nongovernment interference in the exercise of their rights" (Emerson, 1966, pp. 28–29). Contemporary legal scholars point to Alexander Meiklejohn's statement that "The First Amendment Is An Absolute" (Davis, 2020, p. 460). Yet, "Absolutism today enjoys little to no scholarly or judicial support, relegated to the footnotes of yesterday" (p. 460).

Democratic U.S. Senator and then U.S. Supreme Court Justice Hugo Lafayette Black (1937–1971) and Justice William O. Douglas (1939–1975) represented President Franklin Roosevelt's support of political reform and civil liberty through the Bill of Rights and Fourteenth Amendment doctrine of incorporation application to the states. Interestingly, liberals of the time sound more like conservative textualists of the present. They read the U.S. Constitution and Bill of Rights as meaning what was written. Krislov (1964) called "Black's emergent absolutism" as related to the First Amendment: "Black obviously believes that the battle for civil liberties is predominantly one of public opinion" (p. 190):

> Black clearly believes that only if civil liberties are implanted in the hearts of the people can they be protected by the judiciary. This being the case, his absolutist position has given him some advantages in the struggle for public opinion. His dissents are, of course, vehement and unqualified … When, in the area of civil liberties, he is faced with a choice between trying to win a case by technical means or restating a strong, firm opinion, he often prefers to avoid a narrow holding and even to accept defeat on this broader basis.
>
> (p. 191)

Absolutists were concerned that 20th-century doctrine, such as the clear and present danger test, offered government justification to censor dangerous speech. Meiklejohn apparently was the inspiration for Justice William Brennan's groundbreaking expansion of First Amendment rights in a series of important opinions (Russomanno, 2015, p. 117). There were "Madisonian roots" driving an "essential role of speech – particularly the freedom to criticize government and its officials" (p. 119). The "absolute sovereignty" of "people, not the government," however, repeatedly have failed to stop Congress from passing repressive sedition laws (p. 125). Nevertheless, James Madison and Alexander Hamilton extended sovereignty to "the freedom to advocate revolution" (p. 128).

Justice Brennan wrote what many consider to be the most important First Amendment opinion in *New York Times v. Sullivan* (1964) that constitutionalized U.S. libel law. His *Texas v. Johnson* (1989) flag-burning decision expanded political speech freedom. While Brennan was not an absolutist, he dissented in *Hazelwood School District v. Kuhlmeier* (1988) when the Court contracted student press and speech rights from *Tinker v. Des Moines* (1969).

One legal scholar suggested that "the Libertarian tradition" is driving an "outward creep" of First Amendment freedoms (Weiland, 2017, p. 1389). The expansion of speech and press freedom aligns with technological development of the Internet and social media, but "the Court seemingly grounded its doctrinal innovation in the primary goal of protecting listeners' rights, apparently in line with the republican tradition" (p. 1395). The Liberal tradition of protecting "individual rights" may be contrasted with the Republican tradition of "social values, and public good (equality)" (p. 1404). It matters, in other words, whether private individuals or the public are "privileged" in the emerging social freedoms (p. 1404). Expansion of corporate commercial speech rights, for example, can be seen as limiting individual rights. Weiland's "thin autonomy" is conceptualized as "a perversion of the type of autonomy that undergirds the liberal tradition; it is unmoored from the Enlightenment ideals that animate robust ascribed autonomy because it is divorced from natural persons ... associated with corporations claiming an individual speech right" (p. 1460). To the extent that traditional First Amendment expansion was about strengthening political speech rights and limiting government censorship, commercial speech cases shift the conversation, especially in a time of contested online social media communication truths:

> [S]cholarly debates are not the most serious threat to the marketplace model. A robust system of free speech depends fundamentally on widely shared social, political, and cultural commitments, and it would be putting it mildly to say that there is widespread anxiety about truth and the ability of speech – especially but not exclusively online speech – to counter falsehoods and lies.
>
> (Blocher, 2019, p. 441)

In search of "accuracy" or "verifiable truths," the "goal of free speech is not the maximization of truths in the abstract, but rather the development of knowledge" (p. 459). However, Blocher finds that there is an "epistemological crisis" over a marketplace of ideas that seemingly leads to polarized sets of beliefs, as we have seen, found within social network clusters (p. 496).

The U.S. Supreme Court, meanwhile, finds itself split over the "hard cases," such as *Citizens United v. Federal Election Commission* (2010), in which a "bare majority of the Court found these key provisions of federal campaign finance law to be an unconstitutional speaker-based restriction on core political speech" (Weinstein, 2013, p. 1129). Still, it is the promotion of free speech values as fundamentally what define democracy:

> The assertion that democracy and free expression are inextricably intertwined in a symbiotic relationship should hardly be controversial. Democracy could not exist, in any meaningful sense, absent a societal commitment to basic notions of free expression, nor could free expression flourish in a society uncommitted to democracy.
>
> (Redish & Mollen, 2009, p. 1303)

There is a disconnect between representative democracy, as exercised through the vote, and the social media chatter that is increasingly an important measure of public opinion within the electoral process:

> The rise of social media platforms certainly has given individuals the potential to participate in a global public discourse, though whether that discourse is robust or simply too saturated with voices to actually be meaningful is open for debate. The sense of political efficacy among individuals – the notion that their speech will actually lead to meaningful political action – can lead to more robust participation in public discourse. And fervently held ideological beliefs will lead to impassioned participation in public discourse, with or without a concomitant sense of political efficacy.
>
> (Johnson, 2018, pp. 340–341)

Passionate support of the First Amendment has been called "magnetism" in that it functions socially, culturally and politically (Schauer, 2004, p. 1807). A distinct social media communication legal and ethical problem exists within "nonsense" and the freedom to spread it: "Sometimes we speak without intending to "mean" anything at all – exclamations, jokes, doggerel verse, and even philosophical illustrations may all be nonsensical (Blocher, 2014, pp. 1426–1427). We could include memes within this dilemma. A "use meaning" offers even "nonsense" as "entitled to constitutional protection" (p. 1479). Marketplace theory, after all, suggests that falsehoods, in John Milton's classic view, compete for acceptance. Truth is an ideal state of arrival at some future date. We should embrace "robust" and "wide open" debate, as the Supreme Court called for in *New York Times v. Sullivan* (1964, p. 271) and engage in it because social media channels allow us to do so, regardless of our empathy. This also offers no ethical call for social responsibility within conversation on Facebook, Twitter and TikTok. When speech turns to brief violent outbursts, such as with QAnon, Black Lives Matter and other protests or advocacy, social media freedom runs into the limits of legal action.

The First Amendment of the U.S. Constitution has been interpreted by the Supreme Court as providing expansive freedom of religion, freedom of speech or press and freedom to peacefully assemble in protest of government. In times of stress, however, government restrictions found in the Alien and Sedition Acts of 1798, the Espionage Act of 1917 and, more recently, the Patriot Act of 2001 represent attempts to contract freedom of expression. Blackstone's *Commentaries on the Laws of England* (1765–1769) of prior restraint common law doctrine found that free press and free speech are essential to broader freedom, but improper exercise of expression has consequences. The empowerment of individual responsibility is a challenge to the heavy hand of government prior restraint and censorship. Two of the four common law categories – libel and obscenity – remain active under First Amendment interpretation. The others, seditious libel and blasphemy, are of little concern in the 21st–century U.S.A. and many parts of the world. *Near v. Minnesota* (1931) precedent protects individuals against most forms of prior restraint by the government, but *not* restriction of expression by social media sites.

Milton's marketplace and Douglas' nearly absolute right of free speech have been limited by complicated user contracts with Facebook, Twitter, YouTube and other sites. The use of community standards and Section 230 site liability immunity mean that gated social media sites, such as Facebook, are not part of the more open Internet in terms of law. Historically, they have been protected in libel litigation (*Blumenthal v. Drudge and America Online*, 1998). Users, however, must balance First Amendment rights to post against employee, juror and other responsibilities to avoid harm (*Kroger Co. of Mich. v. Granger, NLRB*, 2014; *U.S. v. Fumo*, 655 F.3d 288, 2011). As one example, content moderation of offensive Reddit subreddits by hosting quarantined content or removing it, is an ethical choice for the site (Carlson & Cousineau, 2020). Content moderation has been defined as "a series of practices with shared characteristics," as humans or AI set and apply site rules and polices (p. 205). Additionally, when users report content that may violate community standards, so-called "flagging" must be reviewed by humans, and they may suffer adverse mental health effects (p. 206). Without a standard social media ethics code, platforms are left to decide on "a duty to prevent harm caused by vile speech," a "commitment" to free expression or some balance between the two (Carlson & Cousineau, 2020, p. 207; Johnson, 2017). The use of "digital intermediaries" to review and filter social media posts may present Facebook, for example, with an ethical "duty to prevent or ameliorate harm to victims" (Johnson, 2017, p. 16). Carlson and Cousineau (2020) concluded that, "the most ethical course of action is to remove the community from the site" (p. 211). Any decision to alter or remove social media content must, however, include transparent publishing of details about what was done.

International and European Union (EU) courts have based decisions on basic human rights and **natural law**. Article 19 of the United Nations (1948) Universal Declaration of Human Rights is an extension of "inherent dignity" and the value of global justice and peace:

> Everyone has the right to freedom of opinion and expression; this right includes freedom to hold opinions without interference and to seek, receive and impart information and ideas through any media and regardless of frontiers.
>
> (para. 27)

In the U.S.A., content neutral regulation may not always go far enough in protecting free expression, although narrowly tailored regulation that is not overbroad can limit the power of government to restrict free social media communication.

TIME, PLACE, AND MANNER RESTRICTIONS

Holocaust denial, which is "not protected under the German Constitution," hate speech and white supremacist expression are examples of social media that "are an unprotected form of speech subject to content-neutral time, place and manner regulation by Congress" (Mixon, 2020, p. 401). It is an important point in concluding that a Facebook algorithm "displays content based on user engagement instead of ... the time at which a post was published" (p. 401). Site editorial power over speech is much stronger than governmental limits.

This is quite different from the analog broadcast era that afforded regulators the opportunity to create safe harbors for indecent content in overnight hours when children were not as likely to be in the audience. Congress repeatedly created statute law because of the substantial interest in protecting children from harm. The Communications Decency Act (1996), Children's Privacy Protection Act (1996) and the Children's Online Privacy Protection Act (2003) expressed the view that government should assist parents in their responsibility to protect children.

Traditional zoning approaches, such as those applied by the U.S. Supreme Court, in the city or county ordinance placement of adult bookstores and theatres a distance away from schools and churches, have been upheld (*Renton v. Playtime Theatres*, 1986). In contrast, the Supreme Court has rejected total bans on speech as a violation of the First Amendment. The intermediate scrutiny standard requires government to provide a substantial non-speech interest in limiting free expression. Content-neutral Court doctrine is sometimes applied in context. For example, racist cross burnings and other hate speech are not protected under the First Amendment if there is evidence that the speaker intended to threaten others (*R.A.V. v. City of St. Paul* (1992; *Virginia v. Black*, 2003):

> The language and reasoning behind both the United States' and Germany's regulation of freedom of speech, regarding white supremacist speech on social media, are nearly identical but have been interpreted in varying ways. The limits placed upon the American government's ability to proscribe speech are a valid and representative evolution of the legitimate school of thought that prioritizes "freedom of speech over most countervailing interests, even when the speech is

> filled with hatred." However, this evolution occurred before the advent of social media and the potential for one person's speech to be legitimized and displayed to 2.23 billion people across the globe.
>
> (Mixon, 2020, pp. 419–420)

Application of scrutiny in government regulation of social media communication presents thorny First Amendment questions because nonlinear and algorithmic zoning is less possible than limiting who has access to the site. Age restrictions, for example, are problematic because Facebook and other social media sites adopted age 13 instead of banning minors from participating in the community.

Box 10.1 Thought Leaders Timothy Barouch and Greg Lisby

Timothy Barouch

Photograph by Katherine Terry

Social media are quickly becoming the dominant mode of communication for people to get the news, to socialize with others and to share information, opinions and ideas. Yet, for all of their power to connect people and circulate information to places far and wide, social media have challenged norms of free expression. Hate speech has found a home on sites that avoid wider public scrutiny and regulation. People with malicious intent can discover and publish private information about individuals. Platform design enables circulation of posts, images and video that may elicit strong emotional reactions, but provide little reliable information. Conspiracy theories thrive. Users may not be able to tell whether they are connecting with a friend, a bot or a troll. These are just some of the issues that have posed a serious challenge to the United States political culture of free speech.

Greg Lisby.

Photograph courtesy Georgia State University.

TRUE STORY: NARRATIVE, TRUTH AND DEMOCRACY IN A DIGITAL AGE

Freedom of speech has traditionally played an outsized role in United States' democracy. This belief is grounded in a supposed connection between the human capacity to communicate and representative government. Far more than simply a right that each of us has as individual citizens, we think of free speech as essential to the proper functioning of our political systems. Individuals express their identities through speech. Sharing and being exposed to differing perspectives develops the understanding and tolerance necessary for a diverse society. The press fulfills the function of the Fourth Estate by framing political issues and holding the government accountable for its decisions through adept reporting. Citizens deliberate and make decisions about public affairs after a process of sharing their opinions. When their elected representatives stray from the will of the people, the people hold them accountable in public and at the ballot box. These ideas form the foundation of our faith in free speech.

This connection between free speech and democracy in the United States owes itself to the influence that the Age of Enlightenment had on the United States Constitution. As products of the Enlightenment, the American founders believed in the power of human reason. The human ability to think rationally meant that the people – not God or royal family ties – should be the ultimate judges of a government's legitimacy. This belief supported an idea of government "by the people," committed to liberty and progress. The people gave their reasoned consent to be governed by a social contract. This agreement made it possible for humans to give up their natural freedom in exchange for the government's guarantee of social order.

This founding idea had its roots in a model of free speech that emphasized its truth-seeking function. According to this model, there is an objective reality to the world that humans can know through the competitive exchange of ideas. In his famous argument against government censorship in *Areopagitica* (1644, 1992), the public intellectual John Milton termed this quest as a fight in which truth always would win. Some two centuries later, the political philosopher John Stuart Mill (1859, 1978) described the quest for truth as a mining operation: those who searched for what was right were the miners who, in discovering the rock compounds of untruth, needed to continue working to reveal the elements of truth from within those compounds. Supreme Court Justice Oliver Wendell Holmes offered a different metaphor for the value of free speech in *Abrams v. U.S.* (1919). In one of the most famous dissenting opinions in American constitutional history, Holmes appealed to a "free trade in ideas" in which the best ideas "get ... accepted in the competition of the market ... That, at any rate, is the theory of our Constitution" (p. 630). This ideal model promises many advantages to democracy. It claims to ensure that the people are equally and adequately represented, so everyone's voice is heard. And because the marketplace of ideas values truth, it promises to hold government accountable when the government acts unjustly.

No matter the metaphor, the free speech ideal makes some significant assumptions about us and the world we inhabit, in order to work as intended. Reality has always been messier and more complicated. On a basic level, the free speech ideal assumes that the truth about an issue is knowable and that people can agree on that truth. Yet there have always been moral and political controversies for which the truth may be unknowable. If free speech is to support a truly inclusive democracy, the people themselves must enjoy enough equality, freedom and independence so that each of their voices will count. Yet equality in the United States has been elusive, as the United States' experience with racial and gender equality has all too painfully illustrated. The people also must have access to sound information, as well as the education, time, energy and desire to participate in good faith in a government that serves the public interest. Yet many historical factors have frustrated these goals – gaps in educational opportunity, withholding key evidence on important issues, censorship efforts and so on.

Needless to say, social media use can exacerbate these obstacles. When people use social media, they do so by and large to express the truth as they experience it. This is all to the good when this expression reveals things that are important to know – for example, that police have used excessive force or that otherwise socially isolated people can find others online in a community of virtual support. But these same practices can create flawed echo chambers that drown out different viewpoints. Platforms reward compelling narratives that play on emotions, often times indifferent to any sense of objective truth. The law over time has encouraged people to see their lives as a struggle for self-expression against all those who (however and for whatever reason) would repress that expression. Those who seem to be at the source of those limits are seen as oppressors, censors or bureaucratic minions effectively working to subvert our free will and undermine our constitutional protections.

Social media themselves – driven primarily by the growth of their own private businesses – tend to disavow any responsibility for helping people discover truth. Conspiracy theories can develop and spread quickly in online environments. And because social media are designed to elicit quick emotional reaction rather than reasoned reflection, misinformation circulates quickly among a population targeted by sophisticated algorithms. Those algorithms are concerned more with sharing ideas, images and video rather than scrutinizing them. Moreover, algorithms by their design connect social media users with information similar to what they have already consumed, instead of a diversity of perspectives and sources on an issue.

Given this new reality, perhaps the best hope that we have at the moment for reviving our political democracy lies with us. In the moments after we share, click, read and watch, we are connecting with others and expressing ourselves. Even the sharing of **hyperlinks** communicates ideas. As we do, we might consider whether we also are contributing to the polarization and misinformation that thrive on the internet. Although tweets, comments and posts are difficult to take back in the moment, it may not be too late to alter our own habits for the sake of United States' democracy.

Timothy Barouch is Assistant Professor in the Department of Communication at Georgia State University. His research, which focuses on the relationship between law, communication and democratic practices, has been published in *Communication Law and Policy, Rhetoric & Public Affairs* and *Rhetoric Society Quarterly*. He has a Ph.D. in Communication Studies and a law degree from Northwestern University. He can be contacted at tbarouch@gsu.edu and @tbarouch.

Greg Lisby is a professor in the Department of Communication at Georgia State University. He has a Ph.D. in Communications from the University of Tennessee and a law degree from the GSU College of Law. He is a member of the State Bar of Georgia and practices law in Atlanta.

Sources

Abrams v. U.S., 250 U.S. 616 (1919) (Holmes, J., dissenting).

Mill, J.S. (1978, 1859). *On Liberty*. E. Rapaport, ed. Indianapolis, IN: Hackett.

Milton, J. (1961, 1644). *Areopagitica: A Speech for the Liberty of Unlicensed Printing*. J.W. Hales, ed. Oxford: Oxford University Press.

Olson (2021) outlines First Amendment protections and the historic "distinction between 'speech' and 'press,' including that … 'the First Amendment says nothing about either 'expression' or 'conduct' within the short text (p. 25). While free expression may have a variety of social purposes, the classification of speaker (such as, student or government employee) defines how much "protection" may be found in the courts (p. 31). The First Amendment is open to a range of judicial interpretation and social media law follows precedent that government regulation generally is required to be narrowly tailored and clearly connected to substantial non-speech goals. The 45 words within the First Amendment initially limited federal law that restricts "freedom of speech, or of the press." Social media communication, similar to its foundation in computer-mediated communication (CMC) and **human–computer interaction** (HCI), is a blend of free speech, press and **hybrid media**. The evolving nature of information technologies and computer programming presents challenges for the U.S. Supreme Court and lower courts to balance interests: "They look beyond the category of speech alone to consider the particular circumstances and the harm caused by the speech to determine whether the expression is punishable" (Trager, Ross and Reynolds, 2018, p. 55). Any attempt by government within any U.S. level to regulate content requires application of strict scrutiny and proof "both that it has a compelling interest ... and that the regulation restricts no more speech than absolutely necessary" (Pember & Calvert, 2015, p. 70). As explained earlier, however, narrowly tailored government regulation does not protect social media communication from nongovernmental actors – large social media corporations, employers and other private individuals and organizations. At the same time, international law has emerged "as a new source of freedom of expression because the U.S. Constitution is no longer a global inspiration" (Youm & Sanders, 2020, p. 104). The emerging human rights emphasis aligns with normative communication ethics.

ETHICAL FRAMEWORKS AND ISSUES

Stephen J.A. Ward's areas of activity diagram in Chapter 1 depicts a normative model of ethics focused on evaluation, education and reform. The critique of social media communication is largely centered on improvement of the press, but it raises important questions about how external forces may help reform social media communication. Media councils, for example, appear only to relate to reform of the journalism business – a relatively small slice of social media. For example, debt collectors now use social media channels to contact borrowers (Backman, 2020).

Most examinations of the failings of social media communication ultimately end with a call for media literacy education. If only social media users could learn at a young age that speech has consequences, then they would be in a better position to avoid expression that is unwittingly harmful to others. For example, a three-second video that included a racial slur by a high school senior became a viral sensation, and the social media fallout led a Virginia high school senior to lose her university admission and a spot on the cheer team (Levin, 2020). The release of the information on social media appeared to be strategically timed, and the university bowed to public pressure. The case exposed ethical issues in how information is managed on social media channels. What once may have been exclusively a "pillory of the press" shifted to popular social sites. And, "new ethics" must expand to account for the fragmentation and complexity found within a variety of social media channels – Instagram, TikTok and Reddit to name a few. Legislators and the courts inevitably trail rapid technological, social and political innovation, which leaves it to users and social media site online communities to self-regulate communication behavior. Organizational leadership that emphasizes collaboration, for example, may follow an ethical path of "slow strategy" over "social acceleration" that may harm individuals and groups (Díez, Gauxachs & Míco, 2020, p. 234). The principles suggest a need for increased "transparency, "inclusivity" and "network reciprocity" within a context of care in social media communication strategies and tactics (p. 235). Social media measurement and management should value "trust," "integrity" and "responsibility" (p. 236). In fact, a maturing approach to social media strategies and tactics emphasizes the need to identify organizational values through strategic planning that benefit from use of social media.

At the same time, U.S. government ideas under consideration include federal legislation that would allow newspaper and broadcast outlets an explicit right to negotiate rights with Facebook and other huge social media sites (Mayse, 2021). Australia media law moved more quickly to force Facebook to negotiate publisher payments. One U.S. bill would exempt traditional media companies from antitrust restrictions that keep the industries from making blanket deals. The bill was introduced at a time when proposals would remove Facebook's Section 230 liability immunity, as there was a sense that there was an unfair playing field. This coincided with disclosures that Facebook managers battled with one another over selling targeted advertising that may not be as effective as claimed (Biddle, 2020). Meanwhile, Facebook also argued with Apple's move to limit access to user browsing history – central to the social media business model that sells advertisers' an avenue to buyers (Ingram, 2020).

The social media and technology giants continued to grow with resources to venture into new areas. For example, Amazon followed Spotify into the popular podcasting business (Pisani, 2020). Such social business models threatened earlier podcasting sites, such as SoundCloud. At times, it was difficult to predict whether we were seeing increased fragmentation or future consolidation. Marketplace theories, in practice, do not guarantee fairness, honesty and other ethical values. The Silha Center at the University of Minnesota is one of many excellent resources for tracking legal briefs, comments, statements and publication, as social media law and ethics continue to evolve.

ONLINE RESOURCES

Justia (2020). US Law, Freedom of Expression: The Philosophical Basis. https://law.justia.com/constitution/us/amendment-01/05-the-philosophical-basis.html.

Silha Center (2021). Silha Publications. University of Minnesota. https://hsjmc.umn.edu/ research-centers/centers/silha-center/silha-publications.

DISCUSSION QUESTIONS

1. Which specific legal theories and concepts could be applied to a set of future research questions?
2. How could media ethics offer a useful path beyond current free expression theories?
3. Why would social media theories apply to legal and ethical issues? How could these be integrated into a legal or ethical argument?

REFERENCES

Backman, M. (2020, December 24). Debt Collectors Can Now Contact Borrowers on Social Media. *The Ascent.* https://www.fool.com/the-ascent/personal-finance/articles/debt-collectors-can-now-contact-borrowers-through-social-media/.

Bezanson, R.P. (2003, Winter). Speaking Through Others' Voices: Authorship, Originality, and Free Speech, *Wake Forest Law Review*, 38, 983–1110.

Biddle, S. (2020, December 24). Facebook Managers Trash Their Own Ad Targeting in Unsealed Remarks. *The Intercept.* https://theintercept.com/2020/12/24/facebook-ad-targeting-small-business/.

Blackstone, W. (1769). *Commentaries on the Laws of England* (1765–1769). University of Chicago. http://presspubs.uchicago.edu/founders/ documents/amendI_speechs4.html.

Blocher, J. (2014, April). Nonsense and the Freedom of Speech: What Meaning Means for the First Amendment, *Duke Law Journal*, 63, 1423–1481.

Blocher, J. (2019, December). Free Speech and Justified True Belief, *Harvard Law Review*, 133, 439–496.

Blumenthal v. Drudge and America Online, 992 F. Supp. 44 (D.D.C. 1998).

Carlson, C.R. and Cousineau, L. S. (2020, October-December). Are You Sure You Want to View This Community? Exploring the Ethics of Reddit's Quarantine Practice, *Journal of Media Ethics*, 35(4), 202–213.

Children's Online Privacy Protection Act, 16 CFR 312.10(a) (2003).

Children's Privacy Protection Act, 18 U.S.C. § 2556(8) (1996).

Citizens United v. Federal Election Commission, 558 U.S. 310 (2010).

Communications Decency Act (1996).

Crook, J. (2013, November 21). Don't Spam Facebook with Fake Bieber Porn Unless You Want to Get Sued. *TechCrunch.* http://techcrunch.com/2013/11/21/dont-spam-facebook-with-fake-bieber-porn-unless-you-want-to-get-sued/.

Davis, C. (2020, Autumn). Meiklejohn, Alexander. *The First Amendment is an Absolute*, 1961 Sup. Ct. Rev. 245, *Communication Law and Policy*, 25(4), 460–463.

Díez, M., Gauxachs, A.S., and Míco, J.L. (2020, October–December). Caring Leadership: The Alignment of Organizational Values and Social Media Messaging, *Journal of Media Ethics*, 35(4), 228–240.

Emerson, T.I. (1966). *Toward a General Theory of First Amendment, A Unique Examination of the Nature of Freedom of Expression and Its Role in a Democratic Society*. New York: Vintage Books.

Hazelwood School District v. Kuhlmeier, 484 U.S. 260 (1988).

Ingram, D. (2020, December 17). Facebook and Apple are in a Fight. Your Browsing History is in the Middle.*NBC News*. https://www.nbcnews.com/tech/tech-news/facebook-apple-are-fight-your-browsing-history-middle-n1251612.

Johnson, B.G. (2017, January–March). Speech, Harm, and the Duties of Digital Intermediaries: Conceptualizing Platform Ethics, *Journal of Mass Media Ethics*, 32(1), 16–27.

Johnson, B.G. (2018, December). What is "Robust" Public Debate? An Analysis of the Supreme Court's Use of the Word "Robust" in First Amendment Jurisprudence, *Communication Law & Policy*, 23, 335–385.

KABC-TV (2020, October 25). Rapper Offset Briefly Detained While Live On Instagram, Later Released. *ABC Television News*. https://abc7chicago.com/offset-arrested-detained-was-in-beverly-hills/7330357/.

Krislov, S. (1964). Mr. Justice Black Reopens the Free Speech Debate, *UCLA Law Review*, 11, 189–211.

Kroger Co. of Mich. v. Granger, NLRB. No. 07-CA-098566 (April 22, 2014).

Levin, D. (2020, December 26). A Racial Slur, a Viral Video, and a Reckoning. *New York Times*. https://www.nytimes.com/2020/12/26/us/mimi-groves-jimmy-galligan-racial-slurs.html.

Mayse, J. (2021, January 2). Bill Would Allow Newspapers, Broadcast Outlets to Negotiate with Social Media Giants. *Messenger-Inquirer*. https://www.messenger-inquirer.com/news/bill-would-allow-newspapers-broadcast-outlets-to-negotiate-with-social-media-giants/article_4cb8c28a-274a-56ac-a62c-73339c59b59e.html.

Mill, J.S. (1859, 1956). *On Liberty*. New York: Bobbs-Merrill.

Milton, J. (1644). *Areopagitica: A Speech for the Liberty of Unlicensed Printing to the Parliament of England*. Project Gutenberg. http://gutenberg.readingroo.ms/6/0/ 608/608-h/608-h.htm.

Mixon, G. (2020). Not Your Father's Marketplace of Ideas: Hate Speech and Fraudulent Marketplace of Ideas Created by Social Media, *Emory International Law Review*, 34, 399–433.

Near v. Minnesota, 283 U.S. 697 (1931).

New York Times v. Sullivan, 376 U.S. 254 (1964).

Olson, K.K. (2021). The First Amendment in Theory and Practice. In W. Wat Hopkins, *Communication and the Law*. Northport, AL: Vision Press, 23–34.

Pember, D.R. and Calvert, C. (2015). *Mass Media Law*, 19th edition. New York: McGraw-Hill.

Pisani, J. (2020, December 31). Amazon Gets into the Podcast Business. *Associated Press*. https://apnews.com/article/music-streaming-services-meghan-markle-1ce798d0e-c2e830c1cd2757fc0527e00.

R.A.V. v. City of St. Paul, 505 U.S. 377 (1992).

Redish, M.H. and Mollen, A. M. (2009, Summer). Understanding Post's and Meiklejohn's Mistakes: The Central Role of Adversary Democracy in the Theory of Free Expression, *Northwestern University Law Review*, 103, 1303–1370.

Reno v. ACLU, 521 U.S. 844 (1997).

Renton v. Playtime Theatres, 475 U.S. 41 (1986).

Russomanno, J. (2015, Spring). The "Central Meaning" and Path Dependence: The Madisonian-Meiklejohn-Brennan Nexus, *Communication Law & Policy*, 20, 117–148.

Schauer, F. (2004, April). The Boundaries of the First Amendment: A Preliminary Exploration of Constitutional Salience, *Harvard Law Review*, 117, 1765–1809.

Shankman, P. (2020, September 4). There Are No More Rules. Now Is Your Time. Email Newsletter.

Skeet, A. (2020, March 13). Ethical Leadership Practices in a Pandemic. Markkula Center for Applied Ethics. https://www.scu.edu/ethics/leadership-ethics-blog/ethical-leadership-practices-in-a-pandemic/.

Texas v. Johnson, 491 U.S. 397 (1989).

Tinker v. Des Moines Independent Community School District, 393 U.S. 503 (1969).

Trager, R., Ross, S.D., and Reynolds, A. (2018). *The Law of Journalism and Mass Communication*, 6th edition. Thousand Oaks, CA: SAGE.

United Nations (1948). Universal Declaration of Human Rights. https://www.un.org/en/universal-declaration-human-rights/.

United States v. O'Brien, 391 U.S.367 (1968).

Virginia v. Black, 538 U.S. 343 (2003).

Weiland, M.N. (2017, May). Expanding the Periphery and Threatening the Core. The Ascendant Libertarian Speech Tradition, *Stanford Law Review*, 69, 1389–1472.

Weinstein, J. (2013, Winter). How Theory Matters: A Commentary on Robert Sedler's "The Law of the First Amendment Revisited", *Wayne Law Review*, 58, 1105–1148.

Youm, K. and & Sanders, A.K. (2020, Spring). International and Comparative Law as a Reverse Perspective on Communication Law, *Communication Law & Policy*, 25, 103–112.

Researching Law and Ethics

The values sought by society in protecting the right to freedom of expression may be grouped into four broad categories.

–Professor Thomas I. Emerson,
Toward A General Theory of the First Amendment (1966, p. 3)

Thomas Emerson sought to examine free expression as playing a fundamental role in democracy, as the U.S. Supreme Court began its interpretation just over four decades before he published his widely cited book. Emerson (1966) found four values: "(1) as a method of assuring individual self-fulfillment, (2) as a means of attaining the truth, (3) as a method of securing participation by the members of a society in social, including political, decision-making, and (4) as a means of maintaining the balance between stability and change in the society" (p. 3). There can be little debate that social media communication, at least at times, benefits individuals and the search for truth within the marketplace of ideas. We may activate strong public engagement, political debate, and peaceful release of social tensions. Emerson (1966) argued for individualism in thought, and that each of us "has the right to express" personal "beliefs and opinions" (p. 5). Individuals are seen in this view as members of society in search of "truth" in a rational process of "considering all facts and arguments which can be put forth" (p. 7). Most importantly, it can be argued, the venting of free expression has a potential to help serve the "precarious balance" of social change and stability (p. 11). Social media communication can be caustic in the short term, but we would hope that enlightenment prevails. Emerson (1966) also acknowledged that the marketplace is not absolute, that government is a participant at the same time that it is "regulating conflicts between individuals or groups" (p. 29). An ongoing challenge within social media is the antidemocratic voice of some, yet U.S. free expression has advanced within the nation to include some legal protection for "those which seek to destroy it" (p. 49).

A review of salient legal and ethical theories in the previous chapter should lay a foundation for developing research that can be presented or published. For example, a rejection of balancing First Amendment interests against others, at times runs counter to a long list of U.S. Supreme Court cases over many decades. The current research challenge is to identify doctrine that provide convincing support for protecting the individual right of free expression under the First Amendment. The legal research process serves to: (1) identify existing legal issues and reasoning through specific case facts and decision-making; (2) connect cases to observe emerging law and trends; (3) suggest alternative legal paths; and (4) acknowledge limitation of legal theories and application within case law, state and federal statutes, regulation of speech and conduct, and international common values. In general, most social research follows the following steps that can be adapted for use in legal and ethical research papers:

1. Introduction: The best research papers offer a clear and explicit statement of purpose. "The purpose of this paper" signals to the reader that the author knows and can explain why the research is important.
2. Literature review: A conceptual framework should be developed that builds upon previous research – whether it comes from case law, social scholarship, law review articles, ethics studies, or other journals and books. Through previous studies we can develop theory-based research questions (RQs).
3. Results: If you develop specific RQs, or even theoretic hypotheses based on previous studies, then you should be able to answer specific questions. Court decisions and/or other evidence should help explain findings.
4. Conclusions: The three parts of any strong conclusion are: a) *interpretation* – what do the results mean? b) *limitation* – what were the limits on conducting a reasoned analysis? c) *future research questions* – Where do we go from here? Law review articles frequently advocate changes in law or direction in future court decisions.

5. References and footnotes: Depending on use of APA style rules or Harvard legal citation, the referencing will vary. However, it is important to tell readers the sources of *all information used* to build the research arguments.

Research of complex First Amendment issues that impact social media free expression can be challenging, but development of solid legal and social theories helps scholars organize the social world by studying primary and secondary sources. Legal stability through precedent, or *stare decisis* in case law, offers a somewhat consistent First Amendment framework that serves what Karl Llewellyn placed within "social values of predictability" (Cohen, 1985, p. 7). Legal research proceeds by reading judicial reports, finding relevant cases and statutes, exploring legislative history and administrative law, and placing it within the context of any international treaties or law, such as common or civil law (p. xxiii). Over time, LEXIS (Nexis Uni) and WESTLAW offered access to international primary and secondary resources.

LEGAL THEORIES AND ETHICAL FRAMEWORKS

Levy (1985) offered a comprehensive history first titled *Legacy of Suppression: Freedom of Speech and Press in Early American History,* later revised to *Emergence of a Free Press.* The original backlash to his work centered on a "fear ... that the wicked forces of reaction might capitalize on the discovery that the Framers gave their paternal blessing to suppressive impulses" (p. xvii). Decades later, a divided Supreme Court tussles over originalism and intent of Framers that included landholding slaves. Levy (1985) studied the origins of seditious libel laws motivated by potential effects to destabilize England's government: "Freedom of religious and political expression was feared as a means of triggering conspiracies, internal disorders, wars, revolutions, or some other disastrous train of events that might pull down church and state" (p. 5). By the time of the vast American colonial development, it is noteworthy that "the test of free speech" could be operationalized as "the right to speak openly and with impunity among neighbors" (p. 16). Centuries later, we might substitute neighbors for Facebook friends. Still, Levy (1985) recognized that "American Libertarian Theory" was a matter of historical emergence and Framers' direction:

> What they said is far more important than what they meant. It is enough that they gave constitutional recognition to the principle of freedom of speech and press in unqualified and undefined terms.
>
> (p. 349)

By the time that the 20th-century U.S. Supreme Court began to interpret the First Amendment and Fourteenth Amendment, scholars contrasted authoritarian, libertarian, social responsibility and Soviet Communist models of free press (Siebert, Peterson, & Schramm, 1956). Libertarian concepts may be grounded in human rationality and happiness: "The fulfillment of the individual therefore becomes the ultimate goal – the goal of man, of society, and of the state" (p. 40). However, the post-World War II concern over authoritarian regimes and decline of absolute liberalism led to calls for press social responsibility that included "financial self-sufficiency" (p. 74). One criticism was that: "The press has been subservient to big business and at times has let advertisers control editorial policies and editorial content" (p. 78). This problem remains, not only on newspaper and media websites, but also Facebook, YouTube and other social media platforms that monetize content. Nobody would challenge that ethics demands truthful journalism, but the 21st-century social media communication era has been defined by a willingness of politicians at all levels and corporations to disseminate false information. The distinction between a natural right of free expression and social responsibility is "a moral right with an aspect of duty," including "duty of the individual to his thought, to his conscience" (p. 96). So, normative ethics demand individual "growth," social "intelligence" and "progress" (p. 96). "One's right to free expression must be balanced against the private rights of others and against vital social interests" (p. 97). Indeed, courts frequently have interpreted the First Amendment through use balancing tests when determining rights and harms.

Computer hacking laws, for example, raise concerns about the First Amendment rights of data journalists and researchers (Fidler, 2020). The U.S. Supreme Court agreed to settle disagreements between most of the U.S. circuits. The *Van Buren* Supreme Court case may settle, as the Reporters Committee for Freedom of the Press (2020) **amicus** brief suggested, whether or not the statute violates overbreadth under the First Amendment by "significantly" chilling "both traditional newsgathering and new data-journalism techniques" (para. 3). Under the law, unauthorized access to confidential information is a crime: "The court of appeal's interpretation is so broad that it could sweep in ordinary journalistic activity that is essential to the newsgathering process ... dramatically altering the way in which government officials and corporate whistleblowers relate to the press, the means by which the press gathers and reports the news, and the degree of newsworthy information made available to the public" (Reporters Committee, 2020, para. 8). Access to information is one important legal component, but freedom of expression on the Internet also remains a concern.

Any attempt to backpedal on the *Reno v. ACLU* (1997) U.S. Supreme Court interpretation that Internet communication enjoys publisher First Amendment freedom risks, in the extreme, a possibility that social media channels could face a set of rules similar to those in U.S. broadcast regulation and licensing. Congress and the Federal

Communications Commission (FCC) imposed a variety of rules, enforcement and fines that functioned within the political system (Krasnow, Longley, & Terry, 1982):

> To a great extent these relationships are determined by law – by statutes that are themselves the formal heritage of past political disputes. Such laws, however, are seldom crystal clear; the result of earlier political conflict may have been, and often is, statutes and rules drafted with deliberate ambiguity – broad general mandates that permit the politics of today to determine the rules and standards of tomorrow. (p. 9)

One such ambiguity involved application of a "public interest" standard that also has been suggested for social media companies. As a matter of regulation, it would be impossible to avoid normative values of social media accountability and difficult to predict the future of rapid social technological change. Broadcast licensing existed to address perceived spectrum scarcity and the need for technological, if not economic limits on the number of voices controlling the marketplace of ideas. It favored media gatekeeping that barely exists within social media, except for the most extreme and caustic views. We can learn from the failures of the "broadcast policy-making system," without going into more detail here, that any regulation of social media would be driven by the executive, legislative and judicial branches of U.S. government, the "regulated industries" and "citizens groups" (p. 136). Importantly, financial backing of influential lobbying frequently gives regulated businesses the upper hand on consumers at the Federal Trade Commission (FTC) and other parts of government. In the end, "conflicting goals" and "unequal strengths" should produce symbolic and descriptive "mutual accommodation" (pp. 138–140). However, this model fails to account for hyperpolarized politics, policy deadlock and conflict that offer little contribution to individual development and progress, so defined, demanded by social responsibility theory. In this sense, social media law and ethics over two decades has been defined by a theory of First Amendment liberalism accompanied by a continuing sense of moral outrage. A clear path has not yet emerged to find consensus about how to structure social media that either benefit or at least avoid harm to the democratic ideals found in the search for truth and progress.

LINGERING CONSTITUTIONAL AND STATUTE LAW ISSUES

First Amendment cases are litigated within a complex structure involving interpretation by several influential U.S. Circuit Court of Appeals and the Supreme Court. For example, the expansive language of the *Packingham* (2017) Supreme Court opinion was tempered by legal commentary and lower court application.

Box 11.1 The *Bobal* Ruling

In *U.S. v. Bobal* (2020), the Eleventh Circuit reviewed a case from the Southern District of Florida. Chief Judge William Pryor wrote for a three-judge Appeals Court panel. Bobal was convicted of "attempting to persuade a minor to engage in sexual activity and committing a felony involving a minor while required to register as a sex offender."

On appeal, Bobal cited the *Packingham* (2017) decision in an argument that restricting his computer use was unconstitutional. The court, however, distinguished the two cases and the lower court criminal conviction and sentence was affirmed. In response to Bobal's advances toward an adult woman, a neighbor posed online as a 14-year-old. Bobal eventually "sent the fictitious girl a picture of his penis" and the FBI was called to respond to his text messages. A federal grand jury indicted Bobal on two counts of "using a facility and means of interstate commerce to knowingly attempt to persuade, induce, entice, and coerce a minor to engage in sexual activity." Bobal was convicted and sentenced to 240 months, "followed by a lifetime term of supervised release."

At issue was a special condition that Bobal "shall not possess or use a computer that contains an internal, external or wireless modem without the prior approval of the Court." The District and Appellate courts found the lifetime supervision was constitutional because Bobal could "still use the Internet for valid purposes by obtaining his probation officer's prior permission."

Source: *U.S. v. Bobal*, 19-10678 (11th Cir. 2020). https://mitchellhamline.edu/sex-offense-litigation-policy/wp-content/uploads/sites/61/2020/12/11th-Circuit-Court-of-Appeals-Opinion.pdf.

As a research issue, how we read Supreme Court language – narrowly, broadly or somewhere in between – has significant impact on the degree of First Amendment freedom. In the case of convicted criminals who lose their fundamental rights, the issue is how long free expression rights may be curtailed after time has been served. For the rest of us, the power of social media companies to dictate content decision-making rules for users remains fairly broad and problematic. When non-lawyers read and attempt to understand the social media law, they have a lot to learn in the research process – from **parallel citation** rules to language filled with legal jargon.

Communication law and ethics students also need to learn Latin words commonly used by attorneys and judges within research documents. Legal jargon is one way, *inter alia* (among others), in which the writing of lawyers may be difficult for students to access. For example, within text and footnotes, readers may see ***infra*** to point to a later point made in a decision or ***supra*** for earlier information. Or, a judge may apply **strict liability doctrine** when holding an individual liable for damages – even when there is no proof of fault. News reporters sometimes cover cases in which a **temporary restraining order (TRO)** is issued to halt an action while the court reviews the law. Or, they may see a "writ of ***mandamus***" that directs a government agency or public official to do something. Sometimes, journalists and news organizations use state **shield laws** that protect them from disclosing confidential sources of their information, but most social media users probably are unaware of the law. They most likely have not taken a class that teaches them about **reporter privilege** that offers some protection to a journalist and news source. The definition of a journalist and this protection is made fuzzy because of social media communication and the power to reach global audiences from a mobile smartphone. **Live tweeting** a breaking news event, for example, presents interesting issues when a defamation lawsuit follows. An otherwise private person may be considered a **limited-purpose public figure** when they thrust themselves into the vortex of a controversial public issue. In such a case, actual malice replaces sloppy negligence as the standard in a libel case. We must presume that most social media users would not know this. Similarly, if information turns out to be false, a **retraction** of a false claim can mitigate damages in a potential libel lawsuit, but social media users may dig in against their legal and economic interests.

It is likely that we will see more social media case law that defines how much the First Amendment applies within large social media platforms that function as a quasi-public forum in the next few years.

RESEARCH LAW AND ETHICS ISSUES

A variety of research issues exist relating to the study of social media communication. Grimmelmann (2015) explored the law and ethics of social media experimental research. As early as 2012, for example, Facebook pushed content in an experiment to try to manipulate psychological sadness without consent or disclosure. The "systematic" manipulation of "reactions" did not follow academic processes through an Institutional Review Board (IRB), required under federal procedures, "to obtain informed consent from participants and approval" (p. 219).

A few states have attempted to pass laws protecting social media users from human subject research, but there has been no widespread movement on this front. User agreements also fall short of clear informed consent: "The language in typical terms of service is too general, and the signup process too attenuated, to generate meaningful informed consent" (Grimmelmann, 2015, p. 244):

> The conversation about the right legal rule for consent in social media research should not be a distraction from the underlying ethical role of consent. The real goal, ... should be enthusiastic consent. Social media research should not be an adversarial setting in which researchers and companies try to wring from users whatever minimal threshold of informed consent the law tells them they need. Instead, they should seek enthusiastic consent from users, making them into valued partners who feel they have a stake in the research and are eager to contribute to its success. Researchers have stories to tell about what they can learn from interacting with users. Facebook has a story about how our friends' moods influence our own and another about promoting civic participation.
>
> (p. 271)

SOCIAL LEGAL RESEARCH

Beyond legal and or ethical research methods, there are more than three decades of work utilizing social methods in the study of law (Humphreys, Gill, & Krishnamurthy, 2013; Pritchard, 2009). For example, one might do a quantitative and or qualitative content analysis of First Amendment law. Swann (2021) treats research as "scientific writing" (p. 7) that typically includes an abstract, literature review, hypotheses and research questions, methodology, findings, discussion and conclusion, references and appendices (pp. 22–23). Social media communication content is a form of mediated communication:

> These messages can be shaped and formed by the particular medium to reflect a symbolic representation about our world. Mediated communication may reflect reality as you know it or not. Narrative messages can be examined to see how these powerful societal influences are reflecting a particular reality.
>
> (p. 33)

For example, the *Elonis v. U.S.* (2015) case could be examined to see how the district court, Appellate Court and U.S. Supreme Court used Anthony Elonis' Facebook post language to justify each decision, including majority and dissenting opinions. In content analysis, researchers have examined violent messages, cultural indicators, gender and race.

Armstrong (2021) explored racism within social media conflicts in which white women are called a "Karen" (p. 27). Frequently, cases arise from a video recording and social media post showing a white woman who expresses fear of a black or person of color and threatens to call police. Armstrong theorized that "the racist actions that we see in viral incidents are taken when the intersection of whiteness and womanhood come together as a racist weapon" (p. 28). The narratives promoted by Twitter hashtags and memes, for example, revolve around shifting the women's behavior from "harmless victims to potential racist aggressors" (p. 28). Oregon was one of the first U.S. states to pass a tort law "allowing victims of racist 911 calls to sue the caller" and define unacceptable behavior (pp. 49–50).

Nearly every traditional legal research topic has been impacted by social media. For example, the use of change of venue in moving trial location to guarantee a Sixth Amendment right to a fair trial is problematic given social media content sharing to anywhere (Garfield Tenzer, 2019). "In the past few years, defendants filing change of venue motions have included social media posts in their baskets of adverse pretrial publicity" (pp. 441–442).

Another example is the use of social media as a "weapon of information warfare" and impact on international law (Qureshi, 2019, p. 171). When it comes to misinformation, disinformation and "deepfake" manipulation, international law and treaties do not address the problems associated with social media content. International and comparative law scholars struggle to develop theory-based research about contested factuality. Social media use "by non-state actors, including terrorist organizations" to recruit and "extend hateful and inciteful content to vulnerable individuals" suggests that future legal and ethical research is needed (pp. 201–202). Methodologies to collect group behavioral social media data are important to understanding social, legal, and ethical research questions.

Box 11.2 #StopTheSteal Case Study

The Twitter application programming interface (API) freely allows social researchers to collect large numbers of tweets – about 18,000 recent tweets that can be aggregated to as many as 90 days. NodeXL, a social network analysis (SNA) tool, can be used to track hashtag social movements. Immediately following the 2020 presidential election-night results, for example, supporters of Donald Trump sought to stop counting in battleground states under the #StopTheSteal hashtag that bolstered questionable claims of election fraud. We can see from

November 24, 2020 data that the hashtag was related to key influencer Twitter accounts and other hashtags:

@realdonaldtrump
@millionmagamarch
@jennybethm
@jeffrosetv
@yogagenie
@sidneypowell1
@thejusticedept
@replouiegohmert
@ali
@briankempga
#stopthesteal
#sundayvibes

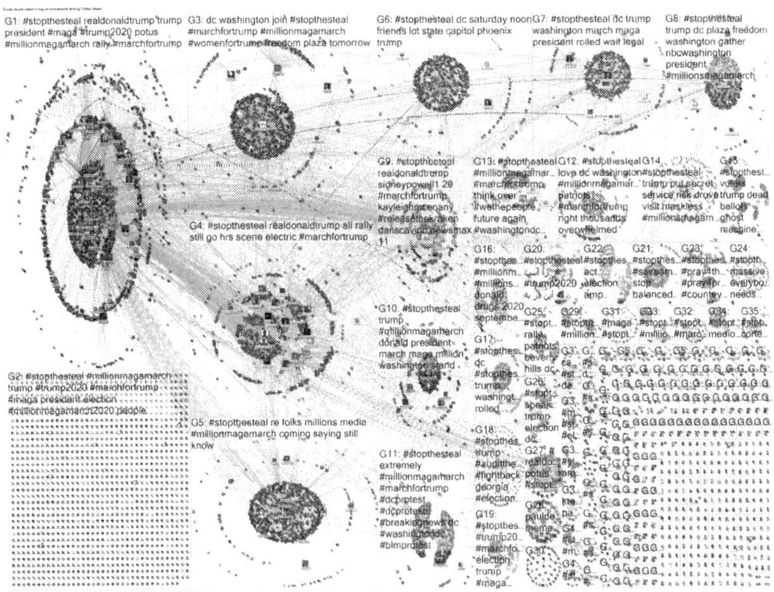

Social Network Data.

Courtesy Social Media Research Foundation. https://nodexlgraphgallery.org/Pages/Graph.aspx?graphID=242141.

#headswillroll
#trump2020
#maga
#fightback

The *mapping* of social media communication offers identification of conversation clusters, links to website content and indicators of account tagging behavior – raising important legal and ethical concerns. In the #StopTheSteal example, some groups were threatening violence through their speech with the #headswillroll hashtag. From a First Amendment perspective, the tweets initially did not present a clear and present danger of immediate harm, although some were related to protests outside vote counting centers. Later, Twitter, Facebook, and Instagram and others forced President Trump to remove tweets, suspended accounts, and banned him. Some of the threats elevated from online harassment during the mob attack on the U.S. Capitol to violence and deaths. At the same time, the law of criminal threats examined by the U.S. Supreme Court in the *Elonis* case, reveals that state of mind must be evaluated. The public NodeXL Graph Gallery is a real-time, open science tool to observe data being collected by researchers around the world. Many current issues relate to social media communication law and ethics.

Source: NodeXL (2020, November 24). #StopTheSteal. Social Media Research Foundation. https://nodexlgraphgallery.org/Pages/Graph.aspx?graphID=242141.

Digital surveillance of social media user data footprints is a growing research topic. Frequently, social media accounts are connected to news sites that may be authorized through opaque user agreements:

> Newspaper privacy policies deserve scholarly attention because online activities (including newsreading) can provide a rich and detailed record of people's interests, attitudes, preferences, attention patterns, social network ties, and purchasing patterns, as well as clues to their fears, biases, beliefs, and political positions, particularly when user data are shared between news sites and social media.
>
> (Adams, 2020, p. 869)

The potential misuses of personal data include economic "exploitation" and "political manipulation" (p. 874). These monetization concerns align with EU attempts to restrain surveillance capitalism. "Respect for human dignity demands that people be respected as ends in themselves rather than as objects to be manipulated for extraneous ends such as profit making and political gain" (p. 883). Social media managers should have a sense of duty, not only to employers but also to their readers. There companies should exercise corporate social responsibility (CSR) that includes "limited acquisition and use of user data by advertisers, exchange of data between sites and shared data with third-party affiliates" (Adams, 2020, p. 878). In the U.S.A., data privacy law is slowly emerging, and there is a need to ethically behave in collection, storage and use of individual data.

LEGAL STRUCTURES AND OTHER FACTORS

Students of law and ethics should review the U.S. Circuit court system. As previously explained, most cases are not considered by the Supreme Court, so appellate courts in the thirteen circuits interpret law within their regions:

> There are 13 appellate courts that sit below the U.S. Supreme Court, and they are called the U.S. Courts of Appeals. The 94 federal judicial districts are organized into 12 regional circuits, each of which has a court of appeals. The appellate court's task is to determine whether or not the law was applied correctly in the trial court. Appeals courts consist of three judges and do not use a jury … A court of appeals hears challenges to district court decisions from courts located within its circuit, as well as appeals from decisions of federal administrative agencies.
>
> (United States Courts, paras. 5–6)

The location of many social media companies in Silicon Valley means that the Ninth Circuit can be very important.

Other circuits in New York (Second), Philadelphia (Third) and Washington DC (DC Circuit) also wield influence over the regulated media industry. The DC Circuit typically reviews cases from U.S. regulatory agencies, such as the FCC, FTC, FEC and SEC. Historically, important First Amendment law also has come from Illinois (Seventh) and Florida (Eleventh). Under Article III of the U.S. Constitution, the Supreme Court has the highest legal authority on the fewer than 200 cases per year it grants *cert.* and hears.

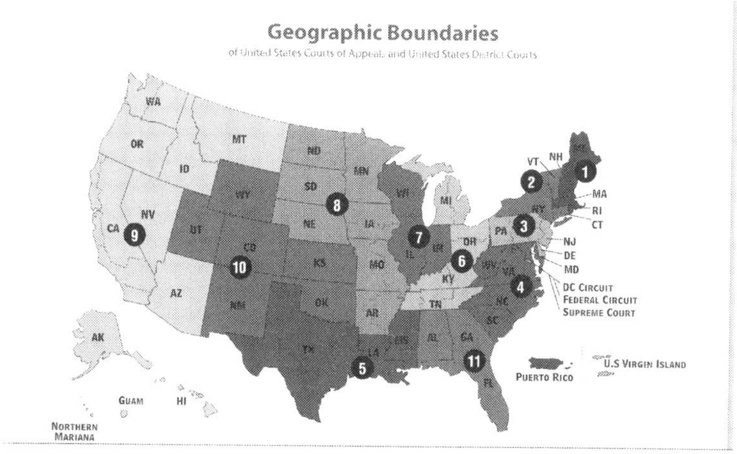

U.S. Courts of Appeals Map.

Courtesy U.S. Courts (2020). https://www.uscourts.gov/file/document/us-federal-courts-circuit-map.

Box 11.3 U.S. Supreme Court Justices

U.S. Supreme Court Justices, 2018–2020.

Photograph courtesy Fred Schilling, U.S. Supreme Court. https://www.supremecourt.gov/about/justices.aspx.]

Name (age in 2020)	State	President (party, year)	J.D.	Replaced
John Roberts, C.J. (65)	MD	Bush II (R, 2005)	Harvard	O'Connor and then Rehnquist as CJ, Reagan (R, 1981)
Clarence Thomas (72)	GA	Bush I (R, 1991)	Yale	Marshall, Johnson, (D, 1967)
Stephen Breyer (82)	MA	Clinton (D, 1994)	Harvard	Blackmun, Nixon (R, 1970)
Samuel Alito (70)	NJ	Bush II (R, 2006)	Yale	O'Connor, Reagan (R, 1981)
Sonia Sotomayor (66)	NY	Obama, D, 2009)	Yale	Souter, G.H.W. Bush (D, 1990)
Elena Kagan (60)	MA	Obama (D, 2010)	Harvard	Stevens, Ford (R, 1975)
Neil Gorsuch (53)	CO	Trump (R, 2017)	Harvard	Scalia, Reagan (R, 1986)
Brett Kavanaugh (55)	MD	Trump (R, 2018)	Yale	Kennedy, Reagan (R, 1988)
Amy Coney Barrett (48)	IN	Trump (R, 2020)	Notre Dame	Ginsburg (Clinton, 1993)

Source: U.S. Supreme Court (2020). About the Court, Justices 1789 to Present. https://www.supremecourt.gov/about/members_text.aspx.

The U.S. Supreme Court likely will be addressing social media regulation in the years ahead. Congress' proposed elimination of Section 230 liability immunity for Facebook and other technology companies is part of what is shifting. From data privacy breaches and hate speech to misinformation during U.S. presidential and other election cycles, lawmakers seem willing and ready to regulation social media communication.

Rochefort (2020) used a governance theoretic framework and policy analysis method to explore alternatives for regulating social media: "Policy *effectiveness* is a central criterion with any comparative policy analysis and is operationalized with respect to the stated goals of a new law or organizational practice" (p. 232):

> In addition to *effectiveness*, the criteria of *administrative difficulty*, *cost*, and *political acceptability* supply relevant evaluative benchmarks for the comparative assessment … Overall, this analytical approach is consistent with the regulatory

> framework … in which sound regulation depends on, first, the identification of market failure or a systemic problem; second, specification of alternative remedial approaches; and, third, selection of the regulatory action that maximizes net benefit to society.
>
> (p. 233)

The spectrum of rules runs from industry self-regulation through limited or comprehensive government regulation. Obviously, Google, Facebook, Twitter and other social media platforms have strengthened self-regulation found within terms of service end-user agreements. Social media ethics codes and principles also fall within a self-regulated marketplace. However, data privacy state law, including the protection of biometric profiles, in Illinois, California and other states represents a shift toward limited or comprehensive regulation in select areas. If states and the federal government go further toward creating a structural public interest, convenience and necessity approach to social media, such as what was done within broadcast licensing, then we will begin to treat these sites as a form of "public utility" (Rochefort, 2020, p. 251). Alternatively, antitrust efforts to break up Facebook by treating it as a monopoly or EU human rights privacy law are fertile future research topics. Calls for greater transparency align with a normative and ethical need for accountability.

Box 11.4 Thought Leader Ming Xie

Ming Xie.

Photograph courtesy West Texas A&M University.

With the prevalence of information technology and social media, the development of online accountability has attracted scholars' attention. Online accountability is defined as "the provision of inclusive and transparent organizational practices serve to demonstrate or enhance accountability on the Web" (Lee & Joseph, 2012, p. 170). Diverse social media activities and platforms allow nonprofit organizations to convey their transparency and accountability to their stakeholders.

SOCIAL MEDIA AND ONLINE ACCOUNTABILITY

In general, the role of social media has been examined from the perspective of democratic theory, public sphere and social capital. Nonprofit scholars have started the discussion of the impact of information technology on accountability and conceptualized the virtual accountability and web-based accountability (Slatten et al., 2016; Dainelli, Manetti, & Sibilio, 2013; Dumont, 2013; Lee & Joseph, 2012).

TRANSPARENCY AND INFORMATION DISCLOSURE

Transparency has been viewed as being able to generate or improve organizational accountability (Anheier et al., 2013). Scholars have argued that transparency is the most important aspects of nonprofit accountability (Bothwell, 2001; Edwards & Hulme, 1996) that allows nonprofit organizations to fulfill their fiduciary and legal duties (Sloan, 2009), to be accountable to stakeholders and to increase the visibility and public scrutiny (Kearns, 1996). Studies have found that nonprofit organizations promote organizational processes, including outcome measurement and strategic planning that contribute to their reputation among influential institutional actors (MacIndoe & Barman, 2013; Barman & MacIndoe, 2012). However, even though nonprofit organizations have been seen as being more accountable for upward accountability (Schmitz et al., 2012), existing literature has demonstrated the underutilization of social media for financial disclosure and performance disclosure (Slatten et al., 2016; Blouin & Lee, 2013). For example, financial disclosure and performance reporting are widely cited ways nonprofits demonstrate accountability (Ebrahim, 2016), Blouin and Lee (2013) found that only 43 percent organizations posted their annual reports, 13 percent posted audited financial statements and that only 3 percent posted their IRS letters of determination, revealed by an examination of 1,769 nonprofit organizations. Saxton, Neely and Guo (2014) claimed that performance and annual report disclosure online is more important than financial disclosure for current and potential donors. They suggested that the decision regarding how much financial, strategic and performance information they should disclose online is critical for nonprofit organizations to get charitable contributions.

VOLUNTARY ACCOUNTABILITY VERSUS MANDATORY ACCOUNTABILITY

Compared to the mandatory accountability that requires nonprofit organizations to be accountable to government regulators, funders and other upward stakeholders, the accountability based on information technology is a kind of voluntary accountability. Without mandatory responsibility and the formal standards and criteria such as the auditing, accounting and reporting system of the governmental regulators, nonprofit organizations have the discretion to decide what information is shared and disclosed over social media.

Through the voluntary information dissemination, nonprofit organizations are able to legitimize their presence, elevate organizational images and perceptions, build reputations among various stakeholders (Manetti et al., 2017) and to monitor the spread of awareness of their mission and issues (Appleby, 2016). For example, Svensson et al. (2015) found that nonprofits share general information about the program or organization, including "events, news updates, and grants and funding approval ... focus on what the organization or one of its programs have achieved such as participation and funding milestones as well as program or chapter expansions" (p. 1094). In their research specific to social media and nonprofit advocacy, Guo and Saxton (2014) found that information dissemination was focused on "getting the word out through the continuing sending of brief messages to the organization's followers" (p. 71). They found that hashtags on Twitter were a particularly useful tool for getting the organization's advocacy message out.

SOCIAL MEDIA AS PUBLIC SPHERE

Habermas' (1974) concept of the public sphere emphasizes the social institution encouraging participation of "all citizens" (p. 49) in the process of public opinion formation. The public sphere is a "communication structure that refers neither to the function nor to the contents of everyday communication but to the social space generated in communicative action" (Habermas, 1996, p. 360). With the proliferation of information technology and social media, the discussion of the public sphere has been expanded from mass media to social media. Discussions have been around whether technologies can create a new environment for democratic institutions that are more participatory and citizen-centric. Chun and Luna Reyes (2012) stated that "social media use in government is considered a technological innovation and a transforming agent in generating citizen engagement from campaigns and grassroots-activism to shared governance promoting democracy" (p. 442). Questions are raised regarding whether social media platforms such as Twitter and Facebook are alternative structures of public spheres by encouraging broader participation.

CONCLUSION

In the social media world, nonprofit organizations are able to take the responsibility to proactively provide information, to generate online conversations and dialogues, to create an online community and therefore to mobilize social resources for their missions and social values. **Communitarianism**, a philosophy of placing community needs above any individual, should be considered. Ethical disputes within social media may center on a competition for scarce resources, but larger community interests could prevail.

The performance- and resource-based accountability focuses on the organizational constraints of social media use and the resource development and solicitation through social media activities, neglecting the mission-related activities through social media including the mission fulfillment, goal achievement and social impact. The broader examination of the relationship between social media activities, organizational mission and the social impact will improve the understanding of social media's role for nonprofit organizations' development and thriving.

Ming Xie is an assistant professor at the Department of Political Science and Criminal Justice, West Texas A&M University. Ming received her Ph.D. degree in public administration from University of Nebraska at Omaha.

She also holds a Ph.D. in cultural anthropology from the Graduate School of Chinese Academy of Social Sciences in Beijing, China. She is particularly interested in intercultural communication, emergency management, as well as non-profit organization management and communication.

Sources

Anheier, H.K., Hass, R., and Beller, A. (2013). Accountability and Transparency in the German Nonprofit Sector: A Paradox?, *International Review of Public Administration*, 18(3), 69–84.

Appleby, M. (2016). Nonprofit Organizations and the Utilization of Social Media: Maximizing and Measuring Return of Investment, *SPNHA Review*, 12(1), 5–26.

Barman, E. and MacIndoe, H. (2012). Institutional Pressures and Organizational Capacity: The Case of Outcome Measurement, *Sociological Forum*, 27(1), 70–93.

Blouin, M. and Lee, R. (2013). Is Your Financial Information Online?, *Nonprofit World*, 31(2), 22–23.

Bothwell, R.O. (2001). Trends in Self-regulation and Transparency of Nonprofits in the U.S., *International Journal of Not-for-Profit Law*, 2(3), 604–622.

Chun, S.A. and Luna Reyes, L.F. (2012). Social Media in Government, *Government Information Quarterly*, 29(4), 441–445.

Dainelli, F., Manetti, G., and Sibilio, B. (2013). Web-based Accountability Practices in Non-profit Organizations: The Case of National Museums, *VOLUNTAS: International Journal of Voluntary and Nonprofit Organizations*, 24(3), 649–665.

Edwards, M. and Hulme, D. (eds.) (1996). *Beyond the Magic Bullet: NGO Performance and Accountability in the Post-cold War World*. Boulder, CO: Kumarian Press.

Habermas, J. (1974). The Public Sphere: An Encyclopedia Article (1964), *New German Critique*, 3, 49–55.

Habermas, J. (1996). *Between Facts and Norms: Contributions to a Discourse Theory of Law and Democracy*. Chichester: John Wiley & Sons.

Kearns, K.P. (1996). *Managing for Accountability: Preserving the Public Trust in Public and Nonprofit Organizations*. San Francisco, CA: Jossey-Bass.

Lee, R.L. and Joseph, R.C. (2012). Survival of the Fittest: Online Accountability in Complex Organizational Populations, SAIS 2021 Proceedings, 30.

MacIndoe, H. and Barman, E. (2013). How Organizational Stakeholders Shape Performance Measurement in Nonprofits: Exploring a Multidimensional Measure, *Nonprofit and Voluntary Sector Quarterly*, 42(4), 716–738.

Manetti, G., Bellucci, M., and Bagnoli, L. (2017). Stakeholder Engagement and Public Information through Social Media: A Study of Canadian and American Public Transportation Agencies, *American Review of Public Administration*, 47(8), 991–1009.

Saxton, G.D. and Guo, C. (2011). Accountability Online: Understanding the Web-based Accountability Practices of Nonprofit Organizations, *Nonprofit and Voluntary Sector Quarterly*, 40(2), 270–295.

Saxton, G.D., Neely, D.G., and Guo, C. (2014). Web Disclosure and the Market for Charitable Contributions, *Journal of Accounting and Public Policy*, 33(2), 127–144.

Schmitz, H.P., Raggo, P., and Bruno-van Vijfeijken, T. (2012). Accountability of Transnational NGOs: Aspirations vs. Practice, *Nonprofit and Voluntary Sector Quarterly*, 41(6), 1175–1194.

Slatten, L.A.D., Guidry Hollier, B.N., Stevens, D.P., Austin, W., and Carson, P.P. (2016). Web-based Accountability in the Nonprofit Sector: A Closer Look at Arts, Culture, and Humanities Organizations, *Journal of Arts Management, Law & Society*, 46(5), 213–230.

Sloan, M.F. (2009). The Effects of Nonprofit Accountability Ratings on Donor Behavior, *Nonprofit and Voluntary Sector Quarterly*, 38(2), 220–236.

Svensson, P.G., Mahoney, T.Q., and Hambrick, M. E. (2015). Twitter as a Communication Tool for Nonprofits: A Study of Sport-for-Development Organizations, *Nonprofit and Voluntary Sector Quarterly,* 44(6), 1086–1106.

ONLINE RESOURCES

First Amendment Center (2021). Freedom Forum Institute. https://www.freedomforuminstitute.org/first-amendment-center/.

DISCUSSION QUESTIONS

1. What role should the original intent of Framers play in how we interpret the meaning of the First Amendment, as it applies to social media case law?
2. How, if it all, should theories of liberalism and absolutism be limited by a need for social responsibility within the exercise of social media free expression?
3. How, if at all, could research address concerns about the global power of Facebook, Google, Twitter and other companies that manage social media communication?

REFERENCES

Adams, P.C. (2020, Winter). Agreeing to Surveillance: Digital News Privacy Policies, *Journalism & Mass Communication Quarterly,* 97(4), 868–889.

Armstrong. M. (2021, Winter). From Lynching to Central Park Karen: How White Women Weaponize Womanhood, *Hastings Women's Law Journal,* 31, 27–49.

Cohen, M.L. (1985). *Legal Research.* St. Paul, MN: West Publishing.

Elonis v. U.S., 575 U.S. ___ (2015).

Emerson, T.I. (1966). *Toward a General theory of the First Amendment, A Unique Examination of the Nature of Freedom of Expression and Its Role in a Democratic Society.* New York: Vintage Books.

Fidler, M. (2020, November 30). US Supreme Court to Hear Arguments on Hacking Law, First Amendment Implications. Reporters Committee for Freedom of the Press. https://www.rcfp.org/tech-press-freedom-nov-29-2020/.

First Amendment Center (2021). Freedom Forum Institute. https://www.freedomforuminstitute.org/first-amendment-center/.

Garfield Tenzer, L.Y. (2019, Spring). Social Media, Venue, and the Right to a Fair Trial, *Baylor Law Review*, 71, 421–465.

Grimmelmann, J. (2015). The Law and Ethics of Experiments on Social Media Users, *Colorado Technology Law Journal*, 13, 219–271.

Humphreys, L., Gill, P., and Krishnamurthy, B. (2013, June). Historicizing New Media: A Content Analysis of Twitter, *Journal of Communication*, 63(3), 413–431.

Krasnow, E.G., Longley, L.D., and Terry, H.A. (1982). *The Politics of Broadcast Regulation*, 3rd edition. New York: St. Martin's Press.

Levy, L.W. (1985). *Emergence of a Free Press*. New York: Oxford University Press.

NodeXL (2020, November 24). #StopTheSteal. Social Media Research Foundation. https://nodexlgraphgallery.org/Pages/Graph.aspx?graphID=242141.

Packingham v. North Carolina, 582 U.S. ___, 137 S. Ct. 1730 (2017).

Pritchard, D. (2009). Rethinking Criminal Libel: An Empirical Study, *Communication Law & Policy*, 14, 3030–339.

Qureshi, W.A. (2019, Winter). The Militarization of Social Media, *Hawaii Law Review*, 42, 169–203.

Reporters Committee for Freedom of the Press (2020, July 8). *Van Buren v. United States*. Amicus brief. https://www.rcfp.org/briefs-comments/van-buren-v-united-states/.

Rochefort, A. (2020, Spring). Regulating Social Media Platforms: A Comparative Policy Analysis, *Communication Law & Policy*, 25(2), 225–260.

Siebert, F.S., Peterson, T., and Schramm, W. (1956). *Four Theories of the Press: The Authoritarian, Libertarian, Social Responsibility and Soviet Communist Concepts of What the Press Should Be and Do*. Urbana, IL: University of Illinois Press.

United States of America v. Peter Robert Bobal, 19-10678 (11th Cir. 2020, November 30).

United States Courts (2020). https://www.uscourts.gov/about-federal-courts/court-role-and-structure.

U.S. Supreme Court (2020). About the Court, Justices 1789 to Present. https://www.supremecourt.gov/about/members_text.aspx.

12 Future Issues

> *First, each platform now serves as a* ***gatekeeper*** *over a key channel of distribution. By controlling access to markets, these giants can pick winners and losers throughout our economy. They not only wield tremendous power, but they also abuse it by charging exorbitant fees, imposing oppressive contract terms, and extracting valuable data from the people and businesses that rely on them.*

—U.S. House Subcommittee (2020, p. 6)

Joe Biden's grandchildren planned to help the new president by offering viral views to young audiences of life inside the White House (Moore, 2020). Naomi Biden (@NaomiBiden), the oldest grandchild, had 188,000 Twitter followers (para. 2). Meanwhile, Ella Emhoff (@meena), Kamala Harris' stepdaughter, had millions of election night likes for a TikTok video celebration that played Ariana Grande's "Positions" song (para. 3). Similar to the Obama and Trump administrations, there was no turning back on skipping around media gatekeepers and communicating directly with the public. This has become so important for politicians that some in both parties have expressed concern over the power that social media companies have over users.

Social media communication and **user-generated content** (UGC) on the open Internet created new First Amendment legal challenges. Social media sites, such as Facebook and Twitter, face enormous difficulties in moderating content for disinformation. At its founding in 2004, Facebook "had few codified rules about what was allowed on the platform and what was not" (Marantz, 2020, para. 1):

> These days, the Implementation Standards comprise an ever-changing wiki, roughly twelve thousand words long, with twenty-four headings – "Hate Speech," "Bullying," "Harassment," and so on – each of which contains dozens of subcategories, technical definitions, and links to supplementary materials. These are located on an internal software system that only content moderators and select employees can access. The document available to Facebook's users, the Community Standards, is a condensed, sanitized version of the guidelines.
>
> (para. 2)

Hundreds of Facebook employees reportedly work to restrict "hate speech, misinformation, and violent extremist propaganda" (para. 5). The concentration of editorial power has caught the collective eye of U.S. elected representatives. The Facebook emphasis on its singular community represents **utilitarianism** that functions to promote utility and happiness at the expense of moral and ethical responses to complex social problems. Too often the black box decision-making of Facebook, Twitter and other social media companies functions similar to a **veil of ignorance** in that "behind the curtain," isolated responses lack transparency and complete honesty.

One reason to be skeptical of Facebook editorial controls is its unsystematic approach to content regulation. For example, a "white supremacist network" connected to United Kingdom "far right" terrorism was allowed to remain on Facebook and Instagram (Townsend, 2020, para. 1). It is not clear if group size matters, although there were about 80,000 followers linked to "40 neo-Nazi sites" selling "Nazi SS symbols and stickers" (para. 2). The network also praised a "teenager under investigation for shooting dead two Black Lives Matter protesters in Wisconsin" (para. 3). Critics have charged that extremists use Facebook and Instagram to recruit, organize, and fundraise, and that the social media company has known about these efforts for years without responding. Facebook reported in 2020 that about "one in 1,000 pieces of content viewed included hate speech," and that the company takes some form of action against millions of posts (para. 9). However, Facebook exercises editorial control with little transparency in the process, as well as their U.S. liability immunity that protects them from many lawsuits.

The contentious U.S. 2020 presidential election and pandemic was a backdrop for a variety of content management approaches. Twitter, for example, not only flagged incumbent President Donald Trump's tweets, it also turned off some retweet features ahead of the voting. The worry was about the promotion of lies that could spark violence:

> The company will essentially give users a timeout, for example, before they can hit the button to retweet a post from another account. And if users try to share content that Twitter has flagged as false, a notice will warn them that they are about to share inaccurate information.
>
> (Conger, 2020, para. 3)

Russian manipulation during the 2016 and 2020 U.S. elections also helped to explain why Congress held numerous hearings, issued reports and proposed laws that would limit the powers of the largest social media corporations.

A growing concern about the four largest technology companies – Amazon, Apple, Facebook and Google – led to a congressional investigation and calls for use of antitrust rules to break monopoly ownership powers that may starve competition from new businesses. A U.S. House subcommittee issued a report that outlined the problems:

> To put it simply, companies that once were scrappy, underdog startups that challenged the status quo have become the kinds of monopolies we last saw in the era of oil barons and railroad tycoons. Although these firms have delivered clear benefits to society, the dominance of Amazon, Apple, Facebook, and Google has come at a price. These firms typically run the marketplace while also competing in it – a position that enables them to write one set of rules for others, while they play by another, or to engage in a form of their own private *quasi* regulation that is unaccountable to anyone but themselves.
>
> (U.S. House Subcommittee, 2020, pp. 6–7)

The report vowed to pressure the U.S. Department of Justice and other regulatory agencies to enforce antitrust law, as has been done in the past with the original AT&T telephone breakup and action against Microsoft:

> Facebook has monopoly power in the market for social networking. Internal communications among the company's Chief Executive Officer, Mark Zuckerberg, and other senior executives indicate that Facebook acquired its competitive threats to maintain and expand its dominance.
>
> (p. 12)

The U.S. House Subcommittee (2020) proposed myriad steps, including: restoring digital economic competition, strengthening antitrust laws, and reviving antitrust enforcement. Facebook shared more than 124,000 internal documents with lawmakers (p. 25). One concern is that while competition breeds "innovation, business dynamism, entrepreneurship,"and whole new industries, recently "there has been a sharp decline in new business formation as well as early-stage startup funding" (p. 46). Additionally, Facebook failed to protect data privacy, such as during the Cambridge Analytica breach:

> The opacity of data collection and use contributes to consumer confusion and the misperception that consumers do not care about their privacy – the so-called privacy paradox – simply because they use services that have become essential.
>
> (p. 54)

At the same time, Facebook and other companies may have contributed to the decline of journalism in the U.S.A. and employment in news reporting:

> A prominent publisher described this relationship as platforms having a "finger on the scales" with the ability to suppress publishers that do not "appease" platforms' business terms.
>
> (p. 64)

The business models for social networks depend on large audiences to deliver to advertisers:

> As another market participant describes it, "attracting a critical mass of users is essential to delivering a viable social network, as there is no reason for users to start using a social network if there is no one there with whom they can connect."
>
> (p. 89)

For newer apps, such as TikTok, the result is a dependence on "niche strategies to varying degrees, and most have far less user engagement, attention, and data and a smaller share of advertising revenue than Facebook" (p. 90). If a social network does attract a larger following, then they may broaden focus or be purchased by one of the giants. This is exactly what happened when Facebook bought Instagram.

Social network market concentration also is being impacted by cloud computing, newer voice command and "Internet of Things" (IoT) technologies. There is increasing market concentration within the ecosystem required to move data and correctly command devices.

Social Media Companies by Monthly Active Persons (MAP) in Millions[482]

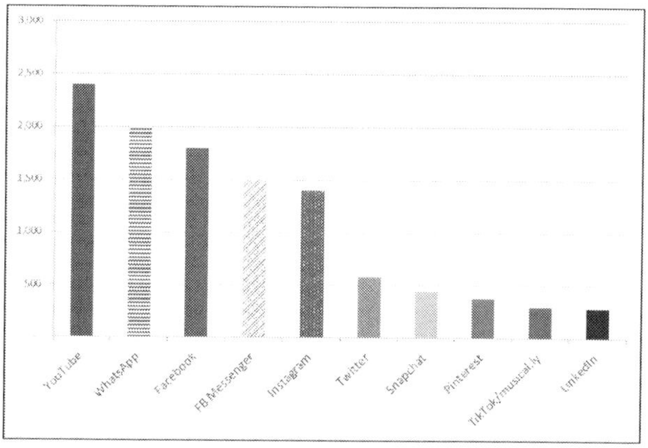

The social network marketplace is highly concentrated. Facebook (1.8 billion users) and its family of products—WhatsApp (2.0 billion users), Instagram (1.4 billion users)—have significantly more users and time spent on its platform than its closest competitors, Snapchat (443 million users) or Twitter (582 million users).[483] TikTok is growing quickly and is often referenced as evidence that the social media landscape is competitive.[484] Although it meets the broad definition of social media as a social app for distributing and consuming video content, TikTok is not a social network.

U.S. House Subcommittee 2020, p. 93.

United States House of Representatives.

Voice Assistant Ecosystem[645]

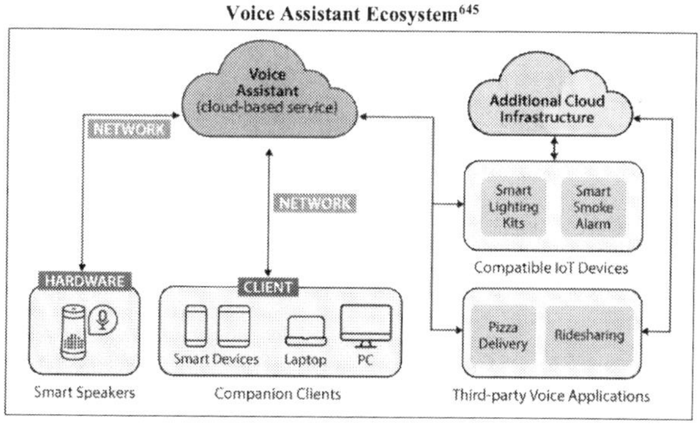

Although there are multiple types of voice assistants within the ecosystem, Subcommittee staff focused primarily on voice assistant platform vendors and third-party hardware manufacturers, including smart speaker manufacturers and Internet of Things (IoT) compatible device manufacturers.

U.S. House Subcommittee 2020, p. 122.

United States House of Representatives.

The infrastructure is creating complex new advertising arrangements. Facebook has been under investigation by the Federal Trade Commission (FTC), the Department of Justice (DoJ) and state attorneys general:

> Facebook has monopoly power in the market for social networking ... Facebook's monopoly power is firmly entrenched and unlikely to be eroded by competitive pressure from new entrants or existing firms ...The social network market has very high entry barriers – including strong network effects, high switching costs, and Facebook's significant data advantage – that discourage direct competition by other firms to offer new products and services.
>
> (pp. 134–135)

Additional evidence comes from the United Kingdom's Competition and Markets Authority (CMA) that identified Facebook market dominance over social networks and display advertising. Facebook has been allowed to leverage its billions of daily users for the foreseeable future and this is a conclusion also found by Australian and German regulators. Facebook has claimed to investors that it controls 95 percent of U.S. social media activities (p. 139).

When WhatsApp launched, it attempted to survive as a subscription service because the advertising model that Facebook exploited means that "a significant portion of their engineering team spends their day tuning data mining, writing better code to collect all your personal data, upgrading the servers that hold all the data and making sure it's all being logged and collated and sliced and packaged and shipped" (p. 157). Ultimately, the app was sold to Facebook for $16 billion in 2014. Later, in 2016, the European Commission fined Facebook for providing "incorrect or misleading information" about its intended changes (p. 159). The U.S. House Subcommittee (2020) concluded that Facebook strategy can be described as "Acquire, Copy or Kill Competitors" (p. 164). Twitter and Snapchat have both suffered from Facebook's copying and monetizing of their innovative ideas. In response, Congress has called for:

a. **Interoperability** – email "is an open, interoperable protocol for communicating regardless of a person's email service or the type of device they use"

b. **Data Portability** – "The difficulty of switching tends to keep users on incumbent platforms" (pp. 386–388)

The shoe was on the other foot when New York University researchers collected and analyzed Facebook political advertising data, and then the company complained

(Connor, 2020b): "Facebook sent a letter to the NYU researchers demanding they just stop it. 'Scraping tools, no matter how well-intentioned, are not a permissible means of collecting information from us'" (para. 1). While Facebook complains about independent research of its platform, it also funds academic research. This may be ethically considered a **conflict of interest** in that privileged actions may not lead to moral or ethically sound decisions. The **particularity** of personal business goals and loyalties conflict with a more universal observance and application of moral ethics. Facebook's attempts to control social media by purchasing Instagram and other successful tools, however, sparked a backlash within the marketplace.

In response to Twitter and Facebook management of content during the 2020 presidential election, some users left the popular sites for alternatives. For example, Parler launched in 2018 as a "free speech platform" by empowering users to "moderate" content (Serrano, 2020, paras. 1–2). QAnon and other conspiracy theories have been filtered by Twitter, Facebook and YouTube, and Parler claimed to offer "a neutral platform for free speech" and "also create a social media environment that would protect data privacy" (para. 5). The once small "libertarian-leaning social network" doubled its users to 10 million after the 2020 election (Hagey, 2020, paras. 2–3), but Amazon AWS removed it from the cloud. The **consequentialism** of Facebook's attempts to dominate the social media marketplace may or may not lead to ethical behavior by those with a track record of bad behavior.

It was unclear if new competition would shield Facebook and Twitter from future regulation. Facebook, meanwhile, continues to struggle with how to address violation of rules, including those by prominent conservative Steve Bannon, short of suspending accounts (Reuters, 2020b). "Bannon suggested in a video ... that FBI Director Christopher Wray and government infectious diseases expert Anthony Fauci should be beheaded, saying they had been disloyal to U.S. President Donald Trump," but Facebook removed the content, not the page (paras. 6–7). The report revealed that CEO Mark Zuckerberg told staff that the account was "offensive," but "clearly did not cross the line" to be suspended or banned (para. 5). As a matter of law, Facebook exercises its end-user agreement powers. Ethics, however, might lead us to a deeper cultural value test over what information could be potentially harmful when it undermined a scientific expert during a pandemic that was claiming historic numbers of lives. Clearly, the FTC and state attorneys general lawsuits in late 2020 that were discussed earlier left legal and ethical issues unresolved at this writing.

The concentration of power by a handful of media and telecommunication giants has led some to argue that the FCC, FTC, DoJ, and other agencies should use their powers to regulate and limit monopolies (Hanley, 2020). At the same time, the U.S. Supreme Court refused to hear a review of §230, but Justice Clarence Thomas wrote a rare and controversial statement about the issues.

Box 12.1 *MalwareBytes, Inc. v. Enigma Software Group* (2020)

Cite as: 592 U. S. ____ (2020)

SUPREME COURT OF THE UNITED STATES
MALWAREBYTES, INC. v. ENIGMA SOFTWARE GROUP USA, LLC
ON PETITION FOR WRIT OF CERTIORARI TO THE UNITED STATES COURT OF APPEALS FOR THE NINTH CIRCUIT

No. 19–1284. Decided October 13, 2020
The petition for a writ of certiorari is denied.
Statement of JUSTICE THOMAS respecting the denial of certiorari.

This petition asks us to interpret a provision commonly called §230, a federal law enacted in 1996 that gives Internet platforms immunity from some civil and criminal claims. 47 U. S. C. §230 ...

This case involves Enigma Software Group USA and Malwarebytes, two competitors that provide software to enable individuals to filter unwanted content, such as content posing security risks. Enigma sued Malwarebytes, alleging that Malwarebytes engaged in anticompetitive conduct by reconfiguring its products to make it difficult for consumers to download and use Enigma products. In its defense, Malwarebytes invoked a provision of §230 that states that a computer service provider cannot be held liable for providing tools "to restrict access to material" that it "considers to be obscene, lewd, lascivious, filthy, excessively violent, harassing, or otherwise objectionable" §230(c)(2). The Ninth Circuit relied heavily on the "policy" and "purpose" of §230 to conclude that immunity is unavailable when a plaintiff alleges anticompetitive conduct ...

I agree with the Court's decision not to take up this case ...

Enacted at the dawn of the dot-com era, §230 contains two subsections that protect computer service providers from some civil and criminal claims ... This limited protection enables companies to create community guidelines and remove harmful content without worrying about legal reprisal ...

... Courts have discarded the longstanding distinction between "publisher" liability and "distributor" liability. Although the text of §230(c)(1) grants immunity only from "publisher" or "speaker" liability, the first appellate court to consider the statute held that it eliminates distributor liability too – that is, §230 confers immunity even when a company distributes content that it *knows* is illegal. *Zeran* v. *America Online, Inc.*, 129 F. 3d 327, 331–334 (CA4 1997). In reaching this conclusion, the court stressed that permitting distributor liability "would defeat the two primary purposes of the statute," namely, "immuniz[ing] service providers" and encouraging "self-regulation." *Id.*, at 331, 334. And subsequent decisions, citing *Zeran*, have adopted this holding as a categorical rule across all contexts ...

Yet there are good reasons to question this interpretation.

First, Congress expressly imposed distributor liability in the very same Act that included §230. Section 502 of the Communications Decency Act makes it a crime to "knowingly ... display" obscene material to children, even if a third party created that content. 110 Stat. 133–134 (codified at 47 U. S. C. §223(d)) ...

Second, Congress enacted §230 just one year after *Stratton Oakmont* used the terms "publisher" and "distributor," instead of "primary publisher" and "secondary publisher." If, as courts suggest, *Stratton Oakmont* was the legal backdrop on which Congress legislated ...

Third, had Congress wanted to eliminate both publisher and distributor liability, it could have simply created a categorical immunity in §230(c)(1): No provider "shall be held liable" for information provided by a third party ...

... Extending §230 immunity beyond the natural reading of the text can have serious consequences ...

Source: *Malwarebytes, Inc. v. Enigma Software Group*, 592 U.S. ____ (2020).

Masnick (2020) was quick to challenge Justice Thomas' reading of legislative history and U.S. Supreme Court rulings. He framed the statement within a tendency by Justice Thomas to want to reverse precedent – including libel law since *New York Times v. Sullivan* (1964):

> This is … an ahistorical reading of the situation … 230 was never meant to be understood in connection with the rest of the Communications Decency Act (all of which the Supreme Court tossed out as unconstitutional in *Reno v. ACLU*). 230 was meant as an alternative approach to the clearly unconstitutional approach that Senator Exon wanted with the CDA, which was a plan to try to ban all pornographic and offensive material on the internet … Thomas ignores this aspect of the history, and acts as if the intention all along was that 230 was meant to somehow work together with the rest of the CDA. That was not the intention.
>
> (paras. 12–13)

Thomas appeared to be exercising a form of originalist interpretation of the law popular since the 1980s that goes beyond the text and ignores legislative history in favor of the context of informed opinion at the time. As we go forward, the method is one way that the U.S. Supreme Court can fashion arguments that allow it to overturn decades of established precedent. Originalism has focused on semantic meaning at the time in which the U.S. Constitution or later laws were enacted. An early original intent theory has given way in recent years to so-called textualism and original meaning utilized by the late Justice Antonin Scalia.

Box 12.2 U.S. Senate Questioning of Twitter CEO

Senator Ted Cruz: Mr. Dorsey, does Twitter have the ability to influence elections?

Twitter CEO Jack Dorsey: No.

Cruz: You don't believe Twitter has any ability to influence elections?

Dorsey: No, we are one part of a spectrum of communication channels that people have.

Cruz: So, you're testifying to this committee, right now, that Twitter – when it silences people, when it censors people, when it blocks political speech – that has no impact on elections.

Dorsey: People have choice of other communication channels.

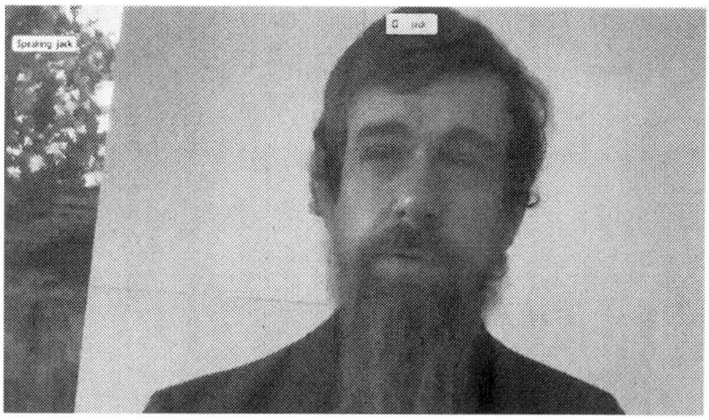

Twitter CEO Jack Dorsey (@jack).

United States House of Representatives. https://youtu.be/5BMJvx5fKvs.]

Cruz: Not if they don't hear information. If you don't think you have the power to influence elections, why do you block anything?

Dorsey: Well, we have policies that are focused on making sure that more voices on the platform are possible. We see a lot of abuse and harassment, which ends up silencing people and having them leave from the platform.

Cruz: All right, Mr. Dorsey, I find your opening questions, your opening answers, absurd on their face. Let's talk about the last two weeks, in particular. As you know, I have long been concerned about Twitter's pattern of censoring and silencing individual Americans with whom Twitter disagrees, but two weeks ago Twitter, and to a lesser extent Facebook, crossed a threshold that is fundamental in our country. Two weeks ago, Twitter made the unilateral decision to censor the *New York Post* in a series of two blockbuster articles, both alleging evidence of corruption against Joe Biden. The first concerning Ukraine, the second concerning communist China. And Twitter made the decision, number one to prevent users, any user from sharing those stories, and number two, you went even further and blocked the *New York Post* from sharing on Twitter its own reporting. Why did Twitter make the decision to censor the *New York Post*?

Dorsey: We had a hacked materials policy.

Cruz: When was that policy adopted?

Dorsey: In 2018, I believe.

Cruz: In 2018. Go ahead. What was the policy?

Dorsey: So, the policy is around limiting the spread of materials that are hacked. We didn't want Twitter to be a distributor for hacked materials. We found that the *New York Post*. That because it showed the direct materials, screenshots of the direct materials, and it was unclear how those were attained that it fell under this policy.

Cruz: So, in your view, if it's unclear the source of a document, in this instance, the *New York Post* documented what it said the source was, which it said it was a laptop owned by Hunter Biden that had been turned into a repair store. So, they weren't hiding what they claimed to be the source. Is it your position that Twitter, when you can't tell the source, blocks press stories?

Dorsey: No, not at all. We, our team, made a fast decision. Uh, the enforcement action, however, of blocking URLs – both in tweets, and uh in DM, in **direct messages** – we believe was incorrect, and we changed it.

Cruz: Today, the *New York Post* is still blocked from tweeting. Two weeks later.

Dorsey: Yes, they have to log into their account, which they can do at this minute, delete the original tweet, which fell under our original enforcement actions, and they can tweet the exact same material from the exact same article, and it would go through.

Cruz: So, Mr. Dorsey, so your ability is you have the power to force a media out. And let's be clear, the *New York Post* isn't just some random guy tweeting. The *New York Post* has the fourth highest circulation of any newspaper in America. The *New York Post* is over 200 years old. The *New York Post* was founded by Alexander Hamilton, and your position is that that you can sit in Silicon Valley and demand of the media that you can tell them what stories they can publish. And you can tell the American people what reporting they can hear. Is that right?

Dorsey: No. This was this was a, you know, every person, every account, uh every uh organization that signs up to Twitter agrees to terms of service. In terms of service.

Cruz: So, media lets us genuflect and obey your dictates, if they wish to be able to communicate with readers, is that right?

Dorsey: No, not at all. We, you know, we recognized an error in this policy, and specifically the enforcement.

Cruz: You're still blocking their posts. You're still blocking their posts, right now. Today, you're blocking their posts.

Dorsey: We're not blocking the post. Anyone can tweet.

Cruz: Can the *New York Post*, uh, post on their on their Twitter account?

Dorsey: If they go into their account.

Cruz: "No" is your answer to that. No, unless they genuflect and agree with your dictates. Let me ask you something: You claimed it was because of a hacked materials, uh, policy. I find that facially, highly dubious and clearly employed in a deeply partial way.

Source: U.S. Senate Commerce, Science and Transportation Committee Hearing, (October, 28, 2020). Facebook, Google & Twitter Execs Testify on Social Media Regulations. https://www.c-span.org/video/?476686-1/facebook-google-twitter-execs-testify-social-media-regulations.

The context of the Senate committee testimony was the 2020 election and partisan disagreement over social media platform power to filter content, such as misinformation. Section 230 of the Communications Decency Act (CDA), protects Twitter, Facebook and other online companies from legal liability for content on their sites. After the election, Senate Majority Leader Mitch McConnell proposed repeal of Section 230, as part of the next round of Covid-19 payments (Sonnemaker, 2020), but that move failed. Justice Clarence Thomas also expressed concerns.

There is growing public discussion about the future of social media. *The Social Dilemma* was a Netflix documentary that, in 2020, challenged the power of TikTok and other platforms. The popular film, however, was criticized for sharing video examples that were out of context. Chelsea Gilliland, for example, had posted a TiKTok video in March of that year that joked about "Coronavirus masks" and conspiracy theories, but the documentary made her "an example of social media's well-documented issues with misinformation," instead of meaning "to mock coronavirus theories" (Alexander, 2020, para. 2). "I had previously posted a video saying that the stuff that I post is sarcastic" (para. 3). However, viral TikToks also debunked misinformation by providing personal accounts of vaccine trials (Rosenblatt, 2020). One such post had 2.7 million views (para. 4). The #CovidVaccine hashtag had 36 million TikTok views (para. 5). This appeared to be because younger users were information seekers rushing to combat misinformation and disinformation promoted by the anti-vaccine movement.

The EU Right to Be Forgotten (RTBF) notion that an individual should be able to remove Internet content seems dangerous within the long-term search for truth. Marketplace of ideas philosophies were built on physical library holdings and information stability. Social media can be used for good or evil, and we see a lot of stress throughout the world over openness. China, India and the U.S.A. are the top three countries for number of Internet users, and developing nations are quickly emerging. China is among those nations officially blocking Facebook and other non-Chinese social media sites. China's comprehensive state security law was enforced on Hong Kong in 2020, and high-profile businessman Jimmy Lai has been jailed amid growing pro-democracy protests (Al Jazeera, 2020): "Lai, a vocal critic of the government in Beijing, is one of the highest-profile figures charged under the national security law that China imposed on the territory … in a bid to stamp out dissent" (para. 2).

Elsewhere in the world, social media participation seems to help promote freedom. Facebook's top cities using it include Bangkok, Jakarta, Dhaka and Mexico City. No U.S. cities are among its top ten cities, so we would expect the social media giant to be less responsive to concerns. Facebook's 2.5 billion monthly active users (MAUs) largely utilize mobile devices around the globe.

No effective international law accounts for state power limiting social media communication that could incite ethnic division, be considered criminally libelous, or fall under blasphemy. While common law and U.S. constitutional law protect against prior restraint, many nations criminalize speech through draconian methods.

Beyond concentration of power by social media companies, such as Facebook, freedom may also be restricted by the large telecommunication companies – AT&T, CenturyLink and Verizon. In the U.S.A., investment in faster broadband access may be limited by the potential for profit. Cable Internet access speeds also may be impacted by corporate interests of advertisers. The commercial internet may not always be open to free expression. Additionally, expensive rates limit access to those with the money to pay.

There continue to be substantial government interests in trying to protect children, and keep all of us from harm. The U.S. Supreme Court has been cognizant that the First Amendment means that we cannot reduce Internet speech to only what is fit for children. Adult content is protected in traditional ways under the precedents of key case law explained earlier, such as *O'Brien, Miller, Central Hudson* and *Reno*. Social media publishers have significant First Amendment freedoms.

Beyond a general lack of prior restraint, there are significant risks for subsequent punishment for speech that is libelous, an invasion of privacy, a violation of intellectual property or deceptive. The technologies also make it too easy for police to violate constitutional rights by searching our mobile devices without a warrant (*Carpenter v. U.S.*, 2018; *Riley v. California*, 2014). Google Street View images also have the potential to "see" us from above.

Social media technologies also make it too easy to spam consumers with unwanted advertising. In one case, Facebook won a, $873 million court judgment against a Canadian who was improperly using the site. Facebook, YouTube, and other sites continue to remove content that they find to be illegal, dangerous or potentially leading to violence. The *Elonis* "true threats" doctrine means that some social media posts can be criminal, if it can be proved that there was an intended threat against specific people or organizations.

At the same time, huge social media companies are rapidly deploying artificial intelligence (AI). Google, however, abruptly fired an "Ethical Artificial Intelligence team" co-leader Timnit Gebru after she was critical of company decisions (Newton, 2020). Apparently, a Google manager found this internal message inconsistent with expectations: "I had stopped writing here as you may know, after all the micro and macro aggressions and harassments I received after posting my stories here (and then of course it started being moderated)" (para. 8). As a leading Black ethicist, Gebru faced resistance on publishing a paper:

> Have you ever heard of someone getting "feedback" on a paper through a privileged and confidential document to HR? Does that sound like a standard procedure to you or does it just happen to people like me who are constantly dehumanized?
>
> (para. 11)

Commenters suggested that research papers at other companies are routinely reviewed for protection of intellectual property rights, but not as a mechanism to internally stifle academic discussion outside the company. The degree to which large corporations offer employees' intellectual freedom and First Amendment rights outside the workplace remains an important and ongoing legal and ethical issue.

Social media communication and the broader media ecosystem currently present significant credibility issues. Bates (2020) quoted the Knight Commission on Trust, Media and Democracy 2019 report that found a "Crisis in Democracy" from political division: "Many of us live inside echo chambers where only our own political sentiments can be heard, and distrust those who do not agree with our particular viewpoint" (para. 2). The amplification of polarization comes through media content from a variety of sources, including those who want to spark hate. Bates (2020) studied the post-World War II Commission on Freedom of the Press that called for social responsibility in an age of media gatekeeping. Social media, however, empower anyone with a Twitter or other account to spread falsehoods. In the absence of traditional media journalism function, recall that some have advocated for broadcast-style regulation of the Internet. This would be a dramatic departure from digital development and U.S. Supreme Court precedent. Still pressure has come from Europe and some U.S. states to protect privacy through data regulation. Nevertheless, a strict new social media law in Turkey requires Facebook and other social media companies to open a local office and "accept liability for harmful content" (Jalan, 2020, para. 1). Companies refusing to comply could face large fines, advertising bans and reduction of Internet bandwidth. Twitter agreed to the rules, as it "promised to continue 'defending open, public conversation and ensuring our service is available to people everywhere'" (Bilginsoy, 2021, para. 2). The "draconian" rules appeared to be part of Turkey President Recep Tayyip Erdoğan's larger efforts to chill or freeze free speech and human rights (paras. 6–7). In some countries, free expression is considered immoral.

At the same time, the posting of fake images created an international spat between Australia and China, as most countries in the developed world struggle to find a balance between freedom and security (Needham, 2020). Beneath the politics and rhetoric is a deeper fight within social media companies, such as Facebook, to define civility, as they limit hate speech and misinformation (Roose, Isaac, & Frenkel, 2020). Facebook applies a "News Ecosystem Quality" (NEQ) score within its algorithm – "a secret internal ranking it assigns to news publishers based on signals about the quality of their journalism" (para. 3). CEO Mark Zuckerberg reportedly "agreed to increase the weight that Facebook's algorithm gave to N.E.Q. scores to make sure authoritative news appeared more prominently" ahead of the U.S. 2020 presidential election (para. 4). Concerned over a contested election, Facebook had "break glass" plans that gave newsfeed prominence to major news organizations and reduced visibility of "posts from highly engaged hyper-partisan pages, such as Breitbart and Occupy Democrats" (para. 5). The *New York Times* quoted two employees attending a Facebook meeting after the election as saying that there should be a permanent shift to a "nicer news feed" filled with less partisan information (para. 6). Later, Facebook offered newsfeed information cues about news organization credibility. A First Amendment issue remains over how Facebook can both serve as a quasi-public forum for free expression and edit the broad spectrum of political communication on most social issues.

Box 12.3 Case Study: Florida Target Anti-Mask Parade

A local Target store is an unusual location for a free speech parade, but a small group in Ft. Lauderdale marched to the Twisted Sister 1984 hit "We're Not Gonna Take It" to protest wearing masks during the pandemic (Tyko, 2020):

> "Take your masks off. We're not doing it. Take off your masks. We're not going to take it anymore," the group shouted, pumping their fists in the air, some wearing "Make America Great Again" gear … "We're Americans, breathe," a woman yelled. "It's all a lie!"
>
> (paras. 3–4)

Twisted Sister band leader Dee Snider (@deesnider) responded to a viral video of the parade by tweeting: "No … these selfish assholes do not have my permission or blessing to use my song for their moronic cause. #cuttheshit."

Anti-Masks Protest.

Twitter @deesnider. https://twitter.com/deesnider/status/1306086822817099778.

The *Miami Herald* called the event a "flash mob storm," and counted ten to 15 protesters (Marr, 2020, paras. 1–2). The event was planned earlier in the week and promoted on social media channels, as some complained about store rules requiring customers to wear masks as a way to limit the spread of Covid-19. A Target spokesperson told *Fox Business* that: "We're aware of the group of guests who came into the store ... and we asked them to leave after they removed their masks and became disruptive and rude to other shoppers" (Fox Business, 2020, para. 5).

Broward County officials enforced a mask law by fining Target and issuing $100 fines to the protesters for not wearing a mask in a public space (Huriash, 2020). Florida counties passed various laws during the pandemic. In Broward County, facial coverings were required in all public spaces outside private homes. Civil and criminal charges included fines up to $1,000, or $15,000 for "intentional and irreparable violations." A business could be forced to close for 24 hours.

"Our priority remains the health and safety of our team and guests," Target Spokeswoman Danielle Schumann said" (Huriash, 2020, para. 15). Target complied with the law by asking protesters to leave "after they removed their masks and became disruptive and rude to other shoppers" (para. 17). The Target corporation went no further in taking a broader brand stand against anti-maskers and instead treated the case as a local issue. Given the many thousands of deaths caused by the spread of Covid-19, it was a missed ethical moment to speak out for facts and science.

As a free speech issue, the protesters could have chosen to select a public park or street for their protest, but they would still have been in violation of Florida law by not wearing a mask. Organizers suggested that they were exercising their First Amendment rights to speak out against the public policies.

Sources

Fox Business (2020, September 17). Anti-Mask Protester Fined After Marching Through Target Store. https://www.fox13news.com/news/anti-mask-protesters-fined-after-marching-through-florida-target.

Huriash, L.J. (2020, September 16). Twisted Sister's Dee Snider Calls Anti-Maskers "Moronic" For Protest Inside Fort Lauderdale Target. *South Florida Sun Sentinel*. https://www.sun-sentinel.com/coronavirus/fl-ne-anti-maskers-fort-lauderdale-target-20200916-aqrfh5fou5dstf6todhz-qixy54-story.html.

Marr, M. (2020, September 17). "No More Masks!" Watch a Flash Mob Storm Through a Target Store in Fort Lauderdale. *Miami Herald*. https://www.miamiherald.com/news/ local/community/broward/article245784820.html.

Tyko, K. (2020, September 18). Dee Snider Scolds Anti-Mask Parade of People in MAGA Gear Playing Twisted Sister Song at Florida Target. *USA Today*. https://www.usatoday.com/story/money/2020/09/17/target-maskless-shoppers-twisted-sister-dee-snider-face-coverings/3485442001/.

The U.S. Supreme Court split 5-4 in favor of an injunction against severe church attendance limits proposed because of the Covid-19 pandemic, in part as Justice Neil Gorsuch said it: "Government is not free to disregard the First Amendment in times of crisis" (*Roman Catholic Diocese of Brooklyn v. Cuomo*, 2020, Gorsuch p. 1). While not specific to social media communication, the larger First Amendment law context is that government must have a compelling interest, and any regulation has to be narrowly tailored. The least restrictive means to accomplish even the worthy state action to save lives also must satisfy the Bill of Rights, First and Fourteenth amendments under U.S. law. The First Amendment issues remain thornier when it comes to Facebook content management during the pandemic given that its live video became an important streaming service for churches and synagogues.

Facebook, in particular, has gone down a bit of a rabbit hole in efforts to define and ban harmful or offensive content. The banning of Holocaust denial or distortion posts may be clearer than regulation of conspiracy theories (O'Brien, 2020). Facebook was "directing people to authoritative sources if they search for information about the Nazi genocide," but the site also targeted "misinformation ahead of the U.S. presidential election" in 2020 (paras. 1–2). Holocaust survivors have urged large social media sites to push back on lies that have been posted using the #NoDenyingIt hashtag and advertiser boycotts. Facebook CEO Mark Zuckerberg has used a balancing approach to content moderation standards: "I've struggled with the tension between standing for free expression and the harm caused by minimizing or denying the horror of the Holocaust ... My own thinking has evolved as I've seen data showing an increase in anti-Semitic violence, as have our wider policies on hate speech" (para. 9).

Box 12.4 Thought Leader Jasmine McNealy

Jasmine McNealy.

Photograph courtesy Christopher Lee Fatt.

To say that one of the major questions of the past few years has been what to do about social media would be an understatement. Since the advent of the commercial web, and even before, the Internet has been used to form connections, to make ties. The strength of these ties we know and have learned can have significant implications for relationships, business, public health and government. While these tools have allowed us to create, strengthen and reinforce bonds, these bonds have also proven to have significant impacts, both for good and for ill, they have been used for fomenting hate, distributing false information, and surveillance. These sociotechnical issues – integrating both the societal or social, as well as the technical (Fox, 1995; Cherns, 1976) – have drawn much discussion from policymakers, advocates and civil society organizations seeking remedies for the impacts related to social media.

FOCUS ON THE CONNECTIONS

To truly understand how we have come to this place, it is important to define what we mean by "social media." As a general matter, all media are social. That is, all media allow the people to relate to one another, to transfer information in some way. Radio, for example, allowed the broadcast of news, music and other content, from one place to another from a distance. Vinyl records, too, allowed for a convenient way to transfer culture in the form of music, poems and speeches. But both radio and vinyl have their limitations. Those able to broadcast, low-powered radio notwithstanding, make up only a small portion of the population. Those able to press their own vinyl, too, are small in number. But truly social media, as we know it today, are different from these and other so-called traditional media.

What we mean when we say social media are the digital tools that allow for a larger portion of the population to connect, to have access to and distribute information, and to transfer and transform culture. Although calling them social network sites, boyd and Ellison (2007) defined social media as providing users with opportunities to: "(1) construct a public or semi-public profile within a bounded system, (2) articulate a list of other users with whom they share a connection, and (3) view and traverse their list of connections and those made by others within the system" (p. 211). In that way, the crux of social network sites, social media, was connection and how connections can be communicated and used for communication.

In the 13 years since the publication of the boyd and Ellison (2007) piece, new digital spaces and tools have arisen that have complicated this definition of social media. While the principle of connection remains the same, new kinds of digital space and mobile app have allowed us to connect and use these connections. All while offering different affordances, that provide the potential for different modes of communication and other functions (Majchrzak et al, 2013; Faraj & Azad, 2012; Leonardi, 2011). And different media have allowed for different communities to spring and strengthen.

THE ISSUES WITH CONNECTING

But not all of these communities are prosocial. Journalists and researchers have chronicled the growth of radical extremists on social media sites for decades. These groups are not solely about transferring ideology, but have put their beliefs into action. The August, 2017 "Unite the Right Rally" in Charlottesville, VA, was bolstered by social media, which allowed White nationalist extremists to connect and organize. This rally ended with one extremist driving his car through a group of counter-protesters, killing Heather Heyer. This is not the only example of social media interactions leading to detrimental actions. Mass murderer Dylan Roof, who in 2015 killed Black American members of the Mother Emanuel African Methodist Episcopal church in Charleston, SC, has been tied to several far right chat forums.

And the affordances of social media are not only linked with racist violence. Large sites such as Facebook and Youtube, along with apps including Telegram and WhatsApp, have been found to be hubs for spreading misinformation. During the 2016 elections in the United States, for example, there was a significant increase in political "fake news" stories (Ali and Zain-ul-abdin, 2020; Allcott and Gentzkow, 2017) on sites such as Facebook. And while the political or election-related disinformation campaigns have been significant, during the 2020 Covid-19 pandemic, social media have been used to spread medical misinformation (Apuke and Omar, 2020; Pennycook et al., 2020). The ramifications of misinformation are important to consider from national security, public health and other critical perspectives. And, of course, this is not solely a U.S. problem; misinformation is a global phenomenon.

Of course, in the U.S.A., the conversation turns to how social media, and the large tech companies behind them, should be regulated. The U.S. Congress has had several hearings calling tech CEOs before it to answer questions. Some members of Congress and, indeed, the US president have called for changes to regulation aimed at the content found on social media. The furthest Congress has gotten was the 2018 Honest Ads bill proposal, which would have required platforms with more than 50 million unique users to maintain a public record of advertisers who have spent more than $500 on advertising per year. The idea is to provide transparency about the ads that users may encounter, as well as identifying foreign ad buyers seeking U.S. audiences. For his part, in May 2020, then President Donald Trump issued an executive order aimed at prohibiting social media sites from engaging in "selective censorship" related to politically related content.

The major problem in the attempts to regulate social media content and why Congress has chosen to aim at transparency instead of prohibition is the protection for freedom of expression under the First Amendment to the U.S. Constitution. Both individuals and organizations have constitutional protection for expression, even for what amount to lies. That these lies come in relation to social and political debates only enhance the protection under the law. Further, federal law in the form of section §230 of the Communications Decency Act, which provides a safe harbor for online platforms not engaged in the development of tortious content. Platforms themselves may make decisions about what kinds of content are allowed.

A CALL FOR A REVISION IN FOCUS

That platforms provide spaces for contemptuous content, the organization of radical movements and the fostering of antisocial communities is a matter of great concern. We also know that expression has impacts. The focus on social media is misplaced. While acting as platforms, spaces and media for antisocial behavior and expression, social media are tools. These tools allow for connecting across far distances and are available to a significant section of the population. But the problem of misinformation, hate speech and radicalization are older than Usenet, one of the first chat and newsgroup forums, developed in 1980 (Hauben & Hauben, 1998). Racism, xenophobia, sexism, homophobia and other divisive ideologies have existed for a significant portion of history. Social media did not invent these issues. Instead, social media have amplified societal disconnects and allowed for the distribution of associated materials at scale. Social media, if anything, have laid bare the foundational human issues and provided space for these to take other forms in. Therefore, any discussion, attempt at regulation and/or teaching that focuses solely on the tools are misplaced.

The antisocial issues with social media such as radicalization and misinformation, along with the others not mentioned here, are sociotechnical. As a complex system of issues, any solutions require more than a focus on the technology. Instead, it is important that policymakers, organizations and educators approach any remedies with attention to the underlying, systemic issues. The focus only on the tools prevents the creation of adequate remedies. Complex systems require true investigation of the issues; ignoring the social only prolongs the persistence of these ills.

Jasmine McNealy is an associate professor of telecommunication at the University of Florida, where she teaches courses on regulation. She researches media, technology and law with an emphasis on privacy, surveillance and data governance. She is also the Associate Director of the Marion B. Brechner First Amendment Project at UF and a faculty associate at Harvard University's Berkman Klein Center for Internet & Society.

Sources

Ali, K. and Zain-ul-abdin, K. (2020). Post-Truth Propaganda: Heuristic Processing of Political Fake News on Facebook During the 2016 US Presidential Election, *Journal of Applied Communication Research*, 1–20.

Allcott, H. and Gentzkow, M. (2017). Social Media and Fake News in the 2016 Election, *Journal of Economic Perspectives*, 31(2), 211–36.

Apuke, O.D. and Omar, B. (2020). Fake News and COVID-19: Modelling the Predictors of Fake News Sharing Among Social Media Users, *Telematics and Informatics*, 101475.

boyd, D.M. and Ellison, N.B. (2007). Social Network Sites: Definition, History, and Scholarship. *Journal of Computer-Mediated Communication*, 13(1), 210–230.

Cherns, A. (1976). The Principles of Sociotechnical Design, *Human Relations*, 29(8), 783–792.

Faraj, S. and Azad, B. (2012). The Materiality of Technology: An Affordance Perspective. In P.M. Leonardi, B. Nardi, and J. Kallinikos (eds.), *Materiality and Organizing: Social Interaction in a Technological World*, pp. 237–258. New York: Oxford University Press.

Fox, W.M. (1995). Sociotechnical System Principles and Guidelines: Past and Present, *Journal of Applied Behavioral Science*, 31(1), 91–105.

Hauben, M. and Hauben, R. (1998). Netizens: On the History and Impact of Usenet and the Internet. *First Monday*.

Leonardi, P.M. (2011). When Flexible Routines Meet Flexible Technologies: Affordance, Constraint, and the Imbrication of Human and Material Agencies, *MIS Quarterly*, 147–167.

Majchrzak, A., Faraj, S., Kane, G.C., and Azad, B. (2013). The Contradictory Influence of Social Media Affordances on Online Communal Knowledge Sharing, *Journal of Computer-Mediated Communication*, 19(1), 38–55.

Pennycook, G., McPhetres, J., Zhang, Y., Lu, J.G., and Rand, D.G. (2020). Fighting COVID-19 Misinformation on Social Media: Experimental Evidence for a Scalable Accuracy-Nudge Intervention, *Psychological Science*, 31(7), 770–780.

GROWING GLOBAL MARKET CONFLICT

A challenge to the unbridled power of social media companies, such as Facebook and Google, is coming from national laws. In the previous Turkey example, a law allowed the country to fine Facebook and Twitter "for failing to appoint a country representative" (AFP, 2020, para. 1). The law requires any platform with more than 1 million users to force the representative to "implement court orders to remove contentious content or face heavy fines" (para. 2). Periscope, YouTube, and TikTok also have been fined for failing to comply (para. 3). The commercial sites could be banned from advertising in the country. President Recep Tayyip Erdoğan previously threatened to "wipe out" social media, and the government prosecutes people for "insulting the president" (paras. 10–11).

At the same time, verification of information continues to be a problem around the world. **Blockchain** technologies, however, are one method for increasing transparency. Verizon's "blockchain-based, open-source newsroom product" called "Full Transparency" was designed to increase accountability in distribution of corporate news releases (Pirus, 2020, para. 1). Under the system, an "alteration" of "text changes" are "tracked" (para. 2). "We invite organizations across the word that prize transparency as much as we do to adopt blockchain-verified communication practices" (para. 5). Blockchain allows messages to be secured, tracked and "contextualized" (para. 6). It is an innovative approach to fight back against "fake news" and censorship by making fact-checking more systematic. Readers can see a red check mark and transparency update notes about any changes since publication (Verizon, 2020). In general, sites are moving to limiting editing of content in a way that displays changes to readers. This heightened transparency promotes a more ethical form of communication.

At the same time, personal responsibility requires that social media users transform values and critical thinking into ethical posts. Too often, however, professionals fail by creating content that misses the mark. Paul Ewell, a dean at Virginia Wesleyan University, slammed voters after the 2020 election by posting on Facebook that: "If you voted for Joe Biden, please unfriend me" (Connor, 2020a, para. 1). "It's flat-out name-calling by someone in a position of authority," one student told the university newspaper.

O'Neill (2001) argued for reframing First Amendment law around the rapid diffusion of civil liability cases on the Internet. This trend continued, as social media communication developed and became central to public life. Untrained citizens may not even be aware of what those with a journalism and media communication education come to understand: subsequent punishment for libel and invasion of privacy are very real threats to free expression. It remains unclear if the increased threats of civil liability litigation are because "the courts have somehow caused the situation or are simply responding to new and stronger claims of liability" (O'Neill, 2001, p. 168). For sure, social media communication amplifies truthful and false information, and some of the content harms personal or business reputations, invades the private sphere, or results in some other harm.

Legal and ethical issues also remain in connection with the mobile devices used to access social media sites. Apple has settled with more than 30 states in lawsuits claiming iPhones speeds were throttled to address a battery life issue (Associated Press, 2020). One class action case resulted in a $500 million payment to users in California, and a multistate settlement of $113 million compensated those in some other U.S. states (paras. 1–2). At least 19 other states, however, were not covered by the case agreements. The litigation lacks equity for consumers in states that did not sign on to the lawsuits.

A patchwork of laws, including defamation and obscenity state standards fail to provide national consistency in First Amendment law. Even when these cases do not survive in the courts, there are meaningful ethical assertions about Potter Box definition of factual information, application of sociocultural values, use of philosophical principles (such as Aristotle's **golden mean**, Kant's Imperative, Mill's utility or others), discernment of competing loyalties, and impact on personal and professional behavior. Christians et al. (2005) conclude that "the closest scrutiny" in ethics "forces us to articulate precisely where our loyalties lie as we make a final judgment or adopt a particular policy" (p. 5). In the end: "Respect for the dignity and worth of others may be the most essential principle for the ethical individual or organization" (p. 231). The current failings of social media communication may be less about Facebook, Twitter, YouTube and other platforms and more related to a loss of mutual respect for each other. The law can find some measure of equity and restitution, but it falls to use ethical communication behavior to bridge divides and respond through our common human values.

Too often, political and economic power are used to push back against social media users' collective community strength to expose illegal or unethical governance. In France, a proposed law "would restrict the filming of police officers," and it appeared to target social media users (Charlton & Adamson, 2020, para. 1). Under the proposal, it would be "a crime to publish photos or video of on-duty officers with the intent of harming their 'physical or psychological integrity'" (para. 2). Mobile phone photos and video frequently have been used as evidence in police brutality cases – including deaths while under arrest. French journalists and other citizens protested against the initiative. Public protests and social media posts can have positive and negative impact amid contested political change.

Employees frequently are at risk of losing a job if they are not protected by a collective bargaining agreement, private contract, or other legal tool. Sometimes firings are based on a company desire to protect branding, or a lack of confidence in their marketing efforts. Tony Piloseno (@tonesterpaints), 22, was a college student fired by Sherwin-Williams "over his wildly successful paint-mixing TikTok account (Chen, 2020, para. 1). The viral story of his dismissal generated numerous job offers from competitors, and he accepted a job at Florida Paints – a company that appreciated Piloseno's creativity. However, it often goes badly for young employees who are active on social media. An Oregon nurse was placed on leave after her TikTok videos that "mocked the state's pandemic protocols ... by saying she does not wear a mask in public" (Hauser, 2020, para. 1). To Salem Health Hospital this represented a "cavalier disregard for the seriousness of this pandemic" (para. 3). Arts employees are another group that became active on social media channels during the pandemic. Furloughed and laid-off museum and gallery employees criticized their employers, as part of a longer term call for "improved working conditions and diversity at their museums" (Wagley, 2020, para. 2). The arts workers used anonymous Instagram accounts to target the intersection of #Covid and #BlackLivesMatter in posts about "layoffs, furloughs, shutdowns, and protests" that collided with "calls against the art world's hypocrisy and complicity in systemic racism, labor abuses, and so much more" (para. 6).

The fear of employer sanctions and firings lead many using TikTok and other social media sites to seek anonymity in their account names and look for ways to hide their content trails. Fleets, for example, are Twitter's answer to Snapchat, Facebook and Instagram Stories that disappear after a day. "There's still no complete control after hitting send," DatChat CEO Darin Myman claimed (Myman, 2020, para. 2). While user intent may be to delete a permanent record of tweeting, most sites do not eliminate screenshot functions. Few even make users aware that images have been collected and stored. This has led to some users leaving major social media platforms and replacing them with encrypted messaging, such as Signal. Some of these tools use blockchain technologies to verify what happened after the post. DatChat, for example, built a self-destruction mechanism that offers user control over number of allowable views, screenshot notification and prevention, as well as non-forwarding security (paras. 6–9). In the end, user behavior and site programming combine to create social and technical boundaries that must be weighed against national and international law and ethics.

Larger legal and ethical issues remain about First Amendment freedom of expression at a time filled with social media communication. Journalists, for example, found "destructive habits" that were "hitched" to the "political class" instead of a "connection to a live public" that serves democratic values (Rosen, 2020, paras. 1, 24). The political news coverage filled with winners and losers failed, in Rosen's (@jayrosen_nyu) view, because it embraced tendencies toward strategies over policies that do not support democracy. Too many news reporters saw social media channels as broadcast facilities instead of spaces for community engagement. Facebook, Twitter and other social channels provide some support for development of healthy **virtual communities**, of the sort Howard Rheingold imagines, where protected political speech could flourish. They also have taken some steps to remove "bad actors" while balancing a right of free expression, limiting harms against others, and supporting human rights. Individually, we have a social responsibility to improve what is wrong about social media – from invasion of data privacy to disinformation. The platforms also must step forward and own their need to exercise corporate social responsibility – even when it conflicts with a fiduciary responsibility to shareholders in terms of surveillance capitalism and profit.

Pavlik, Alsaad, and Laufer (2020) suggested that journalism education could play an important role in the fight against misinformation and disinformation. They identified ten "core principles" to apply, including a "pursuit of truth," "storytelling excellence" and "ethics" (p. 393–401). It is clear that following these principles in training journalism students would proactively limit legal cases and ethical failures by professional journalists. However, untrained social media users somehow need to be educated in media law, ethics and literacy. Media and public opinion happen within a social media context, and the high level of message noise may circumvent news media efforts to promote truths.

Facebook has been most aggressive in banning false information, such as "claims about Covid-19 vaccines that have been debunked by public health experts" (Reuters, 2020a, para. 1). Facebook's Head of Health said the ban was part of support for the global public health community "to keep people safe and informed during the coronavirus public health crisis" (Jin, 2020, para. 1). The company outlined three initiatives:

1. Ensuring everyone has access to accurate information and removing harmful content
2. Supporting health and economic relief efforts
3. Keeping people connected (paras. 3–12)

Facebook's response centered on spending millions of dollars for fighting misinformation, redeveloping the battered news industry, supporting healthcare workers and businesses, and donating to mental health telephone services.

Netiquette, or digital etiquette, is one way that each of us can contribute to avoiding legal conflicts and practicing ethical social media communication (Klassen, Hoekje, & Stevens, 2020). By understanding specific technologies, setting boundaries of time and space, and being "respectful and professional," we can practice law and ethics (para. 11). Ideally, self-regulation and ethics will promote social media progress instead of a need for government regulation that surely would further restrict the fundamental right of speech and press that defines democratic freedoms.

U.S. CONSTITUTION PASSAGES

Article I, Section 8: The Congress shall have Power ... [3] To regulate Commerce with foreign Nations, and among the several States, and with the Indian Tribes; ...

Article III, Section 1: The judicial Power of the United States shall be vested in one supreme Court, and in such inferior Courts as the Congress may from time to time ordain and establish. The Judges, both of the supreme and inferior Courts, shall hold their Offices during good Behavior, and shall, at stated Times, receive for their Services, a Compensation, which shall not be diminished during their Continuance in Office.

Article III, Section 2: The judicial Power shall extend to all Cases, in Law and Equity, arising under this Constitution, the Laws of the United States, and Treaties made, or which shall be made, under their Authority;—to all Cases affecting Ambassadors, other public Ministers and Consuls;—to all Cases of admiralty and maritime Jurisdiction;—to Controversies to which the United States shall be a Party;—to Controversies between two or more States;—between a State and Citizens of another State,—between Citizens of different States,—between Citizens of the same State claiming Lands under Grants of different States, and between a State, or the Citizens thereof, and foreign States, Citizens or Subjects ...

First Amendment: Congress shall make no law respecting an establishment of religion, or prohibiting the free exercise thereof; or abridging the freedom of speech, or of the press; or the right of the people peaceably to assemble, and to petition the Government for a redress of grievances. (1789)

Sixth Amendment: In all criminal prosecutions, the accused shall enjoy the right to a speedy and public trial, by an **impartial** jury of the State and district wherein the crime shall have been committed, which district shall have been previously ascertained by law, and to be informed of the nature and cause of the accusation; to be confronted with the witnesses against him; to have compulsory process for obtaining witnesses in his favor, and to have the Assistance of Counsel for his defence. (1789)

Fourteenth Amendment: All persons born or naturalized in the United States, and subject to the jurisdiction thereof, are citizens of the United States and of the State wherein they reside. No State shall make or enforce any law which shall abridge the privileges or immunities of citizens of the United States; nor shall any State deprive any person of life, liberty, or property, without due process of law; nor deny to any person within its jurisdiction the equal protection of the laws. (1868)

ONLINE RESOURCES

U.S. History (2021). 18a. The Bill of Rights. https://www.ushistory.org/us/18a.asp.

DISCUSSION QUESTIONS

1. Why do you agree or disagree that Facebook and other social media platforms should have immunity from lawsuits?
2. What specific developments within social media law do you believe to be most important going forward? Why?
3. How should social media ethics inform our online behavior? What role should ethics play in the future development of social media communication?

REFERENCES

AFP (2020, November 4). Turkey Fines Facebook, Others Over New Social Media Law. *i24 News.* https://www.i24news.tv/en/news/international/middle-east/1604486899-turkey-fines-facebook-others-over-new-social-media-law.

Alexander, J. (2020, October 8). The Social Dilemma Caught One of Its 'Conspiracists' Off Guard. https://www.theverge.com/2020/10/8/21497218/social-dilemma-tiktok-coronavirus-conspiracy-theories-social-media.

Al Jazeera (2020, December 31). Hong Kong Tycoon Jimmy Lai Ordered Back to Jail Pending Trial. *AlJazeera.* https://www.aljazeera.com/news/2020/12/31/hong-kong-tycoon-jimmy-lai-ordered-back-to-jail-pending-trial.

Associated Press (2020, November 18). Apple to Pay Another $113M to Settle iPhone Battery Claims. https://apnews.com/article/apple-inc-lawsuits-arizona-f25446ea616d8f27a5285501b296a5e7.

Bates, S. (2020, October 7). The Man Who Wanted to Save the First Amendment by Inverting It. *The Atlantic.* https://amp-theatlantic-com.cdn.ampproject.org/c/s/ amp.theatlantic.com/amp/article/616573/.

Bilginsoy, Z. (2021, March 20). Twitter to Establish Legal Entity in Turkey, Comply with Law. https://apnews.com/article/world-news-turkey-media-social-media-e0d122e1856f-8ce3382d55fea93e6029.

Carpenter v. United States, 585 U.S. ___ (2018).

Charlton, A. and Adamson, T. (2020, November 28). French Protesters Decry Bill Outlawing Use of Police Images. *Associated Press.* https://apnews.com/article/police-paris-police-brutality-france-emmanuel-macron-27f4206b9716691e4ba4172e9b6252ac.

Chen, T. (2020, November 24). The TikToker Fired for His Viral Paint-Mixing Account Has a New Job. *BuzzFeed News.* https://www.buzzfeednews.com/article/tanyachen/man-fired-from-sherwin-williams-hired-at-florida-paint.

Christians, C.C., Rotzoll, K.B., Fackler, M., McKee, K.B., and Woods, Jr., R.H. (2005). *Media Ethics: Cases and Moral Reasoning.* Boston, MA: Pearson.

Conger, K. (2020, October 9). Twitter Will Turn Off Some Features to Fight Election Misinformation. *The New York Times.* https://www.nytimes.com/2020/10/09/ technology/twitter-election-ban-features.html,

Connor, T. (2020a, November 14). Virginia College Dean Under Fire for Slamming Biden Voters. *The Daily Beast.* https://www.thedailybeast.com/virginia-wesleyan-college-dean-paul-ewell-under-fire-for-slamming-joe-biden-voters.

Connor, T. (2020b, October 24). Facebook Outraged at NYU Researchers Collecting Its Political Ad Data. *The Daily Beast.* https://www.thedailybeast.com/facebook-outraged-at-nyu-researchers-collecting-its-political-ad-data.

Fox Business (2020, September 17). Anti-Mask Protester Fined After Marching Through Target Store. https://www.fox13news.com/news/anti-mask-protesters-fined-after-marching-through-florida-target.

Hagey, J.H.K. (2020, November 15). Mercer-Backed Parler Makes "Free Speech" Pitch to Conservatives Who've Turned on Twitter and Even Facebook. *Market Watch*. https://www.marketwatch.com/story/mercer-backed-parler-makes-free-speech-pitch-to-conservatives-mad-at-facebook-and-twitter-11605390504.

Hanley, D.A. (2020, October 9). The FCC Has Untapped Powers. The Next Administration Needs To Use Them. *Washington Monthly*. https://washingtonmonthly.com/ 2020/10/09/the-fcc-has-untapped-powers-the-next-administration-needs-to-use-them/.

Hauser, C. (2020, November 30). Oregon Nurse Is Placed on Leave Over TikTok Video Mocking Masks. *New York Times*. https://www.nytimes.com/2020/11/30/ us/oregon-nurse-tiktok-mask.html.

Huriash, L.J. (2020, September 16). Twisted Sister's Dee Snider Calls Anti-Maskers "Moronic" For Protest Inside Fort Lauderdale Target. *South Florida Sun Sentinel*. https://www.sun-sentinel.com/coronavirus/fl-ne-anti-maskers-fort-lauderdale-target-20200916-aqrfh5fou5dstf6todhzqixy54-story.html.

Jalan, T. (2020, October 6). Facebook Refuses to Establish Local Office as Turkey's New Social Media Law Kicks In. *Medianama*. https://www.medianama.com/2020/10/223-facebook-turkey-social-media-law/.

Jin, K.-X. (2020, December 3). Keep People Safe and Informed About the Coronavirus. Facebook. https://about.fb.com/news/2020/12/coronavirus/#roku-latest.

Klassen, T.R., Hoekje, B., and Stevens, S.G. (2020, October 19). 5 Tips for Improving Your Digital Etiquette. *Routledge*. https://www.routledge.com/blog/article/5-tips-for-improving-your-digital-etiquette.

Malwarebytes, Inc. v. Enigma Software Group, 592 U. S. ____ (2020).

Marantz, A. (2020, October 12). Why Facebook Can't Fix Itself. *New Yorker*. https://www-newyorker-com.cdn.ampproject.org/c/s/www.newyorker.com/magazine/2020/10/19/why-facebook-cant-fix-itself/amp.

Marr, M. (2020, September 17). "No More Masks!" Watch a Flash Mob Storm Through a Target Store in Fort Lauderdale. *Miami Herald*. https://www.miamiherald.com/news/local/community/broward/article245784820.html.

Masnick, M. (2020, October 13). Clarence Thomas Doesn't Like Section 230, Adding to His Anti-Free Speech Legacy. *TechDirt*. https://www.techdirt.com/articles/20201013/11283545491/clarence-thomas-doesnt-like-section-230-adding-to-his-anti-free-speech-legacy.shtml.

Moore, E. (2020, December 2). On Twitter and TikTok, Biden Grandchildren May Offer Viral View of White House Life. *NPR*. https://www.npr.org/2020/12/02/ 940891836/on-twitter-and-tiktok-biden-grandchildren-may-offer-viral-view-of-white-house-li.

Myman, D. (2020, November 20). Disappearing "Fleets" Aren't As Private As You Think. Personal Email.

Needham, K. (2020, November 29). Australia Demands Apology from China After Fake Image Posted on Social Media. *Reuters*. https://www.reuters.com/article/us-australia-china/australia-demands-apology-from-china-after-fake-image-posted-on-social-media-idUSKBN28A07Y.

Newton, C. (2020, December 3). The Withering eMail that Got an Ethical AI Researcher Fired at Google. *Platformer.* https://www.platformer.news/p/the-withering-email-that-got-an-ethical.

O'Brien, M. (2020, October 13). Facebook Bans Holocaust Denial, Distortion Posts. *Associated Press.* https://apnews.com/article/election-2020-media-social-media-elections-mark-zuckerberg-14e8073ce6f7bd2a674c99ac7bbfc240.

O'Neill, R. M. (2001). *The First Amendment and Civil Liability.* Bloomington, IN: Indiana University Press.

Pavlik, J., Alsaad, A.A., and Laufer, P. (2020, Winter). Speaking Truth to Power: Core Principles for Advancing International Journalism Education, *Journalism & Mass Communication Educator,* 75(4), 392–406.

Pirus, B. (2020, November). Verison's Newsroom To Use Blockchain In Bid For Absolute Transparency. *CoinTelegraph.* https://cointelegraph-com.cdn.ampproject.org/ c/s/cointelegraph.com/news/verizon-s-newsroom-to-use-blockchain-in-bid-for-absolute-transparency/amp.

Reuters (2020a, December 3). Facebook Bans False Claims About Covid-19 Vaccines. *NBC News.* https://www.nbcnews.com/tech/tech-news/facebook-bans-false-claims-covid-19-vaccines-rcna188.

Reuters (2020b, November 12). Zuckerberg Says in Meeting Bannon Has Not Violated Enough Policies for Facebook Suspension. *CNBC.* https://www.cnbc.com/ 2020/11/12/ zuckerberg-bannon-has-not-violated-enough-policies-for-suspension.html.

Riley v. California, 134 U.S. 2473 (2014).

Roman Catholic Diocese of Brooklyn, New York v. Andrew M. Cuomo, Governor of New York, 592 U. S. ___ (2020).

Roose, K., Isaac, M., and Frenkel, S. (2020, November 24). Facebook Struggles to balance Civility and Growth. *New York Times.* https://www.nytimes.com/2020/11/24/technology/facebook-election-misinformation.html.

Rosen, J. (2020, September 28). "You Might Not Like It, But It's Smart Politics." *PressThink* Blog. https://pressthink.org/2020/09/you-might-not-like-it-but-its-smart-politics/.

Rosenblatt, K. (2020, November 29). Viral TikToks Offer Firsthand Accounts of Vaccine Trials, Debunk Misinformation. *NBC News.* https://www.nbcnews.com/news/us-news/ viral-tiktoks-offer-firsthand-accounts-vaccine-trials-debunk-misinformation-n1249046.

Serrano, J. (2020, November 16). "Unbiased" Social Media Platform Parler Is Unsurprisingly Found to Be Backed by Conservative Megadonor. *Gizmodo.* https://gizmodo.com/ unbiased-social-media-platform-parler-is-unsurprising-1845683193.

Sonnemaker, T. (2020, December 29). McConnel Ties $2,000 Stimulus Checks to trump-proposed Poison Pills on Section 230 and Election Fraud, Likely Sinking Push for Additional Covid-19 Relief. *Business Insider.* https://www.businessinsider.com/ mcconnell-ties-stimulus-checks-section-230-repeal-election-fraud-2020-12.

Townsend, M. (2020, November 22). Facebook Condemned for Hosting Neo-Nazi Network with UK Links. *The Guardian.* https://www.theguardian.com/technology/ 2020/nov/22/ facebook-condemned-for-hosting-neo-nazi-network-with-uk-links.

Tyko, K. (2020, September 18). Dee Snider Scolds Anti-Mask Parade of People in MAGA Gear Playing Twisted Sister Song at Florida Target. *USA Today*. https://www.usatoday.com/story/money/2020/09/17/target-maskless-shoppers-twisted-sister-dee-snider-face-coverings/3485442001/.

U.S. House Subcommittee On Antitrust, Commercial and Administrative Law of the Committee of the Judiciary (2020). *Majority Staff Report and Recommendations*. Washington, DC: U.S. House of Representatives.

Verizon (2020, October 30). Verizon's "Full Transparency" Launches Blockchain Verification For News Releases. https://www.verizon.com/about/news/verizons-full-transparency-launches-blockchain-verification.

Wagley, C. (2020, December 21). More Than Ever, Art Workers Are Calling Out Their Employers – Anonymously – On Social Media. Can It Make Real-World Change? *ArtNet News*. https://news.artnet.com/art-world/anonymous-instagram-accounts-2020-1932998.

Glossary

A

absolute privilege: a form of immunity for government officials, which provides they cannot be named in civil suits – including defamation suits – for acts they committed as part of their official government duties.

absolutism: in law, a belief that the First Amendment means what it says. In ethics, truth and other assumptions that guide human behavior.

access: historically, public access to media channels and technologies and an ability to offer alternative narratives to the dominant media *agenda-setting* process.

act: a piece of legislation. After an act is approved by the legislature and the executive, it is incorporated into the jurisdiction's *code* as *statutory law*.

actual damages: money awarded in a civil lawsuit for actual harm, injury or loss.

actual malice: public figure or official defamation case legal term of art meaning that the content was published after entertaining serious doubt, in reckless disregard of the truth.

administrative law: the body of regulation and opinions issued by the Federal Trade Commission (FTC), Federal Communications Commission (FCC) and other agencies created by Congress to address complex and technical areas of law not addressed by statute.

advertising: paid and commercial messages purchased by an advertiser or agency representative to appear within mainstream traditional or hybrid digital media. Sponsored content or "native advertising" mimics the look and feel of editorial or news content, but it is sponsored as a single ad or part of a larger ad campaign buy.

agenda-setting: a research term for the process of determining political, media and public agendas that guide policymaking and other decisions.

altruism: concern for others rather than the needs and interests of the personal self.

amicus curiae: (Latin, "friend of the court") term used to apply to a brief filed in court by someone who is not a party to the case. *Amicus* briefs usually are filed in an appellate court by an organization, which has an interest in the legal issue the court will be considering.

app: short for *application*, an app is software for use on a desktop, laptop, tablet or smartphone that allows the user to apply the power of system software for a particular purpose.

appellant: the party appealing a case.

appellee: the party opposing the appeal of a case.

appropriation of likeness: invasion of privacy case law use of a name, image or likeness for commercial purposes without consent.

augmented reality (AR): use of geographic data and mobile smartphone data and images to augment physical spaces with vast amounts of computer data.

autonomy: utilizing moral or ethical law to make individual life decisions without external interference.

B

bad tendency test: prior to the 20th century, U.S. courts restricted free expression when speech had any possibility to cause harm.

balance of interest doctrine: when a court rules on a legal issue, it often uses a balancing test: weighing the interests of one party against another. In the context of a First Amendment case, the balance is between the individual's (or group's) right to expression and the state's interest in regulating it.

best practices: standard practices of an industry, developed gradually, that are the processes and social media content that have worked well over time.

Bill of Rights: the first ten amendments to the U.S. Constitution establish fundamental human rights.

blasphemy: disparaging words about churches, religion or gods.

blockchain: connection of big data computing, part of the "Internet of Things" (IoT).

blog: online sites, often owned media, in which somewhat formal and regular posts (information and commentary) are published. Early blogs were characterized by authenticity, which is the idea that the author presents a more "real" and unfiltered identity.

board: Pinterest uses the term "board' to reflect the online space on which users "pin" content to a virtual message board.

branding: the marketing technique of emphasizing a brand for a product, service, organization or individual. A logo, face or even a song may reinforce the brand for consumers.

breaking news: real-time events and news that happen as developing news stories. Traditional media emphasize breaking news and this content is frequently spread on social networks.

brief: attorney-written arguments for a case on appeal to inform judges about formal positions of each side. Court-filed documents in which attorneys present the factual and legal positions of the parties they represent. In trial courts, briefs are filed in support of motions; in appellate courts, briefs present the legal positions of the parties on the issues on appeal. Students sometimes confuse this term with a *case brief*, which is a summary of facts, legal issues, reasoning and decision used to study an opinion.

business-to-business (B2B): business between two businesses rather than between a business and a consumer.

buzz: the aggregate social network activity from a word, term, phrase or other content. On Twitter, for example, we can track #BreakingNews buzz on a graph of time (X) and total number of tweets (Y).

C

categorical imperative: unconditional, highest moral law that ignores consequences.

case brief: a short summary of case facts, legal issues, decision (holding), and reasoning for a court opinion.

cause of action: the specific facts in a case that provide a right to file a lawsuit against another.

censorship: a *prior restraint* by the government that stops publication before it happens. More generally, it is suppression of words that violate norms.

certiorari: the U.S. Supreme Court grants "*cert*" in agreeing to hear a case from lower courts and ordering that the files in the case be sent up. A party files a petition for a *writ of certiorari* asking for review. Currently, the Supreme Court hears no more than about 150 cases each term out of more than 7,000 requests.

chatbots: artificial intelligence that generates an automatic response to a social media user each time she or he responds.

cite: a citation that notes the location of a case by reporter volume number, page number (court for "Bluebook" legal citation) and year.

citizen journalism: individuals use online platforms to distribute news created as nonprofessional citizen journalists. This content may be "hyperlocal" with a neighborhood focus that does not attract large enough audiences to interest mainstream media.

civil action: one party in a civil lawsuit claims a private wrong against another.

civil cases: tort cases over breach of contract or other private actions are heard between parties in civil litigation. Actions include those "at law" for monetary damages and "in equity" involving other forms of "remedies." These may include requiring the loser in a lawsuit to take some action. Federal courts and most state courts are unified systems. All district judges hear both civil and criminal matters.

clear and present danger test: applied when a court finds that free expression has the potential to cause immediate violence or other substantial harms.

click-through rates (CTR): a measure of user clicks on sponsored results.

client: an individual, organization, lawyer or financial claimholder represented by an attorney or law firm.

code of ethics: a set of ethical rules or guidance, such as the PRSA Code of Ethics, that define individual professional behavior within an industry or organization.

commercial speech: advertising, social media influence for a business or promotion of products or services.

common carrier: rules applied to telephone and other universal services requiring nondiscrimination of access and no editorial restriction over content.

common law: is "judge-made" law, as it began in England and spread through the colonies. Lawyers use precedent through careful analysis of previous cases and the legal principle of *stare decisis* to argue cases in and between U.S. states. It is distinguished from statute or other types of law.

communitarianism: a philosophy of placing community needs above any individual. Ethical disputes frequently center on a competition for scarce resources within a community and the degree to which the community can rise above this.

community: a core CMC concept that describes how individuals create groups, including interest groups, by sharing information within social networks. In ethics, *communitarianism* places the community and its needs above any individual.

compelling interest standard: when government seeks to restrict *content-neutral* free expression under the U.S. Constitution and First Amendment, *strict scrutiny* means that a narrowly tailored overriding interest must be proved.

complaint: document filed in court to initiate a civil or criminal action. A complaint sets forth alleged facts that give rise to a cause of action.

computer-mediated communication (CMC): a social and research construct that begins to explain the nature of social network and social media behavior and culture.

confidentiality: contracts frequently require client information to be kept confidential for a variety of reasons, such as business interests. There may be legal or ethical responsibilities to keep information confidential.

conflict of interest: individuals or organizations that either act in their own privileged interests instead of others or have a publicly *perceived conflict of interest* may not make moral or ethically sound decisions.

consequentialism: a view that ethics is based on the consequences or effects of any action.

contempt of court: failing to follow a court order may place an individual or organization in contempt and this could lead to time in jail.

content neutral: *time, place and manner* restriction that is unrelated to the content of expression.

constitutional law: the U.S.A. or other national fundamental framework determines rights as interpreted by a Supreme Court of other highest legal body. In the U.S.A., federal courts determine constitutional and federal procedural questions, as well as common law disputes between states.

controlling authority: a U.S. Supreme Court decision has controlling authority in all federal courts. In cases not decided by the Supreme Court, each of the 13 appeals court circuits may set precedents for the courts within their respective circuits.

convergence: an early description of the merging of previously separate media, such as print (newspapers and magazines), broadcasting (radio and television), advertising, public relations and marketing. So-called "convergence newsrooms" were developed to allow content producers to work across online media platforms.

conversation: within online interaction, conversation monitoring may be used to increase engagement by responding to comments, reactions and posts by others.

conversion: marketers convert social media activity to sales.

copyright: legal ownership protection of the *manner of expression* within a tangible medium. Failure to use copyrighted contented without permission is *copyright infringement.*

cost per click (CPC): a social media alternative advertising measure to the traditional cost per thousand mainstream method for pricing commercial messages. CPC charges advertisers for every audience user click.

credibility: related to trust and believability. In media research, we talk about source and message credibility. The more content has both, the more likely audience members will be to trust it.

critical thinking and reading: learned analyses skills that include *deconstruction* of socially constructed media content, development of critical questions, and application of critical theory and methods in the viewing, for example, of social media communication.

criminal courts: state and federal prosecutors act as the government in criminal cases against individuals.

criminal libel: statute law may make it a crime to defame an individual through publication. Prior to *New York Times v. Sullivan* (1964), this also referred to libels against the government or officials.

crowdfunding: raising money by making online appeals that leverage social networking and social sharing. Increasingly, crowdfunding is used to support lawsuits.

crowdsourcing: social networks allow individuals to interact in real time. Crowdsourcing is defined as a method for gathering, filtering, generating and distributing information within a social network. On Twitter, for example, crowdsourcing is used during breaking news to separate facts from rumors.

C-suite: top-level corporate executives making key decisions that may include social media policies.

customer relationship management (CRM): organizes engagement around customer satisfaction, loyalty and retention.

D

damages: plaintiffs in a lawsuit may recover money as compensation from a defendant in the case.

de novo: within a case, these are new issues that must be reconsidered.

deception: intent to mislead, manipulate or alter facts or truth within the *public sphere*. Social media misinformation and disinformation, such as *deep fakes*, may intend to deceive people.

declaratory judgment: sometimes a court decision declares rights, obligations and legal opinions without "relief" in the form of financial damages or an injunction to stop specific activities.

defamation: injury to reputation that could lead to social ridicule via a published *libel* or a spoken *slander*.

defendant: party against whom a civil or criminal action is brought.

deontology: a focus on *duty* rather than *utilitarian* consequences of action.

determinism: an alternative to individual free will, causes and effects are predetermined rather than influenced by human behavior bounded by moral principles.

dicta: language in a court opinion that discusses an issue or issues that are not before the court in that particular case. Dicta have no precedential value, but may indicate how the court may rule if and when that issue does come before it.

digital rights management (DRM): systems of control over content access to seek user payments.

diffusion: the spread of new ideas, practices, processes or products. Diffusion research identifies the earliest innovators (2.5%), early adopters (13.5%), early majority (34%), late majority (34%) and laggards (16%). The percentage of adopters (Y) is graphed using an S-shaped curve over time (X).

direct message (DM): in Twitter, followers may send private messages that are not broadcast on the larger network.

directed verdict: in the course of a jury trial, the judge may determine that the evidence presented entitles one party to judgment as a matter of law. When this occurs, the judge will direct the jury to enter a verdict in favor of that party.

diversity jurisdiction: involves disputes between individuals or corporations living in different states and the decision about where to hear a case. Under the U.S. Constitution, Article III, such questions may be resolved by a federal court.

doctrine of incorporation: the First Amendment, as well as all of the Bill of Rights, apply to state law under the Fourteenth Amendment's due process clause.

doctrine of preferred position: state laws are normally presumed constitutional until otherwise shown, but this presumption does not apply to the Bill of Rights and the 14th Amendment. This means that states have a burden to prove that laws do not violate the freedom of expression.

duty: ethical emphasis on what is required of an individual, organization or society. For example, duties of citizenship are assumptions based on shared values. Duty may lead to ethical or unethical outcomes.

E

early adopters: in a diffusion cycle, the first to adopt new technologies and/or ideas.

earned exposure: customer reviewer expressions of positive feelings about products or services.

earned media: public relations professionals work to receive positive attention for their clients through content that is not paid advertising. Earned media may be the product of media relations, a campaign, real-time engagement or other activities.

eCommerce: online sales and business.

Electronic Frontier Foundation (EFF): organization promoting free and open Internet.

egoism: self-interests guide action.

electronic word-of-mouth (eWOM): an extension of face-to-face communication applied to social media marketing.

emoji: small, colorful images used to express feelings; these grew from text emoticons developed in the 1990s.

en banc: (Fr., "in the bench") state and federal appeals are heard by a panel of three judges. The party that does not prevail before that panel may request that the case be reconsidered *en banc*, that is, by all the judges of that court. Under certain circumstances, some courts permit the court itself to determine that a case should skip the panel review and go directly to an *en banc* proceeding.

engaged journalism: newsroom use of social media engagement tactics, such as chats, events and other opportunities to interact with audience members in a community.

engagement: the term that describes strengthening social network interaction from passive to more active. It goes beyond passive viewing to clicking on a link, liking content, sharing content and responding to content in some way that can be seen by social media users.

entrepreneur: social media sites have been created and developed by the technology sector, which values an innovative culture. Personal computer *hardware* and software were first developed by young entrepreneurs, such as Bill Gates and Steve Jobs, and the current industry features inventors and their startups.

equity: common law precedent may be rigid, but equity calls for additional flexibility in constructing a fair legal remedy.

ethics: philosophical study or application of moral principles within human decisions and action.

F

Facebook Insights: a dashboard showing social media managers' performance over time of fan page posts.

Facebook Live: a real-time streaming video app within Facebook that allows for viewing, commenting and use of like, love, sad and angry emoji.

fact: in trial courts, juries decide questions of fact and judges decide questions of law; if there is no jury, the judge decides both questions of law and questions of fact. Discovery – the often expensive and time-consuming process by which the parties learn and test their respective factual contentions – frequently leads cases to be settled before the case goes to trial.

fair comment: public sphere criticism based on provably truthful facts qualifies for a common law defamation defense.

fair use: noncommercial use of copyrighted content may be allowed and consent from the rights holder is suggested.

fake news: a term applied to propaganda, distortion and manipulation or lies shared with an intent to deceive readers.

false light: privacy claims that can be made against false information that may or may not be defamatory.

fan: a Facebook user may like a page and become a fan. By doing this, the posts on this page appear on the user's news feed.

fault: a required standard to win a libel suit, applying *actual malice* for public figures and officials or *negligence* under most U.S. state laws.

felony: a crime which is punishable by a year or more in prison.

fighting words: are those that are likely to spark immediate violence and not protected First Amendment expression.

first sale doctrine: in copyright law protects royalties in each first sale, but purchasers may resell or rent the legal copy. When you purchased this textbook, you also bought the right to sell or rent it. However, copying it without permission or limited fair use of quotes would violate the law.

foundationalism: the use of self-evident truths in development of ideas.

G

gag order: a court issues a gag order to prevent communication about proceedings in a particular case. Gag orders against the media have generally been found to be unconstitutional prior restraint, as explained by the *Nebraska Press* decision. Courts are permitted, however, to issue gag orders against the parties and their attorneys in a civil or criminal matter to refrain from talking about the case with anyone, including the media.

gatekeepers: those who perform a traditional news editorial function of story selection.

golden mean: Confucius claimed *virtue* was found at the middle of two extremes.

grand jury: a panel of citizens that determines whether there is probable cause to charge a person with a crime. These are secret proceedings at which only the prosecutor presents evidence. A defendant may, but usually does not, testify before the grand jury. If she chooses to testify, her attorney may witness her testimony, but may not otherwise participate in the proceedings.

group libel: cases hinge on the size of a group. Only small groups of a few individuals have been able to successfully claim defamation.

H

hardware: physical computing equipment, such as a desktop, laptop, tablet or smartphone. We also speak of components, keyboard, mouse, monitor, router, modem, etc., as hardware.

hashflag: a paid emoji that automatically appears when a promoted hashtag is used.

hashjacking: hijacking a hashtag already in use on Twitter for an event.

hashtag (#): the number sign is used on Twitter and, more recently, Facebook as a filtering device. By searching for and using hashtags, subsets of the larger feed can be seen and used.

heteronomy: autonomy is supplanted by factors external to the individual.

holding: a decision of a court, as determined by a vote of judges or justices.

human–computer interaction (HCI): early research into how humans engaged with computer hardware and software.

hybrid media: new media that incorporate some older media rules, such as news editorial practices.

hyperlinks: web links to other content via an Internet URL address.

hypothetical imperative: use of if-then or cause-effect statements without regard for complex interaction of social forces.

I

idealism: an emphasis on the value of ideas and ideals over material objects, such as products and services in the marketplace.

identity: what we present online through the use of words, photographs, sounds, videos, emoticons, avatar or other means. Each time we decide to communicate (and even when we do not), we suggest an identity to social network site users.

impartial: use of equity and equality, such as when a judge treats all parties in a lawsuit equally and with fairness. In social media communication, impartiality would be an application of morality and ethics in all interaction, engagement and online community building and maintenance.

implied consent: weaker than explicit consent in writing, but may be considered in court.

impression: awareness of information, such as from seeing it during a search.

influence: users with a lot of fans, followers or connections tend to be considered influencers. Celebrities' large reach affords them monetized influence, but micro-influencers with 1,000 to 100,000 followers also may be influential due to higher engagement with fans.

infra: used within an opinion to say there is more on the point later in the decision.

injunction: a court order directing a party to take or refrain from taking a particular action.

innovation: a business culture favoring change over stability.

interaction: each engagement with another SNS account reflects a decision to interact. Interaction and engagement are a key foundation for social media use.

inter alia: meaning "among other things."

internet protocol (IP): an address number attached to a user computer or location.

irrationality: philosophical *inclination* to favor emotions instead of reasoned logic.

J

judgment: a court decision that typically is a financial award in favor of one party to a civil lawsuit.

jurisdiction: a geographic or subject area authority of a court.

justice: the ideal of reason may be sought through equality, freedom, common good, consistency and natural rights of fair play and balance.

K

key performance indicators (KPI): continuous monitoring of important business variables.

keywords: words used within SEO to move page placement higher in a search by relating to common user language.

L

law: trial courts make findings of fact and conclusions of law. In a jury trial, the jury is the finder of fact. U.S. appellate and Supreme Court cases apply and interpret the law, such as the First Amendment.

liability: legal responsibility within a case.

libel: within *defamation* law, written and published words that damage reputation through the potential, for example, of hatred and ridicule.

limited-purpose public figure: an otherwise private person who thrusts themselves into the *vortex* of a controversial public issue may be held to the *actual malice* standard in a libel case.

live tweeting: during an event or breaking news, eyewitnesses and commentators may tweet in real time with updates on any new information.

location-based services (LBS): designed to allow users to check in at locations.

loyalty: an obligation to consistently follow decisions and action of an individual, organization or society.

M

mandamus: a court order, usually styled as a "writ of *mandamus*," which directs a government agency or public official to perform an act it is required to do by statute or existing court order. It is also used by an appellate court to direct a lower court to modify its ruling in accordance with what the appellate court has ruled in a particular case.

marketing: promoting and selling products and services targeted at a specific market. Research is usually utilized to focus marketing, which may involve use of advertising and social media marketing.

means: the process and actions used to achieve goals that philosophers call *ends*.

measurement error: all measurement has error and researchers estimate amounts.

media communication: a theoretical perspective that moves away from mass communication and mass audiences toward fragmentation.

media literacy: is a way to describe the need for media audience members to possess skills that allow them to deconstruct and understand media content. For example, an information literacy approach would emphasize knowledge and learning. Media literacy scholars suggest that children need to be taught to realize when they are being sold products and services through sophisticated advertising and marketing campaigns.

meme: social media content that features cultural imitation. Production typically uses easily identifiable characters, iterations and humor. For example, there is a persistent use of an image from the 1971 *Willy Wonka and the Chocolate Factory* movie because of an early meme generator site.

metrics: measurement of behavior within social media. A variety of social media "dashboards," such as Google Analytics, Sprout, Chartbeat, Hootsuite, Cision, Tweetdeck, Argyle Social, Sprout Social, and Radian6 are in use.

microblog: short, or limited space, blogging began with Twitter and its 140-character limit. Microblogging became a genre to comment through without taking the time and energy to publish a more formal blog site. Even for those blogging, microblogs are used to push out links and drive traffic back to the site.

misdemeanor: minor crimes punishable by fines, community service or minimal jail time of less than one year.

mobile communication: smartphones and tablets connected through WiFi or cellphone data. Mobile Internet connections allow for the use of a wide variety of social media apps.

monopoly: commercial business control over supply, processes, products and prices that unfairly disadvantage competitors in the marketplace.

moral calculus: calculating a morally correct decision in a legal case or other circumstance.

moral reasoning: determination of rights and wrongs based on an ethically based analysis.

N

narrative: use of storytelling techniques, such as a story arc.

natural law: historically was seen to imperfectly follow the eternal rules of God. Ancient Greeks, Romans and other sought normative rules describing highest authority about what ought to be done. Classical naturalism sought "the word" and modern naturalism identified ideals. We may derive fundamental ideas of good over evil, a desire for truth and avoidance of harm.

negligence: *tort* law standard of *fault* for most states' libel law determined by what a reasonably careful individual or professional would do.

network visualization: social networks generate large amounts of data that may be viewed as a series of network maps of communication hubs and spokes. Visualization depicts through graphs the social space between SNS accounts.

nihilism: a lack of any beliefs, including rejection of truth as a desired value.

nondisclosure agreement (NDA): information exchanged between parties to a contract may be protected for a period of time covered by the agreement.

nongovernmental organization (NGO): entities operating in the nonprofit sector rather than government or commercial for-profit businesses.

O

objectivity: a norm within journalism placing value and emphasis on balance, fairness and telling at least two sides to every story. In the second half of the 20th century, journalists strove for objectivity. Recent scholars see it as an unachievable ideal. Social media users of social networks frequently emphasize subjectivity and opinion.

obscenity: lacking First Amendment protection under *Near v. Minnesota*, pornographic depiction of sexual conduct in the U.S.A. is determined by applying the three-part *Miller* test.

opportunity costs: the cost of using money on one expense and not having it available for other possibilities.

organic: is a way to describe naturally evolving social media content. Facebook contrasts content that organically circulates on the social network with paid content that is then boosted to the top of feeds or given more prominent placement.

overbreadth: law that is vague and overly broad in suppressing free expression will be found to be unconstitutional under the First Amendment.

owned media: typically company-owned media, such as a website.

P

packet switching: the method of moving Internet data in packet chunks and reassembling content on arrival.

paid search: search engines charge advertisers for top placement within search results.

parallel citation: referencing earlier publication of an opinion, for example, in S.Ct. or L.Ed, as well as the later official U.S. *reporter* about five years after the decision is released in a *slip opinion.*

particularity: attachment to loyalties and individual desires that may conflict with universal and impartial application of morality and ethics.

paywall: a system requiring registration and payment by users.

per curiam: (Lat., "by the court.") unsigned appellate decision issued under the name of the court. The court issues a *per curiam* decision in cases where it believes the procedural and legal issues raised are neither novel nor significant enough to merit a signed decision.

persuasive authority: lawyers may cite a case from outside of a circuit or state as persuasive to a court. Law review articles, scholarly views and other evidence also may be cited that does not strictly carry precedent.

petitioner: the side that appeals a lower court decision.

pin: Pinterest describes any posting on a user board as a pin, which is the online metaphor for placing a scrap of paper on a bulletin board.

plaintiff: the individual, organization or governmental entity that initiates a civil or criminal action.

platforms: online sites that offer various social media services.

pleading: a written legal argument that makes key points a court is asked to consider.

pluralism: recognition of multiple social realities and groups, sometimes controlled through a process of *elite pluralism* that define a democratic agenda through agents of power.

pornography: sexually explicit content that may be protected under the First Amendment, if falling outside the *Miller obscenity* test.

positivism: law is made by humans and based on sovereign authority and the emphasis is on form over fairness.

posting: the act of uploading media content to a social media site. Beyond organic content, the text, photographs or video distributed through a posting may receive wider distribution by paying for a promoted post or sponsored content on a site.

precedent: under common law, previous cases guide decision-making unless other legal authority can be found to change direction.

prior restraint: under common law and the First Amendment, government *censorship* of expression is unconstitutional. After publication, content may be subject to *subsequent punishment.*

privacy: a concept first suggested in the late 19th century that calls for legal protection of intimate details of life, especially when a person seeks to protect these from public view. Private behavior that lacks harm to others may be protected from the public interest.

private libel: constitutional First Amendment interpretation is applied to individual defamation cases.

promoted posts: social media sites charge advertisers to appear in prominent positions that are likely to be seen.

propaganda: information designed to promote or advance a view, cause, person, product or idea. Before World War II, propaganda was simply considered persuasion.

However, World War II propaganda caused people to associate the term with a pejorative meaning such that now it suggests the spread of false information.

public domain: content that falls outside *copyright* law may be freely used without permission.

public figure: general-purpose celebrities or limited-purpose individuals for specific public issues fall under the *actual malice* standard in libel cases.

public official: a decision-making elected or appointed federal or state government employee that falls under the *actual malice* standard in libel cases.

public relations (PR): seeks through professional best practices to present, maintain and manage public images and reputations. Ongoing campaigns use media relations tactics to present perceived positives. Reputation management efforts may be in response to a crisis from perceived negative information.

Q

qualified privilege: accurate and fair reporting of public information.

R

reach: a traditional mass media measure of distribution, social media are also interested in measuring the broad distribution of content.

real-time social engagement: current PR best practices include nearly immediate response to conversation monitoring of social media. Within a relatively short time, sometimes a matter of minutes, a brand engages on a social network about a trending topic, issue or person.

reckless disregard: in a libel case, *actual malice* is proved by showing that serious doubt about truth of the content was considered and disregarded before publication.

Reddit: Redditors are active regular users of the Reddit site drive conversation.

relativism: moral values are considered relative to other individuals, organizations and societies instead of based on rationality in ethics.

remand: a higher court may direct the lower court to abide by a decision and it may also allow for additional proceedings.

reporter privilege: a journalist right to protect the source of confidential information is not absolute and a court may order a news reporter to disclose or be punished with jail time possible. State *shield laws* explicitly create a privilege against testifying in a case.

respondent: the lower court winning side opposing a *petitioner* appeal.

retraction: a correction of an earlier publication that may mitigate *damages* in a libel suit.

return on investment (ROI): calculation of a financial gain minus the cost of an investment. ROI is expressed as a percentage or ratio and is sometimes considered a measure of efficiency.

retweet: redistributing a previous tweet with the letters RT in front of it, this allows Twitter users to easily share content to their social network. Twitter users also post MT for modified tweets and PRT, if an item is a partial retweet.

right to be forgotten (RTBF): European law empowering users to have personal information removed from the Internet and disconnected from search engines, such as Google.

roles: individuals adopt roles, much as an actor might. A social media professional, for example, may perceive and express the role of an innovator or entrepreneur.

RPIE: the Public Relations Society of America PR process of research, planning, implementation and evaluation.

S

search engine optimization (SEO): Google algorithms produce a system for pushing some Internet content to the top of any specific search.

search engine result placements (SERP): using SEO techniques to drive high placement during keyword searches.

search warrant: a court order under the Fourth Amendment that authorizes a legal law enforcement search of a private home or other property, including social media data, to find criminal evidence.

seditious libel: an act of defaming the government or a government official, this is popular in totalitarian regimes sensitive about the reputation of the state. Sedition laws have been justified by helping to quell violence.

shield laws: in some states, journalists have legal protection against testimony that would disclose the source of confidential information. News organizations argue the need to protect anonymous sources in order to publish information disclosing wrongdoing.

skepticism: raising doubts about theories or experience as indicators of morality and ethics.

slander: *defamation* through speech that damages a reputation.

smartphone: mobile telephones connected on cellular networks that provide an Internet connection through devices that have personal computer capabilities.

snaps: Snapchat user postings to the site.

social business: application of business strategy, goals and tactics within social media marketing campaigns.

social graph: on Facebook, this is a user's complete social network.

social justice: equality and fairness of social, political economic and other action, such as found within the social media #BlackLivesMatter and #MeToo movements calling for racial and gender equity, as well as *social responsibility* in the action of government and corporations.

social media dashboard: measurement tools that organize data for efficient analysis.

social naturalism: is a view that law derives naturally from a social system.

social network: an array of online platforms used to connect with others.

social network site (SNS): any online platform that enables communication between site accounts.

software: computer code that allows hardware to be used via an operating system, programs and applications.

sponsored content: paid media content that may appear near editorial media content and free social media content.

stare decisis: the legal doctrine of *precedent* to follow prior, similar cases.

start-ups: new business ventures, sometimes with the funding help of "angel investors," launch social media sites and apps. An innovation culture, annual events such as "South By Southwest" (#SXSW) and the tech journalism community drive interest and activity in the diffusion of new ideas and products.

statute law: law enacted by Congress, state legislatures, county board, city councils and other legislative bodies.

stories: mobile apps Instagram, Snapchat, Facebook and others offer users Stories as a tool to string together a series of postings into a larger narrative.

storytelling: a fundamental concept in journalism and media communication. People have told stories since the development of language and oral tradition. Storytelling techniques, including the use of narrative, drive interest in content.

strict liability doctrine: holding an individual liable for *damages* without proof of *fault*.

strict scrutiny: to be upheld under the First Amendment, government regulation targeting free expression requires a compelling interest and narrowly tailored language.

summary judgment: a motion to dismiss a case. A judge may decide that there is no reason to continue.

supra: within an opinion, this means that there is earlier information within the decision.

T

tactics: strategic PR campaigns devise a set of tactics used to achieve communication goals. For example, if a campaign is designed to raise awareness about an issue, a tactic may be to create a YouTube video that can be shared by bloggers.

tagging: on Facebook, a person can be tagged in a photograph. In doing so, a name is associated with a face and perhaps a place and these data can be shared across the social network. More generally, geotagging is use of a computer software code that identifies location. A smartphone photograph may be geotagged with the location and these data can be presented or used within the context of an application.

temporary restraining order (TRO): a court may temporarily restrict action.

terms of service (ToS): contract law that users click and agree to use software, apps or websites.

third-party litigation funding (TPLF): legal or litigation finance provides money to cover a part of the cost to either bring a lawsuit or defend against one.

time, place and manner restriction: government restriction of free expression may be narrowly tailored to a specific context, such as done within zoning laws that restrict adult dancing clubs or media stores to specific distances from school and churches.

tort: in libel or slander cases, a civil wrong is based on action not found within a contract. These cases usually determine whether or not monetary "relief" is ordered and, if so, how much in compensatory and punitive damages. A civil wrong, such as libel, slander, breach of contract or negligence. These wrongs do not rise to criminal behavior but can subject the person who commits them to civil liability for monetary damages.

trademark: a word, symbol or name that identifies products or services within the marketplace.

transformative: in copyright law, some type of created added value that distinguishes the new content from an original.

transparency: the social media approach of disclosing all relevant interests and not having a hidden agenda or manipulating facts to favor individual and organizational interests.

trending: on Twitter, different words and hashtags trend at any given time. These are the most talked-about items. These can be organic or "promoted" as advertising.

trust: is considered an important and fundamental characteristic for a lot of influential social media content. Trust is related to credibility and believability, which is frequently assessed by judging previous behavior, including communication.

tweet: Twitter originally limited each individual message to no more than 140 characters, but this was relaxed. Twitter Limits also include: 1,000 Direct Messages and 2,400 tweets per day; 1,000 follows per day; and ratio limits after 5,000 follows.

Twitter Analytics: a dashboard for social media managers to track real-time account data.

U

user-generated content (UGC): created content by users, often not sponsored by traditional professional media organizations.

user profile: online descriptions of user identities.

utilitarianism: an emphasis on utility and happiness without regard for moral and ethical implication of behavior.

V

vagueness: a law limiting free expression under the First Amendment may be found unconstitutional if it is not specific.

validity: in social science, the determination that measurement is conceptually what it was planned to be.

veil of ignorance: philosophical theory suggesting that a decision could be made in isolation from society and culture.

verification: verified account authenticity of identity is an important online concern. Twitter created a blue checkmark to identify those accounts that have been verified through its internal process and this also appears on some Facebook pages. Additionally, Facebook users may take advantage of a two-step verification for login that includes a text message code to a mobile phone for account security.

viral: content that is shared quickly and widely because of high interest. Social media enables individuals to post viral videos on YouTube and rise to almost instant fame.

virtual communities: online spaces creating a community experience among users.

virtue: classical ideal of practicing the highest morals and ethical behavior.

vlog: video bloggers use video posts instead of text. Vlogs are regular commentary in a video medium.

W

word-of-mouth (WOM): personal influence is spread through word-of-mouth communication. In the past, this was mostly done face to face. Now, CMC allows for mediated WOM through social media communication.

work-for-hire: under copyright law, employees may transfer intellectual property to employer ownership, based either on job description or a contract covering use of the work.

Index

A&M Records, Inc. v. Napster, Inc. 125, 146
Abrams v. United States 20, 36, 230, 246, 259, 261
absolute privilege 13, 323
absolutism 251–2, 287, 323
access 1, 5, 9, 22, 62, 80, 85–6, 96, 103–5, 107–9, 126, 137, 144, 151, 153, 155, 158, 163, 165, 167, 169–70, 172–3, 176, 184, 213, 233–4, 244–5, 257, 259, 263, 269–70, 273, 289–90, 296, 302, 309, 314, 317, 323, 326, 329
actual damages 13, 46, 130, 135, 137–9, 141, 151, 168, 215–17, 220–2, 273, 323, 329, 340–3
actual malice 152, 168, 176, 217, 221–2, 225, 232, 273, 323, 332, 334, 339
advertising xiv–xv, 8, 12, 21, 66–76, 79–81, 88–122, 129, 133, 152, 164, 189, 204, 263, 292, 294, 303–4, 310, 313, 323, 326, 328, 330, 335, 343
agenda 102–3, 106, 119, 242, 323–4, 338, 343
altruism 324
Amazonians for Employee Privacy 94, 116
American Association of University Professors (AAUP) 44, 48, 61–2
amicus curiae 324
appellant 15, 194, 324
appropriation of likeness 127, 153, 324
apps, applications 8, 25, 34, 144, 154, 156, 162, 292, 310, 336, 341–2
augmented reality (AR) xvi, 164, 324
authenticity 85, 94, 111, 250, 344
autonomy 86, 92, 240, 253, 324, 333

bad tendency test 20, 324
balance of interest doctrine 20, 108, 262, 324
Bannon, Steve 295, 321
Bates v. State Bar of Arizona 79, 88
best practices 92, 94, 109, 114
Bethel School District v. Fraser 46, 61
Bill of Rights 15, 20, 44, 220, 252, 307, 318, 324, 330
biometric 15, 97, 164–9, 175, 178, 281
Biometric Information Privacy Act 167–9
Black Lives Matter 52, 54, 62, 254, 290, 315
blasphemy 21, 187, 255, 302, 324
Bollea v. Gawker Media 149–51
brand 52, 73–5, 77–8, 84–5, 106–7, 112, 193, 240, 306, 325, 339; *see* branding
Brandenburg v. Ohio 21, 36, 230, 246
Branzburg v. Hayes 245–6
breaking news 126, 250, 273, 325, 328, 335
brief 11, 38, 202, 213, 268, 270; *see also* case brief
Bubba "the Love Sponge" 150
bullying 45, 54, 57, 93, 186–7, 190, 193, 243, 290; *see also* cyberbullying
business-to-business (B2B) 23, 325
buzz 72, 325

California Consumer Privacy Act of 2018 96–8, 119, 165
California Proposition 12
Carpenter v. United States 176, 303, 319
case brief 11, 38, 325
categorical imperative 314, 325
cause of action 189, 325, 327
censorship 3, 6, 46–7, 49, 51, 120, 157, 159, 230–47; *see* prior restraint
Central Hudson Gas & Electric Co. v. PSC of New York 21, 36, 65, 69–71, 77–81, 88, 109, 119
certiorari, cert xii, 11, 15–16, 194, 296, 326
chatbots xvi, 19, 154, 206, 326; *see also* artificial intelligence
cite 16, 25, 44, 49, 157, 167, 202, 267, 272, 282, 296, 326, 337
citizen journalism 244, 326
Citizens United v. Federal Election Commission 80, 89, 253, 264
civil action 13, 15, 326
civil courts 14; *see* torts
Clayton Act 26
clear and present danger test 20, 230, 252, 277, 326
click-through rates (CTR) 72, 326
client 92, 106, 111, 113–16, 224, 326
code of ethics 17, 48, 110, 112–15, 117–18. 121, 326
collective bargaining agreement (CBA) 94, 141, 315
commercial speech xv, 6, 21, 51, 65, 68–71, 73, 77–81, 88, 102, 109, 253, 326; *see also* advertising
commitment 83, 85, 93, 199, 220, 253, 255
common carrier 125, 326
common law 9, 14, 16, 20, 23, 26, 35, 142, 153, 215, 220, 233, 254–5, 302, 326–7, 331, 338
Communications Decency Act of 1996 xii, 108, 256, 264, 297–8, 301, 311; *see* Section 230
communitarianism 284, 327
community 3, 10, 20, 29, 39, 41, 43, 45, 47, 50, 54–5, 62–3, 84, 101, 121, 135, 141–2, 144, 151, 161, 166, 170, 186–8, 192, 204, 211, 218, 229, 250, 255, 257, 260, 264, 266, 290, 297, 307, 315–17, 320, 327, 331, 333, 336, 341, 344
Community for Creative Non-Violence v. Reid 141
compelling interest standard 21, 48, 51, 81, 195, 198, 201, 235, 238, 260, 262, 307, 327
complaint 25–6, 37, 42–3, 47, 75–7, 89, 95, 120, 205, 213, 222, 225–6, 233, 327
computer-mediated communication (CMC) 121, 151, 251, 262, 312–13, 327
confidentiality 49, 78, 95, 106, 111, 151, 204, 224, 327
conflict of interest 295, 327
consequentialism 295, 327
constitutional law 11, 14, 20, 62, 302, 327
contempt of court 327
content neutral 198; *see also* time, place and manner
controlling authority 15–16, 327
convergence 60, 328
conversation 35, 110, 152, 208, 210, 253, 274, 277, 304, 310, 328
conversion 72, 328
copyright xvi, 58–9, 112, 123–8, 130–43, 145–8, 150, 207, 328, 332, 339, 343–4; *see also* intellectual property
cost per click (CPC) 72, 328
Covid 7, 18, 34–6, 41–2, 63, 94, 96, 99–104, 121–2, 145, 147, 159, 172, 206, 225, 234, 301, 306–7, 310, 312–13, 315, 317, 321
credibility 19, 84, 111, 222, 303–4, 328, 343
criminal xv, 2, 11, 14, 54, 109, 150, 182–4, 193–4, 198, 208, 211–12, 219–20, 222–24, 227, 230–1, 233, 235–6, 239, 247, 272, 277, 284, 288, 296, 303, 306, 318, 326–9, 332, 338, 340, 343
criminal libel 220, 222–24, 233, 235, 239, 247, 288, 328; *see also New York Times v. Sullivan* (1964), seditious libel
crowdsourcing 328
Cruz, Ted 298–301
customer 19, 84–5, 172, 329–30
CVS Health 93–4, 116

damages 13, 46, 130, 135, 137–8, 141, 147, 149, 151, 168, 215–16, 220–22, 273, 323, 329, 340–3
de novo 329
deception 12, 71–3, 81, 111, 329
defendant 2, 14–15, 133, 194–5, 199–200, 221, 223, 225, 329, 332
deontology 81, 329
determinism 32, 329
dicta 16, 231
digital 2, 18–19, 27–8, 31–2, 36, 38–40, 43, 51, 56, 60–1, 79, 81, 86–8, 102–4, 108, 115–17, 119–20, 124–6, 136, 145–6, 166, 171, 174–6, 182, 185–7, 206–7, 209, 213, 231, 244–7, 255, 258, 265, 277, 287, 292, 304, 309, 317, 320, 323, 329
directed verdict 15, 329
disinformation 17, 27–8, 30, 71, 100–1, 166, 250, 275, 302, 316, 329
diversity 118, 260, 315
diversity, equity, and inclusion (DEI) 118
diversity jurisdiction 14, 330
doctrine of incorporation 16, 252, 330; see Fourteenth Amendment, due process
doctrine of preferred position 20, 330
Dorsey, Jack 171, 298–301
Douglas Marland et al. v. *Trump Memorandum* 156–7, 176, 178, 234, 246–7
duty 23, 26, 81, 107, 118, 144, 175, 193, 245, 255, 270, 278, 315, 329–30

early adopters 191; see diffusion
earned media 72, 330; *see also* public relations
eCommerce 72, 330
Elaboration Likelihood Model (ELM) 86
Eldred v. Ashcroft 125–6, 146
Electronic Frontier Foundation (EFF) 79, 330
electronic word-of-mouth (eWOM) 72, 330
Elonis v. United States xv, 2–3, 11, 37, 109, 119, 274, 277, 287, 303
emoji 11, 330
empathy 83, 254
en banc 37, 120, 330
engaged journalism 32, 331; *see also* community, engagement
engagement xiii, 11, 18, 35, 39, 83–5, 87, 207, 256, 267, 284, 292, 316, 328–31, 333–4, 339
entrepreneurs 116, 331
equity 13–14, 23, 70, 106, 111–12, 118, 164, 176, 314–15, 317, 326, 331, 333, 341
European Commission 102–6, 119, 294
European Court of Human Rights 223
European Court of Justice (CJEU) 109, 137, 239
European law 20, 108, 340
European Union (EU) 12, 21, 119, 155, 163, 180, 186, 255
executive order 48, 50, 62, 149, 156–62, 176, 233–4, 246, 310

Facebook xiii–xvii, 1–4, 7–12, 18–19, 22–8, 32–4, 37–9, 48–9, 58, 60, 66, 74, 88–9, 94–5, 98–9, 102, 107–8, 118–21, 125, 147, 151, 154–5, 164, 166–7, 169, 176–9, 181, 184, 187–8, 190, 193, 202–3, 206, 208, 211, 213–14, 225–27, 229, 231, 233, 239, 245–6, 254–7, 263–5, 269–70, 273–4, 277, 280–1, 284, 287, 290–2, 294–5, 299, 301–4, 307, 310, 312–21, 331–3, 337, 341–2, 344
fact 3, 11, 15, 23, 28, 30–1, 34, 49, 53, 57, 75, 94, 101, 126, 129, 133–4, 142, 192, 208, 210, 215–18, 222, 235, 263, 314, 331, 334
fair comment 35, 331; *see also* common law, public sphere
fair use 59–60, 124–6, 130, 136–7, 140–1, 143, 145, 331–2
fake news 28, 30, 310, 312, 314, 331
false light 152–3, 331; see defamation, privacy
family 65, 74, 87, 92, 107, 155, 193, 195, 216
Family Educational Privacy Act (FERPA) 155
fan 7, 331–2
fault 199, 220–1, 273, 332, 336, 342; see actual malice, negligence

Federal Trade Commission (FTC) xiii, 12, 19, 24, 38, 65–90, 95, 102, 120, 164, 172, 177, 271, 294, 323
fiduciary 23, 26, 40, 92–3, 107, 164, 282, 316
fighting words 52, 205, 238, 332; *see also* clear and present danger
First National Bank of Boston v. Bellotti 69, 80, 89
first sale doctrine 125, 332
foundationalism 332
Fourth Amendment 154, 163, 340
Freedom of Information Act (FOIA) 155, 244
FTC v. Facebook 25–6, 37
FTC v. Lord & Taylor 75–7, 89, 109, 120

gag order 21, 332; *see Nebraska Press v. Stuart*
gatekeeper 289
Gawker 149–51, 175, 177, 179
General Data Protection Regulation (GDPR) 21, 104–5, 108, 175
Gertz v. Robert Welch, Inc. 215–16, 227
Golden Mean 314, 332; *see* balancing
grand jury 2, 11, 14, 245, 272, 332
group libel 216, 332; *see* defamation

hardware 331–3, 341
Harper & Row Publishers v. Nation Enterprises 123–4, 146
hashflag 240, 333; *see* Twitter
hate speech xiv–xvi, 3, 34, 44, 54, 57–9, 181–214, 231, 239, 243, 256–7, 265, 280, 290, 304, 308, 311
Hazelwood School District v, Kuhlmeier 46, 49–52, 62, 252, 265
Health Insurance Portability and Accountability Act of 1996 (HIPPA) 42, 155, 169, 177
heteronomy 240, 333
holding 11, 69, 131, 226, 243, 252, 258, 273, 297, 325, 333, 342
hostile work environment 93
human rights 17–18, 29, 32, 161, 169, 187, 193, 223–4, 227, 239, 255, 262, 266, 281, 304, 316, 324
human-computer interaction (HCI) 262, 333
Hustler Magazine v. Falwell 177, 217, 227
hybrid media 262, 333
hyperlink (link) 22, 101, 139, 165, 331
hypothetical imperative 333

idealism 333
identity 14, 18, 71, 80, 105, 167, 169, 184, 187, 207–8, 213, 224, 243, 325, 333, 344; *see also* personal branding
Illinois v. Austin 194–202
impartial 318, 333, 337; *see* equity, fairness
implied consent 6, 140, 152, 333
influence 6, 25, 33, 65–7, 71–2, 74, 77, 81, 83–4, 87, 100, 108–10, 120, 140, 152–3, 209, 258, 274, 278, 298–9, 313, 326, 333, 344; *see also* celebrities, engagement, fans, followers, influencers
infra 273, 334
innovation 24, 108, 120, 154, 244, 251–2, 263, 284, 292, 334, 341
Instagram xiii–xviii, 3, 7–8, 18–19, 22–7, 33, 38–9, 43–5, 67, 74–5, 77, 88–9, 127, 139–40, 147, 151–2, 154, 164, 178, 188–9, 213, 239, 250, 262, 277, 290, 292, 295, 315–16, 322, 341; *see also* Facebook
inter alia 105, 195, 273, 334
interaction 18, 32, 97, 209, 262, 312, 328, 331, 333–4; *see also* engagement
international xiv–xv, 11–12, 21, 33, 41, 103, 106, 128, 149–80, 193, 207, 211, 213, 219, 222–4, 227, 233, 239, 245, 247, 255, 262, 265–6
International Emergency Economic Powers Act (IEEPA) 156, 233, 247

judgment 13, 15, 18–19, 59, 82, 101, 131, 135, 201, 217, 303, 315, 329, 334, 342
jurisdiction 7, 14, 136, 318, 330, 334
justice 36, 67, 90, 95, 108, 118–19, 137–8, 162, 164, 175, 213, 239, 255, 284, 291, 294, 333, 341

Kardashian, Khloé 65, 88
Katz v. United States 154, 177

Keefe v. Adams 48–50, 52–3, 62–3
key performance indicator (KPI) 109, 334; *see also* data
keyword 340; *see* SEO
Knight First Amendment Inst. At Columbia Univ. v. Trump 4, 37, 109, 120
Kogan v. Facebook, Inc. 225–6, 227
Kroger Co. of Mich. v. Granger 93, 117, 255, 265

Lane v. Facebook, Inc. 154, 177
liability xiii, 3, 6, 13–14, 38, 53, 67, 73, 92, 107–8, 126–7, 141, 144, 215, 218, 220, 155, 263, 273, 280, 290, 297, 301, 304, 314, 321, 334, 342–3
libel 7, 14, 20, 35, 163, 216–27; *see* defamation, reputation
limited-purpose public figure 273, 334, 339; *see* actual malice
location-based services (LBS) 109, 245, 335

MalwareBytes, Inc. v. Enigma Software Group xiv, xvi, 296–7, 320
mandamus 273, 335
marketing 22, 66–7, 71–2, 74, 77–8, 87–9, 91–122, 178, 315, 325, 328, 330, 335, 341
Marland et al. v. *Trump et al.* 156–7, 176, 178, 234, 246–7
Matal v. Tam 129, 147
Mathers, Dani 150–1, 176–7
McCutcheon v. Federal Election Commission 80–81, 89
media literacy 30, 39, 61, 99, 101, 121, 166, 242–3, 262, 335
meme 59–61, 63, 205, 335
MGM v. Grokster 126, 147
microblog 47, 335; *see* Twitter
Milkovich v. Lorain Journal 217–18, 227
Miller v. California 20, 181, 184, 337–8
Minnesota v. Tatro 9–10, 39
misdemeanor 7, 68, 151, 190, 206, 336
misinformation xiv, 3, 31, 33, 71, 100–1, 121, 166, 187, 207, 213–14, 250, 261, 280, 301–2, 304, 307, 310–11, 313, 316, 321, 329
mobile 4, 13, 25–6, 43, 87, 109, 124, 144, 152–3, 158–9, 163, 169, 179, 209, 244, 273, 302–3, 309, 314–15, 324, 336, 341, 344
monopoly xiii, xvii, 24, 26–7, 39, 95, 110, 281, 291, 294, 336
moral reasoning 109, 319, 336; *see also* moral calculus
Moreno v. Hanford Sentinel, Inc. 154, 178
Morse v. Frederick 46–7, 51, 63
mutuality 83, 111

narrative 85, 258, 274, 336, 341–2
Naruto v. Slater 127, 130–6, 147
National Labor Relations Act (NLRA) 93, 116–17
national security 122, 154–6, 158–60, 162–3, 172, 185, 233–5, 245–6, 302, 310
National Security Agency (NSA) 154–5
natural law 21, 255, 336
Near v. Minnesota 20, 38, 121, 220, 233, 247, 255, 265, 337
Nebraska Press Association v. Stuart 21, 38, 229, 247, 332
negligence 138, 144, 221, 224–5, 273, 332, 336, 343; *see also* tort, fault
network 1, 6, 17, 26, 29, 30, 55, 97, 100, 109, 152, 172, 186, 253, 263, 275–7, 290, 292, 294–5, 309, 312, 321, 325, 327–9, 331, 333, 336–7, 339–42
New York Times v. Sullivan 20, 38, 52, 68, 89, 121, 220, 222, 227, 232–3, 247, 252, 254, 265, 298, 328
New York Times v. Tasini 136, 147
nihilism 109, 336
non-disclosure agreement (NDA) 92, 106, 151, 204, 336; *see also* public relations
non-governmental organization (NGO) 285, 336

objectivity 32, 336; *see* balance, fairness
obscenity 6, 20, 46, 49, 181–214, 255, 314, 337–8; *see Miller v. California*, *Near v. Minnesota*
Olmstead v. United States 153, 178

open educational resources (OER) 143
opportunity 6, 33, 59, 173, 240, 242, 256, 260, 337
opportunity costs 242, 337
organic 23, 72, 99, 108, 110, 337–8, 343; *see also* earned media
overbreadth 50, 200, 337
owned media 109, 325, 337

packet switching 154, 337
Packingham v. North Carolina xv, 1–2, 38, 108, 121, 157, 178, 231, 234, 247, 272, 288
paid search 109, 337; *see* SEO
Papish v. Board of Curators of University of Missouri 47, 52, 63
parallel citation 13, 161, 273, 337
particularity 295, 337; *see also* loyalty, objectivity
paywall 337
People for the Ethical Treatment of Animals (PETA) 131–2
persuasive authority 16, 337
petitioner 337
Pew Internet 34, 39, 231–2, 247
Pinterest 23, 325, 338; *see* boards, pins
plaintiff 14, 133–4, 160, 204, 221, 225, 296, 338
platform 17, 74–6, 114–15, 122, 125, 139, 159, 186, 188, 208, 213, 257, 265, 289–90, 295, 299, 301, 313, 321, 341
pleading 2, 338
pluralism 338
pornography xvi, 89, 181–214, 233, 264; *see also Miller v. California*
positivism 14, 338
post 2, 23, 35, 45, 47–50, 54, 56–7, 61, 67, 71, 75–7, 100–102, 113, 116, 149, 151, 155, 181, 188–9, 208, 220–1, 224–5, 239, 255–6, 270, 274–5, 291, 301–2, 316, 338, 340, 344
precedent xv, 3, 9, 11, 14, 19, 43, 47, 78, 102, 125, 135, 140, 217, 230, 232–3, 255, 261, 269, 298, 304, 326, 331, 337–8, 341; *see* stare decisis
prior restraint 20, 35, 93, 157, 161, 220, 233–5, 246, 254–5, 302–3, 325, 332, 338; *see also* censorship, subsequent punishment
privacy xiii, xv, 6, 12–15, 18, 20–2, 24–5, 35, 37–8, 42–3, 45, 53, 55–7, 59–60, 71, 77–9, 89, 93, 95–6, 98, 104–5, 107–10, 116, 119, 121, 127–8, 130, 149-180, 183–4, 186, 189, 193, 196–8, 202, 207, 216–17, 219, 220, 224–5, 227, 234, 239, 245–6, 256, 264, 277–8, 280–1, 287, 292, 295, 303–4, 312, 314, 316, 324, 331, 338
private libel 220, 338; *see* defamation
promoted posts 338
propaganda 160, 290, 312, 331, 338–9,
propinquity 83
public domain 125, 127, 131, 140, 199, 339
Public Employment Relations Act (PERA) 42
public figure 217, 221–4, 273, 323, 334, 339; *see* actual malice, defamation, official
public relations (PR) 6, 37, 48, 87–9, 91–121,141, 145, 174, 227, 242–3, 249, 328, 330, 339–40

qualified privilege 13, 339

R.A.V. v. City of St. Paul 256, 265
racist 44, 58, 186, 193, 205, 214, 256, 275, 310
real-time social engagement 11, 330–1, 339
reckless disregard 152, 217, 222, 224, 232, 339
Recording Industry Association of America (RIAA) 125
red flag words 218–19
Reddit 23, 114, 116, 205, 255, 262, 339
Reed v. Town of Gilbert 80, 89, 202
relativism 81, 339
reliability 29
remand 11, 339
Reno v. ACLU 21, 39, 108, 121, 216, 227, 266, 270, 298, 303
reporter privilege 273
research, planning, implementation and evaluation (RPIE) 109, 340
respect 9, 52, 111–12, 114, 142, 145, 155, 178, 198, 223, 250, 278, 315

respondent 217, 220, 340
retraction 340; *see also* damages, defamation
return on investment (ROI) 108, 340
retweet 139, 291, 340; *see* Twitter
revenge porn xv, 181–214; *see* pornography
right to be forgotten (RTBF) 22, 108, 120, 163, 180, 302, 340; *see also* Google
risk 47, 83, 95, 107, 167, 172, 179, 185, 199, 222, 315

Sanford, Bruce 218–19
Schenck v. United States 20, 39, 230
scrutiny 9, 20, 48, 50, 52–3, 61, 71, 77–80, 158, 161, 193–4, 198–202, 235–8, 256–7, 262, 282, 314, 327, 342
Search Engine Optimization (SEO) 109, 334, 340; *see also* algorithm, Google
Search Engine Result Placements (SERP) 109, 340; *see also* SEO
search warrant 155, 340; *see also* privacy
Section 230 xiii–xiv, 3, 14, 39, 67, 90, 108, 121, 125, 207, 255, 263, 280, 301, 320–1
seditious libel 220, 255, 269, 340; see defamation
Sherman Act 26, 95
shield law 245
skepticism 8, 79, 340
slander 217, 222, 329, 341–3; see defamation
smart 105, 321; *see* also mobile
Snapchat 18–19, 23, 25, 49, 61, 74, 127, 150, 294, 316, 341
Snyder v. Phelps 62
social business 32, 263, 341
social graph 32, 341; *see also* Facebook, social network
social justice 341; *see also* equality, fairness, moral
social network 1, 6, 9, 11, 17, 25–6, 186, 253, 275–7, 291–2, 294–5, 309, 312, 325, 327–8, 331, 333, 336–7, 339–42
software xiv–xvi, 95, 125, 144, 169, 174, 178–9, 203, 225, 245, 290, 296–7, 320, 324, 331, 333, 341–2; see app
Sonny Bono Copyright Term Extension Act of 1998 125
Sony Corp. v. Universal Studios, Inc 126, 147
sponsored 19, 47, 49, 51–2, 65–7, 72, 75, 323, 326, 338, 341, 343; see paid media
stare decisis 14, 269, 326, 341; *see* precedent
State of New York v. Facebook 26–7, 39
statute 2–3, 11, 14, 67, 73, 77–8, 134, 154, 156, 165–9, 166, 167–9, 183–4, 190, 194–6, 200–1, 207, 222, 230, 232, 236, 245, 256, 270–1, 297, 323, 326, 328, 335, 341,
summary judgment 15, 221, 325, 341
supra 273, 342

tactic 150, 171, 342
tagging 167
Tatro, Amanda 9–10, 39
temporary restraining order (TRO) 157, 273, 342
terms of service (ToS) 8, 34, 108, 139, 154, 181, 186–7, 188–9, 213, 230, 274, 281, 300, 342; *see also* contract law
Texas v. Johnson 21, 39, 230, 235–8, 247, 252, 266
third-party litigation funding (TPLF) 150, 342
TikTok 8, 18–19, 23, 25, 33, 54, 66–7, 89, 122, 152, 156–7, 176, 178, 180, 233–4, 246–7, 254, 262, 289, 292, 301–2, 313, 315–16, 319–20
TikTok v. Trump 233, 247
time, place and manner restriction 44, 51, 68, 157, 234, 256, 327, 342; *see also* narrowly tailored
Tinker v. Des Moines Indep. Sch. Dist. 21, 39, 41, 43–6, 51–2, 63, 252, 266
tort 13, 144, 151, 163, 175, 178, 207, 215, 217, 222, 275, 326, 336, 342; *see also* damages
trademark 59, 112, 124, 126, 128–9, 145, 148, 343; see intellectual property
Trademark Act of 1946 124, 148
Trademark Modernization Act 145
transformative 136–9, 145, 343; *see also* copyright

transparency xiv, 5, 32–4, 39, 42, 62, 66–7, 71–2, 74, 84, 107, 114, 150, 164, 173, 178, 223, 245, 250, 263, 281–2, 285, 290, 310, 313–14, 321–2, 343
Trump, Donald xiv, 3–5, 35, 37, 39, 48, 63, 66–7, 90, 98–100, 109, 112, 119–21, 149, 156–9, 163, 176, 178–9, 187, 207, 211–12, 214, 233–4, 246–7, 250, 275, 277, 280, 289, 295, 310, 321
trust 23, 34, 53, 72, 84, 96, 100–1, 107, 112, 115, 119, 121, 178, 250, 263, 286, 303, 328, 343; *see also* credibility
truth xiv, 20, 33, 61, 81, 94, 111–12, 152, 218–24, 232, 238, 243, 245, 249, 251, 253–4, 258–60, 267–8, 271, 302, 312, 316, 321, 323, 329, 336, 339
Turning Point USA 48, 63
Twitter xiv, 3–5, 8, 17–19, 22, 25, 32, 34–7, 39, 45, 75, 84, 88, 95, 99–100, 112, 116, 119–120, 126, 139–40, 143, 146, 155, 164, 166, 170–3, 175, 177–9, 186, 188, 190–2, 205, 211, 213–14, 220, 224, 226, 234, 239, 244, 254–5, 275–7, 281, 283–4, 287–91, 294–5, 298–301, 304–5, 313, 315–16, 319–20, 325, 328–9, 333, 335, 340, 343–4

U.S. WeChat Users Alliance, et al., Plaintiffs, v. Donald J. Trump, et al., Defendants 149, 158–163
UK Competition and Markets Authority (CMA) 67, 294
United States of America v. Bobal 231, 247, 272, 288
user profile 32, 343
user-generated content (UGC) 290, 343
utility 81, 281, 290, 314, 329, 343

vagueness 158, 161, 200–1, 343
Valentine v. Christensen 68, 90
validity 241, 343
veil of ignorance 290, 344
verification 5, 37, 313, 322, 344; *see also* identity, verified accounts
viral 57, 59–60, 92, 100, 127, 205, 240, 262, 265, 275, 289, 301, 305, 315, 319–21, 344
Virginia State Bd. of Pharmacy v. Virginia Citizens 68, 90
Virginia v. Black 256, 266
virtual 71, 96, 121, 172, 207, 260, 282, 316, 325, 344; *see also* community
vlog 4, 344; *see also* blog, video

Weinstein v. University of Illinois 141, 145, 148
word-of-mouth (WOM) 72, 107–8, 110, 330

YouTube 3, 8, 19, 33, 60–1, 91–2, 100, 118, 121, 124–6, 146, 186–7, 190–1, 202–5, 213, 231, 241, 255, 270, 295, 303, 310, 313, 315, 342, 344

Zacchini v. Scripps Howard Broad 153, 180
Zoom 95, 120

the ?. 42 others 85 of 104) however ?. 107

Found 46 than 96 business 96 state, ?. 108

~~to long 48~~ how ?. 115

Shoot ?. 123 the 123